MY BEST MORMON LIFE

BY

JESSE ELISON

A WORK OF NONFICTION PUBLISHED BY THE AUTHOR

ISBN: 1481053590
ISBN-13: 978-1481053594
Library of Congress Control Number: 2012922307

Type design by Barbara Fifer
Cover design by Sarah E. Grant

CreateSpace Independent Publishing Platform
North Charleston, SC

For my parents

Contents

*[T]hough my education had begun in many subjects, it had been conclud-
ed in none.*

—Jean-Jacques Rousseau, *The Confessions*

*With these words I was thinking that I had made an end of the discus-
sion; but the end, in truth, proved to be only a beginning. For Glaucon, who is
always the most courageous of men, was dissatisfied at Thrasymachus's retirement. So he said to me: Socrates, do you wish really to persuade us, or only to
seem to have persuaded us, that to be just is always better than to be unjust? I
should wish really to persuade you, I replied, if I could. Then you certainly have
not succeeded. Let me ask you now...*

—Plato, *Republic*

*Second Questioner: A last query, please? You have given hundreds of words
of testimony—do you realize that you are accountable for each word uttered?*
*The Disciple: Yes, it is a sobering thought. But now you are also account-
able for each word heard! It is a fair exchange of accountability.*

—Neal A. Maxwell, *Deposition of a Disciple*

*Under the true definition of liberalism, the Church of Jesus Christ is pre-
eminently liberal. First, it makes truth and love of truth its foundation. The
whole latter-day work was initiated by Joseph Smith's search for truth...It is
understood that every worthy member of the Church must likewise seek and
find truth for himself.*

—John A. Widtsoe, *Evidences and Reconciliations*

*We will now take the oath. And remember once taken this oath has never
been broken by any man down through the centuries of time in the history of
this fraternal organization. If any member is doubtful of his strength to keep
this solemn pledge, he will please be seated.*

—Exalted Ruler, *Sons of the Desert* (1933)

PART I

CHAPTER 1

CHRISTINE "CHRIS" JANE HARWARD ELISON

Sunday morning, November 22, 1987, I put on my church clothes, wearing a white, long-sleeved button-down shirt with an open collar, no tie, and brown slacks, tight even for an eleven-year-old accustomed to awkwardly fitting hand-me-downs. With three older brothers my closet was not short on worn clothes. I did not see a new article of clothing until I could work to buy my own; and when I began buying, I did so enthusiastically with money earned moving pipe over the summer, every cent spent before the first day of the new school year. The cool styles were rarely available in my size at any of the malls within a half-day's drive. I started the first week of school in an array of fresh-smelling tight shirts and baggy pants (and vice versa) when neither was trendy nor went well together.

This Sunday morning was still a couple of years before I was able to lift aluminum irrigation pipe for three dollars a line in wheat and potato fields throughout Riverton, a rural community southwest of the town of Black-foot, Idaho. Blackfoot sits in Bingham County, where more potatoes grow per square mile than anywhere else in the world, or so boasts the Idaho Po-tato Museum, the world's only potato museum to my knowledge. Billboards hailing motorists on I-15 advertised the town's landmark, offering Free Taters For Out-Of-Staters. As a converted railroad depot on Main Street, the museum sits a few steps west of the train tracks running parallel to the heart of old downtown. I struggled through a lot of potato vines moving irrigation pipe. I do not recall buying church clothes with my pipe-moving money; multicolored rugby pullovers and brand-name jeans that did not fit, yes, but not church clothes that did.

Sitting on my grandparents' couch in the TV room of their basement, I fidgeted, my shirt partly tucked into my beltless slacks taut like a dancer's tights, fitted for a prospective Deacon—the first level priesthood for twelve-year-old boys in the Mormon Church. A thin green carpet separated us from the concrete below. If there was one thing I knew at eleven years old, it was that the floor was concrete. Years earlier, I had held my youngest newborn brother, Jed, while walking back and forth on it. Grandpa Bob warned me that I would drop him if I did not pay attention, and eventually I did. Jed's wails could not drown out Grandpa Bob's seething reproaches.

My brothers and I had spent Saturday night in town at our Moldenhau-er grandparents' home on York Circle, a few minutes and less than half a mile from our Elison grandparents' home on Goodwin Drive. That Sunday morning we planned to attend Grammie Moldenhauer's Mormon Church on York Drive, a short walk between our grandparents' homes.

My mother, Chris, short for Christine, was the oldest of Berna Dean "Grammie" Jones Harward Moldenhauer's four children from her first mar-riage to Phillip Sinclair Harward. My mother had been in a hospital in Salt Lake City, Utah, for nearly two weeks, and had previously been in a hospital in Pocatello, twenty minutes south of Blackfoot, for about four days. On a school night at my older brother Jeremy's wrestling match at Mountain View Middle School, she had complained of a headache, a recurring ailment that often led to debilitating migraines. Jeremy had won his match, and my mother left before the dual meet ended. That evening, with all her sons scat-tered about the house, she lost consciousness in the front living room. Her initial groans of pain—which paled in comparison to her shrill screams later in the emergency room—were intermittently drowned out by my father's helpless pleas for her to respond as he held her. My oldest brother Jami dialed 9-1-1 and my brother Josh ran the ambulance down as it passed Old Red, our old red house on Nagisty Road.

The next morning a girl stopped me in the bus line to ask if my mother had had a stroke. I did not know. I knew her head hurt, but I was not sure that was a stroke. Over the following days, news from the hospital included the word "aneurysm." That made even less sense. After two bewildering weeks I sat on Grammie's couch waiting to go to church, which did make sense. Not going to church on Sunday morning was unusual for a Mormon, but sitting on Grammie's couch, it never occurred to me that anything was out of the ordinary because I knew that Mormon services occurred at several different times throughout the day. I assumed we would attend a later service. Sometime after we ate and dressed the phone rang, and Grammie answered upstairs. Her scream pierced through the walls to where we sat in the basement. Shortly afterward, Grandpa Bob walked down the stairs. Grandpa Bob, Robert Moldenhauer, had four children of his own when he married Grammie. My mother was a teenager at the time and was the oldest of all the children from both families.

Grandpa Bob announced that we would not be going to church. This pronouncement confused me because Grandpa Bob never went to church. It was not until years later that I learned he was even Mormon. Then years after learning that, there was talk one summer about his being re-baptized, which meant he was not actually a Mormon the whole time I thought he had been one. He had been excommunicated and was off the official records—if one ever really gets removed from Mormon records. In any case, a Mormon who has been excommunicated needs to be re-baptized. Mormons believe every single person needs to be baptized by proper priesthood authority in order to enter into the Kingdom of God. It is an important enough ritual that even Jesus, the savior of humankind, was baptized. And if a person screws up in life, like Grandpa Bob apparently had done, that person needs to be re-baptized. The Book of Life must be a matrix written in graphite with names running down the page next to columns of necessary rites to get into heaven running across the top. And it must be a mess of names and corresponding marks scribbled over with smudges from excessive editing and erasing. Most surely one could thumb down the endless list in section B of given nicknames to eventually arrive at my GRANDPA BOB.

I had notable first experiences with Grandpa Bob that only a non-Mormon, ex-Mormon, or inactive Mormon could provide. He was the first person I saw drink beer—real Coors beer before his massive heart attack, and non-alcoholic beer after it. He owned an old Lincoln complete with an eight-track player, frayed leather seats and crushed beer cans on the floor. He took some of my brothers and me for a drive in the Lincoln at speeds exceeding one hundred miles per hour—another first—navigating dirt country roads running onto the Fort Hall Indian Reservation shared by the Shoshone and Bannock tribes, south of Riverton, with my brothers hollering to go faster. He topped the thrill ride with a fishtailing finale to their yelps of joy and my body frozen, clung to the armrest of the door.

Later that Sunday morning, my father and Jami, who had been in Salt Lake City with my mother, came down the stairs. Stepping into the basement with them was Brother Kevin Winthrop, a member of our ward's bishopric, and Brother Bridger Rooney, also from the bishopric and the only person to beat my father in a foot race and who in a few years would be my first pipe-moving boss. I expect Bishop James Patrick would have come too, but our ward had services that morning, and someone had to preside over the congregation. I had seen all the members of the bishopric at the hospital in Pocatello when Bishop Patrick drove us to visit my mother before she was moved to Salt Lake City.

Each Mormon ward, or church congregation, is made up of people within a demarcated area. We belonged to Riverton Ward, covering a rural area with the Snake River as the boundary to the north running west, and part of the Shoshone-Bannock Reservation running beyond the Blackfoot River to the south. Every Sunday many pickup trucks—some shiny, most beat to hell—lined the church parking lot and the north side of Riverton Road. Across the road from the church's main entrance was a fenced pasture running into the river bottoms with dense trees up to the Snake River.

Each ward is led by a bishop, and each bishop has a first and second counselor. Brother Winthrop was the first counselor whose family lived within shouting range of our property. I knew this because one day, my brother Josh's shout had saved Brother Winthrop's son, Bittron, from Brother Winthrop. Jeremy and Josh had turned the corral behind Old Red on Nagisty Road into a bucking arena, using the main gate of the large corral as a chute, swinging it in from the pasture on sturdy hinges and worn side boards. The converted chute held yearling calves, allowing a rider to set his rope to tie on by wrapping one hand for his attempt at an eight-second ride. Riding was the rawest form of excitement known to us boys; the watching alone was enough for me.

Jami and Josh supplied the stock from their calf projects. They purchased newborn Holstein calves, and Jacob and I, for quarters on the dollar, if we were ever paid, took turns rising before dawn to feed them warm bottles of powdered milk. After rounds in the converted rodeo corral, and long after the fruits of the youngest brothers' early morning labors, the calves were weaned and fattened, and Jami and Josh took them to the Blackfoot Stock Sale, just up Main Street from the Potato Museum. They sold them at a lucrative profit of a few hundred dollars.

Jeremy and Josh's desire to ride calves did not excite our mother, and it would not have done so even in an alternate universe. None of what her boys did was what she wanted her boys to do, and there was little she could do about it. I am certain she would have traded any one of us for a child who excelled at music. She eventually resigned her ambitions to encouraging us to do well in school, something we had no choice but to attend.

I remember her steering the station wagon around the winding road into town. It was a shorter distance but took more time than the other route, which crossed the Blackfoot River to the old highway. I rode my BMX on the winding road many times to buy candy at a convenience store, and I knew every turn. On this drive we were headed to town to register me for the sixth grade, my entry into middle school. Approaching the overpass that marked the border of Riverton, I sat beside her on the front seat, peering over the dashboard into the sky.

—Sixth grade was my favorite year in school.

—Why?

Her answer soothed my concerns about moving to a new school. I had not voiced any, and she did not need me to. I worried about most everything. Her father, Phillip Harward, had been a pilot in the Navy, moving his family from base to base, and as a result my mother attended many different schools growing up. For some reason, sixth grade stood out for her. She assured me the subjects were more interesting than in elementary school. I had no reason to doubt her, but it did strike me as odd at the time to choose the sixth grade as one's favorite year in school. Maybe her excitement was connected to the sixth grade requirement to take band, for which I had elected to learn the trumpet. My foray into organized music surely held more promise than my mother's attempt to teach me the piano—an endeavor that never had a fighter's chance. I do not remember when I first brought home the trumpet, but the day we rented it must have filled her with pride during the moments before I placed the mouthpiece in and began to blow it. My memories of my mother are few, my trumpet debut being among the many absent, but another memory included just the two of us, again driving in our station wagon, when she told me that when she was pregnant with me, she believed I would be the daughter she had always wanted. Something about how a fast heartbeat indicated a girl. If she would have traded one of her boys for a musician, and I know she would have, I'm even more certain she would have traded all six of her sons for one daughter.

One afternoon while we bucked Holsteins, I sat next to Josh on top of the fence of the corral with an open blue sky above us. When turned around, we had a clear view of our neighbors' corrals: the Stocks, who had rodeo sons of their own; and beyond their place, the Winthrop's property. That afternoon, I saw Brother Winthrop's son, Bittron, crossing the pasture to join us. Within seconds I noticed Brother Winthrop—a two-by-four in his hands—charging on a direct line at Bittron. Shocked dumb, I nudged Josh to turn around and pointed at Brother Winthrop.

—Run! Josh shouted.

Bittron looked behind him to see his charging father, a two-by-four's length behind, and he began sprinting before he had turned his head back around, hopping irrigation dikes until he reached and cleared the fence to Nagisty Road. Scared through, I wondered what would happen when Bittron went home, realizing even then that before the age of ten, I had likely performed the single greatest act of my life without being able to say a word—an achievement only because of my quick-acting brother Josh.

I acted on Bittron's behalf as the result of instinct sieged by fear of the violence cresting before my eyes. Had I a few seconds to contemplate the event, I may have chosen not to bother Josh, allowing Bittron to receive his comeuppance. A couple years earlier I had played baseball with my brothers and the Winthrop brothers in the pasture next to Old Red. The pasture mirrored the dimensions of the minor league field in the Peewee City League behind Bingham Memorial Hospital in town. After the game in the backyard, Bittron swung an aluminum bat across my head. He claimed it was an accident, but I had been trying to get the bat from him, so I was sure his swing was a deliberate strike to halt my persistence. I did not lose consciousness, nor did I lose my intention of getting the bat, which he speedily gave up. While I earned the welt, the blow was little more than an indefinite excuse for my intelligence plateauing around—with frequent dips below—average and for my unreliable memory. Furious and howling, I caught my breath and headed straight to Old Red to find my mother so she could exact a punishment commensurate to the strike, which she did not. But she did break up our play and sent Bittron home, paltry discipline meted out by any eight-year-old's standard of justice. My brothers could have exacted revenge on Bittron, but my brothers shared Bittron's annoyance with me, and the strike was something they had probably wanted to carry out numerous times themselves, not having the temerity to do it but assuredly experiencing brotherly catharsis witnessing it.

I was an oak tree, unwilling to bend under the most extreme conditions. I was a teaser, a tireless aggravator to my peers, and was stubborn and unwilling to cower before adults. My style was conspicuous and one dimensional: uncompromising. At age five or so, when I started to complain about my shoulder my parents could not make heads or tails of what was wrong until they started to hear a thump at night as I fell from the top bunk in the room across from theirs. After a fair sample of thumps, they decided to have me examined. I do not remember going into the doctor to learn I had broken my collarbone, but I do remember my last visit. After a couple months spent sleeping on the bottom bunk with my shoulder taped in place, I went back to the doctor's office and stood in front of a full-length mirror, staring at my reflection. The doctor started to tear the tape off when it occurred to everyone (including my mother standing nearby) that he had not put on any pre-wrap. This is going to hurt a little he said. He peeled line after line from my bare skin, and as my mother told it, I did not so much as grimace. When I graduated from primary to young adult Sunday school, Sister Teresa, a small, beautiful woman with a young family of her own, timidly congratulated me, stating that being with older children would be good for me. I knew she meant that being around older children might humble me. The primary teachers, at their wits' end since I had arrived, left me largely alone to do my own thing—coloring, mostly—for the better part of my tenure in primary. I scowled at Sister Teresa like I did at everyone, welcoming more mature targets. I did not need humbling. I needed size. I was small and I knew it, and was familiar with all its disadvantages. I figured stubbornness would minimize them until I got big enough to settle them.

My brothers must have made the most of my mother being in the hospital to get a break from me. I alone stayed with Brother Winthrop's family during my mother's hospital stays and I did not overlap in age with any of their children like most of my brothers did. When women from the ward's relief society brought food to our family, they brought it to the Winthrops' home, assuming all or most of my brothers were there. Unbeknownst to the ward, we had split up: Jake and Jed stayed with Grammie and Grandpa Bob;

Jeremy and Josh stayed at the Brickmerrys, who lived farther down Riverton Road; and Jami was with my father at the hospitals. The night my mother lost consciousness, Sister Nancy Winthrop came over to Old Red, cleaned the kitchen, and saw that we all went to bed. The Winthrops were not only helpful in a crisis, they were also an extension of our daily lives, so I felt I was expected to stay with them, even though I wanted nothing more than to go with my older brothers to the Brickmerrys' home, because I knew they stayed up late to watch movies. But I went to the Winthrops, benefiting from their excessive kindnesses. Of all the people we knew, the Winthrops were the most well acquainted with tragedy. Two of their children had died: one from a fall and the other in a car rollover; a third, Jami's best friend, Winston, would die a couple years later in a hunting accident.

One afternoon following church, all of us brothers gathered together in the front room of the Winthrops' home, where Brother Brickmerry shared a dream about my mother, telling us with tears falling from his eyes that God had revealed to him she would get better. Other members of the ward offered similar assurances at church on Sundays and to me when they dropped off food at the Winthrops'. We constantly received news that members in Riverton and members of other wards in Blackfoot fasted and prayed for her since receiving the news that she was in the hospital. The community poured out their sincerest hopes for the redeemable member of our family we reminded them of every time they saw one of us.

One of the nights during the two weeks I stayed with the Winthrops, Brother Winthrop offered family prayer before we went to bed. I knelt with his children in their family room, surrounded by the wood furniture he had made in his shop a dozen paces from the back door. I rested my arms on the arm of one of the grand wood chairs. In his prayer, he asked God to sustain my family during our mother's struggle for life and to hold our family together. That evening I recognized that his prayer was unlike any other I had heard on our family's behalf. He had not asked God to make everything right and return my mother to her family. He alone seemed to understand her condition may have been beyond the sincere hopes of the community and our family.

I looked at Brother Winthrop as he descended into Grammie's basement that Sunday morning, and I got off the couch. My father asked all of us to join him in the middle of the room. Kneeling on the hard floor with all his sons around him, he tried to reach out and cover us.

—Mom died early this morning, he cried.

My brothers bowed their heads and cried. I bowed my head and tried to cry too. Not comfortable faking I moaned, burying my head in my arms, shielding anyone from seeing me, sounding like I had a belly ache while the others grieved. My slacks stretched as I prostrated myself over the green concrete floor. When voices in the room began to quiet, I rubbed my dry eyes over and over again until they hurt to ensure no one would notice I had not been crying. I stood up and sat on Grammie's couch. Grammie sat on my right and hugged me.

CHAPTER 2

BULL RIDING

Twenty-foot wood poles, four inches in diameter and with bark peeling off, hauled and piled next to eight-foot ties, rested in a pasture, separated from an alfalfa field by an irrigation ditch running up to Riverton Road. The fencing supplies were spread out and ready for a grand arena deep enough for steer wrestling and almost wide enough for barrel racing, a true venue for a small show. Months before my brothers unloaded the supplies, my father had visited with each of his sons to tell of his plans to marry Gayle, a recent widow and member of our ward, and to move us to her home on Riverton Road, a few hundred yards east of the Mormon Church.

When it was my turn, my father said, —I would like to speak with you outside.

It marked our most important one-to-one between father and fourth son, and although he was conscious of the consequences of what he was about to tell me, I was not aware of any. He had visited individually with me before. Years earlier, he had asked for my feelings when he decided to move our family to Boston, and more recently, on the way back from a little league football party, he had talked to me about my mother. I had said I was scared of Boston and wished I had told my mother I loved her. I had no idea the one-to-ones were precursors to the personal interviews that would be repeated by many Mormon Church leaders over the next decade of my life. This one-to-one visit extended beyond church leaders to the members of the church. It was the form of their visits, or interviews, with each other. This was the Mormon approach to addressing concerns, with one person in an apparent position of authority directing the other person's choices. I followed my father to a pair of chairs he had placed under the weeping willow tree in the backyard. Nearby, a weakly taut barbed wire fence separated us from our converted baseball field.

—I am going to marry Gayle and move us to her house. Without any delay, he said.

My father and Gayle had been walking briskly around Riverton for months for all to see. Gayle had two sons and a daughter, all older than me. Her husband, a huge man I knew from sporting events in town and at church, had drowned in a fishing accident on the Columbia River in Oregon.

—Moving to her house will be easier on her because she knows where all her belongings are. How do you feel about moving to her house?

We sat, the hanging branches settling, surrounding us. I thought my posters would hang as well on her walls as they did in Old Red. My great-grandparents, Thomas and Estella Bradley Jones (Grammie's parents), had lived in Old Red early in their marriage. A photograph recalls their youth in prominent black and white in the front room, Stella in a white gown, standing straight with an arm on a chair, and Thomas in a suit, sitting. The Bradleys had lived and farmed farther down Riverton Road, having left the area long before Stella's brother was murdered, shot by pistol at close range in small ranch-hand quarters on the bank of the Snake River.

To move or not to move was not a question I gave a flying lute about. The thick-trunked cottonwood a few steps away from Nagisty Road in the front yard, the tall poplars separating the backyard from a ditch, the gravel driveway ending at the tin-roofed garage, and the corrals and pasture running into the west owned nothing on me. I ran freely on and as easily off of them.

—I don't care.

Poplars draped the sides of Nagisty for a quarter of a mile from the

Stocks' property running north to West Riverton Road, their shade hiding the time of day by the color of the season, winter's blinding white to spring and summer's green walls to fall's naked branches waving a spattering of light. An irrigation ditch running south along Nagisty broke due west at our driveway. I played around and in it each spring, undeterred by the Stocks' Blue Heelers, snipping at my heels, and at summer's end unfazed by suckers' putrid smells rotting on the empty bottom. Behind the poplars on the east side of Nagisty, a potato field opened from Old Red up to West Riverton Road. A center pivot rotated in an enlarged semi-circle over dikes and rows of thick vines.

From Nagisty, Old Red sat back on a modest front lawn on the foreground of our eight acres. A more modest backyard met a line of poplars hiding the end of the driveway. Behind the driveway weathered corrals around a small shed opened into pasture, where our mixed quarter horse and Shetland pony, Buster, ran with the itinerant Holsteins. We rode Buster, not often but enough to remind him he was Lord of the land, owing occasional bursts of service. A single poplar oversaw the west end of the property, rarely explored by me. No land was better known by me in my youth except for those explored in my imagination, charted by Lloyd Alexander in his *Taran Wanderer* series, Terry Brooks in his *Tales of Shannara*, and their forefather John Ronald Reuel Tolkien's *Lord of the Rings*. Their fantasies included landscapes real in my mind and far from anyone I walked around. But they were protected by the crowns of trees high above my conscious and unconscious dreamful years living in Old Red.

The thin drooping branches of the willow tree quietly wisped toward us. My father's council of two announced a life I couldn't anticipate in another location. I did not, because I could not, appreciate the branches of my youth would not reach my imagination away from Old Red.

I had none of the pressing questions my brothers had. Jeremy and Josh had converted the corral behind Old Red into the practice realm of their future. Their one-to-ones with my father about the impending move were not likely their first ones, but they were possibly their first not involving belting reprimands. They did not fail to catch our father in an unfamiliar conciliatory mood, and gave their consent to move upon the condition that they could build a rodeo arena on Gayle's property. By their leave, the arena would link all the brothers' past lives at Old Red to our new ones away from it.

Gayle's property was a few acres with a pasture to the east, where Jeremy and Josh built their arena. Friends and brothers helped. They dug holes to set eight-foot ties, spacing them ten feet apart. Then they drilled holes in the poles to hammer eight inch spikes into the ties. The poles were set five high, ensuring no bull could leap over them. My father paid for two custom-built steel bucking chutes, delivered and placed at the south end of the arena next to a circular holding pen. Orange aluminum mobile panels ran across the middle of the arena to shorten the bucking space, ensuring bulls would have to turn back. Over the next half dozen years, Jeremy and Josh rode every ornery bull local ranchers wanted revenge on and young bulls that stock contractors were willing to haul to the amateur Elison show on Riverton Road.

I rolled my leg over the top pole of the arena and set my foot on a middle rung, keeping my other leg on the outside. Sitting there, I watched my brothers' practice from a distance. If they did not have enough hands, they conscripted me into chute help. Generally a bull-riding event had bullfighters, usually two, and rodeos included pick-up men, two as well. Bullfighters helped distract the attention of the bull away from the rider after his ride. Pick-up men, on horse-back, aided bronc riders on their dismounts and cleared stock from the arena, often being called on to lasso a lingering bull. In our arena, there were no bullfighters or pick-up men. A bull rider pulled double duty, playing a bullfighter while he waited his turn, and after a ride the bull found its way back to the holding pen on its own time.

Our custom steel chutes were among the sturdiest ever made, on my Mormon honor if ever a thing I attested has been true. The gates that swung into the arena were doubly sturdy and so were the smaller gates separating the chutes, steel slabs sliding out on a metal extension, not easily opened, or closed. Opening them could be done at one's leisure but closing them could not. As soon as the bull ran into the chute from the holding pen, the gate had to be closed before the bull backed up, and it would back up. I routinely helped load the bulls and as often struggled to close the gate, and Jeremy would have to jump down from the top of the chute to help me push it. Not bumping me aside and without reprimand, we got it closed.

Of the hundreds of times I witnessed my brothers' preparation practicing at our arena and at rodeos and bull ridings throughout the West, they never failed to be wholly tuned in to the challenge before them. Both still quite themselves—Jeremy stern and laconic, Josh unassuming and conversant—they were nonetheless as serious about their ride ahead as your staunchest adherents' commitment to hellfire and brimstone. No action, from preparing their bull ropes to sitting just right on their ropes in the chute as they nodded their heads okay, was inconsequential.

—Do you want to ride today? Josh asked.

—Some time, maybe, I answered.

—How about today?

Whenever he could, Josh brought bulls to our arena. Neither Jeremy nor Josh ever pressured me to try riding. All the brothers tried of our own accord with only the slightest encouragement. Not only did Josh not pressure me, he proposed something completely foreign to me at the time.

—You'll be good at riding like Jeremy and me. If you want to ride, I'll show you how.

He meant "good" as the best. When he competed at anything, he wanted to be the best and often was. Unlike other sports, bull riding was not a direct competition between riders. That was only incidental after the real competition that took place between the rider and the bull. Riders rode on different bulls, and being the best meant trying to cover a fierce ton of thunder quaking below for eight ungodly seconds.

At the time I was content just being me, good at a couple of things and not at a lot of others, and the idea of being the best at anything had never crossed my mind. Sure I was meaner than any of my brothers, but I hadn't aspired to it nor did I strive at being the best at it. Living at Old Red, Jeremy and Josh had both treated my meanness, underscored with stubbornness, but had not cured it or held it against me. During a football game in the front yard of Old Red, which consisted of me and my oldest brother Jami versus Jeremy and Josh, all of Jami's plays—hand-offs to me—had me running through and over Jeremy and Josh for touchdown after touchdown. Bloated with confidence, I taunted Josh into a fight. He obliged, sweetly moving in to deliver punches to my face, taking me to the ground, letting fall a barrage of punches to the sides of my face until, bloodily maddened, I relented in defeat. Jeremy countered my same call one afternoon at the Winthrops' place when I would not release a coveted yellow moped to him, hell-bent on not letting him take it from me at the cost of punches raining on my face. I did not stop being the best at being stubborn. I just stopped calling my brothers out.

Jami, six years my senior, was the exception. I continued to call him out. He answered by throwing me from one wall to another throughout most rooms in Old Red. Well aware of my six-year handicap, I called Jami out because I doubted that he knew everything, although he didn't share that doubt. I may not have known much, but the few things I knew, I knew. The Mormon religion enjoys a fullness of all that God has revealed, and in keeping with our Mormon tradition, Jami claimed a fullness of knowledge, too. Also in keeping with our Mormon tradition, Jami spoke with absolute certainty about everything he knew, but his confidence did not always correlate with information available to both of us. Invariably, my insistence on pointing out the difference conflicted with his ability to continue to know everything, and resulted in me landing into another wall, proving unstable pairings also can cause supernovae when things get hot enough—matter combining with antimatter, the collision of electrons with their counterpart positrons.

My head was not just hitting walls. After one argument, I climbed upstairs to hide behind my open bedroom door. Whether Jami saw me or not, he claimed he did not. Upon entering the room, he slammed the door onto my head and into the wall. I screamed until our father came up the stairs. Unlike my mother's justice, my father meted out commensurate punishment and cupped his hand forcefully against the side of Jami's head. He asked Jami how it felt. Jami did not say anything. I wanted him to do it again to see if Jami would say something the second time, but he didn't, and I went to bed.

Jami was my Kraken. But unlike Perseus, whom I grew to admire from Desmond Davis's *Clash of the Titans* (1981), I did not have a sword, shield, or helmet to make me invisible, nor did I have Medusa's head to turn him into stone. I fought with words, the only weapons available. During one memorable exchange I was no more than six years old outside Old Red, near a red dilapidated shack we called the red shed, and my first vulgarity ever passed my lips when I called Jami a dick. Enraged, he struck me, tumbling me the length of the sand box behind the red shed. Every bit as furious as he, after picking myself up I returned his violence with a promise that he would not be invited to my wedding—a pretty poignant threat for a Mormon still years from the "age of accountability" of eight when young Mormons choose for themselves, with a certain amount of parental prodding, to be baptized into the Church of Jesus Christ of Latter-day Saints (LDS), and subsequently forever thereafter become accountable for sins like name-calling, regardless of its accuracy.

A week after our mother died, Jami's crying from the computer room in the basement, off the eternally unfinished bathroom, caught everyone's attention. Like all my brothers I went downstairs to see if he had accidentally dropped something on his head, but to my surprise and disappointment, he held a piece of paper he had found by the typewriter. I had not been in the computer room since my last argument with him over playing-time on the

Commodore 64, which resulted in my being thrown across the room into the wall. Still pissed off for being bounced off *Jumpman* before breaking my high score, I demanded to know what he was crying about. Jami cried that Mom had been working on an essay, crumpling and holding it close to his chest. Unable to persuade him to release it, we all asked what it was about.

—She wrote a beautiful essay, comparing rearing her children to working in a garden, making sure plants were watered and rows were weeded.

Our mother had graduated valedictorian of the College of Education, the largest college at Brigham Young University, and had given the commencement address. She continued with graduate work in elementary education, and a copy of her thesis, with random crayon marks highlighting various sections, floated in and out of storage to Old Red. Her thesis relied upon the ideas of Jean Piaget to analyze cognitive reading abilities. She probably had more scientific knowledge about child development than all of Riverton combined, and she compared raising her boys to pulling weeds.

I was the best of my brothers at being stubborn, and I was the best at earning a penny a page for reading. Our mother had instituted the reading-for-payment plan as a last resort to encourage her six boys to open books. I read (and reread) many fantasy novels and other books my mother chose from the youth section of the town library. She never specified that the books had to be of a certain literary value. She was satisfied to see any kind read.

Beyond my unyielding disposition and focus on reading, I lacked the inherent motivation to push myself to excellence. Mormon Church leaders encouraged members to obey church rules and teachings so they could reach heaven with their families, but they did not encourage members to be the best individuals they could be, similar to the Army. Instead, the Church and Army developed their members to fulfill roles on their respective teams. Yet both have succeeded in maximizing individuals' potential, which suffers no irony but shows models of commitment. I faithfully worked at my role to do what was right to get back to heaven with my family, and a key to living a life worthy of heaven was becoming holy by shedding natural inclinations, or putting off the "natural man" who, as recorded in scriptures, was an enemy to God. I thought natural inclinations generally were driven by my ego, and I never stopped to consider whether all of them really put me at odds with God.

Outside the influence of my Mormon religion, which taught me to be righteous, I was not subject to external influences encouraging me—and had no personal motivation—to be excellent. And the events of my youthful life were no more likely to introduce new approaches to life than the fights with my brothers would jolt me from my stubbornness. I studied not for enrichment or to develop my ability to think, but with one aim: an A grade, because good grades paved the way to college. I likewise played sports with only one goal: to have something to do, because doing something was better than nothing. Whether it was facing endless boredom playing the infield in little league baseball on weeknights in the summer or wrestling match after match in a round-robin at youth freestyle tournaments on Saturdays in the spring, I just survived to be there. I did not like sports, but did not know what else to do. In school and sports and in all of my early life that I remember, including the Mormon Church, no one had ever suggested I could be the best at something until Josh did. He caught my attention that afternoon.

Mormons did a lot of things well. They generally did not rodeo. One of the Brickmerry boys, Brumthon, rode bulls, and he was far from a shining example of an obedient Mormon youth. He did not pursue bull riding with the passion that Jeremy and Josh did. Their dedication was not foreign to Mormons who pursued BYU football and the Boy Scouts like zealots of a jealous God. Mormons, albeit not every single flipping one (especially the ones who had attended the University of Utah), took on crazed looks each fall as the BYU Cougars began the college football season. They hoped to regain the national title as they had against all odds, in the year nineteen eighty-four of our Lord, with the undersized Robbie Bosco directing a perfect season. And that providential year followed the graduation of the most hallowed of Mormon quarterbacks, Hall of Famer Steve Young.

If Mormons pursued one thing more fervently than another national college football title, it was earning merit badges and completing an Eagle Scout project, the gateway into Mormon manhood. Boy Scouts was as complementary to the Mormon religion as strawberries were to whipped cream and shortcake. Few things have been better suited to make a more perfect union. I do not recall earning a merit badge, but I did join the scouts on a few camping trips. Freshman year of high school I started one campout in the river bottoms a couple miles from the church. As night descended we broke into two groups and played "steal the flag," a game, as one might expect, designed for stealing the other group's flag. It was otherwise very much like the game of tag. During the game one of the scout leaders challenged me to a wrestling match. I do not remember popping off, but my stubborn ways must have rubbed him wrong at some point in the evening. By all accounts he had been a dweeb growing up, but manhood had been kind to him and he'd put on a lot of muscle. He easily manhandled me to the ground and contorted my limbs, mashing my face into the rocks. It was not my first shellacking, but was the most unexpected one. Dazed and not far from home, I left the campout.

Our family did not follow BYU sports and we failed miserably at Boy Scouts. We liked Jim McMahon, but who didn't? Not a one among us rose to Eagle Scout. If we shared a passion, it was bull riding. My father had ridden bulls and broncos growing up, but he did not encourage his sons, and his interest was an aberration from the true family passion of horse racing. His grandfather, Orson Stanley Elison, and all of Orson's siblings loved horses. My great-grandfather Orson's youngest brother Bernell (sibling 12 of 13) was my first home teaching companion. Home teaching was a staple of Mormon fellowship, involving paired priesthood holders (males) visiting two or three families assigned by the bishop once each month. The relief society, the women's organization, had its counterpart, visiting teaching where paired women visited women in the ward. A wise bishop not only made me junior companion to my great-grandfather's brother Bernell, who was in his eighties, but he also assigned us to a family who raced horses. Whether we ever delivered the home teaching message as outlined in the *Ensign*, the official monthly Mormon magazine, I do not recall, but we did visit about great horses and the recent places the family had been racing theirs. We spent as much time next to corrals, spitting on manure, as we did sitting in their living room, fidgeting on a worn couch.

By the time the Elison family descended to my father's generation, the love of racing horses was second tier to the love of riding bulls. And if Brumthon introduced Jeremy and Josh to bull riding, the Young brothers, Dustin and Jimmy, showed them how to do it. At every opportunity that arose, Jeremy and Josh tried to improve at riding, getting on every bull they could and talking theory over light beer with the Young brothers and an enclave of bull riders from Shelley, Idaho. When bull riders got together, they drank beer and chewed tobacco as sure as monks prayed and tilled the earth. Heavens, the starting quarterback and head cheerleader, probably both Mormons in many high schools throughout eastern Idaho, were more likely having sex than drinking beer and chewing tobacco. I did not drink, chew, or get laid, but I did not do anything dangerous. Beer and tobacco carried the mark of Cain in Mormon social circles, which struck me as hypocritical even in my youth, given the young Mormons I imagined were lucky enough to have sex, and whom I despised not only for their hypocrisy, but also out of pure envy. I spent more time hanging out with bull riders than Mormon quarterbacks. But I did log a few daydreams about the cheerleaders, and not just the head one, providing my first great lesson of failed wish fulfillment, albeit fully conscious. I had more concerted fantasies in the privacy of my own bedroom than a year's highlights of all the major professional sports combined. One Sunday afternoon, captivated by a short-skirted blonde, I ground into my mattress, creating enough friction to alarm Smokey the Bear, when I heard footsteps descending the stairs from my attic room. To this day, I don't know which member of the family witnessed me in the act of brutal assault on my innocent bed. No group was more accepting and less judgmental than cowboys, as certain as no group was more exclusive and judgmental than Mormons. And because most cowboys drank beer and many chewed tobacco, and some even smoked, I did not grow up associating any of those activities with being indicative of poor character. Rather the opposite was true: cowboys could be as likable and honorable as any people I knew. And I knew a lot of good people. Mormons like my great-grandfather's brother Bernell and our home teaching horse-racing family were salt of the earth. I could not conceive of better examples to grow up with than good cowboys and Mormons.

To be great bull riders, Jeremy and Josh also watched a lot of hours of bull riding tapes, which meant the rest of the household did too. Jimmy Young gave Josh a tape of highlights from the National Finals Rodeo of the early 1980s, when Charlie Sampson and Ted Nuce were the new class among the perennial greats, Denny Flynn, Bobby DelVecchio, Butch Kirby, and the indomitable Don Gay. Josh watched those highlights endlessly. No tapes were viewed more during my youth. Very possibly no tapes have been viewed more anywhere on Planet Earth. One tape was viewed with impressive regularity, but a far cry from the NFR highlights, Lane Frost's four successful rides of Red Rock in the late 1980s. It captured our imaginations again and again. Red Rock was the greatest of all bulls, more renowned among bull riders than even the mythical Brahma bull Oscar, Tornado, and the most recent whipsaw force of all mother's terrae, Bodacious. A bucking bull might be the most athletic creature on earth—two thousand pounds of quick, brute strength jumping high above ground and twisting as forcefully around it. None was more athletic than Red Rock.

Red Rock had not been ridden in hundreds of trips during the eighties until the young World Champion Frost rode him four out of seven tries in a special match of champions. Frost on Red Rock was as graceful a human triumph as recorded on film. Red Rock turned in to Frost's hand the third and fourth successful trips, with as fast and powerful a first turn as any corner a bull ever made, and Frost stayed right there with him. A year after the last Red Rock ride, we sat in disbelief around the television, watching the local news cover Frost at the Cheyenne Frontier Days Show, where Frost made a successful winning, but final, ride as a bull killed him shortly after his dismount. Jeremy stood and walked out into the still young night far out of our hearing. I have not seen him cry, but if he has, he did that night. The sadness we breathed at every thought of losing Frost went beyond those summer days, eased only with time and the rerunning of Frost's inspiring rides and returning perfect smile. Bull riders experience life at its brink. They seek it knowingly with fierce determination, alone. Their bull rides rock with sheer immediacy, testing their mettle, stretching mortality's limits against a fierce animal seeking to conquer them. If grace can be found atop terror, bull riders get sanctified whipping it.

Rodeos took us across the country. Shawnee, Oklahoma, was a long drive from Blackfoot, and felt even longer to us, traveling on the upholstered benches in the back of my father's shell-covered, extended-bed Chevrolet pickup truck. I stayed with Josh in a dorm on an unknown campus. We had no sooner shucked our bags and were heading out, when a Texas State bull-riding champion, Adam Carrillo, stepped into the lounge. I knew he was the champion before he told us because his belt buckle was the size of Texas. Adam was shorter than I, and I was a thin, one-hundred-pound freshman weakling. Size had no effect on being a real bull-riding champion, because most bull riders were short; the men were often old-looking boys. Adam did not sit to visit, nor did I expect he ever sat or his buckle would have cut so deep into his stomach, he wouldn't have been able to breathe. Hell if it wasn't half his torso. Had it sat a little lower, it could have been a chastity belt for all to see and admire. Adam had not qualified for the High School National Finals Rodeo but his twin brother, Gilbert, had. Gilbert had won the event the year before. And Lane Frost had won it ten years before our trek to watch Josh compete.

Jeremy and Josh qualified for the state finals, and Josh, as a sophomore, ended up taking the final spot to represent Idaho in Shawnee. The year before at the state finals, Jeremy, as a sophomore, just missed qualifying for the national finals. As consolation, he and others in the bottom end of the top ten Idaho finalists competed in a regional high school finals in Panguitch,

Utah. I had doubted a place with such a name existed, but it sure enough did, somewhere in southern Utah between the state's awe-inspiring national parks. Jeremy's bull bucked, and he made an excellent ride, it wasn't the winning ride—the two were not always synonymous. He scored second. For the winning ride the bull jump-kicked the width of the arena with a local favorite. Bull riders did everything within their power to ride a bull but the measure of the ride in length and in points was up to judges who gauged the length by fractions of a second, starting a stopwatch as the bull and rider broke from the chute. Sometimes a deft thumb was the only difference between a qualified ride of 8 seconds and an unqualified, but no less worthy, ride of 7.9 seconds. Rodeo judges had to be more impartial than God on judgment day, or the slightest bias could shape the outcome. Panguitch was an early reminder to Jeremy and Josh that their triumphs were measured in moments atop the bull and not by checks picked up at the pay window. While I had not made the trip to Panguitch, I was not about to miss finding out whether there was really a place called Shawnee.

The highlight of the Shawnee trip was seeing Jerome Davis ride. Jerome became a Professional Rodeo Cowboy Association (PRCA) World Champion a few years later, and would lead the race for a Professional Bull Riders (PBR) title in one of the early years of its inception before he broke his neck, ending the career of the sport's brightest star. Despite Gilbert Carrillo returning to defend his title, Jerome was the name everyone exchanged as the rider to watch. During Jerome's tenure as a professional, he set the bar as a class act, and after his accident, he did the improbable and raised it. Paralyzed and wheelchair-bound, he showed that life on top was always about the quality of the individual and not about winning gold buckles, continuing his life as a beacon of positive attitude. Gold buckles surely magnified the light on him, but he held it on his own, reminding all folks that life should not be taken for granted, a tried and true cliché if ever there was one and a glowing reminder for all in need of one.

Truth be told, the highlight of the trip for me was a dance. I moved alone over concrete in a large open pavilion following a dark-haired cowgirl. She had a number pinned to her back, so I knew she was a contestant—a barrel racer, I imagined. Josh was somewhere in the cowboy hats on the dance floor. I scooted through cowboys and cowgirls on the margins of the room, aiming to be close enough to ask her for the next fast dance. I could not two-step, swing, or line dance, and could not much freestyle, but that did not stop me from trying. I got in a lot of practice at Mormon youth dances.

Local wards sponsored a weekly youth activity night called "Mutual." The peak activities were dances during holidays like Halloween and New Year's Eve, action-packed nights for non-Mormon teenagers. The dances offered the promise of connecting with cute girls from various wards. They were also notoriously dull, but I went to all of them, half-way through finding the courage to move off the wall onto the thinly populated basketball court that served as the dance floor.

I wore new leather high-tops with Vibram soles, purchased hours earlier at a vendor's booth that sat with hundreds of others in a still-larger pavilion next door. The cowgirl was striking even compared to the many fair-looking cowgirls two-stepping about. Her features caught my eye, but so did her excitement for non-country tunes, and I watched her move quickly and in sync to the infrequent hip-hop numbers. When "Everybody Dance Now," C+C Music Factory's ubiquitous early nineties dance hit, came on, I felt electricity run through me, and though I acted immediately, it wasn't fast enough. I stepped directly to her, but was a second behind her own reaction to the opening line and she immediately grabbed her cowgirl friend and headed to the open floor. Beside myself, I followed. She ripped into controlled motions in time with the beat, her arms moving and her body following in fluid rhythm, her head moving quickly but independent of all other motion. Good God, her beautiful head with me approaching. We owned the dance floor, my arms and body flailing madly to keep up. I had no rhythm, and only had one move, the "quirky jerk," but there was little chance The Cars' "Shake it Up" would be on the night's play-list. We could have been dancing in my fanciful mind to the Hooters' "And We Danced," but I was more of an on-looker reverberating to Don Henley's "All She Wants To Do Is Dance." I believe she knew it.

—Where are you from?

—Mississippi.

—I'm from Idaho.

Taking a silent oath, I committed to find her in this ethereal paradise of Mississippi, heretofore damnably unknown to me. But not before I developed some of my own cowboy skills. And no place was better suited for making me a champion than Jeremy and Josh's arena.

—You'll ride better with your left hand, Josh assured me.

A bull rider places one hand palm up in a tightly braided rope to hold onto while atop the back of a bull. Josh and Jeremy both rode with their left hands, so I naturally was expected to do the same. I theorized my strong preference was to ride with my right hand. I based my theory on the fact that I skated goofy-footed, having spent hours in the church parking lot on my Powell Peralta McGill skateboard trying to jump sidewalks and do ollies. I also felt I would be more in control of my torso whipping this and that way with my left hand free. Protesting seemed improper. Josh pulled out his left-handed bull rope, readying it by sliding a block of glycerin and smashing crumbs of rosin on it. He lent me a leather glove, rubbing more rosin in the palm before putting it on my hand and tying the end with a leather strap. His boots were a size too big, but they had to do, and I was hopeful I would not have to run too far, too fast. I did not own a cowboy hat, but it was not required to practice in our arena.

I stood behind the chute, trying to warm up my legs, my arms, my head, and my heart as I stared at the bull inside the bars two feet away. I had suspected it was all a bad idea and now, looking at the bull, I knew it with every fiber of my Mormon being. If the spirit of God ever spoke directly to my heart, he did then and it did not feel good. For the first time in my life, I felt one emotion completely as fear overcame me. Shivering, I felt the need to relieve myself. I had done so minutes before in the house and had tried again before putting on Josh's boots. Certain that if I did not try one more time, I would be involuntarily doing it in a few moments when I got on the bull, I turned around to try.

—Get up on the chute.

Josh may have mistaken my turn as an attempt to flee. He wasted little time setting the rope, aware that the more time I had to think about what I was doing, the more likely I'd be to act in concert with the unmistakable terror written large across my pale face.

—Sit it on him and put your legs behind his shoulders.

I did. He was warm and shifted under me. I suspected he was uncomfortable, but not as much as I was. Josh showed me where to put my hand, the single hole in the rope with the handle slanted down and out for a better grip.

—Keep your chest out and squeeze with your legs.

I knew all the smart tactics from years of bull-riding talk, but at that moment did not recall a single one. Chest out and squeeze, I could do. Josh pulled the rope.

—Is it tight enough?

—Yes.

He pulled again and asked me again. I shook my head. He laid the tail of the rope over my grip, not wrapping it around my hand like a professional would do.

—Now slide up on your rope and stay there.

He jumped off the chute.

—Tell me when you're ready?

—Okay.

He popped the handle and swung the gate wide open. The bull turned its head toward the open space and jumped out. He jumped and kicked, heading for the metal panels in the middle of the arena. Reaching them, he turned and bucked along their orange blur. My father stood in the middle of the arena with Josh, both of them yelling at me to hang on. I rode the bull for eight seconds, jumped off, landed on my two feet and headed for the fence. He was not what a bull rider would call rank; he was just a range bull, but he felt strong enough to throw a fool off. Thankfully, not this one. At the height of my success, I should have packed and moved to Mississippi to find the cowgirl I hadn't yet forgotten from the dance in Shawnee. Instead, I opted for more practice the following day.

—Do you want to ride today?

—Yeah.

We had the bulls for a few days, and I needed the practice, now certain that I was destined for greatness. Josh did all the prep work again, and I emptied my bladder, again. I crushed the rosin in the glove myself and borrowed Josh's cowboy hat. I sat on the bull and Josh pulled the rope tight, then pulled again, having explained to me after my first ride the bull would push out his stomach so extra pulls were necessary to ensure there was no slack. He jumped off the gate and upon my nod, he swung it open.

The bull jumped out and bucked toward the right. I squeezed my legs and focused on staying on top as the bull drew close to the fence. In a matter of seconds, the bull lunged into the fence, crushing my right shin on a sturdy wood pole rung. Bull riders knew not to get off on a fence to avoid injuries from being run into it, but I had not been trying to get off the bull onto it. I howled inside. I tried to let go of the rope, and despite Josh not having given me a wrap this time either, my hand stuck tight. My body was strung out with my butt moving farther away from my hand, until the bull lunged to the side, releasing my grip and me into the fence. I could not stand.

—There's nothing broken, my father said.

—Here, stand up, Josh said, lifting my arm around his shoulder.

I hopped out of the arena and into the house. In the worst pain of my life, I sat on a couch with years ahead to recollect upon my heyday as a bull rider. The sharp pain in my shin continued for the next twelve months, hobbling me each second of the day and causing me to awaken throughout the night. Over the next decade, pain randomly debilitated my otherwise graceful gait for days. My illusory destiny of greatness had no sooner begun than the combined stupidity of me climbing atop another bull and the bull jumping into a fence burst it. I had been content to watch and know a few champions before those rides, and the good god of arenas everywhere found me content to just watch and know a few after them.

CHAPTER 3

VIRGIL

Willing my right leg to rise and rest on the step, followed by my left leg rising and doing the same, I painfully ascended the three steps of the yellow bus, my right arm loaded down with a bag full of wrestling gear. I reached a green bench half-way to the rear and collapsed into it, resting my face against the fingerprinted window. Hungry, but craving water more than anything, my lips were past parched, pruned and withered on my shrunken face, opening to suck in air. The bus ride from Blackfoot to Shelley only lasted about fifteen miles, but to me, it was an arduous event, understood by no one save perhaps Lieutenant T.E. Lawrence crossing the Arabian Desert. Beyond our shared thirst, I recognized in Lawrence a mirror of my emotional plight: both of us were oblivious to our surrounding realities and were single-minded in our different purposes—his to defeat the Ottoman Empire and mine to make weight at 119 lbs.

Earlier, before the ring of the bell to start first period, I entered the locker room at Blackfoot High School and walked between the rows of green lockers directly toward the room serving as both the trainers' and coaches' office, a small room shared by the coaches of all boys' sports. I stopped a few feet in front of the door at a scale. Shucking off my clothes, I stepped onto the scale to see how many pounds I needed to drop by weigh-ins that afternoon at the Russets' gym in Shelley.

Checking my weight the morning of a dual meet was like a religious rite to start the day. If I failed to do it to alert me to how much water I needed to shed from my system, I felt the guilt meted in the pounds over my weight class. Like every other morning of a dual, I needed to cut a few pounds throughout the day to make weight to wrestle my Russet foe. Since freshman year I had gotten used to cutting a few pounds the day of every match in order to wrestle at the 103 lb. weight class. I was a tall, skinny freshman starting the year at a fat-free 115 lbs., planning to compete for the junior varsity 112 lb. weight class until the varsity head coach, Curt Talbot, asked me to compete for the varsity position at 103 lbs.

Being a varsity wrestler was an honor not even a level-headed freshman could pass up, but I was motivated even more by Coach Talbot's asking me to do it than by the prospect of notoriety showered on me by my less than half a dozen friends who followed wrestling. Coach Talbot was beloved by all his wrestlers. He transcended from father figure to hero figure, and was closing in on deity status. He was the most important person in many of his wrestlers' lives. To understate the point, he could do no wrong. I did not hesitate to answer his call and immediately began starving myself to make 103 lbs. In the end I did not wrestle a varsity match at 103 lbs., because a senior who had initially started at 112 lbs., decided to drop to 103 lbs. I challenged for the varsity spot, but he handily beat me each time, and I spent the season successfully making weight at junior varsity.

January 1, 1991. It's the start of a new year. I received this journal as a Christmas present for Christmas '90. It was a good Christmas. I'm starting a journal to benefit those who read it after I'm gone. Hopefully some of the experiences will be beneficial. I'm fourteen years old and a freshman in high school. So I hope I will have some exciting things to write about. I also hope I can keep this as neat as possible. I'm not a great speller so please don't be critical. We have been out of school on Christmas break for a week and I haven't done anything. Last night for

New Years' Eve I went to a Church dance. It was really boring, but one of the only things I have done this break. We go back to school tomorrow and I'm not sure I want to go. It will be good to get back with all the kids though. Wrestling started. This is my main sport. The feeling you get when you use every square inch of your body to do something and be successful. This feeling can't be beat and you only get it from wrestling, after you beat an opponent. I've never found this feeling in any other sport and I've tried them all (the major sports, I haven't tried half of the sports invented). To end this entry I might as well describe myself since I'm writing my life events and you (the reader) might want to know about me. Like I said I'm fourteen. I was born in 1976, July 18th. I have five brothers, two step, and one step-sister. Both Grandparents are still alive. I like to play volleyball and wrestle. These are my favorite sports. I like to collect cards and read fantasy novels (although I haven't read a book in a while). I like to travel and spend time with my family. I like to go to dances (I love to dance) with friends. I take pride in my grades and how I dress. This is just a little about me. I hope you learn more exciting and some unbelievable things about me as I continue to write.

Though succeeding far below the expectations of my modest manifesto set out in the first entry, my freshman efforts exceeded those over the next three years—zero entries in sophomore year, two entries in my junior year, and seven short sentences of an entry during my senior year.

January 6, 1991. Today I went to Church and watched Chicago Bears advance in the playoffs. Today I had a near-death experience. To me I have never been so close to death. On the way home from Church I was walking home and I was asked if I wanted a ride. (I don't live more than a couple hundred yards away from the Church.) I replied no as I had many times before. But I said I would hooky-bob the rest of the way home, which was no further than fifty feet. I was holding on to the door because the window was rolled down. The road was pure ice so I was moving right along. I don't know how fast the truck was going but I lost my concentration and was on my knees. I don't know how I recovered but somehow I pulled myself up only having a large bruise on my leg. This was the most frightening experience I've had. Because when I lost my concentration and went to my knees I could have easily lost my grip and fell under the truck and been run over, being seriously injured or killed. I just thank God for saving my life. I know I'm not the best kid around but from now on I'll strive to do the right. I could have been so easily taken from this earth that I will pledge to myself next time such an experience reoccurs I will be able to say and realize I'm pure enough and righteous enough to see and be with my Heavenly Father today.

February 10, 1991. I haven't made an entry for quite some time. So I thought I should bring things up to date. New York Giants beat Buffalo Bills in the Super Bowl last month. Today the East All-Stars beat the West All-Stars in the All Star Game (basketball). I had a four-hour nap today after Church and I had a nice lunch. I probably ate too much this weekend and I'm probably over weight by more than a few pounds. I'm wrestling J.V. right now behind B Niffan at 103 lbs. I've only wrestled five matches this year, winning three of them and losing the other two. I received three forfeits too. To me it's not worth it losing the weight I have to and not having a match. This weekend I went to the Madison Invitational. There were some really good matches. I really want to do well the rest of the season. It ends sometime in March. J.V. gets to go to one more tournament and I want to win it. I can't wait until this trimester of school is over, only a couple more weeks. It isn't that hard I'm just getting so frustrated and mad. I've gotten so short patienced. I'm doing a lot better on my prayers. I say them every night. I realized more fully there are so many bad habits I can get into. I see them all around me. I try to be a lawful dealer in all my dealings. To take card trading as an example, I don't steal cards and try to be fair and giving but I see so much dishonesty. Every day I try to be a better person and keep my standards straight. I try not to cheat anyone and I try to be a better brother. I love my brothers. I don't know what I would do without them. I love my dad too. He's the greatest man I know today. I'm so thankful for my upbringing. I'm so lucky to have what I have. I don't have that strong of a testimony but I'm trying to gain one every day. I'm proud to be a member of the Church of Jesus Christ of Latter-day Saints. To be a Mormon is great.

March 10, 1991. Again I'm slacking off in these journal entries. The trimester has ended and we've already had one week of this last trimester. This may be my last week of wrestling for the year. Districts is next week. Wrestling has really been tough this year. Losing the weight has really been a challenge. I've gotten beat more than I've won this year. I'm looking at it as a learning experience. I know I have it in me to place at Districts this week. And I will give it my all. I think I got 4.0 again this last trimester. This trimester I know I can do it again. We haven't gotten our report cards yet but I feel I did well. The war has ended in the Persian Gulf. I know this is the first time I've mentioned it but it went for quite some time. Cara should be getting married within the next month. Aaron, Josh, Jeremy and I might have a real business on our hands working with fire extinguishers. It might provide a college education for us. I've been slacking off on my prayers. I'll start up again. It's been a while since I've read from the Book of Mormon. Well it's really getting late. I'm going to try and be a little more consistent on my journal entries.

March 14, 1991. I have to capture this moment. This year I lost more than I won. I learned so much though. The guys on the wrestling team were the best this year. This is hard for me to express how I feel right now. We won the district tournament and I was proud to be a part of it. I know now, more than I knew before, why I chose the road of wrestling. I've never been with better people and in wrestling you never get put down. I don't know if it was just me but everybody was so positive to me. You can't find any better coaches than Coach Talbot, C, B and M. I think the world of all of them. Talbot is the best. I'm proud to be part of his brotherhood. No other coach loves his kids like he does. It was great getting to wrestle with this year's seniors. B Niffan taught me a lot. He's one of the nicest guys I've ever met. It was a privilege to share my shoes with Tom. He's a great guy and always was making me feel like I was something. Everyone on the team I loved. I'm glad I had the opportunity to be district champs with such a great group of guys. WD is one of the guys I looked up to. Boy is he a good guy to know. DJ was the animal of the team this year. I hope I don't forget the MS brothers when I get gray and old. They're the couple of nicest and best athletes I know personally. All the guys were great. JP and DL, boy did those guys know how to wrestle. And to end. Gaston Brickmerry. He taught me a lot. He's one of the best people I know. I just appreciate everything he's ever done for me. I love them all. I just want to write the names down of the guys I remember this year in random order. JM and LL are two of the coolest guys. M was major funny and they are both a privilege for me to know. SG is a stud. He had so much heart. He wrestled with heart. M Stallings is one of the greatest guys. He took a bad spill today and dislocated his shoulder. He goes into surgery tomorrow. I love all these guys and the other ones I mentioned. TN is a cool guy. I'm glad I had the opportunity to know him this year. HM and OF. Gosh I love you guys. I hope I can remember all these great friends and my freshman wrestling season on how it ended today. I wish the wrestlers going to state all my best.

March 17, 1991. I finished reading the book Susannah. It was required in my English class. I didn't do much more than read today. I was pretty sore after districts. The next day went by fast. This whole wrestling season flew by. I was only one match away from getting to wrestle for third and fourth at districts this year. This tournament is the only time I really wanted it this year. But I'm glad I ended off well. State is this week and I'm going to see if I can go with the team. I'll need to get a pass though. Freestyle wrestling has begun and I think I'm going to wrestle in it. I need to get my card next week though. I ate too much this weekend. I need to not pig out so bad. I'm going to start push-ups and pull-ups next week. Probably tomorrow. I'm not sore anymore. Well not really. The fire extinguisher business fell through. We don't get the business. So I'll be moving pipe this summer. I still have a cold. A stuffed nose and sore throat. I haven't gotten used to this last trimester of school yet. I think we're entering our third week tomorrow. I just want to thank my brothers. They're great. And all my family.

As a sophomore the morning of the Russet dual, I stood on the scale and looked over my naked body, wondering where those extra pounds were. I did a lot to cut weight but drew a line. I would not have thought to shave my feathers as I hardly had any as a fifteen-year-old, quite partial to my light crop. During my last season of freestyle in the spring of my eighth grade year, not having followed through with my expressed intention in my journal to wrestle freestyle again after my freshman campaign, I had travelled to Salt Lake City, Utah, for a major freestyle tournament. It was projected to have thousands of competitors, and the organizers brought the world's most gifted American freestyle wrestler, John Smith, to do a wrestling clinic before the meet began. Smith had won an Olympic gold two years before in Seoul, Korea and would go on to win another Olympic gold two years later in Barcelona, Spain. Like other young kids, I sat on the edge of the mat trying to pick up Smith's finer points, oblivious to his instruction but captivated by his legend, his frame not much larger than my own. He had dominated international competition, making his mark on the history of American freestyle wrestling. No modern American wrestler had a higher winning percentage than Smith and none could win so efficiently: his low single-leg takedown was impossible to defend even though each opponent knew it was coming.

The Salt Lake City tournament fell short of its organizers' expectations despite Utah's being a hot bed of amateur wrestling. Small pockets of Mormons rodeoed, but large numbers wrestled. The dismal turnout had me considering participating in two weight classes to get more matches, but I opted to wrestle in just one—the 95 lb. weight class. I had wrestled in the 105 lb. weight class during the eighth-grade school season, easily making weight as I naturally weighed just over 100 lbs. I got into better shape throughout the year and found I was far more competitive at 95 lbs. during the freestyle season following the school year. However, the morning of the Salt Lake tournament, I tipped the scale just over the 95 lb. limit; it was the first time I had been overweight. Not over by much, I put on a sweatshirt and headed out to the mats to break a sweat. Upon my return, surrounded by other wrestlers whom I had travelled with from Blackfoot to Salt Lake, I stepped on the scale again. It failed to break, again. I was a quarter pound over weight. The man monitoring the scale told me I could probably make weight if I took off my undershorts. Horrified, I looked down at the sagging underwear over my bony frame. I had never taken off my shorts to make weight. My shy nature was compounded by my nervous impatience to jump-start the puberty many of my peers had already entered by the eighth grade. I always cringed during locker room riffs about the who's who among eighth-grade boys with no pubic hair. I hesitated only a moment and stood swaying on the scale before dropping my shorts and baring my self to known and unknown peers standing by, entering the annals of infamous locker room lists. I went on to win the 95 lb. weight class, the final tournament gold of my freestyle wrestling career, which stretched just shy of a decade from elementary to high school.

Like most other mornings after confirming my aching suspicion that I needed to shed a few pounds, the morning of the Russet dual, I dressed and exited the locker room, heading straight to the vending machines. I proceeded to spend my lunch money on hard candy, Lifesavers. It had become somewhat of a habit to purchase Now and Laters or Jolly Ranchers at a convenient store when I needed to shed weight. The candies helped me spit, and I kept it up, spitting all day. During classes, a walk to sharpen my pencil strategically led me by the trash can, where I quickly spit out whatever saliva the candy had elicited, believing my day-long efforts were worth at least a quarter of a pound. Often I would desire water so much that just feeling it would revitalize me, so I would find a water fountain to slurp enough water to refresh my dry mouth and spit it out again. Spitting became a habit on days I was not sucking hard candy or trying to lose weight as well, and after years of it, my teeth became terribly sensitive, their surfaces wiped of all bad plaque and any protective enamel.

During each wrestling season I identified a class, preferably overlapping with lunch, where I could miss or attend in part, allowing me time to sit in the sauna on the day of a dual match. The sauna was busy on the days of a match, with other wrestlers moving in and out. The amount of weight I needed to cut determined how much extra clothing I wore. I often slipped into the trainers' room for a piece of ice to suck on before finding a bench to lie on in the sauna. A few wrestlers wore plastic workout suits, sometimes in the sauna, but I did not have a suit so I wore garbage bags, poking a hole in the end for my head and holes in each side for each arm.

The day of the Russet dual I sat in the sauna, sweating out a few pounds and nearly breaking the pin, weighing in just minutes before I got on the bus. I had not eaten for twenty-four hours. Extended fasts were as common a practice during the season as getting dressed.

My sophomore year was my most challenging and memorable one, and I had one goal—to make weight. It never crossed my mind to try to win. I weighed between 125 and 130 lbs. most days leading up to weigh-ins, having started the season over 130 lbs. Losing ten pounds in the world of high school wrestling was no great feat, but for a teenager still growing with a small percentage of body fat, it was like climbing Mount Everest for each match. Making weight meant holding a respected spot on varsity, and while my performances were consistently something less than dismal, making weight carried the significance of ensuring the team would not forfeit the weight class. If I lost by less than a pin, the team benefited from my sacrifice. But making weight took all my energy. Only my focus on my desire for food was more consuming. On all bus rides before weigh-ins, I thought upon that one subject: the water I would drink after stepping off the scale, and the mouthful of food I would consume after I got dressed.

We got off the bus in Shelley and walked directly to the locker room. I do not recall weigh-ins ever being delayed, and the Russet dual was no exception. I made weight. As soon as I dressed I found my way out of the locker room to the bleachers and devoured all my packed food, a candy bar and a mustard and ham sandwich, my regular lunch deferred on match day. Parents of other wrestlers advised me not to overeat to avoid cramping, and I would nod, my mouth full, agreeing completely, swallowing and refilling, nodding again.

My Russet opponent did not stand out on their roster as one of their best, but whether known to him or not, he did not need to be to beat me. Our match developed like others my sophomore year, him taking me down and me fighting to stay off my back to avoid being pinned. While the loss to my Russet opponent was not remarkable, our performance was.

My opponent must have been new to the sport of wrestling because he apparently knew only one move, the half nelson. He spent the entire match, six interminable minutes, trying to turn me with a half nelson, the most basic wrestling move known to humankind. If two seven-year-olds with no training should wrestle, the one who gains the top advantage will instinctively attempt a half nelson.

People in the crowd regularly rallied for their wrestler in close matches. Although many of my matches were close, however, the crowd was always silent. I hoped for an outcry from the numbing silence from a family member like the mother at the end of *The Music Man* (1962) when Professor Harold Hill's boys' band, in sharply minted uniforms, played their first musical number before a hostile city crowd. The overcome mother burst out "That's my Johnny," piercing the silence and turning the very momentum of the entire audience to Professor Hill's favor. My wrestling was as uneasy on the eyes as Johnny's playing was on the ears, but still I hoped that someone, somehow proud of me in my singlet uniform, would ameliorate the pitiful scene of my dizzyingly poor performance with a loud yap, "That's my Jesse."

My Russet opponent used the half nelson indiscriminately from both sides of my head, and it did not matter if his body was on the same side for proper leverage, and still he failed to break me off my base. I used my hips and free arm to brace against his torque, stalling for many seconds until the referee told us to try something new, then smartly swiveling my hips so his force turned us in a circle. After a few circles I braced again to resume our stalemate. The referee, befuddled, stood without moving. Again he encouraged us to do something different, but after the first minute he succumbed to his awe and remained silent over the next two rounds, apparently convinced the match would end sooner without him blowing his whistle, interrupting us. It may have been the most boring match witnessed by those in attendance, except many of the spectators from Blackfoot had seen me wrestle before.

My opponent occasionally made progress, slamming my head to the mat, breaking me off my base. Not unaccustomed to having been there before, I used my head to brace against his momentum, with my face rotating in a circle. Mat burns and rosy rashes ran from temple to temple. I often kept my head down, despite the action, as it took less energy. He jumped from side to side, but with no success of turning me to my back. If victory were a result of showing the most resistance, I won hands-down. But the referee raised my opponent's hand at the end.

Somehow I stood and walked toward my team, sitting along the side of the mat. No one said anything. No one seemed to notice. I picked up a round thirty-two–ounce water bottle and wobbled my way to the corner of the mat, where I stayed for the rest of the dual, sucking from the hard community straw meant for momentary bursts of refreshment. After finishing the first water bottle, I rose and retrieved another and finished it in a few short minutes. I grabbed a couple of empties, walked to the drinking fountain on the side of the gym, filled them up, and drank them too.

Who would have guessed that my walk through hell of high school wrestling had its beginning in a wasteland of the sport in Massachusetts, the place of my birth, where I returned at around seven years of age? A decade into the practice of dentistry, my father wanted a break. He had six boys, a wife completely undeserving of the harrowing task of raising them, a residential mortgage, and a leveraged dental practice including a commercial mortgage. None of that stopped him from taking out student loans and moving his family back to Boston to attend Harvard University's School of Public Health. He thoughtfully ran the idea by each of his sons, and as a first grader I voiced my worries about crime, recalling having heard of the Boston Strangler. He chuckled and assured me it would be safe.

The two oldest brothers had been on the first Boston voyage, when my father attended Dental School at Tufts University. My older brother Josh and I joined the family toward the end of the Dental School stint. Josh was born in Saint Elizabeth Hospital in Brighton, reporting forever after that he came into the world in the same hospital where John F. Kennedy was born. I was born fifteen months later at home with a talented midwife in Belmont. Our two youngest brothers had come along after our return to Idaho, and the whole crew headed back for the second adventure of my father's year at Harvard.

Our family drove through Davis Square to arrive at our new home on Kidder Avenue in Somerville, Massachusetts. We pulled into the driveway next to our multiplex house, and with our ordinary bustle, the brood of our family exited the yellow and brown station wagon. It must have sounded like a triumphant event, fitting to the finish of the cross-country trip, our sighs and groans of relief indistinguishable from hallelujahs. On the other side of our new driveway sat another multiplex with one man, a bachelor living on its first floor. He must have heard the noise unfolding outside his walls and, confused, imagining perhaps a riot, he stepped out onto his front porch. Caught between his surprise and the attention of the large litter of boys before him, he welcomed us warmly to the neighborhood and offered to help unpack. He introduced himself as Steve to each of us, making eight new friends who would impose themselves on him that year and many more.

Steve had a turntable and volumes of vinyl in crates scattered throughout his living room and bedroom, stacked next to books and his sparse furniture, which included one worn, cheap, flimsy gray chair for setting things on. From Steve's apartment, music played from the day we arrived until the day we loaded back into the same station wagon to head back west. Tunes from the Beatles, the Rolling Stones, Led Zeppelin, and other rock 'n' roll groups played for my ears for the first time. Steve became one of the family and part of our lives. Each brother had a night assigned as his night of the week, and Steve regularly showed up as the highlight. On my night he played my favorite memory board game, always willing to play again despite defeat after defeat. He alone would willingly be my opponent, as I had long ago exhausted the participation of any member of my family.

Our apartment on Kidder Avenue had two bedrooms. The front living room became my parents' room, which they shared with the youngest, Jed, who was three years old. This turned the dining room into our living room, leaving the two bedrooms on the right side of the hall to the remaining five boys. These two bedrooms were equal in size and initially divided between three in one and two in the other. Within weeks, Jami, in the eighth grade and in dire need of privacy, claimed a closet as his bedroom. It had steps

ascending to a boarded ceiling and just enough space to prop a twin mattress in it. The other three brothers claimed the front bedroom, leaving the
back bedroom to me. That I was stubborn and contentious, always wanting
to fight and argue, did not earn me my own room. That I was a sleepwalker
who turned on the lights after everyone was sound asleep did.

My second grade year in Somerville, I did not wrestle freestyle because
they did not have a local club. The nearest club was miles outside the city.
Jami wrestled in one tournament with a few of his friends from junior high
who could not believe a sport existed that sanctioned something they routinely did in each other's backyards, minus the punching. By the spring of
our year in Somerville when the freestyle season rolled around, Jami had
grown accustomed to New England deli salami sandwiches and pepperoni
pizza and faced much larger opponents during that New England tournament than he had back in Idaho.

After our family moved back to Blackfoot and my father resumed his
dental practice, Steve came out to visit on numerous occasions, driving
straight through the states on one trip and flying in with live Maine lobster
on another. On one of his trips, he brought me *The More than Complete
Hitchhiker's Guide* by Douglas Adams, the source of recurring adventures
filled with laughter.

Steve made a memorable visit during wrestling season my sophomore
year of high school to see me compete on varsity in the sport he had heard
so much about since meeting our family in Somerville. He saw me wrestle
in two matches. After the first he did not say much. After the second he did
not say anything.

Steve arrived on the day of a dual meet at Hillcrest High School in Idaho Falls. Hillcrest was a new high school, and their wrestling team was the
worst in the district. During all my years in high school Hillcrest had one
wrestler place at the state finals. His name was Judd. Judd finished in the top
six, earning a medal, but he did not actually place because his medal was
stripped after his final match when he challenged the referee and opposing
coach to a fight. Judd's coach sat on the side of the mat watching the melee
unfold, having long ago learned that Judd would do what Judd would do and
nothing would stop him.

I first saw Judd wrestle at a freestyle tournament at Skyline High School
in Idaho Falls when I was in middle school. He wore a brilliantly colored
singlet, and three attractive girls surrounded him like a head coach and two

assistants. He smiled broadly, assuring them he would score a quick pin. I sat on the other side of the mat to coach my friend, M Stallings. With trepidation, M shuffled to the center of the mat to face Judd. In under ten seconds, M pinned him.

During high school Judd became a best friend and traveling companion to my brother Josh. Judd and his older brother Brock, like Jeremy and Josh, rode bulls. Brock and Judd rode in the flagship Bull Riders Only organization, the first widely marketed independent professional bull-riding association separate from the PRCA. Bull Riders Only cleared the path for the entertaining and obscenely successful PBR. Both Brock and Judd also rode during the early years of the PBR, qualifying multiple times for the finals in Las Vegas, Nevada. Similar in their attitudes, both fought indiscriminately, normally against much bigger foes. In Brock's case, most of his opponents were in over their heads, but not so much for Judd's opponents. Judd was no less game to fight, he just did not have quite as much ability to fight.

Judd was not in the lineup for Hillcrest the night Steve arrived, so Hillcrest did not have a wrestler favored to win. Judd grabbed me after weigh-ins.

—Our guy hasn't been wrestling long. You shouldn't have a problem beating him.

He announced his confidence in me loudly in front of the wrestlers from both teams and the members of their families. Judd may have been correct in his assessment of my opponent's experience. However, sometimes experience is overrated. After completing my normal rituals for the day of a dual meet, sitting in the sauna and eating nothing but ice cubes, I didn't share Judd's optimism.

True, the Hillcrest wrestler did not know much, but he was athletic, quick, and hard to score against. He too apparently only knew one move. After breaking me down, off my knees where most wrestlers put up their first line of defense, he put his legs around me and squeezed. He initially locked his legs in a figure four, an instinct to gain more control, pushing any energy remaining in my body out with the air from my stomach and lungs. But the referee stopped the match, allowing me to catch my breath and awarding me my single point because the figure four around the body was illegal. After the referee's explanation of the illegal move, my novice opponent was undeterred and wrapped his legs around me again, but he did not lock them in a figure four this time and instead squeezed them like scissors, holding them tight for the remainder of the first round. Of all the moves he could have known, he knew to squeeze out my gizzards. When he gained top control in the second round, he squeezed again, and in the third round he squeezed some more.

Scissoring the body was not a pinning combination. That is to say, it was not a move meant to force the opponent's shoulders to the mat; there was not a final purpose to it. Instead, by squeezing his legs around my midsection, he split my body into two, fixing in place my lower extremities and moving my torso across an invisible plane, exposing my back across that plane, which resulted in near-fall points. He racked up near-fall points again and again, and beat me by major decision. He would have likely won by technical fall, ending the match early, but new points were only awarded on a new move, and he did not always release his scissors. His win was Hillcrest's only one.

—Your team is better fighters than wrestlers, Judd told me.

He could not have projected his own style on a more unsuited recipient, unless he meant to imply that I had my place because fighting included someone losing.

It was customary to ride home with the team on the bus after the dual meet. I did not. After the last match between the heavyweights, I grabbed my gear bag and walked up the bleachers to where Steve sat with my family, my dour countenance masking the joy at his arrival. He smiled and welcomed me with a hug.

—Looked painful and not like a lot of fun, Steve said.

I said nothing, in full agreement. He stood at six feet two, with broad shoulders and a barrel chest. When he was growing up in New England and during college, his sport was rugby, which he played at Wesleyan University in Middletown, Connecticut, and at Trinity College in Dublin, Ireland. He knew pain and fun were not mutually exclusive, but made no attempt to explain why they were not after seeing me wrestle for the first time.

Days later, still during Steve's visit, the most anticipated dual match of the season took place at Snake River High School, our crosstown rivals. Snake River was a small school located in the heart of the agricultural industry of Bingham County. I lived across from the Snake River. While the outskirts of Blackfoot High involved rural areas like Riverton, Snake River High was made up of a wholly rural area. Snake River athletics was a division below Blackfoot's with a smaller number of students, yet no wrestling program was more successful at any division throughout Idaho. Their coach, Keith Williams, ran one of the most successful wrestling programs in the nation, producing many individual state champions and team state championships, and accumulating more dual meet victories under his decades at the helm than all but a dozen wrestling coaches in the history of high school wrestling in any state.

The week of the Snake River dual, I stopped by my father's dental clinic. Sally, his dental assistant, greeted me with a kindness befitting her characteristic sincerity, smiling and welcoming me as if I had stepped in from a storm. Sally lived within the Snake River School District, and her boys wrestled.

—What is your weight class this year?

—119.

—Oh great! You have the weakest kid on our team this year. You'll do great. He hasn't wrestled very long and is not very good.

Sophomore year most attempts at building me up had no effect on me. I thought well of my coaches and teammates, but cared little for what they said when they tried to pump me full of confidence. Wrestling was pain, and I defined my performance by the cliché "win or lose no matter" because I did not win. I experienced pain. But Sally's faith in me moved me differently. She was one of the few people I considered genuine, and I considered very few people to have any semblance of anything genuine. I tried to smile and told her I would do my best.

Sally's assessment of my opponent was not the only one offered to inspire me. When we arrived for weigh-ins, Coach Talbot gave me a pep-talk informing me of my opponent's lackluster reputation.

—You'll give us an important win. Every win will count in this dual meet.

Coach Talbot displayed more confidence in me than at any other time of the year.

—You can beat their worse wrestler. We need this one from you in a big way.

I nodded in agreement with no reason to disagree, if one ignored the matches I had wrestled over the whole season.

Spectators filled the bleachers in the Snake River gym from the floor to the ceiling. During the first two matches, I nervously moved behind the row of chairs where our team sat a few feet from the edge of the mat. As the match before mine came to a close, I took off my warm-up sweats and jacket. I put on my headgear and headed out to the middle of the mat. The whistle blew and we locked arms, our heads bumping as we jockeyed for position. The lead went back and forth over the first two rounds, no one gaining more than a single point advantage. At the beginning of the third round, I trailed by one point, and it was my choice of position to begin the final round. I

looked over to Coach Talbot, knowing what he would tell me, and he pointed down. If I could escape, then I would tie the match, and if I could get a
reversal, then I would go up by one. The third round began. I got to my feet
and he tripped me down, slamming my head to the mat. I got to my feet
again and he tripped me down again, once more slamming my head to the
mat. I tried to reverse him, moving from side to side, trying to tear his grasp
from my arm, trying to peel his individual fingers locked around my waist.
He was strong, a hallmark of all Snake River wrestlers, who were by and
large farm boys who had worked long days in the fields during summer and
harvest ever since they were big enough to lift pipes and heave bales of hay.
All of my opponents were stronger than me, but none had a more singular
iron grip from which I could not break free.

I had been working in farmers' fields to develop my strength since the
summer of seventh grade. I was not a natural farmhand, but there were
many fields surrounding our house providing opportunities to develop me
into one. I started by moving irrigation pipe in potato fields for a farmer
who leased land on the Fort Hall Reservation. The farmer hired my friend,
Gaston Brickmerry, and Gaston moved two lines twice a day every day of
the summer. One day he asked if I wanted to help, and the next day, before
sunrise, he picked me up in his older brother Ship's truck. Gaston did not
have a license and drove the bald-tired truck with reckless abandon on the
dirt roads connecting Riverton to the reservation. We fishtailed all the way
there, me silent and sick to my gut, praying for God's protection until we
finally pulled up to the potato field.

The field was not large by any standard, a few acres only, surrounded by
other fields and a couple of small, government-subsidized, small box homes
to the east and southwest. One line ran north and another line ran south,
with a main water line running across the middle of the field. After unhook-
ing the head valve from the main line and moving it to the west a dozen
rows, Gaston started me on the south line. Facing south, he showed me how
to unhook a pipe by pushing it in and twisting it. He pulled it out and lifted
it, water pouring out both ends as he glided over the dikes covered by spud
vines, managing to avoid tangling his feet as he stepped to the new row. Facing north, he hooked the pipe into the head valve on the center water line
as seamlessly as he had removed it from the old one, setting it down as the
beginning piece of the new line. He demonstrated the entire feat again on
the next pipe. He turned and jogged toward the north line and proceeded to
set up the new line.

I faced the line running south and pushed the pipe in to unhook it, wrestling the stem of the pipe to free it. Gaston had warned me against pushing high on the stem in case it broke from the pipe. I took a breath and tried again to push the pipe in, using all my force against the base of the stem. It didn't budge.

—Gaston! Gaston!

He ran between the vines, hopping the dikes to where he had left me. I stepped aside and he forced it free, pulled it out, and left it sitting in the row.

—They often jam. You have to keep twisting to free it.

He headed back to the north line. With the freed pipe at my feet, I bent down with one hand gripping the stem and the other gripping the pipe and tried to lift it. Water poured from the ends as I struggled to raise it a few inches off the ground. I had not even considered that I would not be able to lift the pipe. I tried again, pushing it forward onto the dike as it dropped. Again I lifted the pipe and, unable to clear the spud vines, I stepped into them and dropped the pipe. It lay partially over the dike with its end unhooked a few inches from the old line. I attempted another lift, raising the pipe to its highest point at the middle of my thighs, water pouring out its ends. I lifted my leg to brace the pipe, but with my foot tangled in the vines the pipe began to wobble beyond my control. I tripped over the dike and dropped it again. Brooding over my many minutes of failure, I exploded with my frustration of my puny might.

—Fuck me! You fuckin pussy!

Repeating my tirade over and over, I steamed with hate. Accustomed to being at the mercy of older boys and brothers, I had a childhood that was one constant reminder of my physical limits. I had less of a fighting will than I had a purely obstinate one that led me down one path after another of inevitable conflict. I rarely prevailed. My single greatest physical accomplishment was push-ups. During elementary school my older brothers had push-up contests before bed, and before long I was pumping out one hundred straight. One night we decided to max our efforts, and I topped a cool three hundred. No one else came close.

Trying and failing to move the pipe, I cussed and cussed myself, and I cussed God, a lot. My cursing took on a ferocious performance, hollering at God in the open space around me through maddening tears. I tempted God to damn me in exchange for not having to see the God responsible for creating such a weakling as me. Between my rants of self-hatred, I tried to lift and move the pipe. My curses spent every one of my breaths. Our pre-dawn start gave way to a strong sun, hinting at a warm day. Gaston finished and went back to his brother's truck, where he sat on its hood and watched me, waiting for a conclusion to my wailing. I continued to curse God and myself until, seeing no end in sight Gaston ran across the field with an uncontrollable smile and bubbling laughter.

—Okay, okay. Lift there and we'll move them together.

With an inerasable grin he helped me unlock and lift the next pipe and move it, and repeated the process for each remaining one from the old line to the new. He promised to pay me for the whole line. He roared his brother's truck and we fishtailed the whole way home.

Gaston, the closest to a best friend I had in middle school, within days invited me to move the line again, and I accepted, undeterred by inevitable failure. By his second invitation he had spread news of my defeat, and his brother Brumthon instructed me to lift the pipe with one hand on the stem and to set the pipe on the bicep of the other arm while holding it close against my chest. His advice proved effective. I moved the entire line without help from Gaston or any cursing from me. I had bruises on my bicep and chest the next day to show for it. I proceeded to move pipe during the summers until after graduation, when I moved to Provo and worked as a roofer before my freshman year of college. On many summer days growing up, I added hauling hay to moving pipe. I rose from a dependable bale roller to a venerable spot on the bed of the truck bucking bales. All my farm work made me stronger, but my development still lagged behind that of my farmhand peers across the Snake River.

I could feel Coach Talbot's gaze among all the people in the Snake River gym filled to its capacity. I was more active during the third round against my Snake River opponent than I'd been in any of the matches I had wrestled that year. By the final buzzer I failed to escape or gain a reversal, so I lost by one point. I took in Coach Talbot's disappointment written across the furrow of his brow as I walked off the mat. I said nothing, going to the back to gather my team sweatpants and jacket. I sat quietly during the rest of the matches. My loss was Snake River's gain of three team points, and we lost the dual meet within that margin, our best showing against Snake River in years. After the meet ended we formed a line and shook hands with the Snake River wrestlers. I turned around and found my bag full of gear, speaking to no one, no one speaking to me, all of us aware that my loss had cost us the dual meet. Having smartly obtained consent from my coaches to ride home with my family before the match, I walked up the bleachers to them, ready to go. Steve ruffled my hair and we walked out of the gym.

The wrestling season ended and district championships loomed days after the Snake River dual. Within the last couple weeks, I acquired a staph infection, and it caused infantigo. Or maybe those things were the same, but to this day I am not sure, and lack the motivation to know for certain if I had one or two dreaded skin infections. Infantigo was not uncommon among wrestlers exposed to sweaty, unclean mats, and commonly manifesting as rashes on the joints, elbows, and knees. My bout broke out all over my face, with rashes and blisters running from one side of my face to the other, making Queequeg's hideously marred face that of a cherub in comparison. Gaston pointed out my need to see a doctor to clear it up, so after weeks of its spreading, I proposed seeing one to my parents. If Gaston had not taken an interest in my face, as no one in my family did or would have, I could have scabs proliferating on it and beyond to this day. It was not the first time he showed an interest when no one else did. During my eighth-grade freestyle season, I injured my left shoulder and could not extend it for weeks. It was Gaston who took the time to slowly lift it in millimeters, as I cringed in pain, to give it a full range of motion.

Days before districts, a cheerleader, Lacy, approached me under a basketball hoop in the gym and kindly asked me if the thing with my face was from wrestling. I nodded that it was, not thinking to hide my hideous mug and never for a moment contemplating its effects on others. As undesirable as my face must have made me, it saved me from more punishment on the mat, disqualifying me from entering districts.

May 7, 1993. If you read my last entry, you must be thinking, this guy is lame. 'Seize the Day' what for? What the hell made this guy stop writing in his journal? To tell you the truth I don't know why! I think, for a while I was afraid to grow up. I was afraid to wright down my experiences because reading them would only bring back heart ache. I apologize for my absence of writing in the past two years. Teenage life is trying and I just lost interest in writing down my experiences. The best teacher I've ever had is Bro. Livingston. I'm positive I knew him in the pre-mortal existence. He is so great. He has so much love and cares so much about the youth in the Church today. I think he has influenced me to write in my journal and to read my scriptures. He is such a great guy. More so than Bro. Livingston, my brother Jeremy has influenced me to keep positive and read the scriptures through his great example and the letters he writes me. As a junior in high school I have my fears and frustrations. There's only four more weeks of school left. You (the reader) have missed out on two trying and fun years of my life. To quickly brief you on my status, I've kept my 4.0 GPA. I'd like to go to BYU but I take the ACT in June and need to score well. Last June I scored a 19 but it wasn't that disappointing because of how I took the test with as little as interest as I did. I plan on getting in the high twenties this June. I've lost a dear friend in Gaston Brickmerry two summers ago. It broke my heart when he and his brother did a scam on my father and a few others. Wrestling is still a huge part of my life. Coach Talbot is awesome. I have so much love for him. Turner is a stud too. I've made great friends over the last two years and strengthened relationships with old friends. I'm not involved with any girls. I'm taking CH to the Jr. Sr. Ball tomorrow. She is really cool and has a great personality. I kind of like a girl named LT. She ain't a member but is super cool. She is also gorgeous. The best part of the past two years and every day of my life is the continued growth in my relationship with every member of my family. My testimony is growing. I have some horrible habits but I'm trying to get them licked. My family is great. My brothers I love so much. My parents do so much for me. I love Jami and Jeremy. Jami has taught me so much. He's a great example to me and is so intelligent it blows me away. I love Jeremy. I'm glad he is serving the Lord so diligently and through his example my testimony is growing. I love Josh, Jacob, Jed, and Aaron. I hope I've been a good brother to them. I treasure my relationships with them so much. I appreciate Gayle and all she does. I love my father with all my heart. He is such a great man. He is trying so hard to be a better person and there is no one I respect more or cherish one's example more than my father's except Jesus Christ's. I have so much love but yet I have so much fear. The world is so wicked and I truly want the Savior's help to resist all worldly evils. Nothing is more important to me than returning to see my mother and God with Jesus one day. I don't want to miss that chance but I have so many faults and I really need the help of Jesus Christ to make it. I know the signs of the times are upon us and I only wish I will be worthy to meet my savior every day I live. I guess the main reason I started writing in a journal again was to express my beliefs and tell my family how much I love them in case tomorrow was my last day on this earth.

I'm not the most educated person. I'm not the most outstanding, but deep down inside I would like to leave a positive and loving influence on all I come in contact with. I hope I keep diligent with my feelings and experiences in my future days in this journal because there is so much I want to say and so many names of great friends and teachers I want to mention but can't in this one day. I love life and honestly long for the second coming. I more than anything hope I'm ready to meet my Savior and am pure enough to live with him again along with all my friends and family. I'm willing to sacrifice all to live in the presence of God and my elder brother with all my family and friends but I know it will take the help of my savior to get through this world. I know I can't do it alone because I'm so far from perfect. I wish I could write forever because I have so much to say but I'll live it for another day. To all reading hang in there and don't ever give up.

After one winning season during my junior year wrestling at 140 lbs. on junior varsity, I began my senior year with great expectations. I tipped the scale at the beginning of the year at a fit 165 lbs. Then I lost the first wrestle-off for the varsity position at 152 lbs. I later earned it, but I decided after a shellacking at 152 lbs. at the Madison Invitational tournament that I would drop one more weight class. I spent the disappointing year trading off the varsity spot at 145 lbs., ceding the district seat to my teammate who went on to finish fourth at the state finals. I did not qualify for the state championships that or any year. After my final match at the district tournament, I walked by Coach Turner, picked up my warm-up clothes and headed to the locker room. I changed into jeans and put on my team sweatshirt with the image of a crane swallowing the head of a frog, the frog's webbed grip around the throat of the crane with the words below it "Don't ever give up." I found my family in the stands and left the tournament. We stopped at a family-favorite Mexican restaurant for dinner around the time the championship matches began, and I gorged on spicy enchiladas. A few weeks later I missed the team party at Coach Talbot's house, and the morning after the team party, he found me and pulled me out of class to give me my bar for lettering.
   —We missed you at the party, he said.
   I avoided his gaze, took the manila envelope, and returned to class.

CHAPTER 4

THE MILITARY

I made it to Brigham Young University on a lucky break that came during my senior year of high school. One afternoon I received a phone call from an army recruiter. Initially I rebuffed his offer to discuss joining the army, but finally agreed to a follow-up call when I had more time to talk. He scheduled a time and he called me back, pitching the value of the army and requesting to meet. An unassuming teenager interested in experience beyond his hometown, I accepted. I did not consider the challenges of being in the army, let alone the possibility of fighting a war.

My naiveté combined with my larger hope of having found an answer to paying for college. The closer I came to finishing high school, the more daunting paying to attend BYU became, with no savings and no scholarship to support me. School did not come easily, although it may have appeared so to someone not noticing the massive amounts of time I put in to suc-

ceed. But unimpressive national test scores stopped me from competing for
scholarships. Short on natural or developed brilliance, I relied upon putting
in extra time to learn, under no misconception I could rely upon aptitude
that did not exist. Given my scholarship prospects of zero, I resigned myself
to attending Ricks Junior College in Rexburg, Idaho, also an LDS-owned
school, where I would get financial aid.

The recruiter and I met at my family's dining table, in our large eat-
in kitchen, through which people moved from the back door to the living
room, the central artery of our house. A more appropriate place to visit
would have been the living room, but with fortune on my side our visit took
place amid the post-school and post-work bustle. Everyone worked their
way by us to the fridge, then into the living room to watch television and
back again. Because I had not mentioned the meeting to anyone, the man in
uniform garnered me more than my regular share of attention.

During the meeting my father arrived home from work, and I introduced him to the recruiter. My father joined the Marine Corps after his
sophomore year of college at BYU, preempting the draft to do his duty in
Vietnam. He has always spoken of the Corps with great pride and decried
their popular image with consternation. He bemoaned movies like Stanley
Kubrick's *Full Metal Jacket* (1987) for Hollywood's infusion of profanity into
the Marine Corps. According to him, in his day marines did not have to talk
like Hollywood jarheads to be hard marines. Drill sergeants were always
loquacious but, unlike their contemporaries—refashioned by Hollywood
and unabashed about manifesting their intelligence in four-letter-word increments—they had not always sworn incoherently. To this day I have not
heard my father swear (my mother, yes, but she tried to rear six boys), and by
his own word he belonged to a Marine Corps above the vernacular sewage
copied from the silver screen. The use of FUBAR might go back to World
War II, but go a little further back and you won't find that Smedley Butler
used it. And you'd certainly not find that Daniel Joseph Daly did either. Hell,
he didn't likely use the curse word attributed to his famous hailing, "Come
on, you sons of bitches, do you want to live forever?"

My father's eternal brotherhood with the Corps had begun at boot camp
in San Diego, California. Boot camp was hell but even in hell, stripped of
freedom, my father learned that marines could still retain their dignity. One
member of his platoon, a young man from the South, was a bedwetter. My
father had been a bedwetter growing up, so he knew its accompanying humiliation and lasting shame was worth a Thomas Bernhardean reservoir

of physical ailments good for a dozen autobiographical masterworks. And bedwetting did not improve by talking cures. The drill sergeants ordered the young man to walk the length of the barracks with nothing more than an oversized diaper on while all the other members of the platoon stood at attention at the foot of their lockers. The young man began to walk down the middle when another member of the platoon, a young man from the Northeast, turned his back on the scene and faced his bed. Every member of the platoon followed, defying the trainers and leaving at least one marine with an undying conviction to defy cruel, abusive authority.

After completing boot camp, my father moved to Camp Pendleton for BITS, Battalion Infantry Training. Shortly after he arrived there, the "G" Company sergeants invited my father into their office. He entered to find another young marine present. The other had amateur boxing experience, and my father had no illusions that he could take him. Skilled pugilists abounded in the company. Another member, reputed to have sparred with Muhammad Ali, confirmed his skills in the mess hall by knocking out a navy man who refused to go to the end of the line after cutting in.

—Can you take this Marine? a trainer asked.

My father had been in a few fights, but by his own admission, he had had little success. One fight he recounted more than once to his six sons, intent on dissuading similar action, involved a one-sided pummeling behind Arctic Circle, the burger and fries restaurant on Main Street, the main drag in Blackfoot. And he was on the receiving end. His boyhood pards, Ken and Dillon, never shied from fisticuffs, but my father rarely had to fight because of them. But that day at Arctic Circle my father had been with less-proven friends who used the tough engines of their muscle cars to flee challenges more often than sticking around to confront them. Straight-faced, he looked at his BITS trainers.

—I wouldn't be surprised.

The hell. The trainers told him that he would be the Guidon Bearer for Company "G" Flag for the remainder of the training. He never spoke of the honor, but years later Gayle framed a photograph of Company "G" and hung it on the wall of their home, my father immortalized holding the Marine Company "G" Flag at the bottom corner.

At Camp Pendleton my father passed exams to qualify for OCS, Officer Candidate School, in Quantico, Virginia. At Quantico he set the record for the fastest time for the obstacle course, as I learned in a haze of cigar smoke at my atheist Uncle Band's apartment in Salt Lake City. I was surprised to learn of his obstacle course achievement because my father always denounced athletics, and I had always, wrongly, conflated athletics with fitness. My father denounced the pipedream of collegiate or professional athletic careers at the beginning of each sport's season, always coupled with pronouncements of the superiority of classroom education. His distaste for athletics grew from lasting bitterness about having been cut from the varsity basketball team as a junior, which initiated a decline in his grades. Until then he had had grades as good as my mother's. She, along with his best friend (then her boyfriend), and the brothers who founded a global technology company, all graduated in the top ten of their class without my father.

Many state champions across various sports and collegiate athletes had run the obstacle course at Quantico, some who probably had graduated in the top ten of their high school class, and my father bested them all. I imagined his run the day he broke the record was a proud one. Years later I was proud to hear about it and instantly revised my comparison of him to my friends' fathers growing up. Certainly mine was the toughest of them all.

Band told of my father's accomplishment after recounting his own misguided challenge to wrestle my father during Band's freshman year at BYU. Band was a good athlete, having played multiple sports, lettering as quarterback, starting guard, and infielder, and still finding time to be student body president. In his senior year, he focused on debate during basketball season, to the chagrin of the basketball coach, AG Fowler, my driver-training instructor decades later. Upset when Band missed practices for debate competitions, Coach AG required Band to practice with the junior varsity, believing the shame would lead him to a stronger commitment. Instead Band quit the varsity team on the spot and continued to debate. In later years, I never had a discussion with Band I could distinguish from a debate. Band similarly rebuffed bloated authority during his third year of law school when a law professor told him he would receive a failing grade if he missed an exam to attend a friend's funeral. Ranked number two in his class, Band had everything to lose, and the professor knew it. Band told the professor to fuck himself on his way out of the office in a rage. Band missed the exam to attend the funeral and he finished second in his class, continuing on to earn an LLM in tax from New York University, by all accounts wasting his natural disposition to debate and becoming embroiled for decades in parsing federal and state tax codes.

My father, not the accomplished high school athlete like Band, was lanky and fit as a ranch hand, having been a rodeo cowboy in high school and junior college. His organized high school sports career reached its pinnacle when he was a back-up infielder on the varsity baseball team. But when Band, the decorated high school athlete, wrestled the newly minted marine officer it was no match. At once my father controlled Band to the floor, twisting him in excruciating pain, forcing pleas for a quick release. While neither had any wrestling background, my father's grappling portended his six sons' mat-time and success for several, although it was not my lot to be one of them.

The military looked promising, and I agreed to visit with the recruiter again. Then one evening, shortly after the meeting, I again sat at the dining table doing homework and my father entered. He interrupted me and with no introduction told me he would pay for my tuition and living expenses to attend BYU, so there was no need to meet the recruiter again and consider joining the military. His offer was unprecedented, and astounding. My father had received no assistance from his father and believed unequivocally that parents who assisted their children in adulthood impeded their progress, college assistance included. Not to mention that my older siblings had received no assistance to attend college. My father considered that part of his duty in raising his sons was telling many stories about parents who made the right and harder choice by saying no to children, needy or not.

One story still strikes me as bizarre, about a mother who had supported a son for years and decided to stop after learning he was broke in a foreign country. The mother simply responded to repeated requests with postcards stating "I love you and will not give you any help." What the fuck? Even as a young impressionable kid, trusting my father, I asked myself how in the hell did that story end, believing the mother cruel in picking a poor time to teach her son a lesson. At some point my father had communed, probably in the pre-mortal existence, with Chekhov's Father Khristofor and Moisei Moiseich, agreeing with them that all children were bothers, which inspired my father to rid himself of the burden when each of us left home. And he followed through. I did not argue with him about the story of the mother's warped love when he first told it nor did I remind him of it that evening. My long-standing suspicions aside, that night I accepted his offer on the spot and eventually canceled my future appointment with the recruiter.

My father was zealous about ensuring that his children developed independence. I only knew him to be more passionate about one thing, his belief in Jesus Christ, a belief beyond any conceivable barometer in the history of proverbial passions, except for folks with similar beliefs in Jesus, of course, and those with other religious fervors. His belief in Jesus was impenetrable, ranking with that of the most ardent followers of Jesus throughout the history of Christendom. And while it was below his passion for Jesus, but registering high in his non-Jesus passion, he also wanted his sons to be their own men, relying on no one other than themselves, save Jesus. Education was a critical component for achieving that independence. My father's restraining his passion in my case was not insignificant or without contradiction, a monumental swing activated by the army recruiter's persistence and providential visit.

Advocating even for more than education over sports, my father tirelessly professed his belief in Jesus over all other alternatives between Earth and the planet Pluto. That is when Carl Sagan was alive and Pluto was still considered a planet. My father quoted by heart, and quoted often, a passage from the Book of Ether in the Book of Mormon. The book's final editor, Moroni, interrupted his summary of the ministry of Ether to explain the power of faith, highlighting the example of the brother of Jared, whose great faith allowed him to see the Lord and to move a mountain, the mountain of Zerin. That's faith. In his aside, Moroni lamented his inability to write the powerful words of the Lord, and the Lord spoke to him: *And if men come unto me I will show them their weakness. I give unto men weakness that they may be humble; and my grace is sufficient for all men that humble themselves before me; for if they humble themselves before me, and have faith in me, then will I make weak things become strong unto them* (Ether 12: 27). (This same state of weakness was celebrated by the Apostle Paul in 2 Cor. 12: 7-10.) If my father had been required to choose only one thing to remember, he would have chosen this passage of scripture. It explained everything about salvation and about life. He was weak and Christ was the answer. Not only was he weak but also Christ had made him weak so he would be humble, and thus receptive to Christ. He proselytized his weakness and Christ's role in overcoming it endlessly to everyone who knew him, because he believed it was a reality for everyone. Everyone was weak, and everyone needed Christ. Even in an alternative reality these two facts would be true. Weakness anchored his religious personality, and nothing meant more to him than his duty to anchor his sons with it too.

During my years of junior high and high school my father served as the first counselor in the stake presidency. A "stake" consists of multiple wards within a certain geographic region. For nearly a decade my father gave hundreds of talks, and they were all variations of one theme, our need for a savior and Jesus' role as the one. He quoted from memory every saying attributed to Jesus in the New Testament, with a preference for imagery from the Gospel of John, where Jesus referred to himself as the bread of life (6: 35) and as the vine to our branches (15: 5). My father repeated there was no other way to eternal life than through Jesus. He was not making that up because Jesus said that too, that he was the way, the truth, and the life (14: 6). My father ceaselessly testified over the pulpit and over the dinner table that change happened only through Jesus. And since everyone had weaknesses, everyone needed Jesus. No reality could possibly define a man more than Jesus defined my father.

My father was not merely a good Christian, believing Jesus sacrificed for the sins of humankind and conquered death, rising on the third day after his crucifixion to offer salvation and eternal life to all who believe on his name. My father believed Jesus was the only source of real change in a person's life from overcoming debilitating addictions like alcoholism to ending minor but offensive personality quirks. To suggest psychology or therapies could help treat addiction or heal emotional deficiencies smelled of the sin of idolatry because something, that is anything, was being substituted as a cure in the place of Jesus, whose job it was to change people, on top of saving them. My father's militant Jesus must have germinated in the Corps. It surely did not in the Mormon Church.

And on this score my father's household could not have been more non-Mormon-like. During Mormon Church services, members repeat their beliefs in modern prophets, including the living prophet acting as the president of the Mormon Church and also the founding prophet of Mormonism, Joseph Smith. My father offered countless talks as a local leader, and I cannot recall (and dare the thousands of members who also heard him) his mentioning once the legitimacy of the Mormon leadership (the litmus test of genuine Mormonism). What he bore, in testimony about as pure as a newborn baby, was his undying conviction in the power of Jesus not only to save humankind from eternal damnation but also to change humankind through his available divine presence. While it would be an anathema to question or correct Mormon leadership in most (probably ninety-nine percent) of Mormon households, it was the regular course in my father's. Mormon leadership had value inasmuch as they directed the Mormon membership toward Jesus' saving grace. Inasmuch as they did not—and my father never failed to point out when they did not—they were obstructing the Mormon membership from Jesus. And that was not an acceptable position for leadership to assume, according to my father.

Wherever his belief took hold in my father, its roots went back as far as the Apostle Paul's writings in the New Testament. Paul claimed no one was justified before God by the Law of Moses. He went further and claimed anyone proceeding under that law was cursed (Gal. 3: 10). For Paul, and traditional Christianity that embraced his point of view, justification before God came through Christ (Gal. 3: 10-14). Christ redeemed us through his death and resurrection. The law was a mere *schoolmaster to bring us unto Christ, that we might be justified by faith* (KJV Gal. 3: 24). This curse was as much a given (that is, a constituent piece of reality) as all people's having weaknesses, which made Paul a pretty fair interpreter of the purpose of life for my father. But the appeal of Jesus to Paul and my father went beyond salvation, it went to Paul's explanation that Jesus offered to make everyone *new beings* in their lives.

Instead of arguing over Paul's superior view of Jesus that people are saved by faith and not works, or the consequences after it subordinated the Law of Moses—both perennially hot and controversial topics—there cannot be a more pertinent inquiry than his claim *Therefore if any man be in Christ, he is a new creature: old things are passed away; behold, all things are become new* (2 Cor. 5: 17; Gal. 6: 15). A new being arises from a human's being in Jesus, not merely through the covenant of baptism as correctly implied in the New Testament. Many followers of Jesus since Paul locked onto this notion of a new being in Jesus Christ, and they have succeeded brilliantly in providing a plethora of explanations. But is there any proof? Or even more fundamentally, is there proof people actually change? I mean really, really change with or without Jesus' help. Demanding evidence of a new being is not the same as demanding proof that Jesus has saved anyone from eternal damnation. We can and must do the former, because we have evidence from those who claim to have experienced their new creation in Jesus.

And is not whether Jesus changes people in this life a far more pressing question than whether he saves them in a next one? Take one example: the life of the Apostle Paul. What evidence was there he became a new creature or experienced a new creation? Whatever evidence we have to determine that he changed in this life is far more than we have to determine if he was saved in another life. Paul reputedly started his historical career persecuting Christians (Gal. 1: 13) until having a vision of Jesus (1 Cor. 9: 1). After his vision, he reigned supreme as the greatest missionary of the gospel of Jesus of all time, zealously preaching that salvation came through the death and resurrection of Jesus and not the Law of Moses, exerting a lot of effort to

correct people's views about Jesus after his tireless and enormously successful efforts to introduce them to him in the first place. Most of Paul's work to
correct Christians' beliefs is the basis for the recorded thirteen letters in the
New Testament, over half of which were most likely really written by him.
That makes him the single greatest source of Christianity by a tsunami, over
the next closest high tide of say Augustine or Aquinas or Billy Graham.

So what changed? Paul's beliefs changed and so did his behavior—by his
own account he believed the savior story and he quit trying to jail Christians
after he saw Jesus. And the chief recorder of Paul's life, the author of The
Acts of The Apostles, noted this change as Paul went from holding the robes
of Jewish leaders of the Sanhedrin, who stoned the early Christian Stephen
for preaching Jesus Christ's salvation over the Law of Moses (Acts 6 & 7),
to preaching Jesus Christ's salvation over the Law of Moses and causing his
own stoning (Acts 14). That is the New Testament evidence showing Paul's
change. And that evidence is significant. That is real change, if new behavior
qualifies one as a new creature. Or in other words, who we really are can be
reduced to our actions. That may very well be true. I for one am persuaded
that the fairest measure of who we really are is what we do, including speech-
acts like telling someone she did a good job when she did or someone to shut
the hell up when he should. But change of behavior is generally not what's
meant by a *new creation* or *new being*. Change of behavior is more like an
unruly dog's becoming a well behaved one, all the while still being a dog.
A new being is in tune with the divine. It consists of a transformation of
personality, will, heart and *nature* in the service of Jesus, or better stated in
Christ, *For to this end Christ both died, and rose, and revived, that he might
be Lord both of the dead and living* (Rom. 14: 8-9; Gal. 2: 20-21). It involves a
refining of personality, not necessarily weak to bold but no less marked than
Clark Kent's becoming Superman.

So did Paul's being change? If it did, there is no evidence it did (that
is not to say he did not talk about it plenty, because he did, and those who
wrote in his name talked about it even more; but as we all know, people
who tell nonstop about something and that something's actually being the
case are often a canyon apart). There is, however, evidence Paul's being did
not change. Paul ran a hundred miles an hour toward his goal before seeing
Jesus and ran as fast and farther after he saw him. He zealously evangelized
the gospel of Jesus for nearly two decades, suffering multiple imprisonments
and beatings. He succeeded in establishing a correct understanding of Jesus
that emerged from his letters. It told of a savior Jesus that was embraced by

what would emerge as the orthodox church of the third and fourth centuries (which explains how his letters ended up in the Christian canon). But none of this gargantuan devotion proved he became someone he was not already. It showed the same Paul but on a very different mission, headed in a very different direction.

Central to that correct view of Christ he founded was the propitiation for past wrongs. He was *sold under sin* (Rom. 7: 14) and needed help to remove it. Paul's explanation about becoming a new creature certainly meant something more than a change in direction. It meant erasing past wrongs, and change of disposition from natural to divine inclinations. In the end, Paul may have spawned the most powerful and successful belief in the possibility of change recorded in holy or profane writ. He proved someone could have a really strong belief in change, and his recorded aspirations have resonated with Christians who want to be new beings too, for centuries.

So what about the legion of folks who embrace a new belief and are unrecognizable to those people who knew them in their former lives? We have all met these people. Is not that proof? Is it a matter of their having changed or our not having known them? Is not the illusion that they have changed as obvious as the falsehood that we had all the information necessary to have judged them? Exposing our ignorance even further is how awfully lazily and commonly we ascribe someone becoming a different person when she merely develops her potential. Could we be more offensive? And is not this becoming a new person less a matter of the mysterious and more a matter of incremental steps of development done outside of our purview? And the stuff we recognize as change, has not that come through forming new habits in a new direction? Not some dramatic event? Not to mention the various conditions that affect each and every one of us. Those conditions change, but do we? And if we do, is not that change in habits in response to new conditions? I for one am a hell of lot kinder employed and eating a healthy diet than I was as a university student on the dole eating off dollar menus. It is not that we do not recognize differences in these folks any more than we did not accurately acknowledge their failings in the past. We actually saw both parts, but they were parts of a whole picture we did not see. And the real differences we see are reducible to their behaviors and actions (likely linked to their conditions). Any claim of being a new creature is an expression of ignorance, likely both theirs and ours as surely as if a new creature is as superficial as a translation from the name of Saul to Paul.

If people actually experience a new creation, the bar for showing people become new creatures is much higher than showing people will be saved in heaven. Proof for the former of a single lifetime would be thousands of volumes filling one's own Alexandria library. Showing the latter is accomplished in church buildings throughout the world in minutes or by someone attesting he or she has been saved to your rising blood pressure.

My father embraced Paul's belief in Jesus' changing his being, but neither man—let alone anyone else who has lived—showed the life of a new creature as a result of that belief. Paul may have told an even more important story if the evidence from his life showed a life-long responsibility for one's actions instead of pushing them onto Jesus. But the sheer challenge of telling that story would never have created the fever pitch that came from the one he did tell, whitewashing and excusing one's past. A "do over" as a new bird, that caught on, while the other would never have gotten into the Christian record books. If Paul had told the harder story of being accountable, he would have also faced the harder truth that he could only be one creature, the one that he was, during the one life he had to live. Instead, he became a preeminent exacerbator in millions to billions of lives, exerting years of effort seeking the fantasy silver lining one could be someone he or she was not. To his credit, Paul lived an extraordinary life oriented toward his belief in Jesus.

Which raises the question I have already provided my answer to, whether Paul was not already an extraordinary person, and his belief in Jesus, which included a new creation, magnified what he already was? If that is the case, it seems to me the key is finding the kind of belief that magnifies the best in each of us. Paul demonstrated that an aspect of this key to magnify the best in each person ironically is about a reality bigger than each person. Devotion to a bigger reality can change one's behavior from bully to care taker of the poor. It did for Paul. Or did it? According to him, he did not believe in a different God. That is to say, the reality did not get bigger (his God was Abraham's: Gal. 3: 7). For Paul reality got clearer as he correctly understood God's plan included Jesus' making justification before God possible. I am more convinced that Paul's change really was a matter of direction.

Or maybe Paul and my father were right. Maybe the reality of their Jesus has a physical impact traceable on a believer's brain, altering his disposition, as anything short of impacting one's mind would be less than real change. That kind of traceable change seems as likely as an alternative denouncement to Jesus providing a new being. That alternative response is there is actually no being to change, or in other words there is no definable or defensible "self" for Jesus to change. The alternative position goes, for one, that humans are constantly refashioned on the cellular level; for two, identifying what makes you uniquely you is as mystifying as receiving Jesus; for three, the you that you think you are is an amalgam of cultural influences. If a self is an amalgam, how can a self be accountable to external cultural forces beyond its control? If all selves were subject to white-out snow storms without Luke Skywalker's Lightsaber and Tauntaun to take refuge in, then they wouldn't be responsible. But limits on liberty do not equate to negating the actual self. It certainly confines, stumps, and can freeze it. You correctly intuit there is a "you," a receptor of external forces, bank of your memories, and referent for reflecting and responding. Deficiencies to define the existence of the self by the smartest blokes hardly render the absence of it. There is no absence of self any more than it was not really your grandfather whose burial you attended. If there were, enlightenment resulting from recognition of no self would be commensurate with your correctly purporting that was not grandpa in the box under the freshly groomed dirt. I admit that finding definitive answers to questions about the existence of the self are better left to experts like Orlando in Virginia Woolf's novel by the same name. But what seems certain is that folks who deny the existence of a self appropriately find a happy marriage with those who believe Jesus can change you—they both believe in something to make them new beings. Both classes succeed brilliantly to push from them the responsibility of their actions and subsequent responsibility for the bundle of actions that form their lives and interconnect with others'. Or maybe not—both may have found the key to unlock the door to a life committed to a higher good that includes responsibility to one's actions and their influences on the lives of others. I only know this is an open question, and the believers in Jesus seem to be on the right side of the responsibility gap of most humans. What I do know is that the accurate measure to the question of who is being responsible is by the actions of all parties, not by strongly believed changes within them.

Yet I may have completely missed Paul's genius. His writings are the earliest in the New Testament, and he marks a turn in the history of our known world by focusing on one's nature, the intention of one's heart. Jesus never said he made people into new beings, but the realization of what he did say had that effect on Paul, so he rightly went on to profess it. Whether one becomes a new being or not is hardly as significant as asking yourself who you should or should not be, and then following up by asking what it will take to be it. Paul magnanimously asks all who read him to consider how our lives should be spent by focusing on our deepest nature, our longing hearts, and having the courage to go in the direction the answer points us.

Paul and his disciples over the centuries have found power suffering for and witnessing on behalf of a reality of Jesus as the Christ submitting to God's plan of righteousness and not going about establishing their own (Rom. 10: 3). But how often does a belief in a greater reality align with the best of who you are? That must be a question we each answer for ourselves. It worked for Paul but for you and me too? If it will, you better be correct because the tradeoff is potentially a perpetuation of unaccountable illusory new beings built upon the very foundation of a belief in exclusive propiti-ation of past wrongs through one source, the resurrected Jesus. Even more potentially retarding is the commensurate viral dissonance from the end-less legions failing to account for and develop the creatures they actually are (the same consequence as those committed to obliterating any existence of an independent accountable self). If one cannot account for one's own being, then how in Sam Hill can one participate at large with other beings to account for the myriad of challenges confronting the human race? One cannot. One punts to a greater reality or theory and hopes and strives to high heaven everyone else will too. That is to say, hopes everyone will unify in a greater reality or theory, the proverbial unifying of a whole new silver lining.

My parents married just before my father headed to OCS. He went to Quantico alone, leaving my mother with her family in Blackfoot. She joined him in Quantico, after almost missing her flight out of Pocatello, as Grandpa Bob recounted, not having decided to pack until the morning of her depar-ture, still considering what she would take as Grandpa Bob marched her out of the house to catch the flight. Hours later she arrived to the stoic life of military newlyweds. The early days of their marriage were not absolutely blissful ones. My father bore immense guilt because he had nothing, the guilt pervading his meals in the mess hall, his stomach often knotted, unable to eat knowing there was nothing for his wife to eat at home. He was unable to honor the Marine code of taking all you want but eating all you take. Af-ter OCS, they transferred to Orange County, California, and within the first year of their marriage Jami was born, and weeks later my father headed to Vietnam to face the toughest moment of his life. That moment came when my mother stood holding baby Jami as my father departed for his tour. He walked away from his family to board the plane and did not turn back to wave, fearing he would break down in tears, unacceptable for a marine, let alone an officer in the Corps.

He served one tour in Vietnam doing special operations, mostly in his underwear because it was so hot. He worked nights with a small group directing bombing raids on the North Vietnamese, using a slide ruler to determine the coordinates under great stress in real-time during radio communication with the pilots. Decades later the worry about unwittingly initiating friendly fire on troops whose location was unknown or had been misidentified, or were exposed because of his own miscalculations, was still discernible in his voice, not to mention his guilt for contributing to the deaths of so many enemies and innocent civilian Vietnamese. Like the standard Vietnam veteran he did not talk about his experiences at war. I either had to prod him, getting him to relent only after repeated inquires, or I learned from those who knew him, the latter producing most of the information.

During my time in Provo, Utah, attending BYU, I met one of my father's fellow marines. The man had a beautiful daughter, and I tried to combine interests by seeking out stories of my father by visiting him. He told me he and a few other marines once went to a movie with my father, and shortly into the movie, it became clear they had stumbled into an adult feature. Without any discussion my father got up and left, and all his marine buddies followed. He spoke with great admiration for my father and assured me that other marines who knew him felt the same. Our visits ended shortly after they began, his daughter not sharing my interest.

My father's pride in the Marine Corps could qualify as mortal sin until you listened long enough to learn it derived from belonging to his fellow marines. But his contumacy tempered his love for the Marine Corps, and while it preceded his days in the Corps it reached a summit there. It was not altogether different in kind from the rejection of authority expressed by many of his peers protesting the Vietnam War; while he and they differed on their perceived duties, both groups expected people in authority to deliver on their promises. He also expected their actions to be commensurate with their prestige, disliking few people more than those with authority who failed to deliver on his expectations.

After his tour in Vietnam, my father was stationed in Japan. Junior officers were only allowed to have their wives stay with them a short term, but no similar limit was on senior officers' wives. The prohibition angered him, and was compounded by many junior officers' failure to meet his expectations for married men. When he questioned the prohibition on junior officers' wives staying longer, he was told to do what others did and enjoy the Japanese women in his wife's absence. He was incensed. He wrote Idaho's U.S. Senator, Frank Church, a powerful presence on Capitol Hill during the Vietnam War, demanding a review of the prohibition on junior officers' wives. The letter stirred the marine brass, was career suicide within the Corps, and resulted in a review of my father as insubordinate. His colonel hauled him before a two-star general, and my father held his ground. Minutes into his examination—whether the general noticed in my father's dossier his record obstacle-course time, reports of his consistently cleanest weapon regardless of surprise inspections (by constant cleaning and by smartly dry-firing it on the range), notes about his never-unmade bunk (by sleeping like a corpse and slowly wiggling his way out each morning without leaving a crease or loosening the tucked blanket and sheets), or that he could not talk about the Corps without the strongest pride—the general declared it was obvious my father loved the Corps, and dismissed him straight away. On the drive back to the barracks, the colonel smiled, unable to restrain glimmers of pride, for his marine not backing down. How could the Corps discipline someone who not merely personified but in fact was integrity, everything a Marine should be? On that occasion they rightly did not. Subsequently, the limit was removed and my mother extended her stay in Japan, in concert with new Corps policy for junior officers.

It could have been a marine recruiter's pressing me to join the most venerated organization my father ever belonged to, and my father would have paid for my college expenses in return for focusing on my education and not serving in the military. While I knew education mattered to him, it took years piecing together how much the Corps did. The night he offered to pay for college he told me I already possessed respect, work ethic and character that people learn from the military. He also said I would do well to avoid wasting years subject to military bureaucracy with no control in repeated runs of boredom, always facing mind-numbing imbeciles barking orders because they could be given. He said he knew his help would not be wasted because I worked hard and that would carry over to college. True or not, it got me to BYU.

PART II

CHAPTER 5

CALCULUS

An impeccably groomed stretch of grass ran north and east to west, an inverted T, from the Harold B. Lee Library at the heart of Brigham Young University's campus when I arrived as a freshman at the end of the summer of 1994. Student traffic was heavy each weekday a quarter before each hour, crossing diagonally on concrete paths, pouring into buildings facing the green and flowing toward buildings at the far reaches of campus and beyond.

Later, sitting on a worn leather couch, the smell of tobacco rising with every movement, freshly brewed coffee within arm's length, my Uncle Band recounted the most amazing scene he had ever witnessed, superlative as I recollect it, on the green; when a tiger trainer was on campus promoting his show in the late Sixties or early Seventies, or maybe it was conducting the actual show on the green; the accuracy of my recollection is no doubt impeccable. A large group of students gathered to see the tiger, or tigers. The trainer started running at a full sprint, and his associate, or someone not afraid of holding wild beasts, released a tiger. The tiger glided toward the man, and the crowd's awe turned to terror when the tiger reached him and leaped on him, knocking him to the ground. Imagine the unsuspecting student who walked out of a building bordering the green to see the tiger in pursuit of the man. Band had seen the event from its outset, and it was surreal for him even though he knew the man knocked down was a trainer, and it continued to be surreal as he recounted it decades later.

Most of my classes were in the Humanities Building on the west side of the green, along the stem of the inverted T, an unassuming architectural non-feat but practical, a bit depressing with more classrooms without windows than with them. Despite its prison warmth it was a welcome respite from the overlay of campus-wide religious instruction, if only imagined, and the base of the duration of my university career. Here, most of my English and philosophy classes were held, and here I would regularly see the young woman I fell in love with during my freshman year.

I saw her often within the vicinity of Deseret Towers, the freshman dormitories where I lived. I probably saw her first in the Morris Center, the cafeteria, where I could see her if fortune was on my side two times a day. This was my meal-plan limit, stemming not from a calorie-conscious diet but from a gesture of lean gratitude to my father who was paying for it. When activities separated us for days at a time, I was lucky to see her any given Sunday afternoon after church at lunch.

She was tall, easily my height, just over six feet but not quite six-one, with waist length, free-flowing white hair, and a clear pale face with small eyes, a princess gliding above ground only appearing to touch among lesser beings, straight from Lothlórien in Middle-earth, a sure descendant of Galadriel herself. I did not dare address her, not knowing Elvish, a weakness for sure but only one of many communicative shortcomings. Mormons believe a nation of people called the Jaredites in the Book of Mormon spoke remnants of the purest of all languages, the Adamic tongue, and if her appearance merited a commensurate language she must have spoken it, and like Elvish I did not. I was a monolingual speaker and not very good at it, let alone when smitten. Not only was language an insurmountable barrier, I was also plumb sheepish.

My first semester I walked around dazed but with conviction I had met, or at least seen with some regularity, the woman who shared my destiny.

My devotion to her matched only by the "ingenious hildalgo" himself, Don Quixote de la Mancha's purest commitment to the fair Dulcinea of El Toboso, queen of his heart. A day did not fail to pass that I did not think about the girl as I walked through the Morris Center Cafeteria, hoping to see her. I had no plans to meet her, but who needed plans with providence on my side, convinced no one wanted anyone more than I wanted her, maybe ever, of course excluding my BYU peers and all BYU alumni who had also zigzagged across campus, now spawning the world over and beyond.

That same semester I did well in most my classes, too, straight As with the exception of calculus, which I flunked but, benefiting from pandemic flunking, emerged with a B- on the curve. In calculus, I took four exams and earned a failing grade on each. The third and last exam before the comprehensive final was the only exam in longhand. Each exam was ten questions long, and because I could show my work on the third exam I took the exam to the professor, pointing out I had done steps correctly leading to botched conclusions on a couple questions. The professor, toward the end of his tenure but not lacking in enthusiasm, smiled and said my efforts were worth some extra points, changed my grade to a C, marked his grade book, and before I could protest or thank him he stood and dismissed me with one arm waving me out and opening the door with the other to welcome another student into his office.

Mormon leaders and religious instructors encourage the Mormon membership to keep journals. During high school, my seminary teacher, Brother Johnson, one day stood by a pile of journals stacked high on a desk. I could not imagine how he had so much to write about until I tried my own hand at journal writing and learned the result was largely an expulsion of free-association ideas and feelings. After writing a couple of entries, I was convinced she would be a sorry soul who had to suffer through the stack near Brother Johnson, or my own blather. My sympathy for unknown future readers had little to do with my lack of enthusiasm for heeding the recurring exhortation to keep a journal. I succeeded only in spotty attempts during high school and college, and one faithful run during my Mormon mission experience, at which time (and not during the present composition) I edited choice words made in entries at BYU. What remains is presented here.

September 22, 1994. I am really at a loss. I have come to realize I understand little. I'll try and think of a good analogy to create how real my confusion is but I can't just right now. I guess today was a good experience. It is not even over yet. It's only a quarter after 1. I still have another class to go to.

I flunked my first college exam today. I got 5 out of 10 problems right on my calculus test what I think is pretty xxxxxxx good. Had I not put in those 6 hours of studying I may not have ever gotten 1 right. I really don't understand where things went wrong. I prepared so hard. I felt good throughout the whole test. Things just are sometimes really xxxxxxx I work harder than anyone I know. I guess I can use this failure to my advantage. It would just be nice if I had something to set xxxxxxx I do plan to talk with the professor tomorrow, what do I have to lose? I'll just explain my situation. He'll do little but at least he'll know someone is xxxxxxx quite mystified by things.

I guess life ain't so bad but it ain't so good either. I cannot help but smile though. I mean xxxxxxx cares what I get on my first college test. Is it foreshadowing my college career? Who knows? I guess I will find out with time. Ryan asked me to be his best man today. I guess if I had passed that test I would have thought myself immortal so for some cosmic reason I was destined to fail. I actually feel little disgust about my grade. It is really out of my hands. I did all I could do. That's why I am not feeling like a total xxxxxxx. But I am pretty xxxxxxx I flippin live in the math lab. I do all my homework and did 5 pages worth of review. xxxxxxx I do realize my language is pretty poor. But more than you know, my choice of words do reflect who I am. Maybe they are right when they say the choice of words one uses reflects his mentality, or intellectual level. I am not too smart. Thank heavens for Ryan. He and Steve (I also got a letter from Steve) made my day. And the sooner one realizes this the better he will be. My life is so normal. I have so many dreams and hopes and not even the simple ones of passing a college test come true. Well, I am not a quitter. I am going to kick the system xxxxxxx I have only been here at BYU a month but I am not impressed. My kids are going to go to private schools. I am not sure why yet but I think the teachers are better. My argument is valid. I know many public school teachers including BYU, it is not a true private school in the true essence of the word. I only know one private school teacher that is Steve. Well this is enough for now. Good luck to whoever took the time to read this.

Each week calculus included two days of lectures and a break-out section with a graduate student, including home-work problems and a group quiz, taken and passed by one of our group. Five students to a team, two of which I did not see, but I had their phone numbers in my notebook in case of a homework emergency. I shined, a true lesser star member of the team, always prepared, problems finished in hand. I was eventually deemed, though undeclared by anyone including me, but no less true, a reliable bloke, always ready and prompt to share my answers before timely turning them in for full credit. I learned sharing answers with classmates meant I did not recognize the "I" that did not exist in team. In high school I readily shared answers from the mammoth homework worksheets in A.P. U.S. History with anyone who wanted them, high school calculus, and other classes burdened with enough assignments to fill tomes of busy work, and continued my goodwill even on some exams. I carried out the same practice in other courses when my competence allowed and cohorts permitted. Not to be mistaken with the black and white of cheating so easily applied by teachers and administrators the education-world wide, my activities were a commitment to team and above all good grades. The work in A.P. U.S. History was something I could do over the course of eight hours each Sunday afternoon and evening. Smarter minds reciprocated my kindness in chemistry and to my seeming disadvantage, calculus. But how else did teachers of college preparatory courses expect one to finish all the assigned homework given the disproportion between workload and hours in the day? The answer was team. So I was not shocked to find myself on a team first semester, assuming college professors acknowledged what high school teachers did not.

I faithfully did my homework problems, never on my own but that was only because I could not do them on my own. After each assignment, which seemed like after each lecture but it may have just been the second lecture of the week preceding the break-out section—heaven knows I cannot remember—I went directly to the math lab, which I do remember was a room in the basement of an obscure building nestled up to the southern border of campus and populated with graduate students in light blue lab vests, to complete the assigned problems. And I asked for help on each problem. Early in the semester I learned to avoid the minority in the light blue vest, the Caucasian, because he would belabor the process and minutes would turn into hours. I resorted to profiling English speakers with accents, blue-vested Asians, ranging from the far reaches of Asiatic empires governed by history's great civilizations of the Persians to the Mongolians. Their patience seemed to mirror my own and they seemed unburdened and obviously unaware by my ignorant prejudices against the single white man. I went armed and loaded with my Hewlett-Packard 48G graphing calculator, confirmed indispensable on the course syllabus and by the professor on the first day of class, a $110 purchase made the first week of class, the last cash I had all semester, failing to learn how to use it by semester's end. In high school I memorized formulas but did not use a single equation that first semester of college calculus and was convinced no one else did either. Why would they, when they had a computer in hand to do the steps for them? And god almighty I envied those who could use it. Halfway through the semester the professor announced a series of night classes on how to learn to use the graphing calculator. Relieved to know others shared my inadequacy, I attended the first few night classes eagerly, but my impotent attempts of pushing buttons discouraged me, and to avoid further embarrassment I abandoned the extra course, turning instead to dutiful prayer for divine intervention. I entreated heavenly mathematicians during conscious thoughts of integers and derivatives dancing in my tortured calculus-less head. But my dependence went beyond the math lab and failed attempts with technology.

September 29, 1994. It happens to be raining outside. The time is approximately 12:50 P.M. I have math lab at 2:00. For the past few days I have wanted to write a few things pertaining the personalities around me. I shall start with my roommate. What a great guy. BW is his name. Now if I may interrupt. I am listening to the Cranberries. A piece of lyrics is "It's impossible not to dream." I dream of writing a book. I have decided that I shall include those who have affected my life in some way. Back to B. Besides being very intelligent and personable, B is selfless. Before coming to school I just prayed for a selfless roommate and bang! I got him. Before my first Calculus exam this year B was kind enough to stay up with me into the wee hours of the night and help me. He is also always offering me his left over popcorn, not that he couldn't finish it, he is just selfless. He is a perfect roommate.

It came to my attention at the beginning of this week that not only I have big dreams. B is a CS major. This is only something to fall back on. He hopes to be an inventor. My next door neighbor, V, wishes to be a musician. I talked with V a good part of an hour this past Monday. It was refreshing that someone else had such dreams. I hope to right a book. If I needed something to fall back on it may be a MBA or a law degree.

School is going O.K. I keep up and I have survived what challenges have come my way. In my math group there is a S, A, S, and B. S
is a lot like me. He doesn't really understand. Actually B is the savior
for the group. He takes our quizzes. He provides the balance for my
test scores. B is so smart. Not like BW, but very intelligent in his own
right. B is full of logic. He explains the problems. BW can solve them.
Between the two I have learned all my Calculus this year. I thank the
heavens for those two.

I buckled down and prepared for the calculus final exam for days and
days, no memorizing involved but endless praying and reviewing of problems that had given me trouble during the semester, spanning every single
one I had done. And then I met with one of the members of my study group,
who had already taken the final exam. I hoped of getting guidance akin to
drinking a secret serum to produce an A. The student, charitable enough to
meet the day before I took the final, was tall, blond, a civil engineer major,
and the smartest student in the group who attended the break-out sections,
had a laid-back California cool, probably hailing from there. We planned our
meeting before he took the final, including the other member of our group
who attended the break-out sections, conveniently scheduled at meal-time
at the Morris Center, no doubt suggested by me for any chance to see the angel who haunted my every waking hour. Consistent with all group meetings,
he led the discussion because the other student was as inept as I. Because he
had taken the final I assumed, hoped, and most assuredly prayed, he would
review questions similar to those on the exam. If he did, I didn't notice the
similarities when I took it.

Many professors required their students to take exams at the university
testing center, an official test center building with a football field of a room
a thousand desks wide on the second floor. The testing center stood at the
southwestern corner of campus within a tightly coagulated spit of the honors building and within skipping distance of stairs running down a steep
grade that marked the end of campus. The testing center freed professors
and their assistants from monitoring exams but, more importantly, it func-
tioned to enforce the honor code: specifically the grooming portion. If students' appearances violated the code, including bare-shouldered women or
shadow-faced men, save a medical card explaining the violation produced
on demand, then student employees refused admission. Rejected and down-

trodden, violators would have to cover up or shave before returning to pass the sentries to take the exam.

I remember only a few exams I took at the testing center, one being the calculus final, and I took many there. I was ready for the exam, fully rested and optimistic, having set aside an entire morning. I had been expecting to pass a calculus exam all semester, and was convinced I was due to pass this final one. I entered feeling good, and I finished in an hour's time. I exited the football-field room liking my chances, with spirits high because my work produced a correct answer among the four possibilities on each of the ten questions. For a few cherished moments I felt it was not only possible that I passed, but possibly I aced it. I saw myself all smiles walking lightly, tapping toes on the concrete paths all across campus, twirling from side to side, pulling a pirouette before each gathered crowd. Seconds after I handed in the bubble sheet, a student employee called my surname, and I took the half-page printout marked with bold type "5 out of 10," again. I walked with heavy steps down the stairs and out of the testing center. My emotions turned into faintly audible grumblings as I exited, reaching their crescendo of sporadic bursts of Fuck Me by the end of the fifteen-minute walk across campus to the bell tower, a landmark rising above campus and a few measured huffs from my dorm room.

President Hinckley, the lead Mormon prophet and president of the Church during my freshman campaign, remarked on one occasion he had never used profanity, or maybe my memory fails me again and another Mormon leader made the remark. If it was the prophet, it was not the only comment made by him that gave me pause. Years later Larry King asked President Hinckley about the beginning of the LDS Church's practice of polygamy, and the prophet responded the Church permitted it when the Church moved west. But Joseph Smith received a revelation to practice it before his death, which preceded the Mormon trek west. This the President surely knew as the official introduction to the revelation acknowledged Joseph took multiple wives before, maybe a decade, he wrote the revelation down and made it public. The prophet may not have known about Joseph's relationships to additional wives, most notably the reputedly beautiful Nancy Johnson and Fanny Alger, as it is not inconceivable the prophet had not read history perceived at odds with the official versions propagated by the Church in the copious church manuals, teaching guides and books—more than a lifetime of reading could consume, and from which most active members relied upon for untarnished, unbiased, uncorrupted facts.

Even more troubling, if he never swore, President Hinckley appeared not to have worked any cattle, if I used the same tortured logic of assuming facts not in evidence. But then I have a faint recollection that his family had owned a ranch, perhaps making himself a young buckaroo in the era when owning ranches meant work. This of course predated the fashionable hands-off land ownership of today, sometimes not a matter of choice as much as a matter of adhering to a conservation easement. And maybe cowboys of yore were like pre-Hollywood marines who did not swear.

Admittedly, not all the cowboys I knew did swear. I did, but admittedly I was not a real cowboy, merely suffering from the delusion I was, by association. I suffered even further from a conviction of cussing's value, amounting to a cussing crutch. Not to mention I drew on the causal link between cussing and cattle as a valid proof of every philosophical discussion bent on tackling the impossible justification of cause and effect, a proof with its vulnerabilities stemming from the conscious decision to profane, a priority over the involuntary response of habit, conceded to be a bad one yet so damn therapeutic.

Still not willing to relinquish the hypothesis that President Hinckley had not been on the receiving end of an angry cow, and just as unsure he had not read into the events of Joseph's alleged multi-wifery, one thing remains certain to me: As a young man, President Hinckley read the classics of Homer in the original Greek, which established a high bar for reading throughout his life. It was an advantage over many, if not all, his business-prepped apostle peers who were simply unaccustomed to quality literature, upon rational inference of their words, primed to encounter salacious historical accounts as necessary data points to be discredited, disavowed and discounted.

None of that running through my mind at the time of my calculus final, I stepped guiltlessly across campus, sparing not one innocent my soured tongue. A few hours later, thinking and lying on what passed as my dorm bed, it sank in that I got five of ten correct. I actually got half of them right, a feat, upon reflection, worth a pint of pride, which would do since a pint of fine brew was nowhere to be had.

December 3, 1994. How time flies. Lots & lots happened since I last wrote. I can't remember much so it must not have been very important. The story of my life! Well, I am going to get right to the point. I'm a dreamer, loaner, unbeliever, no-nothing, piece-of-shit. This isn't all that bad. I'm actually quite content. I'm surrounded by some great people.

Oh ya, that also brings me to… the fact that I let off leach. I swear, I'm kind of sucker. Then again I'm not such a sucker. I'll let the reader decide about that last bit. Because I sure do not know where I was going with that. School is groovy. Something is definitely lacking though. I'm a pretty weird guy. There's something inside me, saying, well its saying something! "You're missing something." Pretty intellectual innards eh. Then there's another part of me saying. "Who the ---- cares." I don't know what that all means, but I know what side rules over the other. Life… Pretty interesting thing life is. I have all these dreams to be something. To be one of the greatest writers, intellectuals, mean-old-son-of-a-guns there ever was. Then there is this other side of me. Saying "What?" I know, well, I don't know much. But I do know what I am worth. Not too much, but I figure I am worth a sack of black beans. I mean who the hell isn't worth a bag of black beans. Back to school and one thing-and-another. I am not doing all that well. I'm putting in the time. I guess not enough. Sorry just a side note * where would I be without good music?* O.k. I'm back. My main concern, is, is, well, it is, what do I like? What makes me tick? Will I ever find my niche in this old world? And, why the hell is it raining outside? These are fair questions. Basically, I am trying to find a little truth. But who isn't. I wish my thoughts could be recorded in the books of all books (not the Bible, or the Holy Standard Works) The Big Book in heaven silly. O.k., now that I got off all this stuff. Off what you're asking, at least I would be if I were reading this. Off my chest of course. Now, I am no genius. Actually, I am not even the thing under a genius, or under that for that matter. But never mind, I need not state the obvious! O.k. what if I died tomorrow? Hell it might happen. I really wouldn't mind all that much. Deep down, I'm a selfish, evil, well, piece-of-shit. There I go again, stating the obvious. *Another side note. Some of you readers may think I am trying to be comical. You just don't know me. I'm not being negative. Just keep that in mind* Back to my death. O.K. everyone is at my funeral. I mean the whole damn ward. Pert near two hundred people, give or take a few. All funerals say nice stuff about the deceist. I can't even spell the word! Just sound it out. Well, back to the thing at hand. And I've never been more serious. So who is talking but Jami. Naturally he is going to lie for me. Make me look like a real hell of a guy. So he does. And you know what I don't mind one bit. I'm sitting there with a real big grin when he ends his talk with, "… He was a great friend to all, and most of all (especially to himself) a damn good brother, and a damn good son." Jami knows I'm a dreamer. It's my best dream to be what Jami just said. In this case, I believe it was O.k. for him to lie. It won't make a difference really (on Jami's part) he is still going to hell with me even if he doesn't lie. Who would he be trying to kid anyway. I mean he probably wouldn't have it any other way. Jose, Manuel & Josh are going to be there too. It's going to be a real party. Well, I've run out of things to say. Except, I sure hope I do well on finals. Taker easy. Don't Panic. And God will bless you. That's one thing I believe, is that God blesses good folks.

CHAPTER 6
THE ARTS

I headed home to Blackfoot for the semester break and the holidays. I enjoyed the days I had nothing to do between semesters. I was at my very best doing nothing. I did not realize doing nothing was a talent until I noticed and reflected deeply upon the inability of some people to do nothing without being anxious of their idleness, unsettled not going somewhere and doing something. Doing nothing well has attracted its share of critics but defenders too. John Keats celebrated the "blissful cloud of summer-indolence" in his poem, "Ode to Indolence," choosing nothing, or idleness, over love, ambition, and even poesy with his "head cool-bedded in the flowery grass" not wanting "to be dieted with praise, /A pet-lamb in a sentimental farce!"

I too preferred nothing to inevitable farces, though not minding the idea of eventually being caught in a few just to be sure, hooking together Keats' three ambitions, albeit, unlike him, not predisposed by talent or ingenuity toward any of them.

But doing nothing well was not merely about the avoidance of farces and its younger naïve siblings, of passion and the drama of important events, also experiences I was open to some eventual dabbling in; doing nothing was a virtue. Milton defended the same in his poem "When I Consider How My Light Is Spent," where thousands serve God "without rest" while some "serve who only stand and wait." While we may serve different Gods, through various forms of worship, doing nothing had merit in itself and no authorities of any time or religious persuasion would upend a Keats-and-Milton combination for me. My brother, Jake, a poet, assured me every poet has written on the virtue of indolence, these oracles a faithful band and truest of connoisseurs of the virtue of idleness.

After the most meaningful days of my life between semesters freshman year, I returned to BYU. I started my new classes having survived being swallowed whole by the mighty fish calculus. Retracing paths worn from calculus class to the math lab, I involuntarily retched from the unscrubbable old smells of the great fish, but I tried throwing myself into other all-consuming subjects to combat the recent events inside that putrid belly. And my attempts were fruitful as I landed in the arts.

I was reborn and took full advantage of it, that semester in Introduction to Humanities 101: The Basics of Learning How To Be Fully Human. I did not even know there was a process, excited to happen upon it and finally begin. The class was in the largest lecture hall of the Humanities Building, which seated upwards of three hundred students. The professor was Darrell Mitchell, a short, full-bearded gentleman, who spoke with a lisp and an overflowing enthusiasm for the arts. He talked about the worth of film, literature, dance, paintings, opera, drama, architecture and all arts with the reverence the Mormon prophet used in talking about the singular path to exaltation through the one true Mormon Church. I liked him immediately.

Professor Mitchell welcomed his students the first couple days of class with a large video camera securely on his shoulder, removing it only to lecture and lifting it again at the end of class to record students before their departure. He asked each student to repeat his or her name for the camera, kindly requesting students like me to remove their baseball caps. I complied, removing my cap that had covered unkempt blond hair and, when the red light appeared on the front of the camera, I stated my given name, paused and followed with my surname. After recording everyone on his roll, Professor Mitchell proceeded to call each student by his or her given name throughout the semester as sure as I am composing now.

The lecture hall had a floor slanted downward toward the front, and Professor Mitchell treated the space as his stage. He saw his role as teacher of the arts second to his role as lover of them, and he performed his role tirelessly at the highest level of enthusiasm each class. On the first day Professor Mitchell laid out his course through the arts and each day that followed he captained our voyage further along. He instructed us in a tone overlaid with admonishment mistakable at times as entreaty, even pleading, for us deeply to embrace the truth of art. Wasting no time, he encouraged, or commanded, us to start attending cultural activities early in the semester and not to delay until the last weeks of class.

I was easily commanded, and earnestly marching into the unknown as I did not know a cultural event from an ass whipping. I soon learned that I had attended a few cultural events, the iron hand of father's encouragement upon us. A concert pianist (and younger brother of Micron Technology's founding Parkinson brothers) performed at the civic center in Blackfoot, a converted Mormon tabernacle. When the city could no longer afford to maintain it, they sold the building, which is now the town's sole funeral home. At that center, we also saw several community plays, one being a production of Thornton Wilder's *Our Town*, on a stage empty save for tall ladders and a bathtub. The first cultural activity at BYU that semester, which Professor Mitchell did everything but walk us individually to, was the weeklong showing of Ingmar Bergman's *The Seventh Seal* (1957).

Professor Mitchell's enthusiasm made a lasting impression on his students, and he also left an indelible mark on BYU. He reinvented the BYU International Cinema by expanding show times, increasing and expanding the diverse features, and obtaining a larger venue. He was not modest, extolling the greatness of BYU's commitment to international cinema, claiming the theater showed more international films than any theater across the country and possibly throughout the world. Having no basis to contest the claim because it was the only international cinema I knew, and accustomed to claims of "best" and "greatest" consistent with claims of my religion regularly making the same, I converted to one of Mitchell's disciples well before semester's end, saturated by my weekly attendance of thought-provoking and emotionally-moving films, learning to read whole scenes with quick glances at the subtitles, never having seen a movie with subtitles before that semester.

I grew up watching movies, and they typically fell within three catego-ries: westerns, overwhelmingly John Wayne's with occasional breaks toward works of Eastwood and Redford and repeated viewings of *The Man from Snowy River* (1982); comedies with all the short films by The Three Stooges, repeated viewings of Peter Sellers' *The Pink Panther* series, Steve Martin and company in *Three Amigos* (1986), and Bob and Doug McKenzie in *Strange Brew* (1983); and musicals, spanning the repertoire from Rodgers and Ham-merstein to *Annie* (1982), and of course the family favorite with the brilliant performance of Robert Preston as Professor Harold Hill in *The Music Man* (1962), even surpassing in showings and regard the much-beloved Mormon cultural staple, *The Sound of Music* (1965), still widely admired within my Mormon family, but personally taking the greatest delight in the wit, re-sourceful characters, and beautiful production of Carol Reed's *Oliver* (1968).

The prominence of *The Sound of Music* cannot be overstated in Mor-mondom. Julie Andrews holds nothing short of divine status among the saints. Andrews' Maria, an icon of talent and beauty, and a nurturing moth-er, set the standard for Mormon wives. Maria chose the well-being of a family, willing to sacrifice her love for Captain Von Trapp for the good of his children to have a mother, initially not her, eventually renouncing even her vows as a nun to fulfill her capacity as a mother surrogate. The musi-cal celebrated many of Mormonism's most cherished values: Maria's ideals were pure and her character chaste, not like her peers in the nunnery of Powell and Pressburger's *Black Narcissus* (1947). The Archers produced a perfect film of British resilience of modern values spurned by a foreign culture impervious to Western ways in the story of five nuns' attempting to civilize natives in the remote peaks of the Himalayas, brilliantly creat-ed on a set in London. Like Maria, Sister Ruth was unsuited for the nun's life, but unlike Maria, Sister Ruth's desires were primordial and of the flesh. Like Maria, Deborah Kerr's Sister Clodagh was tempted by an alternative to the sacrifice of a nun's life, with a rich social life including romantic love, albeit in her past but with the possibility of more in the future. Unlike Ma-ria, Sister Clodagh kept her vows and remained committed to God. Sister Clodagh's commitment would not resonate with Mormon culture because sacrificing family was incongruent to an ultimate commitment to God, ex-plaining why no Mormon family had a copy of the Archers' masterpiece, not just in the world among those I knew but also projected to the four corners of almighty Utah.

Other movies of far less theoretical consequence but no less celebrated in our home fell within the catch-all category of action, such as *The Double McGuffin* (1979), *Breakin'* (1984), *The Last Dragon* (1985), *Take Down* (1979), *Clash of the Titans* (1981), *First Blood* (1982), and my swashbuckling favorites of *Scaramouche* (1952) and *Ivanhoe* (1952), watched and re-watched long before I saw films with Douglas Fairbanks or Errol Flynn, those masters of the silver screen in the greatest fantasies, performing dashing feats like those of my youthful day-dreams. I do not recall any dramas save those that defy cinephiles' sophisticated classification, the masterworks of the great Sylvester Stallone, chief among his extensive body of work the immortal *Over the Top* (1987).

While I had not seen a subtitled movie, I had seen many foreign films before arriving at BYU, all of them with Bruce Lee dubbed in laconic, broken English, evidence of my father's commitment to broadening our horizons beyond the dusty plains and high-ridged mountains of his westerns, and exposing us to martial arts beyond those of Inspector Jacques Clouseau. I loved more than anything sitting with my father watching both.

The international theater spanned the southeast corner on the ground floor of the Spencer W. Kimball Tower, the tower itself located southwest of the heart of campus, this cornerstone transforming film in my life. The first week of class, Professor Mitchell handed out humanities cards for free admission to all showings like an earnest Mormon missionary handing out free copies of the "Blue" Book of Mormon at doorsteps across the world, the film card like the Mormon scripture offering passage to new enlightenment, and I gladly took one, wearing its corners through, carrying it always in a pocket on my person.

The Seventh Seal was a freshman's awakening. I was captivated by the plot, the knight embattled in a chess game with Death to delay his own, enamored with the humor of the squire and convinced of his wisdom. I was persuaded that death, hiding its identity, cheated in life and enjoyed seeing its unfairness personified on screen. The film was the most philosophically ambitious I had seen, and it worked famously for a freshman budding intellectually. The viewing experience was aided by paltry subtitles barely and intermittently readable and, at times, indecipherable on the bright, worn reel projected on the screen. The quality of the film was atrociously bad, obvious to viewers even years before the dawn of high definition and Blu-ray. The screen seemed to have bright lights directly behind it, highlighting repairs of torn film, scars of repeated showings over many years. I sat, taking it all in, simply transfixed.

I dragged along my best freshman-dorm friend, Jared, who lived on the same floor at Deseret Towers. Uncaring what he experienced during the film and with no discussion of his thoughts after it, I had pep-talked him into going not on the professor's rave reviews but on the news that the girl of my daily dreams was in Humanities 101. All first semester I had been telling Jared of the goddess drifting among us mere mortal freshman who lived north of campus. He heard about her from sun-up to sun-down as we rose early a few mornings during the week to go to the gym and often ended our evenings with me sitting on the vacated extra bed in his room directly across from my own. His roommate, also from his hometown of Chicago, having flown the coup, not having taken to the BYU climate after the first semester, his absence never impeding Jared's and my discussions about life, school, and the providential sightings of the girl who lived constantly in my thoughts and throughout the nerves running through my entire body. For Jared the mere possibility of doing something connected to her mythology was sufficient motivation to see *The Seventh Seal* all the way through.

And providence was on our side as we rose after the movie ended and exited the Spencer W. Kimball Tower, when she walked to our right and exited the theater into the same dark night. Her identity was unknown to Jared who showed no signs of being affected by the film and offered no response or complaint about it.

Perhaps its seedling bloomed years later when Jared enrolled in a professional acting class in Salt Lake City. We were roommates at the time, with him acting as landlord, making me the generous offer to let me live in his parents' house in south Provo. In lieu of paying rent, I was to enroll in acting class with him, making the weekly commute on his gas in his truck to Salt Lake for eight fun weeks.

But, after seeing *The Seventh Seal*, all Jared talked to me about was what I needed to do to meet this girl I could not stop talking about, while time favored us in the same class.

She briefly looked our way and my heart stopped. Surely she was as unaware of us as Jared was of whom he spoke. I eternally hoped with every fiber of my being she did not think we were possibly talking about her. I slowed my pace as Jared kept talking and when she gained enough steps ahead of us, her strides seeming to increase after seeing us, heading north, our direction, too, to Deseret Towers, the second sure thing we held in common. I interrupted Jared, gasping for air, and said that was her. Surprised, he stopped and looked at her back fading into the night before us. I quietly prayed she had been far too occupied with Bergman's contemplation on struggling with Death to notice the sheer terror written large on my face when she glanced toward us, praying even more she did not feel my longing stare as she walked away.

CHAPTER 7

THE FAMILY

The Sunday morning my mother died I believed, as I expected every-one else in Grammie's basement believed, I would see her again. Mormons believe families can be together forever because Mormon rituals and sacred ordinances bind families for the eternities. The belief in families being to-gether forever has as great an influence as any single belief on faithful Mor-mons, and also appeals to many non-Mormons who long to be with loved ones after death. The together-forever part somewhere on another planet interested me as a child because of how long and distant it seemed, and how much fun of an adventure it would be, my understanding of life beyond Earth cemented in the Tesseracts of Madeleine L'Engle and the Closets of C.S. Lewis. My mother designated a time to read as a family on Sunday af-ternoons, and we kept the tradition for years after her death. We read and reread children's classics by L'Engle and Lewis. Tiered Mormon kingdoms, telestial (lowest) and terrestrial (middle) and celestial (highest), seemed plausible after the places the Murry and Pevensie children had been. The idea of eternal families was less an incontrovertible doctrine revealed by Mormon prophets than it was a wardrobe away for an eleven-year-old boy, sitting on Grammie's couch believing my mother was only gone for now from this world, not forever and not far.

The Mormon belief that families could be together forever began with the Mormons' first prophet, Joseph Smith. He recorded the revelation in Mormon scripture called the Doctrine and Covenants, Section 132. Not only did the Lord tell him families were forever but that exaltation was contingent upon the "new and everlasting covenant" of marriage. In its beginning, the Lord told Joseph,

> Verily, thus saith the Lord unto you my servant Joseph, that inasmuch as you have inquired of my hand to know and understand wherein I, the Lord, justified my servants Abraham, Isaac, and Jacob, as also Moses, David and Solomon, my servants, as touching the principle and doctrine of their having many wives and concubines—Behold, and lo, I am the Lord thy God, and will answer thee as touching this matter. Therefore, prepare thy heart to receive and obey the instructions which I am about to give unto you; for all those who have this law revealed unto them must obey the same. For behold, I reveal unto you a new and an everlasting covenant; and if you abide not that covenant, then are ye damned; for no one can reject this covenant and be permitted to enter into my glory. For all who will have a blessing at my hands shall abide the law which was appointed for that blessing, and the conditions thereof, as were instituted from before the foundation of the world. And as pertaining to the new and everlasting covenant, it was instituted for the fullness of my glory; and he that receiveth a fullness thereof must and shall abide the law, or he shall be damned, saith the Lord.

Joseph's hands were tied since he made the inquiry. If he did not obey it, he would be damned. Mormons perennially ask why God instituted polygamy, and the Mormon leadership have provided various answers, always pointing out that the full answer has not yet been revealed. But that explanation only tempts the Lord to repeat himself! He did reveal why he instituted it to the Prophet Joseph—for the fullness of God's glory. Mormon leadership goes to great lengths to distinguish the new and everlasting covenant of marriage from the practice of plural marriage by pointing out Section 132 repeats "if a man marry a wife [singular]" but that passage is first introduced as a direct borrowing from the New Testament quandary posed to Jesus about whether marriage occurs in the resurrection. The revelation taken as a whole, including the justifications of Abraham to enjoy a fullness and continuation of his seed and the presumption that Joseph Smith already had one wife mentioned by name in the same revelation, does not make the distinction between the new and everlasting covenant and plural marriage. That is not a mistake because there was no distinction intended, just as the revelation unmistakably introduced the new and everlasting covenant as plural marriage in the passage cited above. That introduction and the entire revelation include multiple warnings about damnation if one did not obey. The marginalized Mormon fundamentalist groups who actually still take the Lord at his word at the very least cannot be faulted for their integrity for upholding their end of the principle.

The Mormon marriage covenant evolved to a celestial marriage between one man and one woman, or the justly world-renowned William Goldman's man and wife, the Mormon marriage of my parents, Jimmy Keith Elison and Christine Jane Harward. While my parents' marriage was an admirable attempt at eternal family building with six ruffians limiting every imaginable celestial possibility, it was not the fairest measure of the standard Mormon family project. Make no mistake: Mormons boast successful families for good reason. They have many. If you want a healthy, disciplined, rewarding crop of children, you could do much, much worse than give your kids to a Mormon family like the Madsens in Brady Udall's *The Miracle Life of Edgar Mint*.

Joseph's implementation of plural marriage raised the ire of many critics from within and without the Mormon tradition. Many of the early Mormon apostates left the Mormon Church because of their opposition to Joseph's practice of polygamy, and Mormons decades after the end of polygamy struggle to justify the practice to each other and to nonmembers. The success of staging a positive view of the practice in Home Box Office's series *Big Love* aside, the mere idea of the practice tends to draw public repulsion for faithful Mormons as much as non-Mormons. It has an icky feel to it. Many authors have poignantly addressed the practice within Mormonism, effectively describing its inception and consequences, thorough studies made possible by its relatively recent history and continuation among Mormon Fundamentalist groups, and many of these authors have aptly described the plight of the many young victims subjected to it. Polygamy's centrality to Mormon history cannot be overstated, even though most Mormons view the practice as part of a welcomed closed chapter of the Church's history when the faithful were commanded to do it for mysterious reasons at the behest of God's anointed.

Joseph may have made good on the claim that plural marriage was necessary for eternal salvation if he had included women unlikely to have obtained salvation by any husband other than one commanded by God. That practice would have been a marquee precedent for God's chosen: the charismatic handsome bestower of God's modern revelations extending God's richest promises to those heretofore previously denied the bliss of marriage, by bedding the ignored and debased historical category of outcasts: The Homely, The Spinster, and The Ugly. That was the very approach proposed in James Joyce's *Ulysses* by Buck Mulligan when he entered the hospital with his friend Alec Bannon, joining Leopold Bloom and Stephen Dedalus. Mulligan passed out cards with writing in fair italics, "Mr. Malachi Mulligan, Fertiliser and Incubator, Lambay Island," announcing he purchased in fee simple the island to devote himself to the noble work of establishing a national fertilizing farm to offer himself for the *fecundation of any female of what grade of life soever who should there direct to him with the desire of fulfilling the functions of her natural.*

As evidenced in the aforementioned revelation recorded in Section 132 of the Doctrine and Covenants, God did not discriminate among all classes soever of women as the object of his directive to Joseph. But Joseph's actions were not consistent with Buck's inclusiveness in many known cases where he conditioned exaltation upon the holy practice of plural conjugality. Instead, Smith's view on plural marriage shared those of prophets before him, mirroring Guido Anselmi's view of plural bedmates in Federico Fellini's 8½ (1963)—gather the fairest and many of them. If their views differed in kind, they did not in degree, as measured in the impressions of their first wives. The reaction of Joseph's first wife, Emma, mirrored the displeasure and embarrassment of Guido's wife Luisa.

Guido's fantasy sequence of his wife and lovers (trading Joseph's mantle of prophet for Guido's whip, both instruments effectively bringing others within their desires) sitting down for a meal, after upholding the decree to banish a former lover to confinement upstairs, opaquely resonates to Joseph's nascent vision of plural marriage. The acceptance of Joseph's revelation was unanimous in the vision he received like Guido's own, but outside their respective visions the practice was not embraced by all the women it meant to include.

Emma Smith never accepted the practice, even when Joseph, straight-faced but eternally flushed, insisted she do as God directed her and accept the revelation God had given him and to her, as the revelation explicitly mentioned the need that she go along, the requirement of her faithfulness to support him in doing what God commanded him to do, really her full support of his marrying and marrying more women, as God commanded, delivered initially through Joseph's brother, Hyrum, no less. One would be mistaken to conjecture that novelist Italo Svevo relied on a seer stone in his pocket and channeled Joseph's genuine feelings into the motivations of Zeno in his *Confessions*, purely disposed to each woman in his life, including the desire for his lover, which caused an enlarged appreciation of his wife for her unknowing sacrifice and unknowing understanding that completely moved him. Surely the same motive matched Joseph's desires, making him, too, more in awe of his wife's sacrifice. But Emma had none of it, one rightly infers. She rejected his circular pretense when he was alive, as Luisa was re-pulsed by Guido's justification of his wants. Emma left the Mormon Church after Joseph's assassination, providing a marquee example of integrity and a sound mind for all religious women forced to live under God's command mediated by God's chosen husbands.

Joseph's wives, and attempted wives, were often young and among the most attractive in the community, unlikely candidates of becoming old maids missing out on the eternal bond of marriage. Joseph even demanded women to marry him who were already married to faithful Mormon men. Zeno proposed the same arrangement upon learning of the engagement of his mistress Carla to her maestro, whose instruction he had arranged. Joseph defended the demand as a test of faithfulness to God's prophet, while Zeno's willingness to share was a sign of his genuine love. Joseph probably did not fail to see that making such a demand changed the practice of po-lygamy into something altogether not about eternal marriage but something more in plumb with a mix of power and desire run wild.

In Joseph's defense, however, a mixture of this kind of incredulity in oth-ers was often necessary in implementing an otherwise unacceptable divine practice. And if he didn't provide an example of hubris, no one has. Joseph's demand of others' wives tired even his closest friends, who did not share Andrew Semyonovitch Lebeziatnikov's concept of a free marriage in Fydor Dostoyevsky's *Crime and Punishment*. Lebeziatnikov, a social progressive, believed that providing his wife a lover an ultimate form of respect for her. Not a sentiment likely shared by Zeno, his mistress by definition not his wife, but he surely would have been a willing participant to test Lebeziat-nikov's love. Joseph held the same belief for his friends that were husbands and, not unlike Zeno but unlike the inevitable cuckold Lebeziatnikov, not for himself as the tested husband. Despite the spot-on, exact, and utterly uncanny similarities, Lebeziantnikov's point of view borders on the comical, knowing something of his failure to effect any of his progressive ideas, let alone among women, while Joseph's was nothing short of cruel, knowing the genuine belief so many had in him as God's prophet.

Polygamy has always been, in part and likely for the most part, a biolog-ical, unbounded natural desire and, secondly, something blanketed in sal-vation and patriarchal robing. Its universal appeal to heterosexual males is admitted by Robert the Marquis in his lament over the seemingly impossible challenge to explain its naturalness to the poacher-turned-servant, Marceau le Braconnier, in the aristocratic romantic farce of Jean Renoir's *Rules of the Game* (1939). *Rules* is neglected to an unpardonable fault in discussions of that greatest year of film-making and is necessary to bolster the widely and not uncritically accepted claim among cinephiles and cineastes alike, if one's to believe the year 1960 does not reign supreme. 1960 may be film's great-est year with the international release of Michelangelo Antonioni's *The Ad-venture*, Fellini's *La Dolce Vita*, Jean-Luc Godard's *Breathless*—enough but I persist—Francois Truffaut's *Shoot the Pianist*, Ingmar Bergman's *The Virgin Spring*, Michael Powell's *Peeping Tom*, Fritz Lang's final film, *Diabolical Dr. Mabuse*, and Jean Cocteau's penultimate film, *The Testament of Orpheus*, all during a year Copenhagen native Carl Theodor Dreyer and Helena, Mon-tana, native Gary Cooper laid off the red carpet. This was the selfsame year that the western arguably as good as Sam Peckinpah's *Ride the High Country* (1962) and Sergio Leone's *The Good, the Bad and the Ugly* (1966), the cre-scendo remake (heavens if it didn't take three films) of Akira Kurosawa's *Yojimbo* (1961), a bloody anti-hero action tour de force. 1966 was another brilliant year with Andrei Tarkovsky's *Andrei Rublev* and Robert Bresson's *Balthazar*. Back to '60 and John Sturges' indomitable western *The Magnif-icent Seven*, also a remake of Kurosawa's preeminent *The Seven Samurai* (1954), and Stanley Kubrick's best feature *Spartacus*, Richard Brooks' inim-itable *Elmer Gantry*, and Billy Wilder's smart *The Apartment*. And to think the greatest year of the movies was just two years removed from the greatest movie ever made, Alfred Hitchcock's *Vertigo* (1958), '58 in the mix of any discussion of the best year in film with Louis Malle's tectonic *The Lovers* and the greatest film maker ever Kurosawa's greatest feature, *The Hidden Fortress*, which came eight years after his film *Rashomon* that changed film-making and served as the stick by which all subsequent innovative films would be measured. A list of movies from 1960 would not be complete nor the assertion it was film's zenith without Hitchcock's own masterpiece *Psycho*, and something by Luis Bunuel and Louis Malle.

Marceau, fleeing the gamekeeper Shumacher after flirting with Shumacher's wife, comes across the Marquis, downtrodden, smoking in the shadows of a hall in his country mansion away from the chaos developing in the main corridors. Marceau asks that the Marquis pretend not to have seen him, explaining about the gamekeeper's wife. His plea elicits the Marquis to bemoan his own predicament, the Marquis asking in turn if his servant ever wished he were an Arab. Marceau, surprised, asks why, and the Marquis responds with the "harem," and Muslim logic in male and female relations, justifying the unexpected comparison by adding what he presumes to be an astute observation that Muslims have their favorites yet are still keen to the feelings of others. The Marquis' own intentions, he says, are not to hurt his lovers, yet unknowingly he had crushed his favorite, his wife Christine, moments earlier during the evening's entertainment. Before running on, Marceau identifies the linchpin of being able to follow such a widely held and firmly felt natural desire to please many women: money, the currency of power having its equal only in divine mandates.

Modern cultural norms and moralities implore rational denunciation of polygamy. Yet the practice seems less offensive when players have liberty to enter in and to exit out of it. But the absence of liberty in the practice seems as ubiquitous and universal as its being dictated by men. If the practice were inverted and dictated by women, polyandry, it's not apparent there would flow more liberty, given Olivia Judson's endlessly entertaining and informative writings on sexual evolution, chief among them *Dr. Tatiana's Sex Advice to All Creation*. But given cultural mating rites in male-female relations, variables often absent from the insects and bugs Judson warms us to, presumably the practice may be less deplorable if led by women, certainly an indefensible claim worth consideration, so without further ado....

Consider the axis-altering case study of Catherine in Truffaut's *Jules and Jim* (1962), not a bad year itself on the strength of Truffaut combined with Kirk Douglas' fine performance, second only to *Lust for Life* (1956), in the gritty *Lonely Are the Brave*, Peckinpah's best aforementioned western, and the American release of Bunuel's *Viridiana*, a dramatic summit of the highest pinnacle of humanity's potential examined in cinema. *Viridiana*, alone,

enough for full consideration of the best year if one insists on its international release the year before. Catherine enjoyed freedom with Jules and Jim,
which comes at some consequence, with the eventual expunging of Jim's
liberty of the ultimate stripe when he is killed by Catherine, who also dies in
the act. Catherine proved, for a time, a successful alternative to monogamy
(and ultimately proving Judson right). Catherine's relationships may be a
cautionary tale that, short of being told by God to layer spouses, it may otherwise prove impracticable, surely a defensible position, but Catherine still
proved the point while Jim chose to participate.

If Catherine doesn't persuade, Garance in Marcel Carne's *Children of
Paradise* (1945) may not either. She found on The Boulevard of Crime that
she could have multiple male partners. Her lovers retained their liberty, as
much of what remains of liberty in a person overcome by irrational desires,
each lover showing that, where there's liberty in love, chaos follows. Garance's life, like Guido's fantasies, shared the vibrant life of the inimitable—
because of current bigamy laws—Joseph Smith. Unbecoming of one chosen
by God or not, Joseph's religious, political, and amorous actions showed a
person teeming with a life in love with living (for which I, and apparently
Harold Bloom, admire him).

While Garance lived in full view on the boulevard, the depths of untarnished truth, the same mortal plane mined for ultimate truth in the respective versions of Renoir (1936) and Kurosawa's (1957) *The Lower Depths*,
Joseph intuited what many do, that seeing the naked truth with one's own
eyes and experiencing it requires crossing to—and reinventing—a shadier
alley. The mistake of applying Socrates' germane question of piety in Plato's
Euthyphro, in its modern moral form of *whether an action like polygamy is
morally right* because God commanded it or did God command it because
it is morally right, need not deter us from doing so. The distinction may
provide for a justifiable morality (by answering correctly for the second option), but the question also accounts for focusing on an abstract discussion
that leads to actions, as certainly as inserting polygamy into Socrates' words
shows how frustrating any association of God is with morality.

When Joseph claimed God directed him to practice polygamy, he removed the question about morality of God from the abstract, the only safe
haven for questions about God, to events with consequences. Joseph justified the practice as being from God, but where he succeeded was moving
the practice—or only the discussion of the practice—from one boulevard
to another, from the Boulevard of Crime to the yellowy-bright brick road

of exalted and eternal bliss. His revelatory rite was among the greats of any wizard's decrees. While faced with challenges to sustain such truth amidst civil society, at least Garance and Joseph lived (not all that openly as it took Joseph a decade of trying out the divine practice before revealing it) the experiences they considered truth. Pathetic Guido only fantasized or recalled them from the freedom of his youth. We may not agree with Garance and Joseph, but we don't pity them like we do Guido. Still, most by and large don't envy Joseph, yet many would rightly cheers Marcello Mastroianni, who brought Guido to life on the silver screen.

Alternatives to God's directive of multiple people to cohabit, or to go to The Boulevard of Crime to find the barest forms of truth, are relationships outside the vacuum of staid, ideal relationship, and are up against the ideal of the day, the partnering of one man and one woman. Not all alternatives involve multiple-conjugalis matrimony.

One relationship outside the ideal emerges in Annie Dillard's novel *Maytrees*, with unconventional loyalty between multiple people in overlapping relationships. Maytree was not married to both Lou and Deary at the same time, but he was simultaneously each woman's main partner even in his absence. The very strength of the novel relies on what is absent, a non-intrusive view of the most personal and painful. It's not his loyalty but, again, a woman's, Lou's, that proves the point. It would be preposterous, but not uncharacteristic of my reasoning, to suggest Maytree proves plural marriage works, but short of making that claim Maytree's relationships with Lou and Deary prove multiple relationships happen, overlap, co-exist, or do something currently unnamed (but likely described by Judson). The relationships occurred within acceptable norms of marriage, but the relationships had less to do with civil categories of partnership than with Lou's faithfulness to Maytree during their marriage, separation, and reunion, suggesting plurality of ties works in some circumstances. It also suggests that norms are constantly overturned and, at best, are artificial civil agreements, rightly malleable as our capacity for more workable forms expands.

Heartache seems as inevitable in relationships as beating hearts, mine tearing for Lou beyond my cumulative sympathy for Christine and Catherine and Garance, despite being much in love with her. Emotional pain accompanies the modern pristine man-woman celestial Mormon marriage and other, presumably less eternal, in Christian, pre- and post-Reformation sects, the man-woman marriages prevalent today. The fidelity to modern man-woman marriage traceable to the emergence of nuclear families in the

Industrial Age, dutiful fathers leaving home for work and long-suffering mothers remaining at home to rear children, is not without justification. Study after study shows children benefit from having both male and female care-givers, unquestionably a benefit to the state and attacked myopically as not. The centrality of such marriage to the development of civilization, at a cost of restricted sexual life being demonstrated convincingly by Freud (and remnants and records of great civilizations he relied upon).

But does an alternative, such as woman-woman, cause this nuclear benefit to weaken? Is that even a relevant question for attacking the demonstrable benefits of man-woman? I admit it is not a sufficient attack on the benefit. That is to say, proponents of man-woman rightfully carry their burden by establishing the benefit (i.e., their form of marriage produces bigger armies and more consumers for market economies, clear and convincing benefits to the state), and don't have a burden to show an alternative weakens it. Not to mention the less in-vogue yet no less self evident truth of *the key* to successful domestic life explained by Mary Konstantinovna to Nadezhda Fyodorova in Chekhov's *The Duel*: if women were the weaker sex they would not have been entrusted with the upbringing of little boys and girls—the mother care-giver. Just as they are unanimously accepted not as the weaker sex, there's no refuting that their benefit as mother leaves no viable substitute.

Whether an alternative truly weakens the benefit is an apposite question for an entirely separate issue, and that is the issue of equality, by its very definition what is available to all types and not measured by benefits to the state. If it did we wouldn't be esteeming what is spread evenly among everyone, not stuck on what is best for some; while many tire from equal-this and equal-flipping-that when equal cries minimize or eviscerate self-evident truths, i.e., there is no substitute for mother, many realize that state benefits and fairness to all its citizens can both have their due.

Level-headed people readily intuit *natural selection*, the mechanism by which variations that increase our species' fitness, the result of copulation between male and female participants is forfeited in all couplings not of the man and wife stripe because of the sheer impossibility. These same people as readily note in the positive that choosing a partner has nothing to do with and often works against making the species more fit via natural selection, i.e., falling in love is a matter of *sexual selection* and its reasons remain oblivious to rational minds. Sexual selection comes in all kinds and in all degrees; and if marriage is civil societies' formal marker of consensual adult pairing, then marriage is firstly a matter of marking sexual selection. The lack of effect that alternative pairing has on the state's benefit, is a red herring on the benefit analysis. Yet this is relevant to the issue of equality, a constant and pertinent question dogging those not treated equally, inspiring some of the most grotesque and self-deeming parades ever organized by humankind.

That is only the beginning of the harm to those society should be demanding to get married, not prohibiting them from doing so. Gays, and to an indiscernible degree lesbians, celebrate their hallmark promiscuity because it gets attention, not because it correctly identifies them. If they celebrated it because it identified them, then defense for their equality would be no more deserving than defending your dog's. Marriage curtails cads. It does not promote them. Gays do themselves and those who advocate for their equality extraordinary harm by demanding their right to identify primarily by sexual orientation. Lecherous hetero fucks hardly get due justice returned to them, but they also do not receive veneration from the best among us. Imagine the reception of cheating husbands and licentious executives banding together for a parade to celebrate what defines them—a free wandering phallus.

Freedom of sexing is not a recognized entitlement, is indefensible as one, and has been a retarding foundation for homosexuals from the beginning. It is a wonder anyone believes the choice to fuck everyone metastasizes into a basis for equality. Free sex evangelicals selfishly infected the human immunodeficiency virus onto one innocent person after another, many their own lovers, extending it to thousands through innocent exposure of blood transfusions. No matter how sincerely one believes his identity is reducible to the use of his penis, no one should ever be rewarded for that kind of dysfunction and corresponding behavior. If marriage should mean one thing, it should mean fidelity.

Yet the offense on the innocent extends to us all. We all start as teenagers running with the brumbies and well-intending Jim Craigs civilize us in the attempt to get the most value out of us. A part of corralling us is tempering our behaviors, including sexual proclivities, to function among others. We err as a civilization when a majority does all the cutting, separating according to conventions with no regard to individual preferences. And those who will not suffer conventions fight to remain among the free brumbies, resisting the cutters' attempts until some run off cliffs and others resort to extremes from living underground to all types of absurdities to draw attention to inequalities. The fault lies with all of us when any retired executive with a hankering can buy an elite cutting horse to separate one of us as sure as any one-sided belief can unfairly affect any one of our lives. The question crudely and concisely seems to be whether every consenting and faithful adult deserves to enjoy the desserts of the privilege of marriage as currently constituted as a high social good? The answer seems to be an unequivocal yes that all committed humans, all the ones I have met and can imagine, well deserve their shot in a matrimonial institution as long as culture esteems its padded white walls as unparalleled bliss.

An alternative to man-woman unions hardly poses a threat to man-woman marriage if partners are free to quit acting their parts in man-woman unions for preferred coupling. If equal status is gained and stigmas are obliterated, the result may be a mass exodus from the old to the new, and if that is an actual effect from recognizing all forms of coupling as "marriage" a welcomed one for many who are freed, and victory for equality and a harm to the presumed benefit to the state, indeed, it would be—an exodus as likely as Moses leading Israel through a Red Sea.

Facts show that the established benefit of paired man and woman care-givers face far greater threats to their success than alternative forms of partnering. The barrage of forces screams across suburbia as documented in sitcoms, films, and cartoons. And the definition of marriage in the short history of the United States (and I conjecture, throughout most western *and* eastern cultures, encompassing the royal *all*, not just *we* of *Homo sapiens*) has been a male and his fancy. More succinctly, marriage equals man plus fancy (easily notated by $M = ♂ + F$). The fancy variable has persisted, with pernicious effects.

Consider fancy's presence and effect in the very attempt to thwart it, advanced in one of the most illustrious examples of acceptable and venerated man-woman marriage, never more ardently sought than by the pettifogging lawyer Pyotr Petrovitch Luzhin's to ensnare the attractive, admirable, and vulnerable Avdotya (Dounia) Romanovna Raskolnikov in *Crime and Punishment* (a far too common example of matrimony, fortunately not to be for her, thank the Literary Gods). Luzhin's design was not merely reprehensible to us who made it through the book, but at its essence was the unvarnished form of the prevailing category of marriage: a man seeking to satisfy his interests and desires, social and carnal, and a vulnerable woman subject to satisfy them. Unlike Dounia, most young women don't fare so well. Veronika suffers the more common lot by the scheming Mark in Mikhail Kalatozov's supreme *The Cranes Are Flying* (1957). Veronika simply cannot remain faithful to her boyfriend Boris, who has gone to war, because she is subjected to darker forces of male fancy.

Even if the woman is in a position of power over man's fancy, it's still his fancy that is the key variable. For further consideration ponder Saul Bellow's *The Adventures of Augie March* where Augie's brother Simon, poor and previously rejected in his large-breasted amorous ambitions, aims for and succeeds in marrying the rich and hefty Charlotte Magnus. Simon highlights one of the benefits of man-woman marriage in his justification of marrying for reasons other than amorous love (love an exception in the genealogy of marriage and probably for good reasons) for that of family love. Heavens, he could have married a Mormon if Bellow had just known any! Simon's discourse on family love common to the Magnuses is also a common theme in Mormon talks (sermons), but nary a Mormon family there ever was as prudish-less as the Magnuses. Charlotte might appear less vulnerable than Dounia but rich or poor, fair or not, the fence around traditional marriage remains the same, and the man's fancy is the gate to open and to close it (this doesn't ignore the endless failed attempts to open and close the gates of matrimony that are successfully swung by some other less-deserving courter).

Luzhin, Mark, and Simon's cases plucked from the marriage tree of history support the rule that man's fancy remains the one constant among the evolution of marriage as surely as no conscious head can deny the role of wife rising from one of chattel to human agent, echoing the protestation of Marion Bloom that a pat on the ass didn't make her one. If Luzhin, Mark, and Simon (and Zeno where no summary however accurate and concise will suffice) fail to persuade you, reasonably disposed reader, then look to the unions around you, and if you are not only reasonable but also brave, then to your own.

The probability of finding a compatible mate to go through life seems low, even given all scenarios highlighted by Judson and conceivable combinations of male-female, male-male, female-female, male-lots of females, or female-lots of males, etc., etc., etc., as rightly stated by the great polygamous King of Kings, King Mongkut of Siam, nothing less than an unbaptized ancestral, not mere proto, Mormon himself.

The Mormon Church emphasizes marriage at the expense of many things, not least of which is whether a couple is truly compatible. The Church assumes, not unwittingly, the couple will succeed at marriage more for shared purposes in their religion than from a right fit for each other, taking note of many cultures before them. Mormons who support a marriage between a man and a woman knowingly argue its superiority and the state's significant interest in preserving it despite its dismal success rate teetering around the rest of society's. The advocates of traditional marriage across Christian sects point to the specific role of each gender but do not address the inevitable and irreparable damage when the couple splits.

When Mormon spouses realize how incompatible they are, LDS marriages, solemnized in spiritual enclaves called Mormon Temples, their bitter fallouts make Gandalf the Grey's descent beyond hell intertwined in battle with the Balrog seem like a cup of Chai tea with a shot of vanilla. If they, the mighty plural of all great faceless and presumptively egregious bottomless opponents, were correct that children with inherent expectations from proper traditional marriage explained their advantages over lesser unions, then that logic would explain the commensurate disadvantages shown by the terrific tear in the marriage fabric through the death of Cornelius Suttree's young son in Cormac McCarthy's *Suttree*. That logic is as absurd as proposing the boy Cornelius had more benefits when his parents were together because one was a man and the other was a woman when it's sufficient to infer his parents did not get along well, as elements of respect and cooperation far outweigh in importance gender. What we can safely assert based on his mother's grieving at his fresh grave is that, during his short life, young Cornelius experienced the only true thing in life identified by Stephen Dedalus when observing his weak and futile pupil Sargent: having been loved by one who his weak watery blood drained from, his mother, this love the only real and unsurprisingly as often the only benefit.

Whether *successful traditional marriages* produce better able children than the majority of *unsuccessful traditional marriages* is quantifiable, and the *harm from traditional marriages* to children likely is too, and to the parents and to the in-laws, if the kicks to Suttree's head from his wife's peace-loving father and Suttree's own kick to his wife's mother's *cabeza* are fair indications. What the successes and failures of traditional marriages do not prove is that alternative unions cannot also provide upbringings that produce able children and very likely unable ones too.

The main Mormon goal of marriage is sustainability of its religion through propagation of its member species. There is not much individual liberty in that goal, so it's not surprising that official Mormondom does not support alternative definitions of marriage as the ultimate expression of one's liberty, ironically marked in the surrendering of it to a partnership, such sacrifice even known to be scattered among a few Mormon unions. One Mormon Prophet was rumored to boast he and his wife had never quarreled, not once. That is possible marriage when the husband as master retains his liberty and the wife as servant-slave abdicates her own. Make no mistake those roles often flip, as sure as Betty's advice, dutifully recited by her husband Stan at the end of *Sons of the Desert* (1933), that "honesty is the best politics" rings true.

An unyielding support of an empty *endless* (eternal) traditional definition of marriage of man and woman seems an ironic reconciliation, if not a wee bit deceitful, with the new and everlasting covenant's place within Mormonism, vilified by apostates and Mormon haters, old and modern. Adding two ironies does not apparently equal a literal positive but instead it appears to enlarge grotesquely the irony. A better alternative to the American majority's modern ideal of marriage is the value of the literal support of the freedom to partner, including alternative forms of partnering, which would show a religion at peace with its own alternative version of marriage, an elusive peace not to be while Mormons uncritically tread upon, ever squeamish at the mere mention of their history.

And marriage under any definition will not be worth replication unless its ultimate value is a partnership where both parties can share with each other all aspirations and emotional highs and lows without abuse. The greatest abuses in marriage are not physical, mental, or emotional. The worse abuse results in the stymieing or obliteration of oneself, one's identity, personality and soul. This process of destruction happens in increments over thousands of moments of selfish acts, including mean-spirited omissions, ending in a terminable split after years of lopsided commitment or worse a lifetime with a partner where the best one can say is "at least I wasn't alone."

Guarding against this destructive abuse is one reason Milton's "domestic sweets" between husband and wife rank above "casual fruition" between philanderer and uninhibited lassie. He wasn't merely reflecting conservative values over free expression. He wasn't deprived of his full humanity from not experiencing the swinging heydays centuries later in London any more than he failed to appreciate the romping Roman aristocratic orgiastic bliss. Milton described a state of paradise necessarily including one's truest self, and there's no possible pinnacle for the self constantly subjected to others' abuses. Reining in how much one gives of oneself depends upon how the other spends it.

The key is really correct partnering, not a singular kind of partnering, because if you're one of the few not being abused when you give of yourself, with one or multiple partners, then you're being sustained and possibly enlarged in your capacity to reach new horizons. The return on how much of you that you have spent is the critical inquiry. Other considerations are finite but many, from the emotional to the practical. These other criteria are marked in permanent gray depending upon shared expectations and governing norms of your tea party. Despite it all, you might find a partner who shares your purpose and together achieve your goals to bring about progress, effect real change, or create meaning and log rich experience amidst life's intermittent calm and certain head winds. Hell, you might work in rearing redeemable children.

CHAPTER 8
WORLD RELIGIONS

Early in my freshman year at Brigham Young University, I formed the habit of attending devotionals on Tuesday mornings. However, the most memorable Tuesday morning involved a forum, not a devotional, when Rabbi Harold Kushner came to Provo, Utah to visit BYU's campus. I had not heard of Rabbi Kushner or his classic *When Bad Things Happen to Good People*, and I do not recall anything he said that impressed me that Tuesday morning. While his little book has sat respected on shelves following me from apartments throughout various states the years since I heard his address, I have never read it. But his personality made an indelible impression.

He was a first, an example of a person of great faith in a religion not my own. Moved by his passion for his religion and belief in God, I wanted to know more about what made him able to stand before a Mormon audience, instructing the near-capacity crowd at the Marriott Center with unwavering faith in a God from a different religion. I knew Judaism figured prominently in how my own religion explained that God transferred his truth from the beginning of time as recorded in the Old Testament to present day, culminating in the one true living religion of Mormonism. Mormons believe Israel's legacy extends to people of the Book of Mormon, making Mormons literal (adopted) descendants of the Hebrew tradition in line to receive God's promises of Israel, compounding its blessings in Utah for centuries or so, parlaying their chosen-ness in a new Zion in Missouri at Jesus' second coming. But that understanding failed to appreciate Israel's relationship to God outside its role in the Mormon Plan of Salvation, a failure not exclusive to me within my culture. I wanted to know more about the source of Rabbi Kushner's strength, and I knew where I would begin. Professor Jeff P. Tilman introduced Rabbi Kushner to the BYU audience. I decided to take his class.

BYU required students to fulfill a certain amount of religious instruction hours to graduate, not to be mistaken with the study of religion courses, a discipline unknown to me during my university experience and nowhere to be found at BYU. The requirement broke down to about one religious instruction course, two hours, per semester. Freshman males overwhelming took a Missionary Preparation course that fulfilled the requirement but more importantly primed them for their LDS Missions, standard interruption of their university studies for two years. Committed to serving a Mormon mission but not wanting more instruction on the basic tenets of my faith, and expecting I would get more than enough proselytizing training at the LDS Missionary Training Center and during my mission, I avoided the popular Missionary Preparation course. Yet I felt I could use more preparation because of my ignorance about other religions and what people believed about God, as made clear by Rabbi Kushner. To shed some ignorance, I enrolled in Professor Jeff P. Tilman's course "The Gospel and World Religions."

I entered class and took a seat in the middle of the room in the back row, where I sat all semester after signing my name in a box on a seating chart passed around the first day. The other students were older than me. If I was not the only freshman, I was the only one in class who looked like one. Professor Tilman was less of an instructor than he was a guide through the world's major religions. He demonstrated respect for each religion we studied, and he discussed each religion from the view of its adherents, placing a premium on accurate explanations of their histories and beliefs.

He stood tall against the front wall, his reserved demeanor reminding me of my boyhood Mormon Bishop Eddleston. Bishop Eddleston succeeded the much loved Bishop Patrick, the bishop of Riverton Ward at the time my mother died and, like Professor Tilman, Bishop Eddleston had a reservoir of intelligence, superior to most. Even more compelling was how each drew upon their reserve, delivering clear and concise explanations. Bishop Eddleston was my earliest example of one who could deliver religious ideas and beliefs devoid of passion. His demeanor showed a confidence in the message independent of himself, and he was uncannily and uniquely able to harness his personal feelings. Because I had nothing in common with the intelligence or the delivery of Professor Tilman or Bishop Eddleston, their styles contrasting to mine and those of most people I knew, they set what I would much later come to recognize as the gold standard for intelligent discourse. After religious discussions, not during them, recurring shame set in for my pressing the passion throttle. The aftermath of shame was not for making the connection but for my inability to discuss an idea with any restraint.

Like all my other classes before and after, from the beginning of secondary education to graduate school, I never voluntarily participated in class, speaking only when spoken to, despite the oft-made declaration by the professor on the first day of class that grades would be partially based on class participation, coaxing not even a grain of motivating force despite my recognition that exercising my vocal cords would have boosted many A-minuses to As, sliding me improperly among the elite *summa cum laude* of my peers. Voicing my thoughts on subjects I did not know anything about, was a practice widely exercised outside of class. In class it was never to be, and I remained the silent fool, ranked among, given the ubiquitous effects of grade inflation, my equally average, limited-minded peers. I stayed quiet, but the other students in Professor Tilman's class did not. They were older and also more varied in their appearances. An Asian woman sat to my right, Asian students were known to me from the math lab but heretofore unmet in class, and to my left, sitting in the front, was the single black student I saw on campus, a girl who routinely participated, probably earning an A. And while any claim to diversity on campus would be an overstatement, the class had rich chemistry and by BYU standards I credited it being genuinely diverse for the varied interest and sympathy toward other religions.

The emphasis on variety started with Professor Tilman's practice of ensuring the optimal source of the various religious traditions we studied, practitioners of each religion, came to class. I remember distinctly two Muslim students, Masum and Taslim, both fully bearded, no doubt with beard medical cards in tow to provide safe passage into the testing center and other regulated venues on campus. Their discussion of Islam was outweighed by their deep appreciation of Professor Tilman's support of Muslim students, explaining how much it meant to have a separate room for Muslims on campus for noon prayer, obtained through Professor Tilman's efforts.

The richness of the course had limits that were easily tabled while encountering the religious traditions for the first time. Faithful to the course title, "The Gospel and World Religions," Professor Tilman's method compared Mormonism to all the non-Christian religions we studied. Examining subjects in the context of the greater truth of Mormonism was the normative approach to study all topics at BYU, and other religions were no exception. At the beginning of the course, Professor Tilman passed out a document titled, "Classic Mormon Quotes on Religious Tolerance." A few excerpts follow.

> For none of these iniquities come of the Lord; for he doth that which is good among the children of men; and he doeth nothing save it be plain unto the children of men; and he inviteth them all to come unto him and partake of his goodness; and he denieth none that come unto him, black and white, bond and free, male and female, and he remembereth the heathen; and all are alike unto God, both Jew and Gentile. 2 Nephi 26: 33, the Book of Mormon
>
> For I command all men, both in the east and in the west, and in the north, and in the south, and in the islands of the sea, that they shall write the words which I speak unto them; for out of the books which shall be written I will judge the world, every man according to their works, according to that which is written. 2 Nephi 29: 11
>
> But behold, that which is of God inviteth and enticeth to do good continually; wherefore, every thing which inviteth and enticeth to do good, and to love God, and to serve him, is inspired of God. Moroni 7: 13
>
> Seek ye diligently and teach one another words of wisdom; yea, seek ye out of the best books words of wisdom; seek learning, even by study and also by faith. The Doctrine and Covenants 88: 118
>
> Study and learn, and become acquainted with all good books, and with languages, tongues, and people. D& C 90: 15
>
> Verily, thus saith the Lord unto you concerning the Apocrypha— There are many things contained therein that are true,...There are many things contained therein that are not true, which are interpreta-

tions by the hands of men. Therefore, whoso readeth it, let him understand, for the Spirit manifesteth truth. And whoso is enlightened by
the Spirit shall obtain benefit therefrom. D&C 91: 1-2, 4-5

We need not doubt the wisdom and intelligence of the Great
Jehovah; He will award judgment or mercy to all nations according to
their several deserts, their means of obtaining intelligence, the laws
by which they are governed, the facilities afforded them of obtaining
correct information, and His inscrutable designs in relation to the
human family; and when the designs of God shall be made manifest,
and the curtain of futurity be withdrawn, we shall all of us eventually
have to confess that the Judge of all the earth has done right. *Teachings
of Joseph Smith*, p. 218

The final quotation came from a section titled, "Justice of the Great Law-
giver." The Great Law Giver began from the proposition that God, the Great
Parent, possessed wise and merciful judgment based on the awareness of the
diverse living conditions of his children on earth. Joseph's Great Parent was
not restricted by the narrow understanding of men. His God could judge
by a standard assumed by Joseph, and unstated in his sermon, while men
necessarily judged according to their situations and limited understanding.
Joseph concluded all will be right in the end, a tolerant view of fair universal judgment. What Joseph does not mention is how all will be right in
the end in this excerpt—the assumed bit alluded to above. The Great Parent will judge all his many children the same or we'll all cry foul. The same
measure—unstated above—will be the Mormon truths and that will be fair
because everyone will be given the opportunity to receive Mormon truth
in this life from their unimaginably kind Mormon neighbor or from the
clean young missionaries at their doorstep or in the next life where Mormon
proselytizing will increase tenfold beyond the amazing efforts demonstrated
on earth. This is the kind view. A more pernicious view is some people are
smarter and better than other people, and that's why they get more truth
and higher laws to live by. Joseph's elitism is bearable because who doesn't
see themselves as special when they possess something unique, and Joseph's
ladder of value from the Mormons down to the non-Mormons has so many
precedents in other groups with truth that his ignorance is less excusable
than it is expected. And all of this from an uneducated farm boy.

How does Joseph miss the application of this statement to his early life?
And still place such embarrassing restraints on God? If an unlearned, illit-

erate fourteen-year-old Joseph can receive the highest of truths, who the hell cannot, should have been Joseph's conclusion! That would have been marquee divine tolerance indeed.

The passages of scripture and teachings in Professor Tilman's handout either explicitly or implicitly professed a tolerance of other religions in the context of other truths being within the big Mormon box of truth and everyone who ever lived getting an invitation to play in it.

Religion and humanity courses at BYU were always discussed in the context of the Gospel's enveloping every other truth. The Gospel was more like a very large canopy than a very large box, if I'm permitted to mangle metaphors apropos the oft-tortured logic to explain God. The explanation, extending over all time and every culture, spread its superior shade over all, as the folds continually extend over all discovered truth.

As a faithful Mormon, I resisted the notion that the Gospel was cumulative of all truth and resisted the notion that truths in other religions were partial truths or pieces of the puzzle corresponding to truths fitting nicely in the whole puzzle of my Mormon religion. Even though I resisted the Mormon canopy's being the whole truth and nothing but the truth, I came to appreciate its omnipresence because its validity was constantly tested, unable to contain the blinding light of other, valid truths breaking through its seamless folds.

Each professor I remember at BYU, Professor Tilman chief among them, placed a premium on accuracy. And their fidelity to high academic standards inevitably showed incongruities in the cumulative claim of the Gospel's embracing all truths, by showing how incommensurate the claim was with the partial truths scattered about the world in other sacred texts, art and literature. A magnanimously empty claim, supposedly satisfied by the mere appearance of similarity to something within Mormonism, so simplistic few professors dared dwell upon it. I began seeing the incongruities during my second semester at BYU because of the passion and respect of Professors Mitchell and Tilman toward their topics in their courses. This was not as a result of any antagonism, which admittedly was always present, curling my guts when Mormon leaders marshaled up the panoply of holes in their canopy. Had the professors been lesser intellectuals, or replicas of the Mormon apostles like the majority of religious instructors at BYU, I would have been mired in the far-reaching Mormon shadow well beyond the time that I was, with seams still blocking the rays beyond my Mormon world of absolute, complete, and eternal truth.

Professor Tilman's course introduced what made life meaningful for people in religions not my own, and I wanted to know more. And to top off my genuine interest in the material, Professor Tilman offered extra credit for attending foreign films with religious themes at the International Cinema. I was never more game for a semester of higher education.

One final quotation from the handout stated:

> We ought always to be aware of those prejudices which sometimes so strangely present themselves, and are so congenial to human nature, against our friends, neighbors, and brethren of the world, who choose to differ from us in opinion and in matters of faith. Our religion is between us and our God. Their religion is between them and their God. There is a love from God that should be exercised toward those of our faith, who walk uprightly, which is peculiar to itself, but it is without prejudice. It also gives scope to the mind, which enables us to conduct ourselves with greater liberality towards all that are not of our faith, than what they exercise towards one another. These principles approximate nearer to the mind of God, because [they] are like God, or Godlike. *Teachings of Joseph Smith*, pp. 146-147

I do not understand this quotation from Joseph Smith and have reread it many times. And reading it in context doesn't help either from a section titled, "Counsel Against Secrecies" where Joseph decries organizations involving oaths based on secrecy and penalties, stating such groups weakened "pure friendship," and declaring that he and other servants acted in accordance with the "fullness of the Gospel of Jesus Christ" regardless of clandestine actions of others. Mormons had and indeed have their oaths and secrets, so surely not all groups that have them are despicable, the irony of Joseph's lament hardly lost on most of his intended audience. His use of "fullness" has specific meaning for Latter-day Saints, meaning the gospel restored through him, Joseph Smith. The largeness of restored truths through Joseph extended beyond the Gospel of Jesus Christ as known to all sects of historical Christianity, broadly speaking all developments and trends related to the life and teachings of Jesus Christ. The largeness of "fullness" restored through Joseph proved the Mormon assumption that necessary truths of the Gospel were lost throughout Christian history. The largeness also carries a bit of irony for Christians, broadly meaning all sects of the Christian faith who have relied upon a Gospel of Jesus Christ from the New Testament, a gospel lending itself to numerous interpretations not apparently in need of extra trappings of salvation, as Mormonism's "fullness" includes additional truths about God's Plan of Salvation. In other words, Joseph added fullness to something many since Luther have felt in need of correction but not addition.

The trap in discussing Mormon thought like the quote above is the inevitable elided parenthetical at every turn, but I must step about if I am intent on considering a thought or three. I hoped that failed intentions do not amount to having thought I preferred one idea to an absent other or prolonged our imprisonment in failed explanation of unique Mormon meanings like fullness. Take note I did not tip an oath or secrecy.

However much I like the idea that the mind of God conducts itself "with greater liberality towards all," a principle worth building on for viewing other faiths, I'm not convinced that's what Joseph meant. Joseph premised the divine mindset on love from God being shown to Mormons, presumably from other Mormons, and moved through associations I don't quite follow, a development of ideas not akin to the unencumbered and uneducated youth he was, no doubt a strength when he disassociated himself from learned intellectuals, but eventually a glaring handicap when he ventured into their handiwork, theological discourse.

What I gather from the final quote is an outward tolerance where Mormons develop a scope of mind, or perspective, that encourages them to be better behaved toward others than others are towards each other (and towards Mormons). I boldly venture to suggest this passage shares the kernel of the trademark uber-kindness of Mormons toward nonmembers, the common moniker used by Mormons for the billions of people who are not Mormon. Here the requisite guidance of the Holy Spirit would likely provide the interpretive help one needs to appreciate Joseph's words, spiritual help for enlightened minds and unnervingly, too often, condescending ones, the type of help not exclusively Mormon by any whip.

The *Teachings of Joseph Smith* is a compilation of sermons and excerpts of sermons published in 1938, edited by the Tenth Mormon President of the Church Joseph Fielding Smith, who acted as an official church historian for much of his life. The collection is closer to Islam's *Hadiths*, summaries of what Muhammad said as recorded by his followers, than to John Calvin's systematic explanation of the Protestant faith in *Institutes of the Christian Religion*. Joseph Fielding Smith was the son of the sixth President of the Church, Joseph F. Smith, who was the son of Hyrum Smith, the brother of the founder Joseph Smith. Joseph Fielding Smith was also the father-in-law of the Great Mormon Apostle Bruce R. McConkie who wrote the definitive text of Mormon doctrine, aptly titled *Mormon Doctrine*, in 1958, before being called to his apostleship in the early 1970s. McConkie provided coherent and clear expositions of Mormon beliefs, standardizing the teachings and revolutionizing Mormon theology. McConkie's efforts provided a doctrinal reference point for the Church members to emerge unified in the modern area and enabled the Church to effectively proselytize its beliefs throughout the world. He effectively repackaged Mormonism by cataloguing Mormon beliefs, including some of the most outlandish Mormon claims only the most orthodox dared to defend. His book met a fair amount of resistance by some for its unpopular claims, and by others because it curtailed the Mormonism many loved and embraced not as beholden to official parameters.

The text holds a precarious place within Mormondom. The Mormon leadership did not commission McConkie's efforts and initially denied it official status, and some apostles publicly denounced it for its mistakes, but within a decade the leadership worked with McConkie on a second publication in the mid-1960s, confirming its quasi-official status that continued for decades. The book is currently out of print, marking the end of its own great era. While its official status is debated among the faithful, the text's role in standardizing Mormon doctrine is well cemented. While I have not read it, and have no plans to read it in this mortal life, delaying its certain prescribed reading in my Mormon Outer Darkness (hell), I feel like I have read it because its endless recurrence as a primary source for church manuals and pamphlets and commentaries and dictionaries and bibliographic support of Mormon religious scholarship and talks upon talks and even more talks in local wards and general conferences, most often unacknowledged and even more often the unknown source. Its statements will remain unknown for new generations, as the Church has removed all references to it from publications, portending its likely place as a footnote in Mormonism's intellectual history.

Like many of the Mormon faithful I was mostly familiar with the sensational claims edited out of the second edition under the direction of the Church (for which I am overdue a definition of capital "Church": not to be confused with the building, individual members or the body of Christ but specifically meaning the authorities from the first presidency, twelve apostles, seventy, presiding bishopric, and endless committees such as the correlation and strengthening members' committees). McConkie, a lawyer by training, was unencumbered by the standards of a theologian or academic, and assumed all proofs by their very assertion, with no sniveling about an imperative to referring to Christian history. He completed his encyclopedic project as if he was rendering statutory code for Mormons. The book was a mix of codigraphic and theographic. If McConkie had been anything but a lawyer, his ambitious project of standardizing the Church's beliefs would have fallen in with the long line of commentary of tiered general authorities' opinions, following the tradition of the founding members who suffered from no restraints on topics and length by which they could expound every truth conceivable under heaven. Reading the *Teachings of Joseph Smith* or the voluminous teachings of other Church leaders such as *The Discourses* including sermons of the second President of the Church, Brigham Young, McConkie's explication of official Mormon doctrines marks a monumental contribution. And a much needed and welcome one.

However, McConkie's work marked a clear tradeoff. The McConkie tradeoff was a gain of the standardized beliefs at the loss of uncanonized theology, ending a rich tradition within Mormonism, a loss lamented by many of the faithful. The gains of homogenized Mormon thinking came at the cost of obliterating most and reducing what remained of multifarious spiritual truths, by their nature subjective and ethereal. After McConkie, spiritual truth (the remaining reduced type), standardized to acceptable definitions provided by the Church, was anathema to many as the heart of Mormonism, limiting previously and widely celebrated, unencumbered personal revelation from God. And after McConkie, if there was any doubt before him, the deepest truths between individuals and God were subject to the position of the Church, the Church the gatekeeper of acceptable types of religious experience much like the normative strainers within the Christian sects that Mormonism openly decreed as having been in a state of apostasy. After McConkie, Mormonism resembled nothing more radical than your garden variety chapel, with what you could and couldn't experience as God in order to sit comfortably within it at the approval of its guiding rector, in the case of the one true church its local bishop.

The McConkie tradeoff ushered in a stark controversy over the Mormon Church's view of Jesus Christ as well, a controversy that would prove to be the most significant public event affecting my life and that would foretell, and likely cause, by social and biological sources but not likely the misbe-gotten philosophical measure of causation, the evolution of the Christian identity within the Mormon Church. Only one event, the equal distribution of the priesthood to all faithful males in 1978, had such a great effect on the modern Mormon Church. McConkie's views on blacks happened to be a topic he was beside himself to clarify in his first edition of *Mormon Doctrine*, where he claimed, like many Mormon leaders before him including Brigham Young, that blacks sat neutral during a monumental war in the pre-mortal existence, and as a result of their fence-sitting they didn't fall and stump their heads but were marked by darker skin. McConkie claimed the absolute certainty of this by what he claimed was the irrefutable logic that in war one cannot be neutral. I expect his logic appears inane to most people because he implicitly relies upon an understanding of the pre-mortal life not available to non-Mormons' limited reasoning abilities. He also relies upon the conveyance of meaning in language, his case the Queen's English, used by mortals with an inevitable loss of translation from the pre-mortal life into ours, both changes in reasoning and language ever so unsubtly arming every apologetic Mormon. In other words, you just don't get it. It might just be an excuse, and probably is, but I identify these reasons as the basis for much of my recurring confusion, not to mention what I expect for non-Mormons, but one person's confusion is another person's clearest moment of thought in discussions of God, and a lot of other things we have no knowledge about.

McConkie was eager to share other views he knew definitively. One of those views was of the Jews, a view poorly conceived even by your garden variety imbecile, but for him buttressed by what he perceived as irrefutable logic. McConkie knew Jews were responsible for Jesus' death, but knowing this was not enough, because this treachery against God also explained the devastations wrought upon Jews throughout their history. Scoring no points for originality, McConkie ecstatically rendered the denunciation, along with his opinions of black people, in his first edition of *Mormon Doctrine*. McConkie's brazen proclamations were not new outside Mormondom or within, because founders of the Church, like Brigham Young, proclaimed the same profundities. That was in addition to every other idea that came across his prophetic mind, the prophetic mind marked by its ability to announce prophecies but not to discern between a good and bad one, also not exclusively a Mormon prophetic trait. A startling quality of all who were given the gift of prophecy, like McConkie, is the resolute will to propagate irresponsible justifications for actions affecting people far removed from proof. In the Jewish history comment, in exchange for affirming a self-serving story, as in this case, Jesus' needing to die to ensure that Death was conquered, McConkie was beside himself to miss the ever so typical Roman death of crucifixion of messianic Jews for the opportunity to spout hatred on all Jews after a few, no doubt, tired with the Messianic brother of theirs, the *Jew Jesus*, happily giving him up to Roman inquisition. This prophetic tendency toward dangerous imbecility has always been an unenviable attribute of many representing God.

The same audacity McConkie displayed in his project to homogenize Mormon beliefs was also his hubris, but this did not lead to the fallout before it elevated him to the position of Mormon apostle where he applied his standard of certainty to everything within his purview, which was everything known, and mostly unknown, by him, with reckless abandon over a decade of leadership in the Church. His hubris eventually had its fallout, decades after his seminal work, and the fallout sent seismic reverberations throughout the Church, the after-shocks still felt today in the evolution of Mormons' view on Jesus and efforts to portray themselves as Christians.

The McConkie fallout came over his self-induced controversy on Jesus' personal role in the life of Latter-day Saint members, touching upon the very status of Mormons as Christians, but even more important than their constant challenge to identity as Christians to the larger Christian community was the central role of Jesus within the very climax of the Mormon story. Was the LDS Church the very vessel of Christ's one true church restored through the Prophet Joseph Smith as affirmed by Jesus appearing to Joseph and Joseph's translating a new testament about Jesus? Or was that stuff ancillary to a much bigger plan? McConkie explained it was part of God the Father's Plan, and any omission of credit to God the Father in his own Plan was a grave sin.

The most popular religious professor during the Sixties and Seventies at BYU was a man named George W. Pace. He was even more charismatic than religious professor Stephen Covey, who later rose to success outside Mormon culture for his business leadership books. Covey's supporters would claim he was the most popular professor on campus, but the question was settled in an arm wrestling match where Pace dismissed Covey's bravado with a quick and seemingly effortless win. While Covey was declared the professorial wimp, his consolation prize was his popularity grew over the years to Pace's mere footnote in Mormon history, but a game-changing one to be sure. No professor was loved more by his students than Professor Pace, but if one was it was Chauncey C. Riddle who taught religion and philosophy. Professor Riddle endeared himself to his students by his boundless humanity and extraordinary intellect. The best of humans have a combination of both, and Professor

Riddle was among the best. Pace performed his lectures and captivated his students who filled his classes beyond capacity; many students who were not even enrolled attended regularly. My parents were among his many admirers, and my father continued to maintain his friendship after he graduated from BYU. When my mother died, he sought the advice of Professor Pace on how to raise six sons without a mother. Professor Pace pragmatically told him to remarry, which my father in short order did.

In 1981 Professor Pace published a book titled, *What It Means To Know Christ*. In his short book, Professor Pace encouraged Mormons to develop a special relationship with Christ. The book sold like wildfire within the Utah valley and among Mormon enclaves just beyond. McConkie had risen to the role of apostle by then and had, himself, published the majority of a six-volume work titled *The Messiah Series*, the last part coming out shortly after Professor Pace's popular book. Elder McConkie descended on BYU and gave a scathing review of Professor Pace's book, which he likely hadn't read. He never mentioned the book or Pace by name, but everyone knew the object of his derision. He decried efforts of focusing on Christ the Son above the Heavenly Father and the Holy Ghost, the trio making the Mormon Godhead, not to be confused with the trinity. Years before the infamous rebuke, my father attended a lecture Elder McConkie gave to graduate students on campus, at which a student asked Elder McConkie for the reference of a quotation in his remarks. Elder McConkie responded "We don't quote the authorities, we are the authorities." McConkie standard fare.

Throughout his six-volume series on Jesus Christ, Elder McConkie often cited himself. His view of himself was priceless, and the Church membership's veneration of him confirmed it. Church leadership canonized his poem about his belief in Christ into a hymn widely sung today, titled "I Believe in Christ," and many leaders and ardent members have repeated his last testimony as a witness of Jesus Christ independent of any other man, given just weeks before his death, as evidence of the reality of Christ. So Pace's popular book about Jesus was up against not just another proof in support of Jesus, offering to satisfy the Mormon bedrock principle that in the mouth of two or more witnesses truth is established, but his book was up against a very singular proof of Jesus in the testimony of one of the Lord's anointed, amounting to nothing more than a whimpering threat doomed to defeat in the present contest. Pace did lose in the short term by McConkie's rebuffing the silly notion of being "born again" that accompanied evangelical views of Jesus implicit throughout the book.

McConkie's position was not without irony, given his utter disdain for Christian history and unabashed ignorance of it. He insisted the correct approach to God proper, Heavenly Father, and Jesus Christ, the Son, was through the official teachings and rituals of the Church, not separate from them, namely through *his* witness of Christ, memorialized in his hymn and last testimony. He was a witness of Christ and if someone, including me, wanted to learn about Christ it was possible through McConkie (sounding like sacraments available through other hierarchal structures in Christian history). McConkie laid it on thick, never recanting his infamous claim in the first publication of his *Mormon Doctrine* that the Catholic Church was the Great Whore of the earth as referenced in the Book of Mormon. If McConkie had been a theologian or student of the history of religion, he may have appreciated Mormonism's dependence upon the Reformation, the dawn of Mormonism coming centuries later during the Second Great American Awakening, and modified his advocacy for unheralded central role of authority since Martin Luther shoved its importance down proto-McConkie throats, albeit Catholic ones, with his tectonic declarations. McConkie's challenge wasn't his ignorance, which was vast, but was restraining his mortal self ahead of his eternal reward. Mormonism's ambitious theology purports they too can become Gods of their own kingdoms. The conception of what kind of God varies, McConkie being ahead of himself in embracing the jealous one.

Irony pervaded the controversy without discriminating against Professor Pace, whose thoughtful short book and genuine interest in helping Mormons were never intended to stir up the fury of his leaders. Professor Pace wanted nothing more than to please them, including Elder McConkie. He was faithful to the core and publicly and privately venerated Elder McConkie. A sheet of paper titled "Yielding Your Will to the Lord's Annointed" with the name "George Pace" in the upper right corner nicely nestled in the pages of my copy of *Teachings of the Prophet Joseph Smith*, klepted from my father's or another unsuspecting Mormon's shelf, established Pace's innocence beyond a shadow of a doubt. I offer it as evidence here, five sections worth, the second of which surmises, "The main message of the prophets is Jesus Christ," quoting the New Testament Paul, once Saul, and the Book of Mormon prophets Nephi and Jacob, concluding "Our attitude then toward Christ is reflected by our attitude toward the prophets!" (Exclamation in the original.) Precisely McConkie's take-away message! His preeminent witness of Christ is vindicated every time Mormons sing his poem in Mormon meetings the world over. Not Pace, not my father, not any lay Mormon could claim a witness of Christ approaching McConkie's. Those who remain unpersuaded of Pace's innocence should consider the titles of his other sections: Section One "The Lord's reverence for his prophets." Of course! Section Two I've already stated but it merits repeating, "The main message of the prophets is Jesus Christ." Section Three "To accept the prophets is to accept Christ—to reject the prophets is to be ashamed of Christ." Irrefutable logic! Section Four "The Key to being sealed up to Eternal Life [not rebelling against the prophet]." And Section Five "How to keep from losing confidence in the Lord's annointed [a long quote from Brigham Young about excusing the errors of prophets, concluding "...If He [God] should suffer him [the prophet] to lead the people astray, it would be because they ought to be led astray. If he should suffer them to be chastised, and some of them destroyed, it would be because they deserved it, or to accomplish some righteous purpose..." An estimable cure for lack of confidence. Indeed! (And clear indication of Mormons' preference for the Old Testament.) Word for word from Pace's handout. I love the smell of old books, a light woody taste from each page's reef, the *Teachings* as rich as any, where the handout still lies.

Far from resting my case, I introduce here the status of prophet as cornerstone of the Mormon religion. Idolatrous, not at all! Part of the "fullness" of the Gospel of Jesus Christ restored to Joseph was the inseparability of God-Christ-Ghost-and-Mormon-Prophet. To those who believe in all the Mormon prophets goes the prize of celestial glory and eternal exaltation, including the production of children (to populate their kingdoms). The consolation prize for non-Mormons believing merely in the Gospel of Jesus Christ is still eternal life, just on a lesser kingdom as fixed androgynous beings, an eternal sitting about with no offspring. Adumbrating your lack of gentility is really not so shocking.

During Pace's Christ-centered snafu, my father spoke on the phone with Professor Pace, who insisted Elder McConkie did not disagree with the spiritual principles of his book, his state of denial a result of his genuine love of the Church. Professor Stephen Covey made no similar mistake as he too published a popular book on Christ, *The Divine Center,* that same year of the controversy but not before heavily editing all references to Christ, shamefully, yet not unwittingly, to include "a God and Christ" centered life before its publication. All of this uproar of singling out Jesus from God the Father and the Holy Ghost, and Mormons do not even have a doctrine of the trinity, again the contradiction, not likely lost on McConkie, that focusing on one God, Heavenly Father, over another God, Jesus, or not focusing on one more than another was still a breach of one omnipotent God, the monotheistic God of most, if not all (except the Mormons), Christian believers. Mormons believe God the Father, Jesus Christ, and the Holy Ghost are all separate beings, and if that was not enough, the former two have bodies. As proof, they point to the fact that Jesus came to earth, to a great extent, to gain a body. The idea of God's being embodied was an attractive theophany of theological support for the undiluted Biblical claim that man was created in God's image for many including me, through the present day, but the consequence of focusing on the one embodied manifestation of Jesus, over the non-embodied manifestations, lent itself as pernicious to the God-like development—presumably The Father type—of Mormons, like McConkie.

Professor Pace changed the title of his book in subsequent publications, his popularity among students nose-dived, and the bad press stymied his rise as leader in the Church. Yet years later his efforts were vindicated. An Idaho-reared Mormon apostle, Ezra Taft Benson, took the lead as the Church's thirteenth president the same year that Elder McConkie died, making his primary platform reading the Book of Mormon to learn more about Jesus Christ. I'm not making that up. Benson's years at the Church's helm included conference talk after conference talk about focusing one's attention and life on Jesus in an unequivocal, enthusiastic, evangelical, personal savior sort of way. Vindication hardly possible from any other than a Mormon farm boy from Idaho. But he was no ordinary farm boy. He served in the Eisenhower administration as a *sitting* Mormon apostle; he was an ardent opponent of communism and one hell of a life-long Boy Scout. Benson preceded in politics another well known Mormon, George Romney, governor of Michigan and moderate Republican who actively supported the civil rights movement (contradicting the official position of the LDS Church and its modicum of advocacy against civil rights), and in a moment of unadvised honesty denounced the Vietnam War during a presidential campaign (to his own political ruin), later serving in the Nixon Administration. Benson exited politics after two terms serving the White House, returning to his role as prophet and apostle.

Then came the most popular and successful book in the history of Mormondom, from a Mormon BYU religion professor at the end of the twentieth century, Stephen Robinson. His thin book, *Believing Christ*, with its parable of the bicycle and its evangelical emphasis on Jesus Christ's role as a personal savior, was widely welcomed and accepted among LDS members and leadership, and even praised by nonmember evangelical Christians from somewhere most assuredly in the Deep South, or maybe Colorado. Subsequent to Robinson's success, the Church launched a campaign in the mid-1990s to identify the Church first and foremost as Christian and Mormon teachings as complementary to Christianity, a campaign that continues with no small resistance among Christian sects today.

While the Jesus controversy relegated Professor Pace to obscurity, his small current of belief in a savior Jesus, at first overwhelmed by McConkie's rumblings, in the end led to as significant a contribution to Mormons' embracing of Jesus as McConkie's efforts to standardize church doctrines. McConkie has fallen from the Mormon mainstream, his seminal work now available only second hand, an infamous sore like polygamy (except among the most orthodox and correct of members), while Pace lives widely unknown, his emphasis on Jesus began an ongoing facelift for the Christian Mormon Church.

CHAPTER 9
VISIONS

God spoke to his faithful Mormons every day, most of the time on small matters but occasionally on big ones too, and no walls were too thick, or space too ill suited to connect to him. Living in a ten-by-ten-foot cell of a dorm room may have been confining in every respect, but it didn't stop revelations. And I had always slept in confined spaces, with the exception of my spacious room during the second grade in Somerville, spending most of my teenage years at home banished to the attic not much more than a crawl space, bending my head to walk from one end to the other. Most of the time I spent in the dorm room was spent on my bed reading or sleeping, or both. And for an eighteen-year-old unaware of and unaccustomed to opulent living, one mattress was as good as another: my dorm mattress seemed a fair match, if not twenty years new, for my already weathered body.

Yet despite the easiness with which I was pleased, the previous year I began to notice back pain near my upper back running on the sides of my scapulas and extending down the middle. I credited this in equal parts to a terribly inefficient yet stylish rucksack used for the past three years to carry textbooks from school to home every week-night and back again each morning, now faded to a light brown by the harsh Idaho winters and sun-filled summers, still water-tight with secure but thinning straps, and to the consequence of immoral, yet concerted, self-pleasuring, or the dogmatic abuse of my male member. An act of unadulterated sin, declared and broadcast far and intensely often by Mormon authorities, locally and by satellite, as early as my first teenage year and with vigorous repetition thereafter. It seemed like no sin was more decried nor more foul, continually presented to Mormon teenagers, than that aptly named and cringe-worthy masturbation.

I had no reason to doubt it was a woeful sin, given the outcry against it and my feelings of guilt constant, yes felt often, after participating in it, or doing it if one can be allowed to confront it, but a sin I preferred to keep to myself. Its condemnation was universal. At a high school dance I stood under the basketball hoop at the west end of the gym in a small pack of boys. I was a sophomore, and a senior in the group caught my undivided attention when he randomly said masturbators should be killed. Almost bursting out in laughter, I caught myself just as others in the group offered "yeah" and "no kidding" in confirmation. This senior was a likable, and what I would confidentially classify "normal," Mormon kid. The sin was no less egregious on the ecclesiastical front. Bishop interview after bishop interview when I was growing up included queries of presumed (correctly) lost bouts with masturbation, and interview after interview the queries were greeted by me with a stern glare and practiced non-confession that I had no problems with this alleged teenage plague. Although I constantly fretted I'd flinch in response to the barrage of questions about this repulsive act of self-abuse, I never did, but I was also never asked if I participated in group masturbation, shocked to learn anyone would be asked when my brother told me he'd been so interrogated, no doubt sure as a whippoorwill sings I would have flinched out of shock at the mere idea that such teenage solidarity was possible, let alone allegedly practiced among teenage Saints.

My austere commitment toward participating and not disclosing the abdominal practice paid dividends when I moved from very little privacy living in a large family to no privacy living among other freshman males on a dormitory floor in Deseret Towers at BYU. Having little space let alone little time to myself, I miraculously resisted the urges for self-indulgence save for the most opportune moments, almost exclusively in the shower. One morning I weakened, wound up and overcome by some early morning fantasy, believing I had a clear window of time to myself when my roommate left for his morning class. Just as I retreated from grinding my years-old mattress into submission, opting for the rare righteous choice of self-restraint, pulling up my jeans to wait out my energies, within minutes, no within the passing of mere seconds, my roommate returned, announcing upon his entrance to my blank, exhausted, pants and pasty greeting as I turned my head lying upon my unsettled belly that his damn class had been canceled. I noted the incontrovertible right action was inspired by none other than the anti-masturbatory angelic advocacy group active within immortal spheres furthering the righteous work of Heavenly Father and his Son, Jesus Christ, to eradicate this teenage plague, and also shielding me from humiliation during that year and those to follow at BYU, a far worse brand than if I'd been a lecher stealing innocents' virtue.

The divine angelic influence was for all purposes Mormon doctrine, as high school seminary teachers assured their teenage students that souls across this mortal veil, loved ones included, active doing God's will in the spirit world, could and did see us in our most private moments, all in addition to God's power of knowing every secret thought and action, and if that wasn't ample divine chaperoning, judgment day would be akin to a public festival, on par with carnival in São Paulo, where a larger-than-life big screen projected for the worlds' inhabitants of all time a running reel of all one's sins, surely my back-to-back episodes spanning hours would make my bare hams some of the most famous from alpha to omega, finally giving me the fame I have always believed due them.

The Biblical proverb old men will dream dreams and young men will see visions no doubt is true, but young men do a lot of both. One stark vision holds today. After being recently potty trained I toddled to the bathroom door to exercise my new skill, and upon pushing it open my mother gasped reaching for the shower curtain to cover her naked body. Then years later one night early during those freshman days of yore, one like any other, I turned in after a full day of classes with an accumulation of nutrients and saturated fats and who knows what from two square meals consumed from the Morris Center pushing through my veins to cells healthy and not, covered by my dorm issued blanket on my time-tested not quite twin-sized mattress. I fell fast asleep as was my standard practice. I dreamed of the thin blonde girl who captured so much of my thoughts during my awakened state. She did not have the same hold over me asleep. In this dream I had a companion, my oldest stepbrother George, whom I barely knew, and whom I did little to nothing together with in real life, excepting having seen a movie with him once, went duck hunting another time, and played Dungeon and Dragons over the first few Christmas holidays after our parents married. But not much else, if anything, so his appearance made him an unexpected companion. We were not doing anything in the dream either, no twelve-sided dice or vorpal sword between us, and unlike other dreams with recognizable background this dream was like a dream as empty space surrounded us. Then we came across the young elfin maiden, who owned my days, and I spoke to her and she spoke back to me. I was surprised to see on her face a red mark of some kind, a scar, acne, or fresh bout of infantigo I could not tell, her altered flawless features making her approachable but not explaining her response to me. I do not know if I told her my name but she told me hers, and I remembered it when I woke.

Dreams and visions have plagued more than just young Mormons, and to a young Mormon tethered to the whipping wheel of love, these prophecies, fortunes, dreams, visions, et al., have no proper distinctions. My second semester at BYU I enrolled in a prerequisite for English majors, "An Introduction to Literary Theory." To my chagrin, the class enrollment was overwhelming non-freshman. While not upperclassman, many returned missionaries, in their early twenties, were in the class, and I, a thinly exposed reader at eighteen, was furious at my odds of getting an A competing against peers further along in their entanglement with literary theory, a subject I did not know existed before learning its study was required. If understanding the story and development of the characters was not challenge enough, now I was expected to explicate the hidden cultural truths behind them. I tasted the aggravation other schools often whined about annually when they played BYU athletes well into their twenties. I did what any ignorant student would do, I failed to drop the class and take it in a couple years when I returned from my own mission. In addition to being angry at my peers, a skill developed over years of exacting practice, fits of anger emerged toward the BYU English department I would spend the majority of my time in for their literary-theory-crazed emphasis and efforts to push the fever on me.

Professor Soran, the anointed distiller of my introduction to literary theory, did the department honor, explicating the theories and dutifully assigning endless amounts of homework to leave no free minute unused for more isms than my intellectual capacity could imagine, let alone conceive.

He intermittently relieved us from the sheer terror of never being able to read for pleasure or to find meaning again, and eradicated the notion of merely reading a play, novel, or poem by cementing new approaches for identifying the elements and ideology that underpinned a text, the new object of our study. He routinely gave impersonations of general authorities to lighten the gravity of theory, doing them awfully and entertainingly well.

I remember a couple of texts we approached for their ominous visions, from the great creator of texts of antiquity, Sophocles. Sophocles did not distinguish between fate and visions, nor did his culture, if I rightly inferred from the text, in *Oedipus Rex* and *Antigone*. Oedipus was bound to kill his father and did, and Creon was bound to lose his children and he did, both fated thus because they knew better than the gods. Armed with more theory and distinctions than I could kick from sand on a white beach in Cancun during spring break, a beach I would never walk on because BYU did not have a spring break, I did not confuse the medium of my dream—my mattress—with the oracle of antiquity who spoke for those false, non-Christian and non-Mormon, Greek gods to Oedipus and Creon, but that was merely an issue of transmission, immaterial to the fact mine had come from the true God.

I was not the only young Mormon dreaming dreams instead of seeing visions. One Sunday evening I returned to my dorm room, clean clothes in tow from a weekend at my aunt's trailer on the south end of Provo, and was accosted by my roommate, an Idaho lad like myself, with the announcement that I had told him in a dream what beer tasted like. I grinned, unable to produce a false countenance on such news, fewer proud moments in my eighteen years to my credit. Having started drinking alcohol on stealth missions my freshman year at BYU and certain I always returned to my dorm room sober, I was sore amazed. I asked him if I said it tasted good. He said yes and I nodded.

My older bull-riding brothers drank beer, not in any great abundance but beer was more prevalent than water, at least clean water from other than a hose, at most rodeos. My oldest brother, Jami, developed a taste for beer working at an oil refinery one summer between years at BYU, nursing the end of a relationship with a Mormon Texan princess. My first year at BYU overlapped with his first year of marriage to a young BYU coed finishing her last year at BYU. Jami delayed going to law school one year because he was committed to marrying his coed. The transition went smoothly for him because not going to school for a year was not much different from his "going to school" as he rarely attended classes—his first year of law school the single exception, and even then an exception with many days of its own exceptions.

After I graduated from high school, Jami got me a job as a roofer in Provo, where I spent the summer before my freshman year, the same year Jami finished his short courtship, standard practice among BYU students, marrying his sweetheart from the sea of sweetheart-BYU coeds. Jami and I regularly worked out in the gym at the Fieldhouse, a five-dollar alumni fee for him and, as regularly as we pumped iron, we drove around Provo or parked in empty lots or frequented arcades, he with his oversized plastic bottle of pop from the minimart spiked with whiskey, I in the passenger's seat or taking my turns at pinball surreptitiously sipping wine coolers—notorious wimp cheerleader drinks, Zima my preferred choice—from the inside pocket of my denim jacket. I did not explicitly confirm my roommate's dream because his dream superseded my own reality where beer tasted awful and I imbibed chick drinks, but I would burn in hell for lying before I admitted it.

During my heightened sensitivities to my fate through my introduction to literary theory class, I also learned a few new truths and confirmed ones I already knew, in Professor Tilman's class. They were truths I knew, not because they were already in Mormonism. They were true for me, upon assessment then and reflection now, because they fit my disposition and how I understood events and relations. I knew they suited me, sitting without confidence but with more assurance than in any other classroom, within minutes of the opening lecture on Buddhism. I knew I was Buddhist.

The Four Noble Truths of Buddhism were not merely professions of faith, they were realities. First, life was suffering. Second, desires and wants caused suffering. Third, negating suffering was enlightenment. And fourth, certain disciplines helped mitigate suffering. Bingo. These were accurate observations about living, not assertions in need of supernatural confirmation. They were the bedrock of my life, and I was bold enough to assume the bedrock of all breathing, thinking, feeling humans. Naturally I was persuaded by the additional Buddhist teachings, including the disciplines to mitigate suffering, an eight-fold path understood in three categories of wisdom, ethical conduct, and mental discipline. Wisdom was finding the middle way, and taking the middle way made sense. Wisdom also required right view and intention.

I could not get behind extreme positions not only because I lacked a zealous constitution but also because I found absolutisms a bit foul. For one,

I did not stomach the claim that everyone had to be baptized a Mormon to receive the gift of the Holy Ghost and enter into the Kingdom of God. I always believed one had to live well—what I learned in Professor Tilman's opening lecture on Buddhism was called right action in the Eight-Fold Path. The second category of ethical conduct required right speech, action and livelihood. The third category of mental discipline required right effort, mindfulness and concentration. Buddhism emphasized personal responsibility in its doctrine of karma, where one's deeds had certain effects, immediate and lasting.

There seemed no room in Buddhism for an intervening supernatural source as a justification for the bad in the world. I could not stand the credit given to Satan for bad actions and results, over and over again, for what I perceived as excuses for one's own poor intentions and actions, and more often for one's ignorance for misidentifying the true nature of reality, which involved a lot of sadness and suffering, in which Satan had no hand.

One belief that tipped me a bit was the Buddhist doctrine of no soul, but I had not thought upon it enough to Californian-style appropriate it. Belief of no soul meant giving up on knowing thy self, a venerated western pursuit that is the classical examination of self, a doomed task but an honorable one. The Buddhist belief was defensible, I had to give it that, because of the certain failure of knowing oneself. But not being able to know thy self, and there being an absence of thy self, were certainly not the same thing, one meant all the possibilities of the world and the other meant none. And was my lack of soul-self a precedent for lack of unique disposition or personality? I was not hot and bothered by the notion of my personality or self merely being figments of my passing imagination, always in flux and not permanent. Change, or hope of change, a cherry twist to the Buddhist shake-up on a life of set (Mormon) purpose. But no soul? no, I could not quite dig it because it obliterated an internal life I was fur (as in bloody *more*, or even *hairy*, not *distance*) too persuaded existed, in me and *seen* in others. However, no *eternal* soul, I could. That started to make a bit of sense.

But I was in complete agreement with other doctrines, for example and of course, that the result of much of my craving was due to ignorance and was cause of the lion's share of cravings in those I knew. While the role of compassion toward other feeling beings easily echoed pertinently against my empty capacity for it, not a loud echo mind you, it was the emphasis on mental discipline that reverberated the loudest. A sound mind developed through right effort, mindfulness and concentration made them virtues worth developing to focus in the moment, on the little details when life was actually being lived. Nothing seemed more pertinent or worthwhile.

Mormonism's tireless rituals and practices designed to focus me on higher truths and eternal rewards fur, or hair-iously, too often displaced me from the here and now, allegedly a virtue for dealing with suffering, but a displacement just the same. Mormonism's promise was that from focusing on God and related supernatural truths came the benefit of an eternal perspective and a subsequent enhancement of deeper meanings in mortal life. For example, my actions had eternal consequences, a motive lending itself, for me, to being kinder to my younger brothers, and not a bad consequence at that, for me who could use all correct motives, eternal and otherwise, available to an angry kid. But that promise had the nefarious design of hobbling me in confronting suffering in all its immediacy, fully felt because the actual value of the promise displaced me from it. Heaven knows I did not confront suffering and had the advantage of not knowing I had not, until I started to realize I had not, after being aided by teachings like mindfulness, focusing me on moments lived. I did not confront the pain of losing my mother when I displaced it on the promise I would see her again. That displacement measured how pure my belief was, and the question remained: Was my life enriched because of it? And it was, but it amounted to a large bandage slowly peeling away with each realization of whom we had lost, to reveal an open gash too imperiled to heal.

I may have learned during Professor Tilman's class that I was a closet Buddhist, but I soon learned my favorite philosophy was Taoism. The Tao, or way to live life, emphasized nature, both internal of oneself and the natural world. P'u, the uncarved block, was a metaphor made for me. I had an inner nature and part of living the best life was learning what my inner nature was and living according to it. That included accepting myself as I was and not adding expectations. If my nature was to reach the horizon, that was my nature. If it was to guard my muddied rut, then that would do. External influences of work and school and church and family pulled me in many directions, none of which I felt were consistent with my inner nature. The Book of Mormon (and New Testament) taught followers of Christ had to put off their natural man. This typically had a narrow meaning of one's carnal nature, none other than sexual exploits, or thinking about sexual exploits, having logged my fair share, but was often used to lasso mortal desires of success and temporal aims of worldly excellence along with the blasted horny urges to be eliminated in order to be a righteous Mormon. I believed my inner nature included a lot of aspects worth developing let alone not putting off.

P'u's counterpart was the belief in the wu wei, which meant no-action or doing in accordance to one's inner nature, in modern parlance going with the flow, making for perfect complementarity. Wu wei didn't merely mean I would excel at my self-identified, God-given talent of indolence, which I believed it certainly did, it also meant being in tune with the Tao, or energy in nature, and achievement would be mine at these times of harmony, hopefully most of my conscious moments. Taoism also addressed my aversion to Satan and evil receiving unearned credit. To explain the natural world, Taoism believed in the duality of elements, yin and yang, the most well-known symbol associated with the philosophy. Dueling elements were yet complementary and interdependent and not exclusive, a less simplistic view of a natural world of good or evil.

Taoism also emphasized the source of action, the individual, the one responsible for bringing harmony to oneself and one's community. All its teachings I found quite agreeable, my quick conversion due in part to the connection to elements of the natural world like the uncarved block, the body, and water to support the philosophy. I especially liked the assigned reading, The Tao of Pooh by Benjamin Hoff, a wonderful view of Taoism as evidenced by Winnie the Pooh, in which confident Pooh represented the best of flexibility and acting true to one's nature. I gravitated toward Eeyore, just as true but slightly more my stripe, a pessimistic kinship. Convinced when my freshman floor-mates exchanged nicknames I insisted mine was, and had always been, Eeyore, though I had just assumed it after reading Hoff. Mostly my mates shrugged it off but an enlightened one or two responded, Winnie the Pooh's donkey companion? To my quick correction— Pooh's ass of a companion.

The wu wei fit a question looming on my mind's horizon more than any other. And not a small question: how was I to fulfill my measure of creation? A Mormon tag for being the best spiritual version you can be, which I took very seriously. If God had great things in store for me, then surely they would be. I believed to fulfill what God expected would require my best effort. But the fulfillment seemed less about accomplishment than it did about where my heart was, similar to the openness and humility required in adherence to wu wei. The reigning authority on the topic came from the story of the rich young man who sought Jesus for the answer of how to obtain eternal life, in Chapter Nineteen of the Gospel of Matthew. The young man asked the question, and Jesus responded to keep the commandments. The smart young man asked which commandments, and Jesus replied not with the popular ten but with a truncated five of the Decalogue about living well, leaving off the preceding worship and jealousies and prohibition of idolatries about God and the Sabbath but adding loving your neighbor as yourself. The young man responded that he kept all those mentioned and asked what more did he need. Jesus replied if the young man wanted to be perfect he needed to sell all he had, give it to the poor, and follow him, but the young man had too many possessions and went away sorry. The take-away seems to be that one's heart lies with one's treasures. The young man did not reply he had perfected suspending his interest in material comfort at appropriate times to focus on being a disciple, confident in having mastered the ability to displace his heart, returning to but never fully appreciating his soft bed, and clean and roomy domicile. Rather, his silence may have been an honest concession that one's heart cannot be two places, and where it is, it really is. Many Mormons I knew, and many more I did not whose houses I saw along the Wasatch Mountains every time I drove home to Idaho and back to Provo, appealed to alternative readings consistent with Jesus' style of double meanings, concluding in some fashion that surely the rich would have their place in eternal life and a very nice place at that. Mormons may lead this charge but certainly are not alone among Christians committed to God's blessings being commensurate to their wealth, never ceasing to rise to the clarion call in defense of the world's riches. Confirming, not refuting, my unfair reduction of their hearts to their homes, unfair but not altogether misleading.

Even I was vulnerable to extending its meaning to all efforts, not just seeking possessions, to conclude that wherever one's focus stopped showed what one's treasure truly was. Compounding my quandary, I knew the effort to follow Jesus was not always marketable, and for me this was one of few certainties. And discipleship was possibly quite destructive. Heavens, Jesus ended the same chapter declaring that his disciples must be willing to forsake not just possessions but family too, and would then receive a hundred-fold and eternal life. Admittedly I would not need more than my share, eternal life would nicely do. Firm in my belief that eternal life would come from following Jesus largely entailing inaction, averting the endless distractions to Jesus from material gains to noteworthy works of righteousness marked as rites and rituals that took time and focus, as much as a high-paying job and subsequent expensive toys, away from following Jesus. I felt confident about my view, and I knew this understanding of inaction did not come without fierce determination because discipleship of Jesus was no primped affair.

The Tao may have resonated on a deep level because I grew up aware of nature. The Queen of Nature in eastern Idaho was rightly not a bucking bull. She was a river. And she continually came to mind in references to running water in Taoist writings. She was the mighty Snake. Its unmitigated power was terrifying. But not untested. The mighty Snake began in West Yellowstone, Wyoming, winding across southern Idaho then up the Oregon border into Northern Idaho, stretching down into Washington and emptying in the Columbia River. I knew the Snake from the sharp rocks on its river banks in the river bottoms of Riverton. Regretful, rarely remembering to wear a pair of old sneakers, I gingerly worked my way along its banks, far behind my hardened barefooted peers. We accessed the Snake at the point of the Brickmerrys' property.

The Snake offered us adventure, and a way to cool off during the summer, but its currents were never to be mistaken for accommodating. Strong swimmers dared swim it, and the rest of us worked on our summer sunburns, on occasion stepping in. One spring too early in my experience of life to remember, the Snake flooded much of Riverton when it toppled the Palisades Dam and announced its power, which was forever after well-understood by all within its reach. The Palisades Dam sat almost directly due east of Blackfoot on the Idaho-Wyoming border.

To get there by pickup-truck, the route went through Idaho Falls and northeast, turning south through Swan Valley before reaching the dam. One could cross the impressive cement structure on the way to Jackson, Wyoming. If one wanted a steeper route, he'd turn his truck left at Swan Valley and climb over the Tetons through Victor into Jackson. Jackson Hole was more than a landmark of fictional trucker Philo Beddoe's greatest fisticuffs. It was easy money for Jeremy and Josh any summer Wednesday evening. Jeremy and Josh typically spent summer weekends traveling Idaho and bordering states to rodeos. Weekdays they were marooned at home, eager for practice and prone to make the two-hour drive to Jackson for the standing Wednesday evening show for the tourists. The lure was not the pay, with very little money added to the contestants' entry fees, but it fixed their insatiable desire to ride, with a fun after-party to boot.

Before rodeo trips as teenagers, we made many camping trips to Jackson Hole as kids. Grandpa Bob and Grammie parked their RV fifth wheel at the KOA Campground overlooking the raging Snake just miles south of its mouth in West Yellowstone, as it started its run across Idaho. We set our tent next door and played cards and roasted hot dogs in cool mosquito summer evenings. We joined them for days at a time, by day frequenting the open swimming pool and forests beyond the campground. Climbing the mountains, we searched for bears, and I heard my first on my first ascent, it being hidden from view until my father, growling, leaped from behind a tree. The dramatic Teton peaks and dense forest surrounded us in every direction, and the Snake coursed right through.

Many whitewater enthusiasts ran the stretch of the Snake near Jackson. I dared the waters once with my parents, in a paying company of other amateurs on a sturdy raft under the guidance of a professional, and I recall the infamous Lunch Counter but more clearly the young female patrons struggling mightily, before we set sail, to put on wetsuits. We cleared the white water with more excitement than I could remember ever having, and I was just as happy to catch the bus back to Jackson.

An early trip to see Grandpa Bob and Grammie was momentous. On it, I learned to swim. I must have been about four years old, old enough to want to be without wing pumps rubbing my arms raw. My mother, a seasoned swimmer and former instructor, provided my first lesson in the campground pool open to the Teton Mountains and sea of green trees. The pool sat above the Snake with a clear view of its raging by and around the campground. The lesson consisted of paddling, doggy style, arms pushing from the side of the pool powering below me to her, which I successfully did, gaining confidence, jumping from the side paddling when I began to sink. The lesson ended abruptly when someone screamed overlooking the river, and everyone looked and ran to the fence. The person yelled again that someone was swimming the river. Indeed someone was swimming the river as I looked through the fence. That someone was my father. I saw his arms moving madly against the rapids, breaking through white foam enveloping him, his legs hidden beneath the white surface, which seemed to erase his progress as soon as his arms descended below it, slowly watching with everyone in the pool as the small figure advanced, finally reaching the bank. Upon touching land, he climbed out, and sat down.

My newfound religious fervor in Buddhism and Taoism did not remove my belief in prayer or my hope of divine intervention. My innocent and true passions were not eliminated and certainly found no harmony. I implored God's favor as fervently and faithfully and naively, with the same absence of courage, as Reverend John Ames did in Marilynne Robinson's *Gilead*, but unlike Reverend Ames I had my dream of a name undeterred by marred beauty, and having never spoken to her or shared a glance, Ames's advantage, held to the promise of unrealizable possibility, a courtship more similar in suit to Augie March's worshipful blundering of Hilda Novinson than Amory Blaine's elfin love-moods with Eleanor Ramilly in *This Side of Paradise*.

After completing a cultural event assignment, no doubt a summary of a cinematic masterpiece with artistry I missed by being attentive to the subtitles, I walked to the front of the auditorium of Dr. Mitchell's class to turn in the paper. I knelt to open my rucksack, reaching for my notebook, feeling her presence, raising my head to see her standing right behind me. Hiding my shock, which was indistinguishable from terror, I shimmied, not smoothly, to the side to allow her passage, feigning a search for a missing paper. She placed her assignment on the table in front of us, turned and walked away. Seizing the moment of all moments, I quickly stood assignment in hand, as it had been the eternity she stood by me, and placed it on my section's stack but not before looking at the stack with her paper on top, seeing the name known to me. The tabernacle choir contemporaneously broke into concert, its voices soaring to break forth through my chest and voice, which was no more capable of the appropriate resounding pitch than my will for acting on that moment.

CHAPTER 10

A DANCE

A sharply cropped lawn separated my dorm tower from the Morris Center Cafeteria, which sat between other towers. I walked on the lawn in one of two states, either hungry going to the cafeteria or bloated coming back from it. Never with any cash in my pockets, except ten dollars I borrowed, indefinitely, from Jami—himself strapped for cash, a newlywed living in an apartment without furniture, his bed an assortment of sleeping bags and blankets. From lack of funds, I did not snack but relied upon high-calorie meals knowing the next time I would eat was my next trip to the center. Like other freshman, I gained my fifteen and the increase put me just over my weight preceding my senior wrestling season. The meals combined with regular trips to the gym, by year's end, I exceeded one hundred and seventy pounds. Toward the end of the semester, advertisements of an end-of-the-year dance for all freshman in Deseret Towers were plastered on the doors of the Morris Center. I started the mental preparation to attend, visualizing taking the necessary steps toward and practicing the necessary words to invite Sandy to dance.

With the end of my first college year approaching, most of my floor-mates were receiving their missionary calls for the customary two-year break from university studies to serve the Church proselytizing its restored truth to the gentiles throughout the world. The weekly announcements of friends going to France and Portugal and as far as Moscow turned my imagination around for the many possibilities before me. I was younger than most of my floor-mates, as I turned nineteen the coming summer, nineteen the required age to start a mission. I took the necessary steps during the final weeks of the semester to complete the paperwork necessary to receive my mission call sometime that summer before my birthday.

The first step involved receiving my patriarchal blessing, an important although not necessary rite of passage. Many Mormon youths received their patriarchal blessings in their home stakes before going away to college. Each Mormon stake had a single patriarch whose calling entirely consisted of bestowing blessings on its members. The blessings were recorded and stored in the vaunted record vaults in Salt Lake City, or in electronic form in some vast database. The blessings had a general purpose of announcing that the Mormon members shared Israelite heritage, but also the specific purpose of acknowledging and foretelling blessings for that individual. Mormons looked to the blessing as a spiritual roadmap. I met with my BYU bishop and requested my blessing and, after I correctly answered the standard questions, he recommended me to the patriarch of our BYU Stake, encouraging me to fast the day of the blessing to be more receptive to the promptings of the Holy Spirit.

I met with the BYU patriarch on a Sunday afternoon. He invited me into his office and we sat in comfortable red-patterned upholstered chairs directly across from each other. He was bald and plump and handed me his card, which remains stored in my keepsakes to this day. We visited before he rose and turned on a tape recorder. Placing his hands on my head he gave me my patriarchal blessing. He announced the blessing was given by his priesthood authority and by the power of God and proceeded to announce my shared Israelite heritage and outlined God's blessings for me. The formal blessing continued for ten minutes, the remarkable promises pronounced contingent upon my remaining righteous and obedient to God's commandments, ending the blessing in the name of Jesus Christ, and concluding a marvelous experience.

Shortly afterward I received a copy of the blessing, a copy also assuredly sent to the Church headquarters' records division. I read it and was as amazed at its words as I was the day they were bestowed on me. But the formal blessing written down was not the most impressive part of the meeting with the patriarch. His words before and after the blessing were. After visiting about my family, my freshman experience at BYU and my goals, he told me who I was, confirming precisely how I viewed myself but had not told him or anyone else. Patriarchal blessings were often viewed as providing an indication of one's spiritual potential—synonymous, wrongly or rightly, with leadership positions within the Church. Like many young Mormon men I wanted to reach the highest order of righteousness of living in communication with God, and for all practical purposes that occurred in a position as a general authority. But unlike many who genuinely aspired to the position because of its connection to God, I did not want to be a general authority, not even a smidgen of suppressed desire in me. My religious upbringing had not mixed messages, and general authorities by virtue of their callings did not have any advantage to know God's will. The BYU patriarch did not tell me I would be one either, but what he did tell me, that no one else had, over a few minutes of visiting, cemented our shared vision within me.

There were no other dances held at the Morris Center during the year, so this would be the first and final dance I attended there. The dance had no decorations. The organizers moved the tables to clear space for the dance floor. The displaced tables, the dimmed lighting, and loud music transformed the cafeteria into a dance hall. I had disclosed my interest in Sandy to more floor-mates than Jared. One, an energetic, full blond-haired, terribly decent guy, Simon, hailing from Idaho Falls, twenty minutes north of Blackfoot, pumped me full of confidence the days leading up to the dance. His roommate, Brian, the cockiest and fairest looking freshman on the floor, easily an Abercrombie & Fitch model on his worst-hair-day—genuinely unlikable and unaware of anyone but himself on and off the basketball court, where he dominated with a respectable inside and outside game—would be one of many beautiful distractions for her at the dance.

A group of regulars from our floor headed over together and shortly after our arrival I noticed her. I could have broken into Billy Idol's "Dancing with Myself," but I knew I wasn't living in a musical, and while it was a personal anthem it did not quite fit the mood, giving way to Mormon classics like Alphaville's "Forever Young," so I stayed cool on the side for the better part of the night. If she knew I noticed her, she gave no indication of it, surely a credit to my coolness of blending in. My devotion, beyond curbing that night, patiently crested with no ebbs after a fair amount of pep-talking, from my inner monologue and from Simon, and not nervously standing about.

Well into the night, aware the dance would end promptly at midnight, Simon grabbed my arm and told me to ask her to dance on a slow dance, pushing me toward her. Simon was a far better athlete and a lot stronger than me, having excelled at high school football and, while having never wrestled willingly, had battled me for twenty exhausting minutes to a stalemate in the campus swimming pool. I stood my ground out of self-respecting beliefs of manhood but, after pausing, heeded him and walked toward her. Holding my breath I asked her to dance. She graciously accepted my request and followed me to the middle of the cafeteria dance floor. Thoughts went streaming God only knows where, and I attempted to ask those that seemed appropriate for small-talk whenever my voice caught up to them. The communication came out realistically wimpy and broken, asking how was she, her day had gone, she enjoying the dance, my name, a freshman living in tower X, all the time with my hands lightly touching her hips, daring not the slightest intrusion. I struggled to hear her speak, to say anything, a moment's pause winding me again into my hybrid of question-comment babblings until I quieted just before the end. The song ended, I smiled thanking her, and breathed again walking away from the most complete blunder and triumphant act of my young life. We parted for our respective groups, me wearing a grin across my face on lightened steps toward my group of friends, receiving a hardy pat on my shoulder from Simon. I had broken through. I had made contact.

After I received my patriarchal blessing, I took the next step of filling out my mission papers to be sent to Church headquarters in Salt Lake City. Completing the papers required an interview with my BYU bishop and a member of the BYU Stake presidency. The bishop, a young businessman, with a young family, did not know me well because I rarely went to church, which I thought was a perfect arrangement. We met in a small room passing as his temporary office on the first floor of my dormitory tower. He welcomed me and stated he did not see me much at church, and I replied I often visited my divorced single aunt and her son or went home to Idaho on the weekends. He said fine, choosing not to belabor my lack of attendance. He ran through the standard questions, one of which was whether I masturbated. To my surprise, and while I had tempered my self-abusing activities for no other reason than the challenge of having privacy, my stern and well practiced response broke by a quiver, which I felt and was sure he noticed. But my answer was the same right answer, that I did not have any problems, not willing to risk a delay of a few months of repentance to ensure I was righteous enough to serve a mission.

He passed me and scheduled a time for me to meet with a member of the stake presidency where I returned to my normal interview form, passing that one, coolly, and I thought that was that. Until I decided to go to church the next week and, during elders quorum meeting, sitting in the back row of a tiered classroom, looking down at my Birkenstocks, which I regularly wore when I did attend church services after early on being told by a fellow student that sandals were inappropriate for Sunday. I was levels above the student Sunday School teacher in the small pit below, and I perked up when the teacher spontaneously appealed to the bishop for his opinion, not an uncommon move of deference during any lesson when an authority figure was present.

The bishop stood and commented on a subject I could neither recall nor was I listening at the time, but his comments seemed directed straight at me when he said lying about sins to leaders compounded the sin by not only prolonging the effects of the sin and the necessary repentance process but also by doubling it with the serious transgression of lying to one of God's anointed. He stated he knew students lied to his very face and did themselves grave harm in doing so because they halted the Holy Spirit's guidance with the lie, stopping themselves from achieving their spiritual potential until they cleaned up their lives, which required confessing their sins. He was convinced he was right, and while I was not, I avoided making eye contact because the last thing I wanted to do was another round of interviews.

This same bishop on a separate occasion told us with certainty that we would not do as well on our exams if we did not complete our home teaching to the sisters in the ward, a monthly duty of all faithful male members. Within days of his declaration I had taken my exams, earning As and A-minuses for the semester and not recalling but once all year having fulfilled my obligation to my assigned sisters in the ward. Within minutes of taking my final exam, I headed home for the summer break, waiting for my mission call to arrive, doing what I did best, nothing, in preparation of the two-year mission ahead of me.

PART III

CHAPTER 11
HOT ATLANTA

We departed the plane like other passengers, pulling belongings from seat pockets and our backpacks from the spaces at our feet and from the storage spaces above, trying to miss heads rising in the seats around us, swinging the packs over one shoulder then the other, pocketing extra packages of peanuts, with smiles, some scared, among them mine, jockeying for a place in line, moving in lockstep, halting, resuming our pace in a single stream toward the door, stepping into the enclosed walkway leading to the gate, welcomed by a blast of hot air. Each of us big-eyed and wary, the young men with short haircuts, some cropped, like mine, all the young men wearing new dark suits, most fitted within the past couple months, mine initially with extra space but now filled out by my hundred and seventy-five pound frame fixed on three square meals a day over three weeks in the Missionary Training Center, known to missionaries as the MTC, in Provo, minutes north of Deseret Towers.

The men wore their suit jackets over bright-white shirts, knotted ties, some off center but not mine, snug against buttoned collars. That morning two young women in modest ankle-length dresses had joined our group of elders, which was referred to as a "district" while at the MTC. We all wore prominent name tags clipped or pinned high on chests, engraved surnames following ELDER or SISTER in white above smaller print of The Church of Jesus Christ of Latter-day Saints. We stepped into the gate area greeted by a massive smile under large square-rimmed glasses set on a circular head, looking directly at each of us as he clasped our right hands and walked past him and the monitor of flights moving through Hartsfield-Jackson Atlanta International Airport.

President Lonnie N. Mensh welcomed us to the Georgia Atlanta Mission. His two assistants—advisors, trainers and highest-ranking young men of the couple hundred missionaries in the mission—somber at his side and as serious as we were timid, led us through an Atlanta terminal that extended far beyond the walk earlier in the morning to catch our direct Delta flight in the Salt Lake City airport. One assistant stood at the entry of an escalator, preventing strays from wandering off to lose themselves in the labyrinth of the Atlanta airport, while the other assistant led us onto it, descending underground. We stepped from the escalator into a large open hallway with sliding doors on both sides, trains speeding in opposite directions. The assistant on point led us to one side, directing us to get off at baggage claim.

I had not ridden a subway since my last visit to Boston the summer following my sophomore year of high school. After Steve came to Blackfoot during the wrestling season, he invited me to Boston on summer break. He was a high school teacher accustomed to the good fortune of free summer months, inspired to see that I had a better time than what he had witnessed over the few days of his visit. Foolish in many aspects of my life, wrestling at 119 lbs. my sophomore year being one of them, I was no fool in gaining my stepmother Gayle's favor, learning early in her marriage to my father, a union begun almost two years after my mother's death, the key to her good graces was through acceptance and inclusion of her youngest of three children, Aaron, a year older than me and a decent, likable young man in his own right, the only child from her family left at home. When I presented the trip to Boston to my father and Gayle, I expanded Steve's invitation from me to we, to include Aaron before asking Aaron, and they agreed, and later so did Aaron.

I could hardly repay Aaron for his gifts to me when our families first moved in together. "You only pick on me because you don't like yourself," he said. There were a million reasons I picked on people, including him. For one, he got everything he asked for. For two, I was mean and that's what mean people do—pick on people. But I could not have people thinking I did not like myself, so I quit picking on other people, including him, dropped it cold, never to do it again after his declaration.

Aaron's favoritism was only one among many things that hindered the families' integration. Mormons have family home evening (FHE) once a week, typically on Monday night, and one FHE in Gayle's home began with a dessert she prepared but none of us young Elison wrestlers ate, because it was during wrestling season. FHE continued with a game my youngest brother, Jed, introduced that none of us would play. Gayle said something and my father went berserk. He scooped his hands into the dessert and dropped it on Jeremy's plate demanding he eat every bite. After minutes of his Tasmanian twirling about the house, he proceeded to line Jeremy and Josh and me up against the wall, to berate us for our sour attitudes and childish behavior that evening and since moving to Gayle's house.

None of this was shocking. His outbursts at Gayle's house substituted for his whippings at Old Red, and we all much preferred his new form of discipline. Living at Old Red, we proud few Elison boys shared one indelible youthful thing, the recurring sting of his leather belt across our legs, just below our butts and across our hams. During his prolonged tirade I yelled back at him, as loud as I could, explaining that this had nothing to do with Jed's game or us acting poorly and we wouldn't be forced to accept Aaron and Gayle. We wouldn't be made to carry out fake niceness so everyone had the same fake feeling we all liked each other and if he or Gayle raised the matter one more time with any of the brothers it would be the last time I spoke to them while I lived under their roof. He shut up. If he knew one thing, he knew his ferocity met its match in my obstinacy. I turned around and went to my room. Later that night he came up to my room and apologized. I wouldn't look at nor speak to him. A few minutes later Jeremy came up to my room and asked if our dad had apologized to me too. I said yes, but I hadn't and wouldn't accept it. Apologies were not part of my deal.

We rode subways during that summer trip to Boston, the red line to Cambridge, having a walk about Harvard Yard, or as Steve said, Havhad Yahd, where we walked through Johnson Gate toward the statue of the young minister and university namesake John Harvard, crisscrossing paths on the old yard under no illusion I could score high enough on national exams to gain acceptance there, nor convinced of an alternative demonstration of intellectual ability required to walk as a student between the enclosed old redbrick buildings. Yet I walked in the hallowed space believing it fit for my dream of understanding and exchanging knowledge of great and complex ideas.

We rode the red line to Somerville, seeing our old neighborhood from Davis Square to Powder House Park, where the junior high kids hung out and smoked and teenage girls crudely dressed eliciting my attention wandering from our apartment on Kidder Av'. And we rode the green line to Fenway Park on a summer night when tickets were still available and affordable as a school teacher's treat. Our summer night was spent off the third base line in talking distance of Wade Boggs in summer 1992, when Red Sox fans still went through their annual ritual of mid-season hoping to post-season suffering, cresting with prolonged bitter playoff disappointment, still years before developing hardened resistance to the puritan guilt of performance-enhanced euphoric World Series wins.

The Atlanta airport subway was cleaner than I remembered the Boston T's red or green line. We stepped from the subway when the voice on the intercom announced baggage claim, looking for the assistants, spotting one headed up the escalators and beyond to the mini-mechanical-volcanoes spewing forth luggage onto elliptical conveyor belts. He located our belt and we followed anxiously standing about examining each piece of luggage passing around us until we all gathered our bags. Behind the assistants we carried them outside into the heat of the parking lot. We stopped at a large white van with its back doors open and President Mensh smiling.

We loaded our luggage and stood at attention ready for the order to enter the van for the ride north through Atlanta to the mission home in the Dunwoody suburb. President Mensh straightened his arms and placed them on the shoulders of a bright-faced elder near him, and announced to all of us with his enormous smile that our work as missionaries of the Church of Jesus Christ of Latter-day Saints to share the restored Gospel of Jesus Christ began tonight by speaking with people on the Atlanta rail, MARTA. He demonstrated an approach with a short introduction about the Church followed by questions about the subject's feelings, similar to those we had been practicing for weeks in the MTC, with the elder firmly within his grasp playing the role of the contact. He invited each of us to make similar introductions to find people interested in learning more about the Church and the restored gospel during our ride on MARTA. He said the key was opening our mouths, and encouraged us to do so. Then he and the assistants gave each of us copies of the blue paperback copy of the Book of Mormon, the free gift to share with those who would accept it. The assistants led us back into the baggage claim area through sets of parting glass doors to the MAR-TA stop, the airport being its southernmost station. They bought tokens and passed them out, directing us to spread throughout the cars, and without being told many spread in pairs. I found myself alone and slightly relieved. I took a window seat and spent most of the next hour looking through it on Atlanta.

I glanced around the car trying not to make eye contact with any of the other riders. I noticed one of the young women missionaries who had joined our group of elders earlier that morning. She was tall, red-haired, and beautiful. She was talking to a person about the Church and the work she did as a missionary for the Church. I tried to listen to the conversation mostly blocked by the moving train's din. She wore a serious face and did most of the talking. One of the assistants, Elder Barkwood, came through the connecting door behind us and sat next to me. He asked me how it was going and like all queries from superiors in the Church in official interviews or not I answered it was going well. He then asked me if I had spoken to anyone, and I answered I had not but had my eye on a couple targets. He wished me good luck, stood and moved to the connecting door in front of us and through it to the next car. I turned back to the window and the sprawling landscape moving past me. When I turned from the window minutes later the beautiful missionary had moved down the car and was talking to someone else. I watched her for a few minutes and turned back to the city.

The train ran past weathered small houses along Main Street, stopping first at College Park Station. It started again running north across Harvard Av', passing more houses, eateries, and industrial buildings along the way. At stop after stop, black people got on and got off, more black people than I had seen in my lifetime, including the NBA finals in the early Eighties between the Lakers and Celtics, some of my earliest television memories. As the rail curved to the east, approaching the heart of the city, I saw, to the south and across interstate lanes, Centennial Olympic Stadium within hundreds of yards, and due south of Atlanta-Fulton County Stadium where the great Atlanta Brave and Mormon Dale Murphy played for many years, winning consecutive Most Valuable Player awards and multiple Gold Glove awards in center field, putting up impressive hitting and on-base percentages year after year in the Eighties before the clouded decade of juice-induced performances within its infancy when I arrived in the summer of 1995. MARTA moved us through the city's business and retail districts and skyscrapers, crossing over the interstate toward North Atlanta, passing newer developments through areas like opulent Buckhead running to the northern lip of Interstate 285, "The Perimeter" that encircled Atlanta, and moving beyond to the suburbs bordering suburbs leading into Dunwoody.

When we rejoined the van, driven by one of the assistants, it moved through a neighborhood of large houses separated by trees and sprawling lawns. It pulled up in front of a large red-brick house, and leaving our luggage stored in the back, we stepped out. The assistants led us up the driveway to the front door where President Mensh and his wife, Sister Mary Mensh, welcomed us into their home. They introduced us to their many children living with them in Atlanta, their oldest boys in college at BYU and on missions of their own. President Mensh picked an unsuspecting elder to offer a blessing on the food and upon its completion we picked up our plates and filed into the kitchen where President Mensh stood in an apron behind an island covered with assortments of foods, scooping on our plates large helpings of Sister Mensh's chicken broccoli casserole, within minutes determined unanimously delicious and filling. Our day ended with a testimony meeting in the family room, during which President Mensh invited each of us to his study up the stairs to the first door on the left of the balcony for our first mission interview.

An elder tapped me on the shoulder and I rose from our circle of stories and thoughts of the day and expressions of the unknown experience before us to climb the stairs to the appointed door. I knocked and President Mensh's voice welcomed me from within. He sat at his desk with an open file before him and, raising his head, emitted the same large smile, which now beckoned me to have a seat on the open chair to his side. He asked me how I did on MARTA. I told him I enjoyed the ride through Atlanta very much but had not spoken to anyone. He said it was not easy to do and that I would have many opportunities ahead of me. He asked me about Idaho and my family and about my mother, and I told him all I knew. He asked me about the experience of my first year at BYU, and I told him I enjoyed school and made good friends. He asked me my major, and I told him it was English and he told me his had been the same. He asked me what my grades were, and I told him and he asked me if I was in the honors program, and when I said I was not he asked me why not and encouraged me to enroll when I returned. He told me he appreciated having me in the mission, and I thanked him. He said tomorrow morning he would assign us to our first missionary companions and the match was important and he took the process seriously. He excused me, giving me an elder's name and asking me to send him up behind me.

Like other male Mormon missionaries, I was set apart and confirmed by the laying on of hands as an elder in the Church days before I entered the MTC. Elder was an honorific title as only full-time leaders of the Church called general authorities bore it, and with the title came the mantel of chosen messenger of God. Both male and female missionaries abstained from using given names during their missionary service going only by the title Elder or Sister and their respective surnames. No one had called me by my first name for weeks and no one would for the next two years.

We filed out of the van into a dark parking lot at the assistant's apartment just inside the northern lip of the perimeter. The two sister missionaries had parted company after the dinner, meetings, and interviews at the mission home, to stay with sister missionaries in the area. The night air blazed us its extended welcome of heat as we removed our suit jackets for the first time that day to haul our luggage one more time. We walked into a large air-conditioned apartment with worn couches, a cheap table set, pale white walls and small bedrooms shared by companionships on both ends. We met two more missionaries who were companions of the assistants and worked in the mission office nearby. The assistants directed us to find space on the floor or couch reminding us of our early start. I dressed down into shorts and a t-shirt, leaving my suit draped over my large piece of luggage ready to enter into it again on short notice, and propped my head on some extra clothing. Exhausted I lay down and tried to fall asleep but if I did it was quick, and I woke as quickly nearly frozen. I pulled more clothes from my luggage and covered my legs, pulling my suit coat over my chest, wondering to high hell if someone hadn't turned up the air-conditioning, starting my contemplations slowly and letting them rise by the next morning's end, cussing the assistants and their companions and the whole dastardly mission plot for its indifference.

August 9, 1995. I've arrived. It's a quarter after eleven and I'm going to write until the lights go out. I'm sleeping on a hard floor with no comforts. It's been a long day. I really am a missionary. I'm not sure I feel like one just yet. I had an interview with President Mensh. He is a fine man. I shared who I was. I'm more content with who I am than

I ever have been. I'm an Elison, a Christian, a servant of the Lord. A brother. My head is ringing. I haven't had a headache for quite some time. I'm not sure what kind of missionary I'll be. I won't be a leader. I won't be a pillar for all to see. I'm not these things. I'm just me. Dang I'm happy. I'm one to build things up in my mind. I hope, I hope, and at the same time I know things don't happen like a fairy tale. But today, seeing my brothers, knowing that Jami was pissed as hell for missing me. Knowing that my best friends love me. I'm happy. Indeed I am! It was a fairy tale time for me at the airport. Well, the lights have been turned down. I'm going to pray for my family, friends and all my families' friends. I hope to God my family is well. I love them. Tonight I shared my testimony. I love Jesus Christ. I'm not in Georgia to help everyone. I'm here to help anyone.

CHAPTER 12

THE MTC

Miserable, rising from the lost night's battle, the district unified by far more than the purpose of our day and, dressed in the same clothes as the previous day, lugged bags to the parking lot, loaded them back into the white van, found an open seat, and drove to the Glenridge Ward to meet our trainers, our first companions. But we drove through the hot Atlanta summer morn to meet our second companion if truth prevail, because we arrived in Atlanta in the company of our first companion assigned the first day we arrived at the MTC.

The MTC was spiritual boot-camp on stilts minus the humiliation and disciplinary push-ups and guard. I walked through one of the complex's many front glass doors in the company of my father, stepmother, and younger brothers. Official greeters directed us down a long hallway to doors opening on the left to a deep conference room where we joined future missionaries sitting with family and friends. The official welcome on our first day was brief, including a hymn, a prayer, and a few words, and the time to say our goodbyes was briefer. The massive group stood, people crying hugged and one missionary left the room after another leaving family and friends behind to exit the building the way they had come through the front glass doors. I took my place in the buffet line of introductory stages, handing in my document of current immunizations, a recent tetanus shot duly noted. An elderly lady reviewed the form, unaware of my disappointment over how my immunities paled by comparison to those obtained by missionaries headed overseas. An older missionary who was in his mid-twenties, an ostensible deviation from the standard trooper, with his sleeve turned up and a rubber-band around his arm awaiting a shot, startled me from my self-pity when he accosted me with "Semper Fi, Elder." I averted my eyes from his gaze out of unadulterated ignorance, not a bit of spite, so he accosted me again, and so I answered him with a puzzled tight smile shaking my head. He pointed to my tie-clip, the Marine Corps insignia with the eagle, anchor, and globe, asking me if I was a Marine. I apologized and said I was not but my father was and the clip was his. With eyes covered by large glasses, he kindly told me Semper Fi meant "Always Faithful." I thanked him, unfazed by another pinch of sheer stupidity, but under no illusion I was one of the few and the proud and apparently always faithful. I moved on to the next station humbler and anxious to find my bunk.

July 19, 1995. My first day in the MTC. I love to write. Even more so than that, I love to think. Kind of crazy I know. Well, the MTC is just another trek. I saw three old compadres from the Y. It made this day worth being around for. People are pretty good. Some people I just wish I could spend all the time in the world with. I'm just taking the Wu Wei. I'm doing what's asked of me. I'm not one to do much more. This mission experience will be an interesting one. I hope my family knows how much I love them. Right now I wish my companions could be my old friends from the Y or my good bros just because I know they understand me and I love being around them. My companion for the next three weeks is something special. He has a handicap but it only makes him stronger. I hope with all my heart I can give him something, some part of me that will make him smile whenever he remembers the MTC. Besides that I just hope to get a few push-ups in every morning and maybe a pull-up or two every week. I know my entries sometimes are a bit hard for the young. I don't ever plan on reading this but whoever reads it know that my friends and family are everything to me. I am a dreamer. I always imagine how something will happen and it hardly ever does. I've been hoping these last couple of days that as soon as I walked through the doors to leave my family I would find Jared waiting to greet me. He wasn't just standing around. I found him minutes later helping people with their luggage. Jared or more properly referred to as Elder Lonergan is a great friend. They don't get any greater. Tomorrow I look forward to writing the family at home and Jeremy & Jami here in Provo. They'll be short notes but I still look forward to it.

My companion and I readied and emerged from our sleeping quarters, a room larger than my dorm room at Deseret Towers, with two bunk-beds lined against one wall opposite desks secured to the other wall, and small closet space and dresser-drawers between them. We walked across the MTC campus and entered a tall, layered building full of classrooms on all levels, and found our classroom filled with other missionaries and three older gentlemen. Our small group constituted our MTC "district," the building block of missions everywhere, similar to a squad. We numbered twelve, ten elders, eight of us headed to Atlanta, the other two elders and two sisters also headed to state-side missions. In the mission field, a few districts made a zone like squads make a platoon and many zones made a mission like platoons make a company, missions combined to make up the sixty-thousand-some missionary force spanning the world. The difference between mission and military divisions is that mission categories are synonymous with geographic regions. While the MTC was technically part of the mission field, counting toward time served, it was more a microcosm of the whole shebang than a part of it, where missionaries practiced being the missionary and played the investigator—all in preparation of heading to their assigned corners of the globe.

The three older gentlemen were the district's ecclesiastical leaders during our three weeks on the inside, not to be confused with the leadership of the entire MTC, which had its own mission president and counselors, also older gentlemen. Our gentlemen presided over Sunday services in addition to welcoming us. They visited with us as a group briefly and met with each of us individually, more briefly. I passed my interview fine. The primary reason for the interview was not to determine our worthiness but to pick a district leader. The leadership role was an honor. It was not only an honor on a grand scale because Mormon missionaries were told, and most believed, their two-year missionary service for the Church would be the most spiritual and important time of their lives, but it was honor in the quotidian, all of us unsure and green-faced in need of guidance with hours and hours on end in activity after endless activity ahead of us.

July 20, 1995. Day two on the inside. I won't be writing every day. If I do it will be a miracle. This is a bit of info about who was in charge during my stay in the MTC.

MTC Pres. B. 1st Counselor Pres. W. 2nd Counselor Pres. D.

Mission District B Pres. C.

Branch 32 Pres. H. 1st Counselor Pres. B. 2nd Counselor Pres. S.

Assistant to Pres. Elder M.

District 32-A District leader Elder Y

Coordinating Sister – Sister P.

President H is a very kind man. Pres. B is awesome. He put on a devotional while I was at the Y. He is a marine biologist. He teaches at the Y. How I would one day love to swim with such life. It's getting late. I need to turn in. I did some pushups this morning. I'm getting up early to do some pushups & situps tomorrow. I want to improve on the old figure. Take care.

July 21, 1995. I'm going into my third night here in the MTC. I haven't slept well these last couple of nights. But I can function just fine. My district is going to the temple tomorrow. The temple will be closing for a couple of weeks and tomorrow morning is the only day we can go. I'm not terribly excited about it all. I just don't know.

Tonight I laughed. I have a real problem. I laugh like a little kid when something strikes me funny. It's a sign of my immaturity. Especially in meetings like tonight I just don't know what to do about that.

Having the spirit and teaching by the spirit is the biggest thing here. People feel the spirit like they feel anything else. In all honesty I haven't recognized this Spirit everyone talks about. I wonder if I'm alone. Everyone, well probably not everyone, passes having the spirit as if they feel it so often. It doesn't bug me. I'm trying. I'm not real comfortable about the whole system. I like many of the teaching ideas, but I don't like forcing the spirit or claiming it is always present. Humans have shown love for ages. That's all I want to do. In 2 Nephi 2 a couple versus in is all I want to do. I want to share the Savior with others. I'll never measure up to how things are expected. I don't know. Hell, I'll give things a try.

People are so worthwhile. It has taken me a while to appreciate my roommates and companion. I hope to become good friends with them.

I have some friends in here. It makes it worth it to hug a close friend at a place where things are kind of different.

I try to be humble and I'm trying to learn. I'm giving it the old college try.

I think about my family all the time. I love them. If these 19 years of my life haven't shown that I've failed. I hope I can be a good friend. I don't know why but I think about Sandy all the time. I'll never see her again but the so many times I saw her on BYU campus was worth a lifetime. I wish her the best.

To all take care. I try to do the same, or should I say tried to do the same.

July 22, 1995. Today was long, yet it was worth it. I attended a great meeting tonight. I hope I can serve the people in my area with as much love as possible. Somehow, someway I'm going to use the love I have for my family to love those people in Georgia. Maybe I can show my Savior I love him by doing this. I love him. I love my family. I love my family. [Insert of scrap paper dated July 22]. Expressing my love for my Savior is hopefully something I can accomplish the rest of my life. I am nothing. I really am. There is so much I wish I could express. I just hope I can live for him. These next two years is a golden opportunity for me.

July 23, 1995. My first missionary Sunday. Pretty interesting. The second counselor gave a really good lesson on overcoming fear through love. He shared 1 John 4: 7-11, 16-21. Great Scriptures. Well, I'm going to turn in. My comp became district leader today and he is pretty gung ho. Nice kid. Real nice kid though. Take care.

We rose before dawn to prepare for the day's training broken into a morning, an afternoon, and an evening class, each a few hours in length. My companion told me when his mother was pregnant to cope with being sick she took a drug, likely a sister drug to thalidomide, and as a result he was born with short arms. He couldn't throw a baseball or swing a bat well but got along fine in most activities with a little more time. I hadn't asked but he had kindly offered the explanation preempting any inquiry. He was as normal as the rest of us and loved his sleep. We dutifully woke at the expected time like the rest, but his fidelity to a good night's sleep including its final seconds before the sounding of our alarm extended our time to get ready in full uniform of suit and tie. The extension made arriving at any meeting on time a challenge, which I didn't mind.

Tired when I woke and exhausted throughout the day with repeated role-playing practice, I struggled to embrace the overall missionary spirit. That spirit wound up in a belief that success came through the Holy Ghost (The Holy Spirit). The Spirit, a supernatural feeling witnessing the reality of God and all things related to God, was for missionaries what the categorical imperative, right action regardless of circumstance, was for Immanuel Kant. I resisted the emphasis on this key to success not because I didn't believe it but because I didn't believe it could be conjured by me just as I doubted the application of a—not merely the many—right action across the plethora of my life's circumstances, let alone the same right action for everyone across them and more. While the spirit and categorical imperative are coherent in the abstract, neither have the consistent application to experience as supposed by their most ardent proponents. One only need to go on a Mormon mission where their application supposedly couldn't be easier to chart they don't.

The Holy Ghost was a constant companion to members of the Church who remained righteous because members received it as a gift by Mormon authority at baptism and confirmation into the Church, while only an infrequent Comforter or manifestation of the Holy Ghost could be experienced by people who were not Mormon, just like the enclave of über-duty people who always practice right action distinct from the billions of others who merely dabble in it. The purpose of missionary work is to share this gift of the constant companionship of the Holy Spirit to the world by offering membership into the Church of Jesus Christ of Latter-day Saints and its path to eventual salvation, a moral order no less ambitious than Kant's imagined result of all beings acting rightly, both more possible than comprehensible. Hence, no goal was more important and no measure more accurate for the success of missionaries than the presence of the Holy Spirit. Given the singular charge of getting and keeping the Spirit, missionaries strove to bring about the success of others' conversions by it.

Missionaries tried to maintain the Spirit by obedience to the rules, constantly reminding each other of attitudes and actions conducive to it and those that offended it. In addition to having the Spirit, missionaries sought to develop the skill to identify its presence. The Spirit provided ultimate confirmation of the truthfulness of the missionary's message, unlocking proselytizing greatness, but also, and more importantly, the Spirit confirmed in missionaries the same conviction they sought for others. From day one, missionaries were gaining convictions of the truthfulness of their message in addition to learning how to help others believe their message through the tightly designed and strict MTC regimen. Focus on maintaining the Holy Spirit circled twenty-four/seven as general authorities, ecclesiastical leaders, and teachers witnessed to missionaries, and missionaries witnessed to each other. The emphasis on getting the supernatural in the immediate didn't faze me because I had logged enough sessions of Dungeons and Dragons as a cleric or magic user, or wizard, shunning the brawn and weapons of fighters and paladins, some of my clerics even obtaining respectably high levels with strong healing and protection spells, and failed not to appreciate a belief in commanding supernatural powers, but the transition to applying this power to proselytizing proved unnatural.

Church leaders personified the Spirit. The top-tier missionaries replicated the serious dispositions projected by general authorities whom we saw, many missionaries for the first time, live at the MTC. General authorities were somber, speaking in controlled monotones in clear symmetry to their certainty of the truthfulness of their message, and even more importantly to the certainty of their "callings" as witnesses with authority to speak on behalf of God. Rarely a few of the top tier broke the mold, shucking the status quo condescension. The missionary capable of being a strong witness was rare among so many playing ones.

July 24, 1995. What a fine day or I should say, evening. I met some fine elders by the names of E and H that are going to Boise. My comp, Clementine, and I taught them a couple of principles. We were taught by Elders Z and G. G played college basketball. A guy I could talk to or at lease hang with on the outside, maybe. He is a fine guy. Good looking as can be. I'll see him again because we'll get taught again by him and his comp. Elder G was a sincere guy. I look forward to meeting with Elders E and H again. They're good guys. Elder B, Simon a friend from BYU, is leaving early this morning. We got a picture and said our good-byes. I have some really good friends. These friends, my family, and the opportunity to share this love is worth living for.

July 25, 1995. The days here at the missionary training center seem to drag on. The evenings are worth all the slow drags throughout the day. President H gave an incredible lesson on the atonement. It was incredible in the sense that through sincerity and simplicity he explained and shared his feelings on the single most selfless act that of Jesus atoning for the sins of mankind. I hope for the ability to share my love of the savior. I don't want to kill myself helping everyone. I'd like to help anyone. Right now things are going by slowly, yet I seem to lack a firm grip. I don't know. I've discovered my favorite hymn. I think this is an answer to my prayer last night to whether or not I was in the right place. "A Poor Wayfaring Man of Grief." I love these words. Hopefully I will be able to help those that are unfortunate. I'm not looking to baptize. I'm looking to help others be happy. Knowing that God loves them and that our elder brother does to is what I want to share. I hope I can be a true servant of my savior. Hopefully throughout my mission I can share experiences in my journal. As much as this, I would hope to share my testimony, hopes, and love for my savior. I pray that my family may be blessed with safety and the spirit of Christ. I hope that I will be of some help to someone, anyone. God lives.

July 26, 1995. This will be short. I shall write tomorrow, being that the day is Preparation Day. And a beautiful Thursday it will be. Take Care. God loves you. I know because he loves me, the lowliness of the low.

July 27, 1995. Today was the first preparation day for my district. I accomplished my Book of Mormon reading, laundry, and the writing of a few letters. My district is a pretty nice district. We all went and played volleyball this morning. We get along pretty well. My roommates are interesting people. One, Elder S is very young. I mean that he just graduated from high school and has not experienced. He is a nice kid with a good heart though. His companion, Elder M, is an individual with an identity. He's very sure of who he is. He uses sound reasoning and he cares for his family a great deal. He has experienced. My companion is the middle of these two. The interesting thing is that he is challenged. He was born with his arms shorter than most. He is nice. He is confident that is self-conscious because of his challenge. He wouldn't ever admit it, but Elder M has brought out the insecurity a couple of times. Elder M being a wee bit wiser holds his tongue in this case. While if it were someone different or more the same in person he would probably have continued. Elder M is a selfless person. I respect him a great deal. He cares. Not that others don't. In this situation I just sit back and try and make these individuals real. It's o.k. being my comps companion because he never follows up. Even with our scripture sharing, I do all of it. He never takes the initiative. It may be that he is more concerned with following rules. They are all good guys. They're much different than anyone I've ever lived with or been around. They're not exactly the type I would be with on the outside just because of differences in personalities. I hope for the best with them though as I do the rest of the district. There is one Elder in the district I wouldn't mind being a comp of in the field and that's Elder Whitely. He's active and knowledgeable he isn't pretentious but definitely has a testimony. He's a tall kid from St. George. He would be a fine companion. The sisters in the district are nice. Sister B, going to Lansing Michigan, seems very young and inexperienced. Sister S, going to Detroit, seems much older than Sister B. They are both very nice. Sister S is someone that would be worth learning from. She's African American and a believer in the Church. She's a convert. She is a very nice person. Well, now my district at the MTC is known to the reader for the most part. There are a few other Elders going to Georgia. Elder G, K, S, and L. They are good guys. Hopefully I will add to this tonight.

July 28, 1995. People, People. Hell, people. Once again, I lost my composure during the hymn before class began. Once again, my lack of control was contagious. I'm just having a tough time here being serious all the time. I'm pretty immature. I Guess. But I wouldn't change my personality for anything. It's my identity.

Poor Elder M. He's a stud. He's sound as can be but he's too intimidating for my companion. I wonder what I'd be like with a disability. Would my personality be totally different? It's easy to say no. But I don't know. I think of my family every day. Today in the afternoon class I was asked to play the investigator during the family approach. Nothing else is important to me. To share my family is sharing Jesus. In

my sinful and lowly state I will never give up on my family. I shared at
the end of the trip to the Bahamas with Jami and my bull riding brothers Josh & Jeremy. I love sharing my family. I hope I'm chosen to speak
in sacrament to share my father. If not, I'll share him often enough
in the field. I leave you with the words of Enos (from memory if you
can believe that). "Knowing my father, that he was a just man – for he
taught me in the language – and also in the nurture and admonition
of the Lord, and blessed be [inserted: "the name of"] my God for it."
AND I CLOSE. Shoot, I had to look. I didn't get it word for word.

Our teachers were all BYU students who had served Mormon missions.
Getting a job at the MTC was a major success because of the huge number
of applicants from the legions of returned missionaries attending BYU and
high endorsements required from former mission presidents in the mission
field. The teachers were tasked with primarily developing proselytizing skills
in us but also with teaching the basic tenets of the faith, which were the core
of the missionary lessons, on top of keeping order, teetering on baby-sitting.
Days before we were all in T-shirts and jeans counting the times we wore a
suit between us on any elder's fingers, the sisters' comfort in their dresses
excepted, being their Sunday standard fare, and we all were watching television and talking to friends, and sleeping in and staying out late. As part of my
transition I snuck in contraband, a two-volume set of William Shakespeare's
plays in small print, the Bard's works not on the short list of church approved
reading and listening materials. Facing the lifetime of service ahead of me I
was sure I could cycle through the plays within the next two years.

The contrast between who we were, old teenagers, excepting the two
sisters who were in their early twenties, twenty-one the age requirement for
young women and nineteen for young men, and who we were expected to
be, special servants of Jesus Christ, surfaced every minute in the day. The
MTC regimen was designed to reinforce the expectation of who we were
supposed to be, starting with companion prayer seconds after rising in the
morning to every meeting, some small with multiple districts and a few large
with the largest the entire MTC missionary body when a general authority
visited. Trying to act in accordance with the expectations revealed glaring
discrepancies and damn near made me mad. And the challenge to fashion
us into missionaries largely fell on our teachers, our daytime teachers both
women who confronted the challenge with vigor, the morning teacher with
an indomitable cheerfulness and the afternoon teacher with a headmaster's

sternness. They met our spiritual immaturity and ineptness with the same results, there was only going to be so much progress made and it was not going to be measurable. After the first few days no one was under the impression it would be more than in millimeters. The morning teacher faced this reality with a routine smile assuring us of our eventual progress, and the afternoon teacher faced it with well-earned scorn, decrying our sloth, with predictions of paltry service if changes were not made. As expected, our group usually responded in kind content believing our chances of successful service were fifty-fifty.

I followed my companion out of class and down the stairs through the door into the summer night. We walked among the missionaries in our district to another building on the MTC campus for a small group meeting. Our night classes varied from large group meetings of many districts with one charismatic teacher giving highly motivational lessons to small group meetings with a few districts with a few teachers directing trainings, joining other districts always a welcome relief, a break in routine with fresh faces. Like all meetings this night began with a hymn and a prayer, followed by breaking into smaller groups to practice the proselytizing skills of that night's lesson, consisting of practice scenarios of contacting and teaching non-Mormons, or investigators, with one missionary playing the role of missionary and the other missionary playing the role of the investigator.

This evening numbers were not matching up and a teacher separated me from my district, assigning me to a group of elders who I didn't know but quickly learned were familiar with each other. During an opening prayer I involuntarily started to laugh. Various things would have stirred me to laughter but most likely nothing did as I regularly laughed for no rhyme and no reason. I laughed during prayers, during role-playing, during conversations with elders, my diaphragm sore from continuous contraction and my innards hemorrhaging at the slightest comment or gesture. I had caught a case of the laughs with no known cure. Not taken unawares of my condition during the prayer I quickly muffled my outburst by clenching my jaw, squinting eyes closed, holding my breath. To my surprise the elders I had joined broke out in laughter, their voices louder and their laughter more uncontrollable than mine.

As soon as the prayer giver concluded, their teacher pounced on them, scolding and declaring herself at wit's end with their promises they would behave. In this intense censure in front of all the missionaries in the classroom, I learned, through recurring fits of levity, they were in the same district. Still laughing, one sheepishly exclaimed they hadn't started it—pointing to me as the instigator, and I returned the comment with an expression of surprise, tears welling up, trying to stop laughing, but my confession brought them no peace because she had obtained nothing short of blood oaths they would not misbehave that evening, rejecting their pleas for mercy and intensifying her berating, relenting only when it was apparent not a one of us could stop laughing.

July 29, 1995. Another Saturday night in the MTC. I had a nice experience in the evening class. Everyone there had a nice experience. I felt of my Heavenly Father's love. I do believe Jesus is the Christ, and that he is my Savior, and that he loves me. Life is worth living. I learn from others every day. I wish I could share myself. I wish I knew how to completely turn myself over to my Savior. I wish, I wish... Until then I'll just try and be a friend, and try and be a servant of my Lord and Redeemer Jesus Christ. I'm in a state of not knowing but really being. There are some good people here in the MTC. I wish I could be more Christ-like and love them all. Time is so precious. I need to make the best of what time I have. It's good for me to not have any knowledge of what's in store. For me this is good. I will continue to try. I will try and pray. I hope to live. I mean really live. I love my family.

July 29, 1995 [Inserted unsent letter addressed to my Dad]. I just have one thing to say. You're my dad, and man, I love you. (Said with a little emotion). Now it's been a while since I've seen this commercial. I know you don't drink Bud Light, but there have been a few nights when I could have used a COKE.

It's 7:30 Saturday morning. We are suppose to attend gym. My comp can't do a lot of things so today we are just going to have personal study time. I shouldn't say can't do a lot of things, referring to my old comp of course. He actually plays volleyball real well.

I'm looking forward to going to Georgia, but it still pains me so when I see all my friends from the Y with their respected name tags. What an opportunity, to learn a new language. But the barrier would have consumed me. I study too much. I would have lost focus and just been there to learn as if I were in School. In Georgia I'll actually get to be me. For me, this is the greatest opportunity a mission affords. Because me, is you and the rest of the brothers, me in Gods.

The MTC is an interesting place. I am trying to make the best of it. I'm making some good friends, and since I have a camera I'm getting some pictures with my old compadres from the Y. I'm having a real tough time with having a sober mind as the days turn into evenings. We are in class so long towards the end of the day I'm just tuckered out. We sing and pray before and at the end of every class. I've more than once chuckled during the opening hymn. Sometimes hymns are picked that not everyone can sing. I just lose it in a way. The bad thing is I'm not the only tired, vulnerable one. My loss of control is contagious. I'm working on this little problem of mine. Even worse than this, I believe a little laugh, even though at an inappropriate time, is good to break the monotony. As a side note. I don't believe the most sacred experiences are those found in structured or set up settings. Mine have been while toiling with others or feeling of others' love. I don't think sacred things are to be planned or forced. Sacred, if you will, involves sharing God's love through being a friend.

Basic skills are being taught here. They're good things to have down, but they won't come until a person has got a chance to truly experience the real thing in the mission field. If nothing else, here at the MTC I've gained a greater desire to learn from the Book of Mormon. I look forward to sharing it with others.

One person out of our district will get called on in sacrament meeting to speak tomorrow. The time limit is 5 minutes. The topic is how the Book of Mormon is a testament of Jesus Christ and explains the Plan of Salvation. In 5 minutes, yea right. I plan to use 1 Nephi 8: 12 and then talk about my own father. I hope I get chosen.

I share my family all the time. It's all I have. I begin to understand my Savior's love through my family. My family incorporates all of my personal philosophies. Sharing this part of my life, the greatest part of my life, with the people of Georgia will be an ultimate high. Hopefully those I come in contact with will indeed come to feel our Heavenly Father's and our Savior's love for them. I could care less, well I shouldn't say that, but I'm not concerned with baptizing. I just want to share my family and let people know their loved. I hope I can keep my mirror turned around. I think that is the key, focusing on the Savior. It seems like two influential people installed this upon me. I thank them. One is still around. I pray the other knows of my gratitude.

Well dad, I look forward to the 9th of August. Hopefully this plan is the one. If it changes I'll let you know. Thanks for everything. Thanks for giving me the love of God to partake of. Lehi was a fine man but he was nothing like you. All your sons, in all their imperfections, have tasted of that fruit which is most delicious of all fruit. I hope I'll be able to give my children that gift as you have. Why I belong to my family, I'll never know. I know why I'm in the middle though. I've had the opportunity to get to know all my brothers. I've had the angles. I could have never survived or amounted too much at one of the ends. I couldn't have handled being the one older or the one younger. I'm too weak. I need my brothers' help. You're the greatest of all fathers, but you are one of my brothers. We don't include you as Adam in *Seven Brides for Seven Brothers* for nothing. We few, we happy few, we band of brothers. In this I find true happiness.

July 30, 1995. Well, I didn't get chosen on to speak in sacrament meeting today. However I had the chance to seal and anoint for W.A.S., a sister in the district who was feeling ill. This was my first experience where I took place in a blessing. It was good for me. It was as much a blessing for me as it was for Sister S. One more week at the MTC. I'm getting to know and become friends with an Elder G who is in the district. He's laid back and a good kid. He'd make a fine companion in the field. He's from Idaho Falls. I'm reading the Book of Mormon. I'm really becoming one who enjoys Book of Mormon study. Hopefully this last week I can get the chance to become better friends with all the district members. Take care of yourself. Be excellent to each other and party on. I love life. I look forward to making new friends.

July 31, 1995. Brother F is awesome. He has been off his mission for about 3 years. He went to Las Vegas. He puts on the large group meetings for the group I'm a part of. What a humble yet enthusiastic, sincere individual. He has put on three of these presentations. There is one more. I hate to say he has "put" them on. He has just held them. He has been the main contributor to my best experiences and times here at the MTC.

The first night he "put" on one of these large group meetings he suggested all the missionaries write in their journals what Jesus Christ meant to them. I didn't have the time so I would like to now. Jesus Christ has made it possible for me to live with my family for the eterni-

ties. He atoned for me. I can't express my gratitude. I can simply hope
to show my love through being a servant of him the rest of my days. I
love him. Hopefully with his help I'll return to him one day. Until then
I will fight the battle at hand with my feet firmly planted in his palm.

August 1, 1995. Dear Journal readers. Today was a pretty decent
day. I'm learning, trying, and sharing. Elder Y and I had a good discussion. We're pretty good friends now. Elder G and I have a lot to talk
about. Someday I'm going to go rock climbing with him after the old
mission. We talk college a lot. "Timshel" is Hebrew for "Thou Mayest."
Free Agency baby. That's what it's about. I hope I'm a good missionary. I
hope I'm a good friend. Tonight I'm going to try and pray more sincerely than I ever have. President S gave a great lesson on prayer in district
meeting. The best on prayer I've ever been given. Take care, I love life.

August 2, 1995. Boy oh boy, I'm starting to find my zone with the
scriptures. Getting in this zone may take a couple of months but I've
started. My poor comp is having a tough time. I'm trying to be his
friend. Some people aren't cut out to be a so called "leader." Dealing
with people isn't easy. You have to be willing to sacrifice. Keeping
my mirror turned around allows me to deal with anyone, I'd like to
think. The only catch here is that I don't always have my mirror turned
around. Damn I'm going to try. I hope the letter I sent home to my dad
was well received. I hope he felt how much I love him and hopefully
how much all of his boys love him. If I die I hope my brothers know
in them I live. Because All I am is an incarnation of all their souls. I
believe this with all my heart. Without them I would be nothing. I talk
about keeping my mirror turned around but with those I love most I
fear I haven't. Just the same, I hope they remember the couple of times
I did remember my mother's advice. I'm so blessed. Every day I get to
express my family. It's great. Take care.

August 3, 1995. A few more days in the MTC. Today was preparation day. It was a relaxing day. I wrote a few letters, did some wash, and
read a little bit. I'm looking forward to seeing my family at the airport,
but it's going to be tough to say good-bye. Two years isn't too long but
with limited communication with my main source of being will be
difficult. It should make me a man. I'm looking forward to being on my

own, with only the help of my Savior and family from afar. The truth of the matter is my family goes everywhere I go. There in me. I have a picture I carry in my backpack. I need Jeremy to make some copies of the picture sitting on Mary's cupboard. I'm running out of stamps. I have only a couple left. I wrote Steve Hickey today. I bore my testimony to him. Not using the typical words, but I told him what matters to me. I'm going to keep this up for a month or two and then let him know I'm sending the missionaries his way. I'm going to try and write my Uncle Rocky a few times. Then after a bit I'm going to share with him my love for my family and Savior. I want him to know families are forever. Hopefully he'll become active. If not, at least he may feel my love for him and especially for my family. I hope in these journal entries it doesn't come across that I'm full of it when it comes to my family. Am I doing anything to show my love for them? Good question huh. Probably closer to the truth is I'm not doing enough. But I hope I'm doing something. Well, Dad wrote me today. Told me Jeremy bucked off at a Pro Show. I think it was one of Jeremy's first. I hope that vest works out for him. It's the best investment or use of money that I've ever had the chance to spend. O.K. I'm tired, even with the rest I got today. Take care. Oh ya, I'm going to start writing in my Journals the thoughts my dad shares with me in the letters he writes. I can't remember the date I received his first letter but it was written on the 23rd of July. I think I got it on the 25th. The thought reads "'He does the Saving and the healing. All the rest is intended to nudge us closer to him." Today I received another letter written on the 30th. The thought reads "There is a lot of hullabaloo out there, but the only real source of peace, power, and freedom is a person named Jesus." I love my dad.

August 4, 1995. Brother D. F. taught the last Large Group Meeting. It was a fine meeting. Sister S wrote me a thank you note today. She is really something else. Elder G and I are getting to know each other well enough. He would be a fine friend. I think we could do well as companions. I don't know. I'm looking forward to seeing my brother Jeremy on Sunday. My comp doesn't know about the meeting but a few other elders in the district do. They are to keep Elder Clementine entertained while I spend some quality time with Jeremy. I'm going to bed down for the night. I'm happy to be a missionary. I pray my family is well. I look forward to seeing them Wednesday, 4 days away. Take care.

August 5, 1995. Do I see colors? Does a person's identity reside in part to their color? I do not believe so. I think identity comes within. Do I incriminate myself by entertaining the question above? Once again, I don't think so. In treating a person and the feelings of the time answer that question. I can say, and say, but until I am brought to the point that reveals my character, only then will I know. Sister W.S. is the first African American that I've shared with. She is the only one of the race I had a chance to know. We shared, we are friends. In Atlanta I'll get the chance to share again. Then I'll truly be able to answer whether or not I see in colors.

Tomorrow, my last Sunday. A chance to hear from the Branch Presidency again. I look forward to it.

My comp is interesting. He likes to talk. He doesn't trust. Man, I'm trying to like him but he isn't real. Not in the sense that he doesn't care or have a desire to truly serve the Lord. The kid has a testimony. He tries hard. He just doesn't exist in a real world. I hope if I ever become challenged my personality with my sense of humor in tact will remain.

My districts P.M. teacher (Sister J) told us to write down three attributes we want our investigators to see in us when we have left. Mine are (1) Selflessness, (2) Sincerity or genuine interest and (3) good humored or good natured. If I can keep my mirror turned around, and leave people with a smile, having them know that their Savior loves them, I will have succeeded. Good day and be strong. Book of Mormon, Mosiah 2 vs. 17. Wisdom is gained from serving and interacting with others. I hope to become wise on my mission through these means. I pray to know God. I'm not sure I do. Maybe if I lose myself (Matthew 10: 39) I'll indeed find myself. And in doing so find God. Until the next time.

August 6, 1995. Elder S, one of my roommates, works out every night. He jumps rope, does pushups, and situps. He is a skinny kid. He is near 6 ft. though. He should try doing more than 5 or 6 pushups or situps. I'm not degrading this kid as a wimp. I mean that is blatantly obvious. A person must start somewhere. This kid needs to start pushing himself. As this goes on, his companion Elder M studies away. His mind is filled with knowledge. I haven't found out if this boy is very open to new ideas. At the same time my companion, Elder Clementine, writes a letter. He has hopes of being a great writer and lecturer. My roommates are great. It's been a fine learning experience.

Today as a district we went to the temple. Jeremy met me there. I actually had to have Elder G go get him. Elder G is a cool ELDER. On the outside, he is probably the only one I could buddy up with.

It was fun to see Jeremy. We took a few pictures. Jami & Traci pulled up on his bike a little while after that. I had a few snaps taken after that. It was good to see them. I love my brothers. I hope the best for them.

It was a good Sunday, I fasted and for the first time I had something in mind. I prayed that the letters I write in the mission field will be received with the same feelings that I send them with. God bless you. I sleep.

August 7, 1995. Sister A's class! WHAT KIND OF MISSIONARY I WANT TO BE! It's now 5 after 11:00. My district has thinned out a bit, and in class today we have listened to Sister A share missionary experiences. She is pretty cool. I learned to appreciate her.

I want to be an other-centered missionary. I truly want to love others and help others come to know their Savior and redeemer Jesus Christ. I want to be Christ-like. I want to obey Jesus' command to 'love one another, even as I have loved you, that you love one another.' I want to leave people with a smile or something to chuckle about. I want to leave them thinking that a sense of humor is an important thing. At the same time I want them to have something to hold to. I hope to be humble. I don't think I am the best instrument, well I know I'm not, in the Lord's hands. But I know I'm in my Lord's hands. If I try and love I'll remain in his palm. I hope I can be a friend. I hope I get the opportunity to serve in hard work. I like to work hard. I've had the best examples to help me work. I hope to be sincere and to bear a simple and pure testimony which is MY testimony. I know that my Savior, Jesus Christ, lives. I hope to do what my father has done for me and my brothers. I hope to introduce the iron rod or word of God, that word which is the Son of God, Jesus Christ. Helping others come unto their Savior to partake of the Love of God, which is the greatest of all gifts according to Nephi in Chapter 15, the last verse. What an opportunity I have. I hope to keep my mirror turned around. If I do this I truly will be a reflector of my Savior's love. To share my family. I comprehend my Savior not, but I come to understand him and my Heavenly Father through my family. I love my family. I love my God, for giving me my family and for giving to the world his only begotten, and giving him for me.

It's still the 7th. Just a wee bit later. All right. The MTC has been a good experience. Good night!

A large gymnasium, comparable to the Fieldhouse on campus at BYU, at the south side of the MTC campus, was the main facility for the largest meetings of the entire missionary body. The meetings started with a hymn, a most impressive sight and sound, even for one with no musicality. I couldn't sing on key if Madonna herself appeared and persuaded me, but I didn't have to among the unified chorus of missionaries in the gymnasium! So I sang loud. The power of our group was never greater than during our singing of church hymns, equal to our overt and oft-reminded task of thwarting the designs of Satan. In the MTC we were reminded that Satan was everywhere, never taking a day off, slipping into every situation when righteousness waned, despite Satan's heavily favored counterpart the Holy Spirit. This paradox was beyond theologians, not beyond their abilities to pontificate, of course, but beyond their abstract realm and securely in ours. Satan and the Spirit's presence battled in hearts and minds of missionaries during every conceivable situation where missionaries found themselves. Letting down one's guard in the slightest was chink enough for Satan to create doubts and distractions for developing one's own testimony, and helping investigators find the truthfulness of God's restored gospel through gaining knowledge of his prophet Joseph Smith and sacred scripture, the Book of Mormon. Nowhere was the fight more real between God and Satan than in the extraordinary efforts of missionaries in the mission field. Each general authority spoke about this fight and our need to be resolute and always pay attention to how we either were thinking thoughts and doing actions that invited the Holy Spirit, or made way for Satan's unrelenting influence. There was no in-between as a full-time servant of the Lord. We were either going toward God or away from him. It was impossible to sit still. Make no bones about it, we were Christian soldiers committed to entering the fray for God versus Evil. Entering a field of mixed influences, certainly, but a Satan with that much energy and influence, of this I was not persuaded. I knew my weaknesses but needed no scapegoat for my defining proclivities toward fear, laziness, and cowardice.

The MTC days were longer than normal days and the weeks were longer than any normal weeks I had ever known. During days on the inside, the idea of completing two years of service was as far off as reaching another galaxy. So the end of three weeks came as a mighty feat, first in a line of many.

August 8, 1995. It's early in the morning. I just thought of a couple of goals. I'm not a goal setter, but just the same. Since I'm taking my books to give to the folks at the Airport I suppose I'll plan on reading the scriptures for two years.

My goals. Memorize 2 verses of scripture a week.

Read the Book of Mormon at least 5 times.

Read the New Testament at least 2 times.

Read the Doctrine Covenants at least 2 times.

Read the Old Testament at least Once.

Read the Pearl of Great Price at least once.

Read the 5 approved reading materials at least 1. I love to read. These are reading goals. My all enveloping goal is to help others feel of our Savior's love. Also learn ten new words a week. I have a dictionary! Who-HAA.

CHAPTER 13
ANOTHER BEGINNING

The Glenridge building was a standard Latter-day Saint meeting house, a shade of brown and a single story with an ample parking lot surrounding it. We pulled off the road lined by trees into a driveway running along and up a manicured sloping front lawn, following it around to the parking lot, stopping in front of the back doors amidst many compact cars with bike racks on not a few trunks, vehicles that were part of the mission fleet. Many of the missionaries chosen to train our new crop of arrivals held leadership roles as district and zone leaders, and most missionary leaders had cars, a perk not lost on the rest of the missionaries who rode bicycles, and not lost on our groups' aspirations for our trainers.

We sat in a plain room, a few pictures of the Church leaders and Jesus Christ hanging on the white walls, with recently distributed hymn books on our laps. We knew the trainers by their mature faces and confident steps in worn suits and unpolished dress shoes, and they were new to our company. They were tall, one stood like a light pole and another was mistakable as a Greek god except he moved among us. President Mensh arrived and the meeting promptly began with a hymn and a prayer. President Mensh introduced a trainer and called his trainee, a member of our district, who took his seat by his trainer, and so it went with each of us, and we closed with another hymn and a prayer.

The car moved around the winding, rising and descending road lined with trees into the suburbs of East Cobb County. Brother Bores navigated the turns as aggressively as he shook hands. He drove us north from Glenridge, passing kudzu-draped trees and others free of the parasite, moving speedily over the curvy, hilly roads to his home where we would live in a partitioned space in his basement. His white balding head and unkempt hair rose as he gracefully lifted my luggage into and out of the trunk of his old dented car. His thick, small frame complemented his large face, and he spoke few words recognizable above a mumble, offering an almost wry grin, piercing my recent proclivity toward self-pity. My new companion, a small, young elder, spoke little, hopping about with rounded shoulders. He was a district leader and smartly enlisted Brother Bores' help to save precious miles on his assigned mission car. Each mission car had monthly mileage limits based on the size of the proselytizing area. After the meeting, he acquired a bike rack from another elder, and we drove by the mission office to pick up my new Schwinn bicycle: Red and big. I had not owned a bicycle since purchasing my BMX on layaway a summer between years as a student at Stalker Elementary on West Center Street, a trek on bike from Riverton and only blocks from my Grandparent Jones' house, having owned my BMX long before Hal Needham's *Rad* (1986) and long before my siblings possessed anything as cool. Straight spine and chest out, I peddled the Schwinn in the office parking lot, leaning, braking, adjusting atop the large padded seat.

August 10, 1995. My first day as a missionary. I received many blessings. I got a good companion. He'll make a fine trainer. He's not much older than I. He has been out almost 7 months. His name is Taudrey. He is an Idaho boy. He's not too big. He's cool. We really didn't have much planned. We lucked out and got fed. We then went biking. Georgia is beautiful. The trees are beautiful. We went to a part-member family. Just to visit. We then did a follow up on a guy name Allan.

Allan is sincere. He is sincere about learning. He has good questions. I pray to God that I may be an instrument in his hands. I got among the finest of Georgia Atlanta missionaries today during the training meeting. Hierarchy means nothing to me. God is not a respecter of men. I love my Savior. Hopefully my companion and I can get to know one another over the next couple of days. I pray that I may speak through the Holy Ghost. My heart is so full. It's after eleven. I don't know if I'll ever make it to bed before 10:30. It was a good day. I was skeptical at first. I like being with just one other person. I'm that kind of person. One on one. I love to share. It wasn't long tonight, but I look forward to another. I'm all alone, yet accompanied by angels. I carry my brothers with me in my heart. When I bear testimony, I share my family, as I did last night. God bless you. I love Jesus. It's like I want to get it out all in one night. Wisdom. Keep that mirror turned around and everything will work out.

Lying on the top bunk on old but trusted-clean bedding in my holy top and bottom garments cool and exposed to the darkness seeping in from Cobb County into Brother Bores' basement I shifted sick with no fever. Enthusiastically leaving home shortly after graduating from high school and having spent desirable time away from family including most of my freshman year, not altogether partial to spending time with family except on holidays and with no best friends, I was not homesick. But I had also never been so alone. Despite my zany state caused by being directed every minute in the MTC, I hadn't felt despair there. For nights I tasted Brooks Hatlen's life in Frank Darabont's *The Shawshank Redemption* (1994), in and now outside prison, craving confinement to freedom in my solitary cloud of sadness, too, though as sure as hell was my witness I was bound never to return, the humors of my life blurring those first nights in the mission field. The poignant sadness left with sleep, and unlike Brooks I woke with a much lighter feeling and in time felt it no more.

A missionary's life was bound to his companion's and to instructions from the Missionary Guide and the Missionary Handbook. Calling it simply the Guide, missionaries practiced its lessons each morning to develop their proselytizing skills. Then there was the White Bible, the Missionary Handbook that missionaries read and practically memorized each morning to ensure they made all right actions and avoided all wrong ones. And so began my first morning with my trainer. We picked up in the Guide where the MTC left off, role-playing, one of us as the missionary and the other as the investigator and switching roles. And we read the rules, the White Bible reminded us of our divine purpose on top of what to and not to do.

I rolled up my right suit pant with my backpack straps tight, helmet secure, ready to peddle my beliefs to those in need, effortlessly sliding my leg over the padded seat to follow behind Elder Taudrey, who moved quickly onto Bryant Street leading into the beautiful green forest of East Cobb County. We rode up and we rode down. We stopped at houses Taudrey knew, and did some tracting at many more he didn't. Personally contacting people wherever we found them was the soul of missionary work, and tracting, going from house-to-house engaging people on their doorsteps, was the main activity in this suburb. Sweating in my new cotton short-sleeved white buttoned shirt, I knocked on my first door and more that day, and on many others, often getting no response, and when someone did crack a door typically getting no further than a few words of introduction before being kindly excused, sometimes not so kindly. But I began to open my mouth and share the message of the restored gospel of Jesus Christ.

August 11, 1995. Elder Taudrey is all right. Next couple of weeks and we'll be pards. He treats me as an equal. He's trying to teach me a bit. Today I took my first spill. The office missionaries who put my bike together didn't do very well. I scraped up my hands. I'm all right. This bike riding is tough. I did my first tracting. It was fun. Well, I'm turning in. I met a few new people today. Tomorrow we are scheduled to teach three lessons. I don't know what I have to do or be. I don't understand how Jesus Christ will use me. I'm going to keep trying. I'm having a tough time with prayer. There's like this barrier I can't get across. I want across.

August 12, 1995. Today I took part in teaching the 1st discussion to RW. R is something else. His wife died a couple of years ago, and he hasn't been happy since. It seems like I learn to appreciate my companion a bit more every day. He is a good kid. I've been meeting a lot of the members. There are some fine folk in East Cobb, Marietta East Zone. I need to pray and bed down. Man, I need to learn a lot. I don't know much. I'm broke. I spent some money on groceries this good day, at lunch time. Well, I'm signing off. I need to brush some pearly whites.

• • •

August 13, 1995. Today was a pretty fine day. My first Sunday in Georgia. East Cobb, Ward II. My comp gets radder (cool word eh) every day. We're getting to be pretty good friends. We've covered enough ground as it is to be friends. I had the chance to take part in the 6th discussion. Elder Taudrey, and a stake missionary, Brother Johnson (originally from Idaho, oh ya, my comp is from Idaho too. I think I've mentioned that before) and I, taught the discussion to Amanda D. Amanda will be the first person I have the opportunity to see baptized. Tomorrow morning and from then on I'll be getting up at a quarter to six. I need to start getting the first discussion memorized and then the rest. My mission is going to be a good one. It will take a while to get to know everyone but once people get to know me, shoot I'm going to have a lot of friends. Brother Bores, the landlord member who lives above Elder Taudrey and I is a great man. Well, take care. I'm going to keep learning. I just noticed, well not just, but in this journal of mine I don't paragraph things. I just keep writing from one idea to the next. Take care.

August 14, 1995. We had dinner at the Williams' tonight. Brother M Williams is the ward mission leader. He's pretty cool. During dinner I was reminded of the second "Trinity & Bambino" movie. It was a free for all. Different. I did a few pull-ups today. I feel good. Amanda has postponed her baptism. She'll go through but it won't be for this Sunday. Elder Taudrey is cool. We talked a bit today about girls. Mostly his past girl friends and one in particular that is waiting for him. Nothing too in depth. It's so green here. Trees everywhere. The roads are up and down. It was very hot today. It was a slow day. I've memorized the first and half of the second principles of the 1st discussion. Diligence. I'll keep at it. It ain't so bad. Good night or good day to you. The Book of Mormon is truly a testament of Jesus Christ. I'm enjoying reading it. I'm reading the New Testament. Good Stuff! Take it easy and be excellent to those around you.

Having completed a quarter of his mission, Elder Taudrey was a relatively young missionary to train a greenie, missionary parlance for newbie. He was a responsible elder determined to follow the "Lord's Way," a catch phrase for exact adherence to mission rules for every situation and during every minute of the day. He wanted to do what was expected of him and wanted others to see it. He wore a tight countenance to be taken seriously, quite aware of the need to overcome his young face, small size, and inexperience. He regularly repeated the mantra to work smart not just hard, and he set a goal to see that my first baptism would happen during our time as companions. Part of working smart meant working to obtain referrals from local members. Elder Taudrey worked hard to work smart in the East Cobb Second Ward.

Part of working smart included diligently arranging splits, members accompanying us in our proselytizing efforts. A true split involved two male priesthood members, one going with each missionary, splitting us to double our efforts of contacting and teaching. Getting two members to commit was not common, more often a split involved just one member driving us to and fro, serving as unofficial liaison for the local ward, more bananas with caramel than divide and conquer. We arranged splits for the coming week each Sunday at church during priesthood session, the Mormon male organization, synonymous with the Church governing and administrative authority. We also arranged for dinners for the coming week by passing out a calendar in relief society, the female organization not without its own hierarchy but devoid of priesthood authority exclusive to men. If we combined a split with dinner, we'd completed a mini triumph, and if we combined a split, dinner, and referral, we'd pulled a true coup, rare among members worn over and through from repeated missionary requests.

A member of the Quorum of the Twelve Apostles designed a program for missionaries to involve members in missionary work. He called it the set-a-date program, and its essential parts involved praying with the member family to set a date by which they would invite a nonmember friend to learn more about the Church. The success of the set-a-date program depended upon having the Spirit and applying the commitment pattern. These happened to be the keys to success of all missionary activities. Missionaries relied upon the duo in their dealings with initial nonmember contacts, investigators (those showing interest in receiving missionary lessons), members, and, annoyingly, on each other. The ubiquitous role of the Spirit was only as effective as the skills of the commitment pattern were sharp. The commitment pattern consisted of building relationships of trust, helping others feel and recognize the Spirit, presenting the message, finding out and resolving concerns, inviting others to make commitments, and following up to ensure they did. The MTC structured training around the parts of the commitment pattern as did the Guide. The first day of a missionary's life in the MTC and in The Field began by practicing commitment pattern skills and trying to apply them. Most missionaries applied the commitment pattern in parts as steps to a goal, greenies often with some trepidation and frequently seasoned missionaries by rote. Many missionaries applied the skills seamlessly, some so effective in their use of the commitment pattern that the application seemed indistinguishable from the good feelings and increased understanding associated with the presence of the Spirit, and still others so effective making the Spirit altogether unnecessary, bordering on salesman-like manipulation. We pared the commitment pattern in personal contacting, on doorsteps tracting to stay busy during the day, and amplified it when visiting members in their homes to keep busy during the evening, trying to find someone interested in learning more about the Church.

August 15, 1995. I know the purpose of missionary work is to bring souls unto Christ through the ordinances of baptism and confirmation. This is a goal one finds in the scriptures and it's laid out in the front so often. I'm going to try and obtain Christlike attributes through being more other centered and sincere. Through diligence, learning, and experience I'll develop proselytizing principles and skills.

It's morning time. The above were assignments from the Missionary Guide. I'll check back in tonight.

It is night. A few minutes to 10:30. Today was a nice day. I had the chance to go on splits this afternoon with a Bobby C. Nice guy. A convert of 1 year. He served in the Marine Corps for 4 years. Nice guy. Tonight was interesting. Not really. There was no mystery to what happened. The mission leader of the ward and his wife have little faith in my ability. My companion and I had decided how to use our splits and because I was going to teach a discussion to the mission leader's "investigator" there was a fear that I would not be competent. So, I went with brother Williams to teach a new member discussion instead. All he did was talk. I'm not expecting people to trust or respect me in just a week. But as a missionary, for only two years and such a short period of time will I stay in this area, why not let the Elder share? It's not too tough for me. I can sit silent. It's probably better that I don't say much. I don't know much so I'll just sit. But dang, some people talk too much. If nothing else, even though I want to share, I can learn just by sitting and observing. I can learn. I will learn. Give others a chance to share. Even though you may not know them. They have 10, 12, 20,

or however old they may be, years of experience and feelings that you don't have. Listen to others. Don't just talk you don't know everything. Share on what you feel, not on what you know. Everyone knows. Not everyone feels. Just keep your mirror turned around. That's all I try to do. I'll try harder. I'll try harder. There isn't a day goes by my family doesn't enter my mind. I thank God for them. I know Jesus lives. He's my elder brother. I have some fine brothers.

August 17, 1995. Shoot, I believe I missed last night. Well, anyway. Yesterday was my first P-day. That's probably why I was thrown off. I'm learning. My comp and I are getting along. Brother Bores is a great man. Well, I'm going to keep plugging along. Good day to you. Take good care of those around you.

The high of each day was reading mail. And the high of each week for me was producing it. One day a week, just as in the MTC, missionaries took a preparation day from eight to five, in many missions on Monday although in our mission on Wednesday, leaving the evening open to proselytize like the other nights of the week. Preparation day consisted of doing something different, including going into the city or visiting Civil War sites, with the president's permission to leave our area, always doing laundry, our one day to shop, rationing groceries, lots of spaghetti, baked beans, and rice from the one-hundred-plus dollars of our monthly allotment, and letter-writing.

And I wrote a lot of letters. I wrote my family at home, brothers, step-brothers, grandparents, and friends. I enjoyed writing letters, trying for phrases to match my mood and experience but motivated more by self-interest to get them to write me, knowing the more I wrote the more I would likely receive. I wrote my parents in a family letter, my brother Josh serving his own mission in Dallas, Texas, where he learned Laotian working in Lao communities, my brother Jeremy who had returned from his mission in Ventura, California, to eastern Idaho to attend Idaho State University, my brother Jami who had returned many years before from his mission in Taiwan, Taipei, and was in law school at Willamette University in Salem, Oregon, my younger brothers Jacob and Jed who were still living at home attending high school, Steve Hickey who I had been corresponding with since my family left Somerville, and others from Riverton Ward and friends from high school and freshman year at BYU. Some preparation days I spent the entire day letter-writing.

Rules prohibited writing letters on other days of the week, so the rest of the week I kept a journal. I managed frequent entries during my months in northern Georgia, typically at the end of the day sitting near an air-conditioner, trying to describe my hopes and emotions and some of the day's events.

The neighborhoods had a fair amount in common, trees and cul-de-sacs. And they were all hot and more humid than hell. We knocked on a nondescript door of a member we had prepared to use the set-a-date program having practiced our skills that morning. Elder Taudrey believed the program was a great tool. We were taught, and any missionary worth his or her salt knew, members were the best source for finding interested investigators. This member family was an interracial couple with young children. We tried hard to set an appropriate tone to invite the Spirit, but I noticed early in our attempts the father had plenty else on his mind. He responded briefly, if at all, to our questions about who among his friends would be most receptive to the gospel. In the middle of our conversation he volunteered he was out of work and didn't expect he would be much help, the weight of the world on his shoulders but still giving us time, hearing us out. Elder Taudrey, committed to show me how to do missionary work, focused on setting a time to come back to set a date as the father saw us out. Furrowing his face, pinching his eyes, slightly moving his head in disbelief, closing the door, he did not answer. He watched us leave through the screen.

Dinner appointments with members were ideal for trying to set a date. Because we didn't take any time off from being missionaries, and members knew it, they acted uncomfortably around us knowing we were going to hit them up for a referral. But they wanted so badly to be kind because they knew we were likely sitting at their dinner table after a full day's helping of unadulterated rejection, so they boldly bore their irritation. Rarely, a member, exclusively the husband, would antagonize us like the best of annoyed folks timing our steps up and back down their doorsteps. If the wife didn't want us there, she would not have signed the dinner schedule during relief society meeting on Sunday when we passed the calendar like the hungriest of vagrants outside the local supermarket raising his empty cap. Elder Taudrey wouldn't be deterred by disagreeable husbands.

Another young family with an inactive—that is, a member who didn't regularly attend church and most likely did not live in accordance with the standards of the Church—husband, tested Elder Taudrey. We walked to the front door in anticipation of dinner one beautiful evening at a house on top of a hill with a sweeping view of trees and houses hidden among them. The wife greeted us and welcomed us into the front room and excused herself as she completed dinner. The red-haired and tall husband walked in a few minutes later. Not warmly but not rudely either, he asked how we were doing, looking at me, having met Elder Taudrey, asking where I was from and how long I had been in the mission field, standard questions from active and inactive members.

After dinner Elder Taudrey requested permission to share a message, and the wife quickly agreed. Elder Taudrey proceeded to prepare the family for his invitation to set a date by which they would invite a friend, coworker, neighbor, or known breathing person to learn more about the Church. The father resisted and as Elder Taudrey persisted the father resisted more. Within minutes we moved from the father's not being willing to invite a friend to learning how his mission president had invited sister missionaries in his mission to become his spiritual wives. I did not know how to respond, but I knew encouraging him to pray to ask our Heavenly Father for a timeline and inspiration to be led to an open-minded friend had little prospect of success.

Elder Taudrey acted nobly, shifting gears to bearing his testimony about our work and the truthfulness of the Church, as much for the distraught and embarrassed wife as in defense of our purpose. Interesting mission stories came up in our mission, elders going to clubs, unsanctioned sporting events, and movie theaters, but the stories were not as unbelievable as the ones told by members about their own missions. Missionaries were young men and women bound to make a few mistakes, and I learned that even mission presidents were too.

August 18, 1995. It's about 12:30. We just got done with service. We stack books. We spend a lot of our time in the children's section of the library. I decided to start writing down books that I will one day read to my children and my children will read to me. This first list is just a start.
[Inserted paper]
Tikki Tikki Tembo retold by Arlene Mosel
Hansel and Gretel
Dr. Seuss
The Giving Tree by Shel Silverstein
Where the Wild Things Are by Maurice Sendak

Crow Boy by Taro Yashima

The Little Red Hen

Alexander and the Terrible, Horrible, No Good, Very Bad Day by Judith Viorst

I was just reading my dad's last letter. I don't think I wrote his thought down. The letter was written on the 4th of August. He says "The covenant is so very much more potent than we have any idea of. Remembering our Savior and having his Spirit (his peace) is so real that it is over looked. It's too simple. Looking to the Brazen Serpent was too simple!" He also gave me a scripture. Psalms 46: 10 "Be still, and know that I am God." Just relax.

The day was long today. We didn't do much. It's hot here in Georgia. Even though we mostly drive, the heat still ways on me. Well, I'm going to plug away at the work. I had the chance to share with my companion why I don't believe in expectations and one thing and another. Put off self. That's what I'm trying to do. That is all.

August 19, 1995. It's tough. I'm getting to know my companion well enough. He is a nice guy and all but I fear we will never click. I've spoken a couple of times and I fear I've intimidated him. He wants to be in control. It's important now that he points out everything I do wrong in a pointing out way. He is a good kid. He's just pretty young. We will get along fine. I won't offend him. It's too bad. I was hoping for a real compadre. Dang, he is just so young. He is naïve. An investigator depicted the Persian Gulf War to him like some holocaust and he believes it straight up. He gives me a chance and what not, but he is so inexperienced he feels I am who he was months ago and that I will learn everything as he has. He's cute, I guess you could say. Besides being from Idaho there is not more we have in common. He likes to talk a great deal. He's cool and all but it's tough for me. It isn't tough to sit back and say nothing. But the situation is tough. He's just never had any experience before the old mission. He comments on me not being able to deal with certain types of people or what not. Says I need to personalize the discussions. Dang, I wish I had someone real. Before his mission he never did more than worry about his hair or whether or not he had enough rusty attire. Missions do funny things for people. The situation I fear gives them a false sense of being. My trainer hopes to be a great leader. He hopes to be a master missionary in a couple

192 MY BEST MORMON LIFE

more months. Tonight at the dinner appointment he told the young couple he is on the road of being a "stripling warrior" missionary. Whatever that is. I'm sorry this entry was so negative. I have a great deal of patience though. I'll survive. I'm praying for a lot of double splits. That's all I'm praying for. Take care and be nice. Even though I've written all this, but I still would never intentionally offend. I'll hold my tongue. I'll persevere. I'll keep my focus. Jesus lives.

CHAPTER 14
COWBOYING UP

Ten days into the mission field I was in for the test of my life, when my positive aspirations met a brick wall of reality. Over the next many weeks I found peace in writing and reading letters and in the children's section of the county library. Twice a week, two hours at a time, we stacked books, and I learned on my first service assignment the books checked out most often were children's books selected by committed mothers reading to their young children. Their dedication was our justification for the community weekly good deed of putting books back on shelves for other hopeful mothers.

Our mission president required missionaries to do four hours of community service each week, volunteering at hospitals, nursing homes, food banks, and various community centers, the variety of which I would experience as commitments in my assigned areas and as I moonlighted on companionship splits with other missionaries in their areas over the next two years. The only services during which I recall having no interaction with any people was at the library, my first months serving with Elder Taudrey, and no service did I like more. I enjoyed sorting, hauling, and stacking books. And I didn't mind not having to talk to my companion for a couple of hours. I looked forward to discovering familiar titles and thumbing through pages of books I knew from my own childhood. Twice a week I relived a positive part of my earlier life.

Young mothers passed by us as we read numbers to return our pile of books, and as they looked around for appropriate titles. I worked at a bookshelf chest-high, slowly returning books, distracted by the titles I couldn't resist pulling off, leafing through their pages. A mother intent on finding a book for her young child at her side, carrying her newborn in a sturdy car seat, moved behind me. The library-frequenting mothers knew they had a window of cooperation to get in, find some books, and get out before the library's silence broke, to their child's credit. This mother worked the bookshelves in my section as her window closed on her allotted calm. The child at her side was pressing for attention as she set her newborn on top of the bookshelf and moved with her child to retrieve books. Moments passed and we turned around at the shriek of her newborn, the car seat having fallen four feet to the ground. The baby's screams were heart-stopping, and her mother, in terror, reached to the floor to pick up her baby. Holding her baby tight to her body while the screams continued, she sheepishly warded off persons offering help, not once revealing the cause of the baby's fit, the secret we shared. Staring, I said not a word, sick for the young mother, picking up the remaining books of the pile as I moved out of the section.

My mother encouraged her sons to do two things: read books and to keep their mirrors turned around, or not to be self-centered, selfish, and all about me. The mirror metaphor implied one thing—you were not always looking at yourself. Seeing the back of a mirror did not mean one would be other-centered, altruistic, and compassionate: all far too ambitious goals given her projects. She just asked you simply to succeed at being focused on anything, hell the back of a dirty mirror casing would do, other than you. She also advocated for developing mature personalities with the frequency but minus the zeal of my father's profession in Jesus' influence. She explained we would do best to resist our initial response, relying upon the popular Transactional Analysis of the Sixties. The analysis used a model of Parent/Adult/Child to accurately describe how people acted. In this model, parents were essentially grown-up children acting selfishly on learned behaviors. The goal was to act like an adult: dispassionate, reasoned, and responsible. After years of advocating the model and weighing the possibility of whether any of her family could ever fit into the category of adult, even temporarily, she must have resigned herself they never would.

Jeremy recalled on numerous occasions finding our mother in a room by herself, broken down in tears. The surprise was that she had any moments of sanity. For one, I didn't succeed in keeping my mirror turned around during her lifetime, and haven't since it ended. One morning, years before she died, she struggled to get me to behave, exasperated and honestly declaring that if she had known she would have to help my dad run his business, cook, clean and keep up the house and rear six boys, she would not have had so many of us. In less frustrated moments, she conceded she had the last three, starting with me, determined to have a daughter so her angry declaration was not without truth. But what was unequivocally true was the effect we, the collective six—and no one son more than me—had on her.

That effect resonated with me when I witnessed the bewildered and helpless young mother cradling her fallen newborn in the library. The comparison seems off-kilter, and likely I would need to multiply the newborn's blunt fall by six to appreciate what my mother experienced, regularly. Children certainly have the right to complain about their circumstances, of which I've always been most capable of and willing to do, having entered them beyond any choice of their own, but the disappointment and failure are no less felt in a well-intentioned parent, and surely amplified. My mother experienced days after days of frustration unsettled too by sounds like the shrieks I fled to a different wing of the library.

August 20, 1995. It's about 5 o'clock. Sunday was nice. I need a boost. I really do. I wrote a letter this morning to my dad, but I just ripped it up. He doesn't need to hear my sob story. Heavens, it isn't that bad here. I'm going to be all right. I miss my family. I truly do miss them. Well, I'll enter a bit more tonight. I just read my dad's last letter to me. I'm going to relate the last page. It gave me a brightness of hope.

"It seems to me that however philosophical we may wax, however intricate our thought process may become, or however extensive our information bank, it all comes down to a simple solitary soul whose power, peace, and freedom are the only true source of happiness."

He goes on to write "Ezra Taft Benson asked the question, 'Why is it expedient that we center our confidence, our hope, and our trust in one solitary figure?' The more I learn to center my heart and mind on Jesus, the more peace I feel in my life. They wouldn't look to the brazen serpent because of the simpleness of the way! It's the same today. 'Remembering him always' is so simple that it is a mystery. So we forfeit the peace, power, and freedom that could otherwise be ours." My dad rocks. I love the man with my whole soul.

August 21, 1995. Today was my first zone conference. It was a nice day. It was good to learn and reinforce things taught in the MTC. I had a nice day.

It's getting late. I need the sleep so I'll sign off. Today was a good day. The mission ward leader once again surprised me. Oh boy, it's going to be a couple of interesting months.

August 22, 1995. Today was another day. Pretty profound, eh. I received a couple letters from Sister S and my good brother Jeremy. They were fine letters. I received a phone call from an alias "Ryan Morrison" last night. It was a great to hear Jami's voice. I love that guy. I'm going to be an o.k. missionary. I like meeting new people. I'm getting to know the members. Tonight I met the Billings family. They are good people.

I'm getting into the New Testament. I love learning about Jesus' life. It's time well spent.

Tonight my split was Bro Harrison. The guy just poured out some serious stuff tonight. I think it may just be that name tag I wear, but he told me about his wife leaving him with their kids. He just went into detail. I just sat there. Poor guy. Some people have it mighty rough. They're strong people. Bro Harrison is a strong person.

This is a busy week. I had the chance to teach a first discussion to Sam Gill. He is a good man. My comp told me not to bring up latter-day prophets before he started to talk about them. I don't know. He is a nice guy. He is really surface though. He uses "The Lord's Way" as a title too often. It has no meaning. They use this title here, at least my comp & the Mission President (the only two people I've heard), to quell any questions. It seems like things are caught up in showy stuff. My companion is crazy about splits. He isn't concerned with members when we talk about it but his actions are the contrary. I'm going to turn in. Tomorrow is the second preparation day. I have many a letter to write tomorrow. Hopefully I'll get to my journal, that is the paper that this pen is gracing at this time with its beautiful ink. Take care. I love my family. Getting letters from them makes everything worth it. They bring me closer to my Savior. Because I know that I am loved.

August 24, 1995. I'm not sure what it is with P-day, but I forget all about writing in this journal. This journal has a scent about it. I am not sure if it's good or bad.

I'm going to be honest. I'm not sure what I'm doing here. I'm presently listening to my companion talk with another missionary. Off "the plan" music is the subject. My companion believes in blessings coming and blessings not coming. He knows a lot? I'm confused because we go on so many splits. We are concerned with doing so much to go beyond a standard. I'm having a hard time with the focus. Maybe my focus is off, I don't know.

Tonight I went on splits with Bro Williams and a Bro Bishop. The latter works for the military. He has been a lot of places. He is working on a masters at Georgia Tech. He has an undergraduate degree in aerospace engineering. He is pretty bright.

I'm yet to receive a job well done from anyone yet. I almost got that from brother Williams after we had visited an investigator and his sister. His sister didn't see the need for organized religion. She also wasn't sure there is a God. I said a little bit. I regretted it afterward. But Brother Williams said I had said some good things. Maybe I had and maybe I did not. I don't know.

Things are well with my companion. He was concerned yesterday morning that I was not taking his "constructive" criticism as he would like me to. We talked. Whether we got anywhere I'm not too sure, but we talked.

I'm not looking for a pat on the back. I'm just hoping someone will have the same focus as myself and we will have an understanding. I liked sharing this evening.

At service today, at the library, I copied down a couple titles of children books as I had down on previous occasions. I'll leave this list in this page.

[Inserted paper]
The Wayward Bus (The only Big Kid Book) by John Steinbeck

Miss Nelson is Back by Harry Allard
Curious George books by H.A. Rey
The Story of Little Black Sambo by Helen Bannerman
Casey up to Bat by ...
The Biggest Bear by Lynd Ward
Corduroy by Freeman

As we walked out my companion asked me why I did that. I tried to explain. I've come to realize we will possibly never click. I hope for good experiences but we will never be great friends. He said "You will catch the vision, I'm convinced of that." My list making is not a good thing? One thing I know. I have vision. It's hard not being able to share it. But I can only see though my eyes. I do see. I thank God for that.

I received a letter, actually three today. I think this entry will be the first I actually write my father's comment on the day I received the letter. The letter is dated the 19 of August. He doesn't give a thought this time but rather relates a scripture. He does say before the scripture "It is He (his grace) that does the saving!" The scripture he gives is "And under this head ye are made free. And here is no other head whereby ye can be made free. There is no other name given whereby salvation cometh." Mosiah 5: 7,8.

Take care. Remember that Jesus considers us family if we come unto him. "For whosoever shall do the will of God, the same is my brother, and my sister, and mother" (St. Mark 3: 35). I am His brother. My brothers are my best friends. I think of them often!

August 26, 1995. It is 9:30 A.M. We are cleaning the apartment for an inspection. We are giving blood in a couple hours. It will be a nice Saturday! I have never given a whole pint of blood.

This weekend is Stake Conference. Since I am an adult I'll be attending the session tonight along with tomorrow's session.

It has been pretty nice weather these past couple days. It has rained off and on. There has been an overcast a good part of the time. It is not so hot when this happens here in Marietta Georgia.

Well, I will get back to the pen & paper this evening perhaps. Hopefully I gain something tonight that gives me a bit of inspiration. I will just have to wait and hope for the best. Until then, Good life and happy steps may indeed make up your being.

The blood giving experience was a not-so-good experience. I'm turning it into a positive. I hope my blood tests well. I worry about these kinds of things.

I heard an outstanding talk given by Elder Hill of the 1st Quorum of the Seventy this evening in the stake conference. He talked of seeing, actually seeing the glory of God. Not just the ceremony or the things of man. It was a great talk. I learned a great deal. He spoke of experience. He shared scripture and why they were important to him. I haven't enjoyed a talk from one so high up in quite some time. It's not that I even go away angry or with an attitude that general authorities are wrong. It's just a matter of hearing truly moving talk where the individual speaks from the heart not some list of answers.

Take care. I'll try and do the same. I've come to realize I need to keep my mirror turned around. The WuWei. I've got to quit fighting the situation and just go with it. My comp shouldn't have to be something he is not. I'm accepting him for who he is and it seems to help my attitude. Things are well. I am way too blessed. Later.

August 27, 1995. I enjoyed stake conference today. Elder B. Fallon Hill is my favorite general authority. He is a real human being. I really like the man. He is a great man.

Well, I enjoyed today. I'll be honest with you. By now the reader (you) of this journal knows I am one to complain ONCE in a while. Well, maybe more than not. I wonder how the reader (you) will perceive me? I can't imagine that who I am can be inferred from my words on the paper I've written upon. Well, anyhow I've taken some time, hopefully you had nothing else to do.

Differences are sometimes the real part of my life. In real situations. I've come to realize my companion and I will end up being good acquaintances. But we are too different. I love to listen and to share. This is no existent. Being "happy" that is with a smile and go get-um attitude is not my style. I have never been in this sort of situation before. Two years. Oh my heavens. Will I make it? Hold my tongue. I've brought to mind the scripture found in the 7th chapter of Matthew, verse 6. I can't be superficial but I need to quit casting my pearls. I have been these past weeks. I want to be appreciated just like anyone else. I have so many who love me. I'll just hold it from the dogs. All will be well.

I hope when my day comes I will be referred to as "most excellent theophilus." If Theophilus was indeed a real person what a person. I hope to be a "Theophilus." Truly I do. I love my God. I love his son, my elder brother. And I love my family.

August 30, 1995. Today is preparation day. Our splits are suppose to be here in 15 minutes. I thought I might write a few words. Last night was my latest night thus far during my missionary life. A member of the ward left around midnight after fixing the air-conditioner. Brother Don Carson. He is a good man. Today I accomplished many things. I wrote my family, Jami & Traci, Aaron, Ed Griggs, and Ryan Morrison, Cara & Pete, and a missionary friend Jim P. We went to Kennesaw. This was the first time we did anything on P-day that had to do with getting away from our area. We went to the Big Shanty Museum. There was a lot of civil war memorabilia there. The "General" is in this museum. This locomotive was the object of great excitement in 1862. Some union spies stole it and there was a great chase. The best part of the day was getting to spend time with an Elder Anselm. He is Elder Johnsons', the zone leader, companion. We met them at the museum and then all went to the mall. Elder Anselm is a good person. Talking with him was a great chance to let things off my chest. It wasn't like speaking to my companion. This kid has some experience. He was just someone I could talk with. It was a blessing to me.

Well, I am off to teach the 3rd discussion in a few minutes to one, RW, A 48-year-old man who lost his wife a couple years ago. He is a pretty good person. I enjoy taking part in teaching the discussions to him. Take care and God bless you.

When my brothers started riding bulls my father started fighting them. In his mid-forties he learned like other novices, attending schools, working amateur shows, and studying tape, but unlike most of his bull fighting peers he got into ironman shape. He surmised that, since he would be in the arena for Jeremy and Josh's rides, he might as well dress the part and be in a position to really help, so when they attended bull riding schools he attended with them, as a student bull fighter. They all attended all-around professional cowboy champion Lyle Sankey's school, my father spending each evening soaking in the tub after getting trampled on the first day. Every bull rider gets run over by a bull during his career, and bull fighters do too, and my father completed that rite at the school long before he fought at his first show. He took physical fitness seriously his entire life, and his commitment increased when he began putting on cleats, and hip and rib pads, to step between bulls and the riders. He bought a treadmill and put thousands of miles on its belt and motor, and reintroduced free weights into his long-time dips and pull-up workout routines. A forty-year-old bull fighter was an anomaly. Heavens there was probably a fifty-year-old fighting bulls at shows somewhere in the badlands of South Dakota, but we didn't know of anyone close to fifty except Pops fighting them in Idaho.

His first official shows were as one of the bull fighters at junior rodeos where Jeremy and Josh got their starts traveling around small Idaho towns during the summers during junior high and early high school. Rodeo people knew our name as much for the old bull fighter as the young bull riders. My father's life as dentist by day and bull fighter on Saturday afternoons during the spring and summer reached its culmination at two professional events, the Professional Old Timers Rodeo Association show in Blackfoot two summers in a row. The Blackfoot arena was home to the Intermountain Professional Rodeo Association finals at the Eastern Idaho State Fair in September of each year, the IMPRA a tier just below the PRCA Wilderness Circuit. It was also home to a lot of fair events, including country and heavy metal concerts, with nothing in between. You were either a Chris LeDoux or Iron Maiden fan or neither, but you were not something else because there was no something else. No either-or dichotomy had starker application than the music selections enjoyed on those wooden bleachers. I saw my first concert there, the Nitty Gritty Dirt Band, mouthing lines to "Fishing in the Dark," a song so well known I didn't know I had memorized it.

The legendary Montanan Ronnie Rawson entered the Old Timers Show at Blackfoot both years my father fought it. Rawson was legendary not merely for his two bull-riding world titles won in the Sixties or for the seven bull-riding titles won on the senior tour, but also for the fifty-three-year-old's being the epitome of tough. He broke his jaw his first year at the National Finals Rodeo, had it wired and continued competing, and his career followed suit. For generations of bull riders, Rawson was synonymous with the meaning to "cowboy up."

He arrived at the show in Blackfoot banged up, years of injuries having made him more cautious. He drew the bull Tressbraker, a powerful brindle, one of the stock contractor's rankest. He inquired about the bull, and the contractors assured him he would be fine as numerous high school kids had been on him. Rawson had been in the game long enough to know stock contractors had common interests with bull riders but not the same interests. Both wanted a bull that would buck, but the rider wanted one that would result in a high score and the contractor wanted one to eject and trample the rider for good measure. Contractors cared about their bulls, and few cared about bull riders.

When the owners of the infamous Charolais bull Bodacious retired him after he caused horrific injuries to multiple bull-riding world champion Tuff Hedeman and long-time professional Scott Breeding, they explained the reason was to avoid being labeled as contributing to the death of a bull rider but not because Bodacious could kill a bull rider, which he was hellbent on doing. The white leviathan developed a hop-skip that brought numerous bull riders down on his head, a move designed to deliver a knockout blow. Looking for an objective view, Rawson asked my father what he thought about Tressbraker. Never shy to tell the truth despite backlash, my father told Rawson plenty of high school bull riders had got on but he never saw one ride him, adding he was the rankest in the pen. Rawson turned out that night. The contractor confronted my father, beside himself with anger a bull fighter would think it his job to dissuade a bull rider from getting on one of his bulls. Providing bulls that buck and the safety of bull riders is a contradiction too few contractors have ever been able to get their heads around, and while not the only ones, an unpardonable failing. A few contractors got it, and those enjoyed membership in eternal bull rider brotherhood.

The next summer Rawson climbed on and won the bull riding at Blackfoot. He fell off in front of the bull's head, and my father moved in between the bull and Rawson, diverting the bull's attention and averting a likely trampling. A small framed picture of Rawson hatless and balding at fifty-four, sprawled on the ground beneath the bull with my father in full bull fighter's attire reaching for the bull's head sits next to the unchristened silver beer mug commemorating my father's commission as an officer in the Marine Corps. They are nestled among other mementos and nearly hidden in his closet. Saving Rawson was his job, nothing special but extraordinary.

Bull riders knew Rawson because he was tough, but they also knew him because of his character, central to one of the most well known stories of rodeo lore. Rawson ran a bull riding school like many former world champions, and a young boy was killed there. Rawson sold all that he had, gave it to the boy's family, and hit the road, leaving many to speculate the boy's death was the reason for his inimitable extended bull riding career. A month after winning the Blackfoot show Rawson made another winning ride at an Old

Timer's show in Rock Ford, Colorado. He dismounted, and the bull kicked him in the chest. Two hours later Rawson died. Few lived like Rawson doing what they loved for so long and doing it the best.

The Blackfoot Fair Grounds, home to the Eastern Idaho State Fair held every year in early September, sat on the west of Main Street directly north of Martha's Restaurant (and a half-mile north of the Potato Museum) and directly southwest of the stock sale across the tracks on Rich Lane. The arena, home to rodeos, concerts, the demolition derby, and horse races, sat not quite in the middle of the fair grounds but was its epicenter, with food booths offering anything from tiger ears to cotton candy sprawling before its entrance and a beer garden to the far west of the eateries. Prominent among the food booths and a few feet from the center entrance into the arena sat my great grandparents Thomas and Estella Jones in lawn chairs for every year of my childhood. We headed to their spot, no one else sitting in the vicinity, to say hello for a hug and a dollar, chief among all fair experiences.

Behind my great grandparents rose a vast green wood wall and entrance into a tunnel with bleachers rising up both sides leading to a fenced, elliptical arena with freshly groomed dirt. The bleachers faced bucking chutes, with the announcer's booth above them. The first act of the fair was the IMPRA finals, held the first two nights, always sellout shows. I never bought a ticket. If Jeremy or Josh didn't have an extra free companion pass they knew a bull rider who did. Josh entered the finals near the top of the standings, having secured rookie-of-the-year honors the summer before his senior year. At the state high-school finals he placed outside the qualifying spots to return to Shawnee, Oklahoma, for the national high-school finals, but made up for any disappointment by making more trips to the pay window at IMPRA shows than any teenager had the right to expect. Jeremy returned to riding bulls at IMPRA shows late in the summer after a devastating wreck in the spring, early in the high school season. For his senior campaign, Jeremy added the event of bareback riding to his repertoire of bull riding and steer wrestling to make his trifecta attempt at winning an all-around title. He returned for his senior year as the defending divisional bull riding champion, having bypassed a return trip to the regional championships in Panguitch, Utah, and its dismal judging, for paying events the preceding summer. Despite his thin frame, he was a top steer wrestler, and he had ridden broncs so his bid for an all-round title was realistic. Bareback riding opens a rodeo, and Jeremy started the season and ended it under the belly of a horse, his left knee kicked and for months immobile, missing his senior year atop bulls and tossing steers. He went to all the high school rodeos, upright on crutches, religiously limping to the physical therapy tent each weekend. I followed like he was going behind the chutes to prepare for a ride but headed for more certain pain at the hands of trainers.

I sat in the bleachers facing the bucking chutes. I could see Josh sitting on the bull setting his rope. Next to me sat a friend of Jami's, Ryan, a former missionary companion from Salt Lake City. He had never attended a rodeo but heard plenty about bull riding and Jami's singing praises of Jeremy and Josh. He looked anxious and unsure if he should cheer or hold his breath. For years since my first rodeo I opted for holding my breath for run-on prayers from when the bulls ran into the chutes to my brothers' running from the arena. I never made a more sincere plea to God throughout my life than for God's help to keep them safe, and if it humored him to help them ride well.

The chute-help popped the gate and swung it open and a large black bull lunged out with Josh fixed on it. The bull lunged from side to side without committing to turn back, not spinning (a bull that spins is hard to ride and fun to watch and more likely to produce a high score), fading to the right then making a strong move to the left that whipped Josh down onto the bull's head, knocking him silly, if not out. His body fell to the right with his left hand still in his rope. A bull rider with his hand caught in the rope was said to be hung up. Damn accurate. No bull rider wanted to be hung up, but when he was the foremost rule was to stay on his feet.

Half unconscious, Josh flipped atop the bull to his side. The bull threw his head back hitting Josh's flimsy body, Josh slipped under the bull, and the bull's strong hooves stepped over and over Josh's body. The bull fighters leapt onto the bull trying to free Josh's hand, one moving in on the bull and twirling around with only a second to reach for Josh's tied hand before the back end of the bull swung around and bounced him off to the ground.

My father jumped over the chutes and headed at the bull, jumping at its back for Josh's hand, but bouncing off unsuccessful like the others. An eternity of seconds passed with the bell on Josh's bull rope heard deep into the sky when a chute-helper jumped on Josh's tied arm, wrenching it from the rope and bull. Josh lay in the arena for minutes until the medics carted him away to an ambulance headed to the hospital.

Physically shaken, Ryan said nothing. I did not recognize his countenance. I had not seen complete concern, fear and defeat before. I told him Josh would be all right but nothing reassured him, and he did not respond. He had seen the wreck for himself, and Josh was something but not what I said, and he knew it and I did not.

I sat curled on a bench in the lounge looking into Josh's hospital room. All hospitals had the same effect on me, wanting out and wanting it badly. A drape hid his bed from the open door, and my father sat at the end of the bed with his cowboy hat on a vacant chair. I couldn't hear him as he rose whenever a doctor or nurse entered the room. Josh had not competed in rodeo his freshman year after suffering a concussion, but he spent the season preparing for his next ride by watching a lot of videos and going to many bull ridings.

Josh was deft, with a quick first step, and succeeded at basketball and football. In his junior year he started as free safety on the varsity football team that made it to the state semifinals against Jake Plummer's Capital High School, our school's deepest run in the football playoffs in decades. Josh's athleticism aided him when every movement on top a bull mattered, staying up with each jump, twist, and dip, keeping in sync with the bull's momentum. The slightest movement behind a jump or twist or dip could be a costly mistake. And, even though a bull rider did everything right, he was still at the mercy of forces beyond his control. I could not tell what happened this time.

Josh faded in and out of consciousness hung up on the bull's back, and had recovered consciousness before we reached the hospital, but then he continually fainted when he tried to rise and leave it. So they admitted him for the night. The doctors discovered broken ribs when he arrived, but did not discover until the following morning that the ribs had ruptured his spleen, this delay causing some concern about internal bleeding. He spent the next few nights in the intensive care unit and returned home the next week.

Josh's first night in ICU, Jeremy healed from his injury earlier that spring, then filled in for Josh the second night of the IMPRA finals. Whether Jeremy was next in line to qualify for the finals and by rights got to ride, or the organizers simply made the right choice by granting his request to ride, he got on Josh's draw. The bull bucked hard and Jeremy stuck on making a great ride to a chorus of cheers reaching the hospital a few blocks away where I sat spending the evening.

Football practice began without Josh his senior year, the season passed without him, and it was doubtful he would play basketball in the fall, but he surprisingly made the basketball team then a few weeks later quit. Unlike other high school athletes, Josh's time on the court was not as important as his pride on the side of it or his time off of it. Team players are unselfish and committed to any role to win, qualities measured in play, not watching. High school coaches often meant well but their best argument for teamwork too often amounted to high-top cheerleading with doses of locker-room and bus-ride camaraderie, amounting at its best to temporary emotional diversions from TV and video games, and not establishing habits for a fit life.

I opted for avoiding the illusory value of teamwork for the constant thwarting of self-improvement and self-confidence in wrestling, where I managed just to avoid wilting. But, unlike the herd and lost souls like me, Josh had better ways to spend his time than wasting it or having it waste him. He bypassed going out for basketball his sophomore year because he wouldn't play for the coach, a predictable goofball he had butted heads with earlier in the year in football. He was a rare teenager, what every teenager wanted to be, autonomous but also wise. When he didn't play his senior year behind less skilled players, he walked.

The rodeo high-school season rolled around and Josh still had not returned to form, but you wouldn't know it talking to him. He smiled his usual confidence and climbed on every bull like he had already ridden him and only had to go through the motions. He and Jeremy attended numerous bull-riding schools and none suited them more than Gary Leffew's in Nipomo, California. Leffew talked their positive language and emphasized attitude as an essential skill. For years, they had spent time studying the best bull riders and visualizing their own rides, practices advocated by Leffew.

Josh's formidable attitude and dismal performance his senior year unsettled me. He knew better than anyone else he was not performing as he had but it didn't affect him. I felt like defending him despite no known accusers. Compounding his poor performances were injuries. He took steps to mitigate them by wearing a rib guard, stiffening his torso but limiting his fluid style, and switching riding hands from his left to his right. No one knows more than a bull rider playing a sport hurt leaves him more vulnerable, and Josh got more hurt into the season. After an unsuccessful attempt, launched early, Josh exited the arena behind the chutes at the American Falls arena. I stood near Josh as he unwound his bull rope, cleaned it with a steel brush and placed it with his other gear into his duffle bag, offering no excuse, coolly shaking his head, disappointed and already talking about what he would do different on the next ride. He took off his shirt and removed his rib pad revealing a pouch of fluid at the base of his spine half the size of a baseball. He sent me in search of ice, the surest remedy for every ailment.

The division finals were at the Blackfoot Fair Grounds Arena. The competition was not as stiff in years past, and Josh made enough rides to be near the top of the standings, needing to ride in the final round to win the district. He started his ride out of position and out of pure try rode the second half on the side. Not showy, he won. He returned to the state finals for his third time but for the first time didn't make the short go-around where the top ten riders compete based on the combined scores of their first two rides. But all contestants were guaranteed a third bull. Josh had ridden one of his first two bulls and rode his third bull the night before the short-go, and after all the bull riders bucked off the following day he ended up in fourth place, filling the final spot to return to the high school national finals in Gillette, Wyoming.

Weeks later we arrived at the rodeo arena in Murray, Utah, as they loaded horses into the chutes for the first section of bareback riding. Bull riders competed at the end of the rodeo, so arriving on time never meant early. Murray was a straight shot down Interstate 15 about three hours from Blackfoot. Josh unlocked the trunk and grabbed his gear bag from the old red Ford car my father bought from our great grandmother Jones when she quit driving a few years earlier. It ran great directed by a steering wheel with exceptional play, sporting a few notable dents from light poles, cement blocks, and cars that wouldn't get out of Grandma Jones' way when she backed out of parking lots or pulled into them, which had inspired her children to negotiate the sale.

My first rodeo in a cowboy hat and boots I stepped out the other side of old red. Only cowboys in hat and boots could go behind the chutes, and if I aimed to pull Josh's rope like he'd asked me to I had to dress the part. We walked past holding pens of horses and bulls through the smell of fresh manure to an open space of gear bags neatly spread on the ground with saddles and riggings nearby, and bull ropes tied to and stretched from the top of corral panels. Josh dropped his gear bag in an empty space and headed behind the chutes into the crowd of cowboys, many in groups conversing, a few stretching and walking on a line, others in motion shadow-riding, getting their minds and bodies tuned to the job at hand. I hung back trying to get used to the heels on the boots, fidgeting in my tight Wranglers between straight legs and slightly bent ones, spitting in the dust immediately groomed by the toe of my boot. The stands were packed and it felt like a pro show, Josh's first. He had a few weeks before the national finals in Gillette; having purchased his PRCA permit he planned to fill it starting in Murray.

The rodeo ran swiftly from one event to another to the first section of the bull riding, unlike the many high school and amateur rodeos I had seen. The bulls ran the length of the chutes and hands closed the gates behind them. Josh drew a huge brindle that was in the first chute. He nodded that direction, and I followed, jumping up to the ledge behind the chute after him. He swung himself over the inside bar and sat his knees on the back of the bull and slowly placed his legs behind its shoulders and lifted the ends of his chaps onto his thighs. He dropped the lope in his rope on the right side and directed me grab a wire hanging near me with a hook to jump over the chute and to the ground to hook his rope and pull it across the chest of the bull. I brought the rope to the bar that separated me from the bull and slowly brought it up as Josh reached below and grabbed it. He ran the tail of the rope he was holding on the right side of the bull through the loop. Letting the loop drop back down the side of the bull, he pulled the tail until the handle set in the middle of the bull's back. He shifted the handle down the left side, marking its placement by his left pinky finger on the bull's spine. He tied a loose knot and rose, careful to keep his spurs from touching the bull. He jumped off the chute and began to loosen up, moving his torso in controlled spins, his chaps kicking up as he set his heels.

Jimmy Young, not far off, threw up from an empty stomach. Jimmy's older brother Dustin had won the PRCA Wilderness Circuit multiple times, placing at the Dodge National Finals Rodeo in Pocatello, Idaho, back when only one show was bigger, the PRCA Finals in Las Vegas, years before the TV-driven PBR bonanza. Dustin walked among Tuff Hedeman, Jim Sharp, Clint Branger, the best of the era, and rode as well as they did. He made the finals at the Calgary Stampede one year, a feat so great it had no equal among any mortals we knew. The Young brothers were legends in Eastern Idaho. Josh revealed that Jimmy's throwing up was nothing new as he did it before every ride. He was the only other bull rider I knew at the Murray show, unlike other shows where I knew about everyone because about everyone knew Josh and Jeremy, and I had never seen a bull rider so obviously scared, and all the ones I'd seen previously had been amateurs. Jimmy was a champion, too.

Among the many bull riding tapes Jimmy gave Josh was the college national finals where Jimmy ended up head-to-head against Ty Murray in the championship coming down to the final ride. Like a champ Jimmy rode, but Ty made a finer ride, winning the title. Through Jimmy we knew of Ty's prowess in the sport of rodeo long before he won his first PRCA all-around title and emerged as America's most famous Wrangler-wearing cowboy since the Marlboro man. Jimmy went on to place second two more times at the college national finals rodeo. Seeing Jimmy compete against Murray caused me to well up with pride second only to seeing Jimmy's wild ride captured on the front cover of the *PRCA Rodeo News*, the definitive print medium pre-Internet, the ride that won him the final big show of the summer at the Ellensburg Rodeo.

Josh hopped back on the chute, directing me again to jump to the other side to pull his rope. I moved quietly behind him and stood a few panels down, bracing my shins against the top of the chute for leverage. I pulled the rope and stopped at his signal. He moved the rope up the back of the bull, setting it perfect and told me to pull more, and I pulled and I pulled. He took the tail from me and wrapped it around his hand, threading the tail through his pinky, laying the tail high across the bull's back. He slid his hips up with his thighs on top of the rope running down the bull's sides. He nodded and called for him.

The bull kicked high and made a few big jumps, then turned back bucking parallel to the chutes, covering little ground with fierce, power kicks. The horn blew at eight seconds with Josh tightly in control. He rode and the judges gave him high points, so he left the arena that night with nothing short of the bull rider's quip of the eternal present, having "win" him a second at his first pro show. I knew that with that ride the world had turned back to normal, but driving home Josh wouldn't have noticed it had ever been off kilter. I didn't make the trip to Gillette but Josh made it to the short-go in third place after riding his first two bulls before another brindle (notoriously bad draws being hard to ride and not typically spinners) bucked him off. Another Mormon, Arizonan Cody Hancock, competed at Gillette. Hancock and Josh crossed some of the same trails in the years ahead, Hancock winning a PRCA world title at the turn of the new century. Featured among Eastwood, Brynner, and McQueen in the living room hangs a framed picture of Josh in Gillette, the bull's front hooves deep in the dirt rolling its body to the side with Josh gritting his teeth, bearing down, making a ride he did, while standing behind the chute between gray and black dressed bull riders, chute help, and cowboys in an all white shirt and cowboy hat with his arms raised looking on is my father.

• • •

August 31, 1995. Last day of August. It has been a pretty nice day. Missionary work is sure slow during the day.

A split (stake missionary) is suppose to be here any minute so I'll more than likely continue this entry tonight. I received a letter from Josh and my dad. I shall share a couple thoughts by each of them.

Today district meeting occurred. I had a chance to chat with an Elder Thompson from Orem, Utah, for about an hour after district meeting. His companion was passing off a discussion to mine. Elder Thompson (I'm not sure how he spells his name. There may be a 'U' in there) goes home this next Wednesday the 6th. We had a good talk. He shared his mission with me. He was very honest. He wished he would have kept a journal throughout, more than anything. This was his one real regret. I hope to keep my thoughts throughout these next couple years. I really do. We are both admirers of Steinbeck. That hour made my day. Elder Thompson is a great guy. It was hard for me talking with him. I miss my family and long to see them. He is going home. I wouldn't mind the same. Sure my time will come soon enough. When I say hard I don't mean communicating and what not. Just the fact that he is going home.

Well, I'll continue in a couple hours.

A few hours later. I've done a few pull-ups. I do a few every night. I've found a doorway with ample finger room. Every morning I try to do a few push-ups. In the White Missionary Handbook it says to exercise regularly. So I have tried to do just that. I feel pretty strong.

Now to Josh's sound advice. He starts (It's dated 8-28-95) off a paragraph by saying "Well bro it's good to hear you're happy. Hell that's all I care about. [Where did he hear that, I must have lied to him in the last letter I wrote him. Now he quotes someone, I think it is his own quote though] 'Hell just keep your head above water. It don't matter if you can do the elementary backstroke or just doggy paddle. Either one you ain't going to drown if you keep your head above the water.' That's just one of my thoughts [why did that kid quote that?]. Take it however you want, or don't take it at all. I just wanted to say something so it sounds like I know what the hell is up with life. But as you can tell, I still don't."

Josh is such a man. He is one of my best friends. He and some other guys by the names of Jimmy, Jambo, Jer, Jake, and Poob. Pondo is just one of my best friends. I have a few, six.

Now for my dad's advice. He has dated his letter 8-26-95. "Hang loose my compadre. Don't ever lose your sense of humor. I love you! Dad" This isn't the thought yet but I hope I don't lose my sense of humor. I really hope I do not. "For in Christ Jesus neither circumcision availeth anything, nor circumcision; [than he goes on to write] but a new creature." Galations 5: 15. He gave the wrong reference and on top of that verse 6 reads "… uncircumcision; but faith which worketh by love." I am going to bring to my Dad's attention this mix up because I want to know where this "new creature" comes from. My Dad goes on to say "The 'new creature' requires the savior's touch—spiritually begotten sons and daughters of Christ. Mosiah 5: 7,8. He is one only [I don't know the next word] hove [damn I know now]. He is our only hope/our only joy!"

There it is. It was a tough one tonight. His penmanship and references made it difficult. He is still my friend though. My best friend. At least one of the six. Take care, I'm tired. See ya. I am tired because my companion and I tried to work out our differences for a couple hours last night. We got, well, particularly nowhere. Be happy and have a sense of humor.

September 1, 1995. First day of September. Time flies by quickly, when one is having fun or whether one is not it still flies by.

Today went pretty well. I bought myself a couple Bach tapes. Bach & Handel are the only two classical composers we are allowed to listen to in this mission. I look forward to p-day to listen to my tapes & write a few letters.

Nothing really comes to mind except a visit with an Atheist. His name is George. We contacted his sister Bobby Claiborne. We had a good little discussion on his porch. He was pretty set, yet his eyes showed something more than his verbal communication. I felt good. My companion, once again demonstrated his naivety or whatever I should call it when he commented after the discussion. If he doesn't lead or feel important he tries to down play the situation. I'm coming to terms with dealing with him. It hasn't been easy and the next few weeks will continue to be a learning experience. Good day or good night to you.

September 2, 1995. Today we did a fair bit of tracting. Today was the first day I actually felt comfortable being a missionary.

We encountered a woman who used some choice language and gave us a couple seconds to get off her property. Everything else went pretty well.

We had dinner at Bishop Thorne. He is a great man and he has a nice family.

I received a letter from Gayle and believe it or not, from my good brother Jacob. He wrote me a letter which really boosted my spirits. He closed by saying "I don't know if anyone ever deserves what they get or get what they deserve but I think you should get the best." I love my two younger brothers. Jed wrote me a letter a few days back. I love those two. I hope I was and am half the older brother they are younger brothers to me. In Jed's letter he wrote "I love you with all my heart, and so does our savior, so hang tough, and as Johnny and Josh put it, Stay Gold." Jed's letter was dated the 24th of August and Jacob's was the 26th.

Jeremy has written a few letters to me. He lends some encouragement. I'm keeping all my letters. They are kind of a history for me so hopefully they get stowed away with this journal and any others I have.

Well, all in all, it was a good day. I'm still memorizing the 4th principle of the 1st discussion. I'm trying to kick it in gear.

I sure love my family. Hopefully, some day I can give back what they have given to me. It will take the eternities.

I think of my Savior, and how I'll never be able to repay him for his loving sacrifice. I have some of the greatest brothers, I really do.

September 3, 1995. Today was nice day. I tend to enjoy Sundays just as much as P-Days (or preparation day). It was a fine fast Sunday topped off with a pleasant evening at the Copelands. Bro Copeland and I played chess. I ended up winning the game although I had lost on time. That was buggers though. I had more points. Well, that's about it. He played Cat Stevens and then switched to Handel and Bach contemporaries towards the end. My comp had a tizzy fit. I enjoyed the soothing and relaxing music. I had a good time.

September 4, 1995. Today went well. I tracked all day. During the morning, I was with my companion. I spent the afternoon and the evening with Elder Anselm. I've spoken of him before. He is a new missionary too. We spent the time tracting. We gave away 5 Book of Mormons. Four of these people said we could come back. Today was my first real day. I had the chance to be myself. I loved it. I had a constant peace. I love sharing my testimony. I love sharing the gospel.

It was a great Labor Day. Elder Anselm and I did well. We get along well. I feel good about today. We knocked on quite a few doors. All went real well. No one freaked out. Everything went well. I hope when I read this I'll be able to recall this day. I actually felt like a missionary. I really did. I hope those we follow up on will continue to be receptive. Jesus loves all. All need to know that He Lives.

September 5, 1995. Today was pretty easy going. It didn't drag on but we did not do much.

I made some minor waves with my memorization. I hope to finish the 1st by the end of this week.

Tomorrow we may go to the city. I doubt we well make it. It is a transfer day. Two new elders are also coming into our ward. We are splitting the area in two. We are losing the car so we will be on bikes. On top of all the "so-called" confusing transition the elders will be living under brother Bores' roof along with the two of us all ready here. Things will be tight and it should be interesting.

Well as long as I get my wash done and letters written tomorrow, I don't care what happens. I would like to see the City of Atlanta before long though.

Take care, I'll keep in touch.

September 6, 1995. I finally toured a wee bit of the City of Atlanta. It was fun. The Coca Cola Museum is pretty fun. A guide, by the name of James Godwin, became an acquaintance. Hopefully I'll see him on a return visit. Just a bit after we entered a guide was humming "Come, Come, ye Saints." I picked up on this and it just so happened that we ran into this guide throughout our tour. James, 41, was baptized many years ago. He was active for a while but he got too busy with work. He is married now but they can't have children. He said they hold family home evening every week. He commented that the LDS Church had the family structure that all should follow. He was a good guy. I hope someday he will return to activity. If not he will still be a good guy. Today was an enjoyable day. I talked with a guy by the name of Ray who works at the Federal Reserve in downtown Atlanta. He took a Book of Mormon. I hope he sees some value in it.

Well, take care. I'll try and do the same. The two new elders are cool. Elder Samson and Elder David, both from Utah. The first has been out 20 months and the latter has been out 5. They probably will be living with us in Brother Bores' home for a week or so. Watch it be for a whole month.

September 7, 1995. Today went o.k. My companion and I are having a little friction. He told me today I was a load of bricks on his back. He is tired of carrying the weight of the both of us. Who would have known I was such a pile of .... It went well. Should this kid phase me? Fortunately he does not. I am o.k. I feel bad for him though. I am going to fast tomorrow. Hopefully God will provide a way to make it through this next month or whatever it takes. We tracked today. Not too effective. It was fun bike riding. My legs got a work out. That's about it. Take care. I'll be o.k. Heavens, you knew or know me after this little entry I hope. I'm o.k. am I not? I hope so.

September 8, 1995. Today went pretty well. It is a good thing I wrestled. I know how to run on little energy. My fast went well. Around 3:00 I refused a glass of water but the member brought me one anyway. It says in the New Testament somewhere not to make it a show when fasting. So I accepted. Riding a bike in this Georgia heat isn't the easiest. I made it though. That in and of itself is a testimony builder to me.

I received a package from Gayle today. It contained some goodies. I also received a letter from my father, my good friend. I've written him and expressed my difficulties somewhat, with my companion. His letter is dated the 25th of September or 9-25-95. It should be 8-25-95. Oh ya, I still haven't written dad for clarification on the last scriptures he shared with me.

Here is what he wrote, "It seems like interpersonal relationships are some of the biggest challenges in life. I think all my boys are better at them than I. To see the real qualities in others is so difficult when the differences are sometimes so great. The way we see others may be a reflection of our view of Jesus. He said "Verily I say unto you, in so much as ye have done it unto one of the least of these my brethren, ye have done it unto me." Matthew 25: 40. Have a good week compadre! I love you Dad" I love you too Dad, thanks for helping me. Indeed I need to find the positive, the good in my companion and all others. I love my Dad.

September 9, 1995. Today was a fun day. The bike ride this evening was beautiful. Riding over the rolly, small hills with the breeze running by, trees everywhere. It was a special night. I am not sure if I have mentioned Alice D before but Elder Anselm and I tracked into her over Labor Day. It was a great experience. When we first met her she didn't really want to talk yet she asked a few questions. I shared 2 Nephis 26: 33. "He inviteth them all to come unto him and partake of his goodness…" It was something else to help her see "Mormons" in a different light. This afternoon she shared with us that she had even told her friends about our first meeting. We were going to follow up in the next couple of days. We have set an appointment for next Saturday at 3:00. I also met "Big Joe" a lover of life. He would not kill a thing. He is an Easterner. It was fun to chat with him. The Ansong family is awesome. We helped their father George a while back.

I really like the account Luke gives in the New Testament. It is so detailed. I found a favorite scripture. "In your patience possess ye your souls" (21: 19). I love this verse. I love the scriptures. Happy road, may you find it.

September 10, 1995. The time is 20 minutes to eight. I am sitting on a little block right outside the door to our apartment. There is a type of haze in the air. It may be pollution. I am not really sure.

There sure is beauty in all places. One must seek this beauty out though. The trees are so very green. Before long they will be changing colors. It is fascinating to me that I will have been a missionary for 2 months this coming Wednesday.

I can see my family at home. Jacob is still napping, and Jed may be watching the end of a football game. It is almost five so Dad will be getting home from meetings. Gayle is engaged in something as she always is. Cara & Pete may be visiting this evening. I am sure George dropped in to say hello sometime this weekend. Jami may have called. He and Traci are enjoying the beauty of Oregon and of being young, full of hope and love, and I am sure a bit of anticipation of what lies ahead. Jeremy is visiting with some old compadres. There is a possibility that his class assignments for tomorrow may cross his mind. Josh is plugging away at learning Thai on top of perfecting his Lao accent. Aaron is planning away for the upcoming week somewhere in Ohio. I love my family with all my soul. I wish the best for them. I know my chance will come to share them with others. I thank my Heavenly Father often for his kindness in allowing my family to let me fill that last slot available before this world began.

I will truly miss the new elders when they move out. Elder Samson & David are good guys. I enjoy visiting with them. My testimony grows every day. I love to read. I love to learn. I live to love, I guess. I really don't know. I really don't. Take care and God bless you. I am so thankful for my savior and elder brother. He has made it possible for me to be with my best friends for eternity.

September 11, 1995. Today I received 5 letters. Wow. My parents are going on vacation with my Dad's folks to sunny southern California. I hope they have a good time. I hope Jed & Jake have fun at home. Today was a swell day. I had the chance to go on a split this morning with Elder Anselm again. My companion is interesting. So are the other elders living with us. They are good men. Well, take care. Enjoy life. It is fun to hear from family. I like to keep in touch with my good compadres. I need to get to bed. Good night.

September 13, 1995. Today was P-day (Preparation Day). Last night was a late night so my Journal was neglected. However, yesterday, I passed off the first discussion. I haven't really started on the 2nd yet, but I plan to.

I got my clothes washed. It was a relaxing day. I wrote quite a few letters. Whenever I do this I feel my P-day went well. This evening I went on a split with a Karl Landon. He is in the bishopric. He has a young family. He sure is a personable kind of guy. It was a fun split.

Well take care. Keep fighting a good fight.

September 14, 1995. I find myself lying on the floor of the apartment quite often, looking up at the fan. The fan spins & spins.

This morning was a rainy morning. It rained hard. We were out on bikes during the afternoon. My companion mentioned biking is not for him. I love to sweat. I don't mind. To hurt once in a while is a good thing.

There was an accident on the street out front today. No one was seriously injured. I sure wish I had the nature to go right up & see if I could help.

I received a letter from my good father today. It was dated the tenth of September. My folks are on vacation, just north of San Diego. He tells me to have a good week and then quotes Heb 4: 16 "Let us therefore come boldly into the throne of grace that we may obtain mercy and find grace to help in time of need." He then says "He is real!"

I have a real good family.

Now to the missionary work. It seems like every teaching appointment we have been having cancels of late. It is kind of depressing. I guess the work must go on. I wish I had the opportunity to share my love of the scriptures more often. They truly testify of my savior, our savior, Jesus Christ. I am so grateful for his sacrifice and love for me.

September 16, 1995. We were engaged in a great deal of tracting today.

Reading in the New Testament tends to blow me away. It seems to me that Jesus wanted so badly for those he taught to know him. Even those closest to him did not really know him. Do I know him?

The two Elders (Samson & David) are good men. We get along great. The new situation has improved my relationship with my companion, Elder Taudrey.

I have had many a chance now to meet people of numerous denominations. Many are truly believers of Christ. How does a person like me share His message with them? I wish I could be that disciple of Jesus Christ with His power. I realize my own role, somewhat. Alma said it best "But behold, I am a man, and do sin in my wish; for I ought to be content with the things which the lord hath allotted unto me (Alma 29: 3)" I feel like these words of Alma, only if I were the missionary Alma was.

I am learning a lot. A mission is truly a learning experience. I sure wish I shared my testimony more often. We hardly teach anymore. We keep busy but it seems to no avail. Am I doing enough? I doubt it. I shall try harder. I am happy, but I want to have that joy that comes with introducing others to Jesus Christ.

• • •

September 18, 1995. I missed another evening. It did not even cross my mind last evening to make an entry.

Zone conference # 2 was today. It was a nice Monday. President Mensh gave a nice talk on Love. He brought out that one of Jesus' greatest sermons was on avoiding contention. This was a sermon of example, it took place in the latter hours of his life.

Whenever I travel I always keep my eyes gazing out the window. For a while I tried to be memorizing or doing some study. Lately I just enjoy the trees and the new terrain. I try and enjoy what short time I have to myself to enjoy the beauty of the area.

Tonight, at the Jettsons, we took part in family home evening. We sang "A Child's Prayer." One of my favorite hymns, primary or not. It was a fun experience. It reminded me so much of the family home evenings I once had a part in.

Sister Jettson made the comment that as missionaries we could never be lonely. I held my peace. Some people make the analogy of feeling like they are all alone in the middle of the sea. I tend to make the connection that I am on main street of downtown New York City, and I feel all alone. My perspective is a bit different. Not unique, but different. I haven't felt that alone for some time, actually I never have felt totally alone, I guess that is why I make that latter analogy, it is an analogy, isn't it?

September 19, 1995. Hello Journal Reader. I am fine. Earlier today I had a thought I really wanted to share this fine evening. But I forgot.

Today I received a couple letters. One from Steve & one from my Dad. My Dad's letter is dated the 15th of this month. The letter got here in a hurry. He sent it at the end of his vacation, they vacated to Escondido. He finishes the letter by wishing me a good week and then he wrote, "There is a lot of theology out there but to me what really matters is that Jesus is real. He cares. He changes lives! His love never faileth." Take care Journal reader. I will do the same.

September 20, 1995. I accomplished a few things today. I got my wash done, shopping, and some letter writing. I went on a split with Elder David today. We went to the post office among a few other things. It was a pretty good day.

I don't know why my companion rattles me. But he does. It is more of an anger of late though. I have been working on not expressing it. I think this is good. Every chance he gets he tries to degrade me. He is such a kid. It wouldn't be fair to pick at him. I guess I have done that too often in previous entries. I stand being around many a person but a fickle person is tough to be around. During our first real discussion so long ago he wanted a list of things he could work on and I told him one simple thing. To be honest with me. I don't know what to do. I don't know if the Christlike thing is to bring things to his attention or endure in long-suffering. Life can be so pleasant. Yet things find there way into causing a bit of disruption. Take care. One thing I am is pretty tough. I am not real slow either. Sometimes my mind works. I will be all right. Well of course I will be. Good day to you and God bless you.

September 21, 1995. The day started off with a bang. I neglected to wake my companion. He rose an hour late angry as a hornet. We then proceeded to talk for a couple hours. For the first time I believe we covered some ground as a companionship. I do indeed have a lot to work on. It is great to be with so many imperfections yet be so content with every single one.

There is a young couple in the ward. Tyler Hunter and his wife. I believe her name is Christine. I am not sure. But just the same, the point is, they are awesome. He served a mission to Ecuador. They live in a beautiful home. They are in their early thirties. They fed us steak this evening. They always feed us well. Tyler then went on a split. We taught a second discussion to A.S. It was my most enjoyable discussion thus far. It was fun. A.S. did not commit but I think he will find what he is seeking. I pray that God will bless him as he reads & prays.

Take care. There are some pretty good people out there. Keep your mirror turned around. I'll try to do the same. My good mother didn't tell her boys that for nothing. I wish my mom would have known how much her boys loved her and still do.

September 22, 1995. Today was interesting. I am on a split. I am not sure how long it will last. It may end tomorrow or go until Monday. It will probably end tomorrow.

Elder David & Elder Samson moved out today. They are good men.

I am with Elder Short. He is too a good man. We rode, and rode, and rode this fine afternoon and evening. So many hills in this area, so many hills. I had an enjoyable time. My legs are getting stronger. The roads are great. Trees everywhere. It was beautiful this evening. For the most part the roads were free. It was fun to ride these roads. It's too bad I can't paint a vivid picture.

Take care. I am going to turn in. Elder Short is currently talking so I will show him more attention. Life is exciting. Be excited about it. Be selfless and decent to others.

September 23, 1995. I miss good friends. I miss those good brothers of mine. Time goes by. My split ended earlier today. My back has been aching for a few days now. I think it is getting a wee bit better. Now that you are all updated, take care. I am not sure my role in the overall scheme of things but I am here. I have hope. Take care, again.

Boy do I write coherent, or maybe not so.

Quality time for me is stepping outside the apartment to have some room to breathe and hope freely. It was a cool evening tonight. I enjoyed it. I love life. I am just not sure what I am doing in it.

September 24, 1995. I learn and learn every day. I have decided to never, and I mean never down talk any one. If I have nothing good to say, I shall say nothing at all.

Today was a good Sunday. I enjoy Sundays or at least sacrament meeting more than I ever have before, I think.

Brother Bores called home for me this evening. He talked with Jake. Hopefully Gayle will send my overcoat before transfers on the 4th. I may be leaving this area.

Take care, once again I say unto you to be excellent to each other. Have fun. I am doing well, I hope you are too.

September 25, 1995. As I contemplate on this day that has passed, and now is a dream, I shall never forget it.

This morning started off with another discussion with my companion. It boiled down to my countenance. I have been bringing my companion down. He let me know once again, how I was affecting him. I can handle being degraded and put down but when it comes to an end that I have been a hindrance or negative aspect of one's life, it hurts.

These past couple months have been trying for me. In President

Mensh's interview I couldn't help it, I wept. It hurts to know I have been such a problem to another. I take very serious the insight my father shared not so long ago. How I view others is a reflection of how I view the Savior. Matthew 25: 40. It hurts to know I have been whatever it is, it is how my companion perceives me. I know I haven't been doing enough on my part. I haven't shown my companion any sort of love.

I do not know where to go from here. I want nothing more than a friend. Transfers are in a week or so, I hope for a change. I need a change. I need a friend.

My back has been aching for a few days now. I have stopped doing push-ups and pull-ups for the time being. I plan to start up in a couple days. Yoga. I have been doing Yoga stretches to help my back. My back has improved tremendously. Hopefully it will continue to heal so I can start my pull-ups again. It's hard to lay off.

Life is tough. The last couple months have been a growing experience. It has been tough to be happy, there have been many a time I have not been so happy.

Well, on a good note, I love reading the Book of Mormon. Today I read 3 Nephi 11 through 13. The Savior's teachings are so real. I wish I could follow His teachings and life. I wish I could "come unto" Him. I truly do. Be decent to one another. Be decent.

I don't know what gives such a surety that I am all right. I have been bombarded in such a way I have never been before. I can only thank my Heavenly Father for his love and the tools he uses. My family. I just have to think of my family, and I know I am an o.k. guy. I don't deserve their love, but without it I would be lost.

September 26, 1995. My back is feeling pretty good. The Yoga stretches really work. I've laid off physical stuff these past few days, I guess that has helped too. I started my pull-ups, again this fine evening. I even did a few push-ups. Why do these two things mean so much to me? Your guess is as good as mine.

My companion and I had another discussion while tracting today. It ended better than any other has of yet. I shouldn't say this but I really hope I get transferred a week from tomorrow. I believe I will leave this companionship on a positive note, but just the same I need a new companion. I need a friend.

I am doing well though. I am going to keep with the Yoga stretches for a couple more days. Tomorrow is P-day. I already put a load of wash in this evening. I am going to knock my wash out first thing tomorrow. That's just me. I like to keep up. I love the scriptures. My love for them grows more every day. Take care & be other centered. Through caring for others you will find true joy & peace in this life and I would suppose in the one to come.

September 27, 1995. Yesterday I memorized the whole 4th principle of the 2nd discussion. Today I did not do quite so good. I did memorize a single verse in Acts 2: 38 which reads "then Peter said unto them, repent and be baptized everyone of you in the Name of Jesus Christ for the remission of sins, and ye shall receive the gift of the Holy Ghost." From memory. I'm going to see if I got it correct... Shoot. I missed the first word and I put an 'a' instead of 'the.' I've already went back and changed it.

It is a good thing I got my wash done early this morning because we were painting all day today at LH's home. She is a new member. She is going through a tough time. It was a long day but a good one.

The day ended with a visit to the R.B. Bacon Family. We watched the "Tree of Life" video or "Lehi's Vision." It was one of those animated videos. It was good. A great discussion followed. R.B. is so in tuned with who is the source and where the focus should be. Dang, he is a good man.

Take care and be strong. Be happy along the way. Your compadre, friend, brother, son, old stinking grandfather, who knows maybe I am your great grandfather...

September 28, 1995. Today went pretty long. This evening went by quick. Tyler and Christine Hunter fed us and then they went on a split with me. It was a lot of fun. We covered some ground. These two are a young couple. They are so kind. They have fed us every Thursday night for the past few weeks. They are not only kind but fun to be around.

I had a chance to share Chapter 12 of the Book of Mormon with RW this evening. Every chance I get I like to use the Book of Mormon.

I am doing well. My companion and I are getting along real well. I believe we will part on good terms. I still hope for the parting. I need that new chance. I do like this area though. I do indeed.

Take care. Keep working hard. Be decent and kind to others. Love life to love. Be Christlike and love. Be tough don't weaken. And good night. Oops I almost forgot. My dad gave me this scripture. Prov 3: 5,6 "Trust in the Lord with all thine heart and lean not unto thine own understanding. In all thy ways acknowledge him and he shall direct thy paths."

September 29, 1995. The cockroaches are pretty bad in the apartment I am residing in. I've killed a few since I've been around.

I enjoy riding my bicycle after dark. It is kind of an adrenaline rush. It's fun. The evenings are beautiful here. I like the cool air running across my face.

I received a letter from Jeremy today. He is awesome. I love the guy. I also received a letter from Nick, he is awesome too. He told me he gave a fireside and the title was "When you know you don't know that's when you know, and that God loves you." Then he goes on to say "to be able to convey that message to people would probably go farther than anything. God is Love he's Really Big and he loves you and your work. Keep the faith. Nick. P.S. use this money any way you like. He sent me a check for a 100 bucks. He gave me a 100 bucks at my farewell. I don't deserve it. I surely don't deserve the kindness behind it. It's the act, not the amount. I am going to have to tell him that if he continues to send money he'll break my heart. He is such a great guy. Take care, God bless you. Good night (at least I am going to be shortly).

September 30, 1995. The first day of conference was well spent. I enjoyed it very much. The time went by so quickly. Never has it before. I shall reflect upon it more tomorrow night, hopefully. It is late and I am tired. Good day to you.

October 1, 1995. Day two of conference was very nice. Elder David B Haight gave an exceptional talk. He is a real person. I enjoyed hearing him speak.

I am doing well, still plugging along. I'll be passing off the second discussion before long.

These last couple of days I have had some good thoughts to write home about. I always look forward to letter writing day.

I hope for change in a couple days, yet I hope for a companion I can get along with. A decent individual who wants to share the word and is willing to do just that. Take care, may God bless you.

October 2, 1995. Today I received a letter from my Dad. It was great. 5 pages front and back. My father is so wise. I hope that letter lasts the ages. It is priceless.

I'm currently on a 24 hour split with Elder Anselm. I have mentioned him before. He is a friend. He has been a good person to talk with these last couple months. He has been a friend.

Well, tomorrow morning I'll find out whether or not I am to be transferred. What happens, happens.

Take care and God bless you. Read, read, read. Read holy writ, and read other books of value. Read Steinbeck, Chaim Potok. Read, it opens and teaches. I'm strengthening my love for the scriptures daily. I sure wish I were more bold and loving. I'm just not sure what it is going to take. I love my family. I love life. I love to learn. I know my Savior lives. I want to know him better. I truly do.

CHAPTER 15

ANOTHER GO-AROUND

Thump. An unannounced Doc Marten with black stitching struck the right temple of my head. The preferred shoe of English goth, punk, and nineteen-year-old Mormon boy missionaries. So many missionaries started the MTC in their shiny new pair of Doc Martens that part of the official introduction included instruction to color in the yellow stitching with a black permanent marker. Mass coloring followed throughout the compound as the newly-admitted dutifully put Sharpie to shoe stitches during their first days on the inside. Swinging off his bottom bunk, my companion did not miss a step, kicking me on target, his other colored-in Doc Marten clearing my chin.

My back had been killing me, from my riding the new red Schwinn up and down humidity-laced East Cobb County hills. Muscles high in the middle back hardened into knots between my scapulas, rope-taut as they descended around my spine, so I rode and walked, sweating profusely, in constant pain. Relief came in sleep and lying on the concrete basement floor of our apartment. We did not take naps because naps were not on The Plan, but we did frequently turn the air conditioner to high and lie down to rest shortly after returning to our apartment, faithfully conjecturing, but never asking, such action was not off it. The open floor space extended a few feet in front of our bunks. I took my spot and gazed into the spinning fan, legs fully extended with toes slightly leaning out, arms to my side, breathing deeply, sure I would make it another day, hoping for a welcomed one.

After our first weeks together, my companion wore a permanent scowl. It varied slightly from his stern countenance, an assured facile change I had missed coming as surely as I misread everyone the first fifteen minutes we met, believing myself a few handshakes and backpats away from another decent, well intentioned, potential best friend, unable to relinquish one of those misbegotten personal absolutes that everyone would like me, never considering fully what I found so likable about myself, assuming it as some first cause, an ultimate truth, an incontrovertible reality. Like others before him my companion proved it wrong.

We had been fighting, to put our conversations politely, hours at a time for days after days, making for the longest weeks in memory. I laughed off, slipping his words like jabs in the first few rounds of a prize fight, tiring only in the later rounds. Not about to throw in the towel, god as my witness, I worked the ropes feinting combinations and fancy footwork to set up a knockout, bent only on making the final bell.

Each day my companion repeated that I was taking steps contradictory to The Lord's Way, which was one way and all other ways amounted to Satanic byways. His words exactly. "You're doing what Satan wants you to do." To understate the situation: my every comment and my every action elicited that I was not following The Lord's Way. To accurately state: The Lord's Way was following The Plan: all the mission rules, inclusive of all those in the Guide and White Bible and all those directed by our mission president, all atop rules in the standard works of the Christian Bible and the triumvirate of Mormon scriptures (BOM, the Book of Mormon; D&C, the Doctrine and Covenants; and PoGP, an acronym heretofore unknown to me for the "Pearl of Great Price,") and all latter-day revelation from all latter-day prophets and all general authorities since the time of Joseph Smith. Obedience was the first law of, and presumably in, heaven, as sincerely retold as the single most important eternal truth by earnest general authorities bi-annually at general conference. And its role amplified on a Mormon mission. I got it, and I was not breaking any rules, stolid like the choir at the bi-annual conference. To be a good Mormon was synonymous with being an obedient one. And I was both.

Yes, I flirted with writing letters on other than P-days, my desires assuredly condemning me, but nary fool enough to announce them. If Satan couldn't read my thoughts, I wasn't worried about my companion's reading them either. Although, he, my companion not Satan, like every variation of a conversant constituted of insecure, ignorant, and controlling features would attest that he knew them. A bloody unavoidable recurring type of *Homo sapiens*, and one all too happy to spend your time doing everything he can to get himself center on your conscious stage. Did my companion's malcontent amount to wanting my admiration, longing for me to show dependence on him, the senior companion, my gladiator trainer, satisfied by seeing me break under his virulent barrage of instruction and feedback? I wouldn't give it, show any, or bend a hitch. I was obstinate if I was anything. It reigned supreme over a slew of other fervently held beliefs, including that in my undying and unconvincing likability. At first I handled the horror of our minutes together with light steps of levity. By the end I still barked back straight backboned but holding my shoulders under genuine despair.

I picked up the phone as directed by my companion to confirm our dinner appointment at the bishop's house. A voice answered my call on the other end, and I disclosed myself as one of the missionaries in the ward, asking to speak with her mother. She laughed and explained I was speaking to her. I confirmed dinner and laid down the receiver. My companion, monitoring the phone call, glowered as I turned to meet him. He coldly sentenced my joke as the gravest indiscretion. He had taken precious minutes to explain the delicate situation at the bishop's, him knowing it well as he had been born—missionary parlance for beginning one's mission—in East Cobb. He explained with conviction exceeding all previous declarations the necessity of the strictest right behavior at the bishop's. This was truth, because success in local congregation life came from support of its chief leader, as one might surmise, but that was not the reason for my companion's anger. There were three reasons for that, none of them remotely related to proselytizing: the bishop's three most exquisitely beauteous daughters.

The slightest look, the most fleeting eye contact was utterly unpardonable, presumably leading to a steady gaze, which in turn implied the greatest of Mormon ambitions—eternal union. Inevitable pining would follow, which was grievously inappropriate and far off The Plan. The overpower-ing beauty of each daughter ensnared missionaries in chivalrous fantasies for weeks—which in missionary time equated to about six years in civilian late-teenage angst and early twenty-something ignorance years. My com-panion offered as proof his charismatic and handsome trainer: even he had not dared to speak directly to the bishop's daughters. The mission president, himself, had even directed missionaries not to participate in idle chit-chat and unchecked glances when dining at the bishop's table. At the slightest mistake, Satan would pounce on the open heart. I anticipated testing my mettle like brave missionaries who had gone before me, dining in this celes-tial realm, welcoming the warnings as any knight errant would.

Turning through pine trees and crape myrtles that glowed yellow and lined swirling cul-de-sacs, we entered a quiet grove swallowed by the Geor-gia red sky, and parked the mission car. An uninitiated knight errant in a pledged life of good deeds and virtue by inspiring maidens I was not, step-ping briskly erect behind my companion, bumping him, nearly toppling his little frame onto the sidewalk, marching to the front door of the bishop's home. Brushing me aside with an exaggerated shoulder shrug and side glare, my companion rapped his knuckles friendly on the great wooden door. The bishop sternly greeted us, "Welcome elders," directing our entrance, "please come in." We entered the hot room and the challenges lying before us. The bishop's wife, a most beauteous lady, with bouncing shoulder-length blonde hair, smiled. "Hello, elders," she greeted, ushering us into the dining room. Grinning wide, I stepped to. Without counting I gracefully surveyed the scene, five chairs surrounding the table, probably not round, magnanimous-ly stepping in front of my companion to beat him to a chair next to the bish-op. I stoutly pulled it out, waiting for all to sit.

The Bishop's handsomeness pushed him over the precipice of beauty, tall with striking features, chalky clear skin and manly high cheek bones, dark healthy hair, slender muscular shoulders, unmistakably, in part, re-sponsible for what he cultivated. I froze as I noticed the wall of truth direct-ly opposite me. There, finally ending weeks of speculation, hung a portrait of his oldest daughter, a face so lovely, smiling in golden flowing curls, that I could not deny having seen divinity. No sooner had I seen the first angelic face, I noticed within centimeters of her picture, that of the second oldest daughter, even more beautiful than the first, a nugatory claim if ever one were made. Breathless in a stupor of abounding beauty, I turned to stone upon the entrance of the third and youngest daughter, upon any report in any language possessing more beauty than the second, now joining us for dinner.

The bishop began the blessing on the food and the perfunctory prayer for protection of the missionaries, us two and all those sharing the truth of Jesus and his one true Church the world over, guidance for the Lord's living prophet and the twelve apostles and all people furthering the work of the Lord, including the important temple work for the many dead who had passed on without having heard of the gospel of Jesus Christ and consequently not having the opportunity to receive the necessary saving ordinance of baptism and temple ordinances, and for the constant companionship of the Holy Ghost.

Unable to close my eyes, I gazed on her, yes, the third, who was impossibly fairer than the first two daughters on the wall and who was beyond all words. She sat in a heavenly glow, youthful and full-bodied. Truth emanated throughout the room, rattling through the sinews within me. During suspended moments of bliss I must have slipped a flash of exasperation realizing all the chairs were taken or curiously fixed my brow, befuddled where the other two would sit. My flash or fixed glance surely read large, eliciting, shortly into dinner, the unsolicited explanation, which I interpreted as a profuse apology that the older two sisters had returned to BYU just days ago for the new semester. My fears confirmed or my confusion cured, but certain my one soul cried aloud and, suspecting the bases for the said warnings also orchestrated the delay of our dinner appointment, I tried to avoid our utter and complete ruin. But no despair could linger long, consoled nearly instantly in the recognition of the pinnacle of all challenges less than three feet away in the singular and solitary fairness of all maidens among us, dear reader.

But no purer heart than that of yours truly has existed since the days of the hidalgo, Don Quixote de la Mancha, the Knight of the Sorry Face. Confronted by beauty after beauty, Quixote remained true to the Fair Dulcinea of El Toboso, and like the noble Quixote I remained true to the fair coed of Deseret Towers, the elfin beauty Sandy. Not unaffected at the Bishop's table—quite to the contrary, in point of fact, raptured in dining bliss—I remained committed to the one maiden who held the combination to the lock on my heart, albeit unknown to her, again not unlike Dulcinea, the asymmetry of devotion and its reception no more lost on me at the bishop's table than on Quixote during his errands. My singleness of purpose, matched only by the purity of my romantic vision, sustained me at beauteous affronts.

Dinner ended, and my companion tried to set a date with the bishop's family to invite a friend to learn more about the gospel, succeeding in setting a date when he would follow up to see if they had set a date to pray together to set a date by which they would invite a friend to learn more about the gospel.

Missionary work hurt: its emotional licks of constant rejection, its psychological bumps of transforming from a footloose teenager into a full-time proselytizing missionary, and its physical separation from contact with family and friends, so a blunt shot to my head did not seem out of the ordinary. But if a part of it did, it was that someone on my side did it and then did not apologize. My companion proceeded naturally over me into the kitchen, surely having kicked many logs during his wee days seeking adventure as a youth in the public forests of Idaho. Weeks into the missionary trenches I was fighting battles of all kinds, including those we constantly reminded ourselves of during companion training, district training, and zone conferences, against Satan who worked overtime to keep people from our message. But I also had to fight my companion's campaign to fashion me into what he considered an acceptable missionary type. Within my own mind and heart there also continued the most trying battle, trying to find truth in my circumstances and to understand my purpose, such truth and purpose (intentionality and the life of the author) having survived my freshman introduction to literary criticism.

From a young age, I had expected to serve a Mormon mission, and a hell of a start did not diminish my commitment to the two years ahead. I did not think about going home, not once. At first I didn't think about hurting my companion; thoughts of punching him came much later, after we had been separated. My trial of understanding was not a matter of "should I stay or should I go?" or "should I be or not be a missionary?" It was something else entirely. It was finding truth in such miserable conditions in the suburbs of Atlanta with a missionary's plastic The Church of Jesus Christ of Latter-day Saints badge clipped to my white shirt. I wanted to find truth and discover its connection to who I was and who I would become, sure of some connection during my Mormon mission.

Mormon theology resoundingly answers all Capital-W questions, the 'Whats' and 'Whys' about life, and their siblings. Who are we? Answer: children of God of various degrees of "chosen," Mormons being God's elect; hence the importance of missionary work. What is our purpose in life? Answer: to glorify God by gaining a body and living righteously and being happy by becoming Mormon and having big families. Where did we come from? Answer: the presence of God, where we lived as disembodied spirits prior to the creation of the world. And to Where shall we go after death? Answer: back to the presence of God eventually with a physical body, if we keep the commandments and become Mormon. Universal questions about life from the unrefined to the most esoteric answers interested me, especially stuff outside Mormon theology. All questions and answers vying for the category of truth got my attention, and none more than the Ws cousin: How to live the most meaningful life? As a late-teen on a Mormon mission I knew what the most meaningful life looked like. It was devoted to Jesus Christ and living it was no small challenge.

I struggled with the conditions of my situation but that was nothing new. After setting the latest treasured fantasy book down to sally forth into activities outside my attic, I struggled in everything: getting along with my brothers, working for money to buy clothes and soda pop, getting good grades, curbing my sarcasm, making weight to wrestle, trying to score points when I wrestled, talking to girls, breathing around ones I liked, stopping the spread of infantigo, getting my folks to take me to the doctor to address it, coming up with reasons like The Man with No Name in Sergio Leone's spaghetti westerns to explain my scarring, two years later treating severe acne, again convincing my parents I was worth taking to a dermatologist to treat it, ingesting Accutane faithfully during wrestling season, my bones and tendons struggling to function while this cure destroyed them from inside and singleted competitors on top of me torqued and broke them from outside, stunned by integrals and derivatives, tried by graphing calculators, and high school lunch, and dormitory meal plans, and affecting in times of consciousness to like other humans.

I did not struggle about my convictions. I had the truth about Jesus and aimed to share it. I learned the truth about Jesus from my father, not the Church. To investigators I testified of the truth about saving grace of Jesus and the restoration of Jesus' true gospel not the restoration of Jesus' one true Church. In a letter to my father, I asked him to write down his many beliefs about Jesus he shared with his sons and community during my years growing up in Blackfoot. He did, and shortly after my request a manila envelope arrived one humid afternoon, and in it, bound in a blue plastic cover, were my father's thoughts. He proceeded to write his thoughts about Jesus in short essays and post them intermittently during my mission and for the next many years after my return. I had an advantage as a missionary. I dealt with everything in relation to the truth about Jesus. I didn't merely believe in Jesus, but tried to apply his teachings in my efforts. Those things that were unrelated, or less related, to the truth about Jesus were disregarded or ignored. I focused on what would get our investigators, and me, to him.

Truth seems like a category as large as life. Asking what is truth seems akin to asking what is life, and saying truth is life is only slightly less absurd than Vinnie answering Sean that trust is life at Bunker Hill Community College. But they are absurdities with connections, the compelling long-standing kind of truths. Truth is found in life as trust is. Knowing truth presents challenges beyond corralling it with meaningful definitions. Of all the ways of knowing truth, having lived it is the most persuasive, with our best attempts to explain it always a distant second.

No one has ever established truth in real-time exhortation. But damn if some haven't come close. The truth always lies somewhere else, with its subject invoked from clouded actualities in the past or immaterial projection of certainties into the future. Yet it's not truth if it's not present in the present. Truth is not as big as life at present and is not without paradox, always bigger behind and beyond it. It is part of life, immediate, immanent, a companion measuring and underlying it. Truth's door is always the present, our efforts made in real time to understand the past and to shape the future.

Knowing truth helps people live life. And if it does not, nothing contributes more to living well than faith that truth does. Truth guides our greatest aims and achievements. Truth is knowledge of what actions to take to fulfill immediate needs and to reach aspirations. Truth is multi-dimensional like life, it takes the form of ideas and concrete, ocean floors and mountain tops, plates and coils, electricity, glucose, synapses, load-bearing walls, algorithms, sand and chips, cells and circuits, bears and other mammals, nipples and milk, logic and code, bending moments and stress points, stone and wood, soil and reeds, chisels and pigments and canvas, pigskin and cork, atoms and neurons, and many foils to madness. It exists in the abstract and practical, psychological and emotional, with planes in the physical and theoretical, its parameters often challenging to locate, ever changing.

Spiritual truth seems as difficult as any kinds of truth to find, understand, and share. The same difficulties in obtaining spiritual truth have been used to attack spiritual truth, the attacks often being used to suggest spiritual truth is something other than truth, a position taken for the genuine purpose of maintaining the integrity of truth as wide and broad as it is, but well laid defenses of metaphysics coupled with mystical confessions dually ward off its most ardent critics. Truth defined neatly can exclude unwanted assertions for truth like spiritual truths, but the predicates of that neatness will be limited as will the truth's integrity. Inclusive predicates sampled in the paragraphs above support a much broader integrity, supported by but not conditioned on tight definitions, quite able to stand on their ageless and repeated existence and functions not on the scale of alpha and omega but a scale emerging and evolving.

I sought spiritual truth along with all other kinds of truth, but learned early—long before my mission—of my handicap in finding it. I appreciated its importance for others because of the reverence with which people I respected talked about it. But I had no access to it myself. My handicap may have resulted from my lack of disposition to experiencing spiritual truth, and may have been supported by my belief that spiritual truths were so utterly and completely personal that advancing them beyond the personal diminished them, far too often diverted others' efforts away from more pressing truths towards their alluring and unattainable lush fruits, save in some changed second-hand form.

Truths are elegant and messy, hard-earned and free, clear and absurd, known by laborers and laureates, and parsing them is one of life's great joys and challenges. That's why, among other reasons, talking of spiritual truths was like watching a circus, never without spectacle and always more fanciful than real life, and mostly about the performers and ringmaster. Be that as it may, allowing for the possibility of spiritual truths as surely as acrobats landed their flips and clowns made audiences laugh, the spiritual has amazed and amused. Sure their benefits, as their advocates proclaim, have informed and infused mortals with more meaningful and enthusiastic lives. But the claim relies on the premises that they were not life. They would not be spiritual or other than our physical desires and emotions and mental processes if they were life. If one avowed they were part of life, all that stuff we come to know in the mortal realm of physics, including red shifts, fallow dirt, clean air, and rich excrement would be like miracles being normal occurrences, random and infrequent but normal. A contradiction if maintained is simply meaningless, well, not simply for everyone with opinions on it. The spiritual realm was not equal to the physical realm.

So what was the practical sell of Jesus to one with no more predilections for the spiritual than a stone hinge? Conquering sin, weakness, the actual stuff of failings beyond my power to change, the kind of truth I could believe in because it stared back at me. And I believed, synonymous with knowing, it. And I wanted to share it, the part about the reality of Jesus' changing us, making us better, removing and healing our sins. And as a missionary I got to share it all the time. People expected it. And I wanted to embrace disciplines, including missionary guides and bibles that enhanced my ability to do so, and to reject diversions that did not.

One of those I rejected was leadership. Leadership didn't enhance the message, it didn't deliver it to investigators for us inexperienced, unknowing teenagers, nor did its condescension trickle down to hearts of sincere truth seekers. Elder B. Fallon Hill, a member of the Seventy, an honorific group of leaders directly below the twelve apostles and prophet, visited our mission during my first two months in East Cobb. He had a lazy eye, so his piercing look gave the appearance he could scrutinize no fewer than two objects at any one time. A glowering presence he was not. A stricture of comments and movements he was. And for once I didn't mind. He was not affecting, or if he was, he was a supreme player, and I bought his performance. Serious as a beating heart, he instructed the LDS members at stake conference and the missionaries at zone conference during one of my last weeks in East Cobb.

Elder Hill claimed to have read the entire book of the Doctrine and Covenants, no great feat in itself as my father had memorized it in its entirety, and when I challenged him after a local member passed the rumor my way, he confessed he had, allowing the memorizing could have been any number of books given the downtime in the Marine Corps.

Elder Hill's more modest feat was his commitment to mark each reference to leadership, finding many, some three numerals in total if my memory doesn't mislead me. He concluded the instruction of the Lord to his servants, mostly Joseph Smith, the recipient of the lion's share of revelations recorded in the D&C, was that *aspiring to leadership was a sin akin to the sin of adultery*. He delivered his message with wide open eyes and his head resting against one hand for long stints, simultaneously looking at elders directly in front of him and those of us to the side of him. He may have cited a passage in support, or declared it as revelation given to him and offered to us from one of God's servants. It matters not as he was right. Only the sin of denying the Holy Ghost, a sin declared in scripture, was more damning. Like the unpardonable sin of denying the Holy Ghost and hard-to-repent of sin of adultery, I expected the sin of aspiring to leadership often remained a sin when one became a leader, and the few leaders who repented of it still had its accompanying scars.

Mormon Sunday school teachers taught that Jesus removed sins, but the scars of sin remained; their favorite illustration being nails in a piece of wood, and the nails represented sin and upon acceptance of Jesus' atonement (through baptism in the Mormon Church and regular Sunday attendance and partaking of the holy sacrament) the nails were removed but the holes remained, the take-away being that immoral acts carried consequences forever.

Elder Hill minced no words that aspiring to leadership was extraordinarily immoral; aspiring to and assuming leadership to affirm one's holiness was an act of idolatry replacing God—even if just a smidgen of him—with oneself. Carried in constant motion to the pulpit, it caused harm to potentially hundreds or thousands of people, far more dangerous than adultery, which, though it affected two families and sometimes entire communities indirectly, only affected one other person directly. Identifying scars of sin could be challenging but identifying the unrepented sin of aspiration in Mormon leaders was as easy as recognizing the residual free love on liberals from the Sixties. No thread of sin was more blatant than leaders' abnegation of their duties to truth when they responded to criticisms they didn't have it by asserting that questioning leadership was a sin.

The Golden Excuse—the notion that questioning leaders was tantamount to questioning God (maintaining that idolatrous strain)—is simply a justification for avoiding criticism on the merits. Each leader who raised The Golden Excuse as a shield to criticism seemed as blind to its illusionary protection as they were amnesic about their sinful aspirations to be anointed of God. It is money in the bank: If you ever hear a Mormon leader declare that Mormon leadership—often coincidently including himself— should not be questioned, his aspirations still run strong, albeit recognizable mostly as insecure blathering. It was never more obvious to me than as a missionary.

Elder Hill could not have missed his mark as his bull's-eye extended as wide as the walls of the chapel and as deep as the base of the Wasatch Front—the metropolitan area encompassing Mormon headquarters in Salt Lake City and the beating heart of Mormonism at BYU in Provo. He couldn't have found an audience more in need of his correction and mass repentance than Mormon missionaries, even if he were addressing his peers in the Salt Lake City Tabernacle. Mormon missionaries were repeatedly told, and most believed, their Mormon missions were the two most important years of their lives and the surest measure of success was escalating through the leadership ranks from senior companion to one of dozens of district leaders to one of a dozen or so zone leaders to one of two coveted positions as assistant to the president. And there was no surer torpedo to sink mission morale than a mission president awarding aspiring missionaries.

I could not confirm or deny his conclusion, but like most other truths of religious instruction I accepted, the rumbling in my gut was as sure a sign of concurrence as it was of a needed lunch break, which we shortly took. Aspiring to lead was bad. I believed it, which aided my acceptance of it, gleaming among the ranks thereafter flowed easily to remind everyone who heard Elder Hill or should have heard him, all of us followers of prophets, of which he was nearly one. My enthusiasm for hearing the truth outweighed the importance Elder Hill attached to it. I didn't believe the Mormon mission was the most important two years of anyone's life, and found aspirers and adulterers more annoying than sinful, but I was happy to have another arrow in my religious quiver of contentions.

In our cat fights in every respect except without claws, I may have reminded my companion of Elder Hill's talk at every ruffle but by the time my companion, a young district leader, and I heard the truth about aspiring to leadership as one of the greatest sins our two months together was closing and our fighting, while still at full tilt consuming hours of exhortation and rebuttal, had me exhausted in a victim's phase of giving up any attempt to wound him, bracing with a shield only, tired of holding it, hoping I could soon drop it for longed-for respite with a fervently-believed-in possibility of a better companion.

I anticipated our president interviews with Power Ball expectations. The president interviewed each of the one hundred eighty or so missionaries every month, and since our companionship had been flaring up I'd been looking forward to the time I would make my case for change. Having lost our car with the split of our proselytizing area, we biked to the church. Gray skies covered us after an early morning round of bickering. If our arguments ran over companionship study and personal study time, we did them at lunch or dinner or not at all. With the interviews that morning, my companion assured me we would complete our studies later that day. Our efforts tired me but sharpened the issues, freshening the script I'd prepared for my appeal to the president.

We rode our bikes up to glass doors, passing the white Crown Victoria in the otherwise empty parking lot. I didn't know much about automobiles, but I knew about engines in Ford sedans because of the old one in my grandfather's Lincoln and in my father's, the fastest car known to me during senior year of high school. After my bull riding brothers moved out of the house, my father traded his silver Chevy Silverado extended-cab pickup truck for an extended length Lincoln Town Car. The white Victoria our mission president drove was the sporty wide police model and my father's Town Car was the long boat. A boat but with power, which I had tested in grandfather style with my senior ball date against a member of our group in his green Mustang, speeding past him and up a hill on a blind two-lane country road, slamming on the brakes not to avoid unseen oncoming traffic, which was indeed oncoming and divinely lucky to avoid the Mustang rear-ending us, but to skid into the unmarked driveway of the property for the dance's after party of movie-watching and soda pop drinking with Mormon peers with the exception of my non-Mormon date. My date said nothing and how could she, terrified and without breath. I asked her to the ball knowing she had a boyfriend a couple years out of high school, having known her for years, liking her cute side, but mostly motivated because I heard other people hadn't asked her out of fear for her beau.

I followed my companion inside the church. An outer hallway circled the interior of the church with the gym on the south half and the chapel on the north half and classrooms, offices, bathrooms, a kitchen and a nursery lining the exterior walls. We walked the split circle until we found a small room opened for our interviews a few steps north of the door we entered. President Mensh welcomed us with his enormous smile, inviting us first to visit as a companionship. He smiled again and asked us how we were doing. I did not say much and for all the life in me could not muster a smile to return his, the only such failure during my mission. My companion said something about us having challenges but we were working them out. President Mensh asked to visit with me and straight away told me I did not look very happy. I forgot my script, cried, and admitted I was not. I had never broken down in defeat before, but I also had never been so beat. For a fair share of my treasure built up in heaven I wish I could remember what President Mensh said to me, but I can't. I seem to remember he told me he had been in a similar situation on his mission, and I want to remember he said he'd broken down before his mission president too. I left lighter than when I arrived. If the gray skies hadn't broken during our bike ride home, they would begin to.

Mormons do not have a strong doctrine of penance but its recurrence in the Book of Mormon suggests they should; I expect it just hasn't been officially introduced at general conference. One of my all-time favorite movies, Roland Joffe's *The Mission* (1986), was about this unmined Book of Mormon jewel. And while I loved Ennio Morricone's soundtrack which, combined with Jones and Edelman's *The Last of the Mohicans* (1992) soundtrack, were the limits of my cultural cultivation, I liked even more De Niro and Iron's performances of religious devotion.

As a young teenager and as a young adult wrapped in this reminiscence, I regard the act of asking for forgiveness as ineffectual as the ability to grant it. If someone makes an egregious mistake, there is absolutely nothing that person can do to change what happened and asking for absolution achieves a double affront if it achieves anything. Asking for forgiveness is the cheapest form of bandaging consequences and granting it merely abets this meager triage. The person asking for the impossibility of forgiveness is at best delusional and, at his lowest, worth leaving in the past. What the person can do is take actions to attempt to right his wrong and to demonstrate he will not do it again, but most importantly not do it again and not require the slightest obligation on those he offended. Inhalations of sorry only have value when held in trust to draw upon later, reminders for both the offender and offended of the past failures. If there's efficacious rhetoric, it's to promise not to repeat errors and to track that promise. My undeveloped or absent capacity to forgive, probably an important component lacking in my mutated capacity for sympathy, left me with the single option of doing penance, succeeding rarely but in that instance of failure with Elder Taudrey I made an attempt and almost another.

I slipped three crisp twenty dollar bills into a generic best wishes card. I did not sign my name and sealed the envelope. On my split that evening I directed him to drive by the interracial family we had committed to pray to know a date by which they would invite a nonmember friend to learn more about the church, a wellspring of shame as he walked us to his door still overflowing. We had not followed up with them about praying about a date by which they would ask a nonmember friend to learn more about the gospel, and we managed to avoid the father at priesthood meeting at church. I had no plans to go to the door, but let my split know of my intention to drop off a letter when we arrived, asking him to pull along the side of the mail box, allowing for a quick delivery.

News reached us the night before p-day that I would be transferred out of East Cobb. I had tortured myself with the possibility President Mensh would see value in leaving Elder Taudrey and me together to work out our differences, certain I could have plunged further into my despair and been all the more worthy after surviving it. I celebrated his wisdom for ending my righteous development, immediately packing and gathering my belongings within the hour. We committed Brother Bores to drive us to transfers, and nothing was left to chance. I'm sure I slept. Before leaving our apartment the next day I laid a sleek grayish green tie, the solitary object of my companion's single compliment during our two months together, on his made bed, the tail neatly folded behind its trunk, placing next to it a brief note expressing my hope he would enjoy it. I looked at the tie, a favorite among the ties I owned, purchased a few weeks before I entered the MTC. Then I retrieved the tie, along with the note, and placed them in my coat pocket. I turned, stepped through the door, and closed it behind me.

CHAPTER 16

THE FALL

On my first night in my new area, rain pelted loose windowpanes and wind howled against the walls of our apartment above the garage. Shifting under layers of dirty, old blankets I pulled them up to cover me from water and air coming into our bedroom. Earlier we had driven under dark clouds, neither of us giving them any thought, from transfers at the Glenridge Church west to Dallas, conversing the whole drive about nostalgias not only belonging to a former life but to an entirely different life than the one in our white shirts, dark ties, and LDS Church nametags. We were living our first fall in Georgia, and we expected overcast skies in October. Trying to sleep, we were getting more than we could have expected.

Mormon missionaries do not watch television, listen to the radio, read newspapers, or surf the Internet, a form of information gathering still a few years away from the quotidian on October 4, 1995. If they did, we would have known Hurricane Opal touched down in the panhandle of Florida bent on moving across Georgia to Alabama and beyond, undecided about staying a hurricane or lessening to a tropical storm on the evening of its passage through Dallas.

I awoke to the blurry backside of my new senior companion, a short brick of muscle mass in white garments, T-shirt top tucked into loose knee-length bottoms, bobbing from window to window in our bedroom, to the windows throughout the apartment, with a flash light shining wildly on the walls, yelling his approval at each passing of a fire truck or police car with sirens and lights blazing on the darkened front street. He kindly abstained from addressing my trying to sleep, but I heard comments that the storm was real, the power was out, which I could see, winds knocking power lines down and felling trees around us. The glass broke in the window and the storm whipped in. Undeterred I pulled the blankets farther over my head.

I had been in danger before. There were summer days moving pipe when I got caught in rain showers and thunderstorms and did not tarry a second too long before heading to the car. After a summer of hearty pipe-moving, I set out to spend my money before school started. Driving our white late-eighties four-door Camry was a rare luxury I earned for being a responsible teenager. I used it for twenty-mile shopping pilgrimages to the mall in Idaho Falls, due north of Blackfoot. Blackfoot did not have many retail options, and it was fun to leave town. Idaho Falls offered a mall the entire size of all retail stores combined in Blackfoot, with a lot more hip options. My brothers and I knew one car well during high school and it wasn't the family Camry. We drove a yellow late-seventies Chevette to and from town each school day. Our paternal grandfather Keith, who ran an insurance company in town, had given it to us, providing the opportunity to learn a standard transmission by driving on rural roads before we earned our licenses, at the early age of fourteen, and could drive lawfully into town. The Chevette was dependable on unpaved roads to get to work during the summer and formidable at billowing through snow banks to get to school during the winter. It had seat belts, a working heater, and when the bulb on the stick vanished it required an initiated shift involving a forceful push down from the palm onto the small steel rod and strong push forward to get it into reverse. Getting into the Camry seemed like a dream.

I turned the Camry off the old highway running south from Idaho Falls to Shelley to Firth to Blackfoot, to the two-lane connector road running to the interstate where we enjoyed ten more miles per hour and no stop lights through small towns en route to home after an afternoon walking around the mall, looking at clothes, buying a few, and drinking Orange Juliuses with my younger brothers, Jacob and Jed. I was in high school, Jacob was starting his last year at Mountain View Middle School, and Jed was finishing his last tour at Stalker Elementary School. We were on the cusps of top-tier social castes, the jocks, and needed a few new shirts and trousers, and sneakers if we found any on sale, to show it. We ventured out to complete our school shopping on our own for the first time, handling the crowds and cashiers deftly on this occasion. On the connector to the interstate we approached a truck with an extended trailer full of ATVs driving the speed limit, and as eager to get home as I was impatient, and with a clear run ahead of me I moved into the oncoming lane to pass. I floored the Camry's pedal, and to my surprise the speed increased slightly. I pushed harder, but it didn't respond. Over a few long seconds I advanced alongside the extended trailer with all its cargo and noticed an eighteen-wheeler turning the curve in the distance, headed directly toward us. Believing I still had room I continued to pass the trailer loaded with ATVs and approached the back of the truck, no-ticing the distance closing quickly between the tractor and our car. I honked my horn and looked at the driver beside me who had not slowed down but who I imagined had sped up and also imagined, or saw, shake his head in confirmation of my stupidly self-induced predicament. I looked behind me and saw Jed, his back straight and halfway up the back seat behind Jacob who sat stiffly next to me in the passenger seat, and I felt cold. Fear covered me beyond any feeling of desperation I had ever felt.

I had not attended Jeremy's dual meet with my mother and brothers the night my mother went into a coma in our front living room. I stayed home, and when my mother came home early from the meet I followed her into the living room. She commented that her head hurt more than usual, took aspirin, and lay still. My father had followed her home and shortly after their arrival searched for his first aid kit. Returning to the room, he wrapped my mother's arm in a synthetic cuff to test her blood pressure, squeezing the plastic ball to inflate it, holding her wrist with his other hand. Seconds later he released it, stating it was not working. He said he would need to go to the office to get one that worked. He asked me to watch her while he was gone.

Behind her sat a piano, the object she had worked tirelessly to introduce to each of her sons. She loved music. Whenever a concert pianist did a show at the city civic center, our whole family would attend in our best long sleeve shirts and ties. She signed us up for choir and encouraged us join the school band. When it came to her fourth attempt to successfully connect one of her children to one of her greatest joys, the piano, I asked if I would get a BB gun in return for taking lessons. I either heard my older brothers make similar requests or believed BB guns were customarily given to young boys for embarking on musical chores. She agreed. I had no interest in learning to play the piano, and a few minutes into the first lesson my mother recognized my aptitude matched my interest perfectly. A few more seconds in I stopped and asked when we could go into town to buy my new BB gun. She responded I would have to do more than one lesson. Sitting on that bench for more minutes than I could imagine was devastating. I told her I didn't really want the gun so that was enough playing for me, and asked if I could go. My early retirement must not have surprised her, but having another set of hope dashed against a life full of culturally inferior boys, devoid of so much beauty she wanted so much to share, must have cut deep within her, as she frowned for me beyond my immediate failure.

I woke to our apartment shaking. A bulldozer pushing the building got me out of bed. I looked in the dark toward the ceiling. My companion came into the room and said a tree must have fallen on the apartment. He put on a coat and pants and went out into the night, and on his return reported that a tree had in fact fallen on the apartment on the corner side of our room, directly over my head. It looked stuck and there were still a few more hours before the sun was due up, so I got back on my bed and went back to sleep.

The next morning we were up at dawn when the landlord knocked on our door to ask if we were all right. We were. We dressed, ate cold cereal and stepped out onto the porch and down the stairs to view the storm's damage. Trees were uprooted, one large pine lying across the back corner of the apartment. We took pictures, and set out on my first full day in Dallas.

The charging eighteen-wheeler noticed my feeble progress around the pickup truck and trailer and honked his disapproval. I pushed the steering wheel forward too far into the pass to brake and return behind the ATV trailer. My blame extending into the eternities and all my own, I cursed the Camry, my father for buying such a weak piece of shit, and God for creating so many buffoons. I kept screaming inside what a dick this guy to the side of me was, wanting to side-swipe him if only I didn't have my brothers along.

Then I cleared the pickup truck and swerved in front of him as the eighteen-wheeler charged past. No one swerved to avoid our coming head-on collision, but it's not in an Idahoan's DNA to give up the right-of-way. The pickup I finally passed celebrated our luck by laying on his horn until we reached the interstate's entrance. Too sick with fright to respond I slouched forward, breathing against the tears of the loss of Jacob and Jed I nearly caused.

No informed soul would have called me a great, or the best, or an exemplary brother any more than a sentient being would have called me any of those adjectives before calling me friend. I was indifferent to other people, a respecter of no one. I had calculus sets and A.P. history packets to complete believing in one reality, that good grades would get me out of my home, town, state and life into something else. I didn't hate any of those surroundings nor was I ashamed of them, I had nothing to compare them to, but I knew I wasn't free in them. I wanted the freedom to make choices and believed I needed grades and somewhere else to gain it. In some large part because of my focus to get out, and in some significant but smaller part due to my antagonistic disposition, I passed up each opportunity to be a decent older brother to Jacob and Jed, failing in every respect an older brother enjoys to support and to inspire his younger brothers, eternally unpardonable behavior, so I was as surprised as anyone who knew me would be, to feel such terror at their prospective non-existence, the first recognition I felt strongly about someone other than me.

Behind me the front door led onto the front porch of our home. I stood and looked through the large window for lights in the young night. I sat back down and watched my mother breathing quietly with closed eyes. I had started playing the trumpet that year and at our first competition for first chair I came in second behind Ray and before Kent. The following week I sat in the second chair of the trumpet section under the basketball hoop at our concert and blasted the brass horn. Later I had my permanent lateral incisor extracted on the left side of my mouth to make room for my molars. I couldn't blow for weeks until the socket filled and sealed up. I felt guilty when I went to class and wore the cotton in my mouth days after it stopped bleeding.

My mother announced we would be handing out apples to all the trick-or-treaters on a Halloween afternoon I could not forget, sitting dazed from the news on the couch in the front living room. Apples? Could she be serious? Much of the community knew of the prohibition in the dentist's home on trick-or-treating, but we had never affirmatively opposed others' participating in the pagan holiday, and now my mother was, not on religious but wellness grounds. Some of my brothers silently disappeared into other rooms. I stayed, seeing the perversity of dishing Granny Smith and Golden Delicious forbidden fruits, willing to try it on others enjoying a night I wasn't able to, but not as willingly handing out an apple as the first costume approached, feeling guilty and smiling dropping one in her bag, receiving the same response from each who followed her onto our porch that evening, "An apple?" Treat seekers' numbers thinned and the trick seekers' humor soured over the next years, with eventually no repeaters.

My father returned with the working blood pressure kit but rendered no diagnosis. My brothers filed into the house sometime shortly after him. Without warning my mother failed to respond to my father's comments and moaned quietly. I got up and moved through the kitchen and climbed the stairs to the upstairs bedrooms until I reached steps near the top and looked through the bars at them lying together on the floor, my father holding my mother and my brothers scattering to help.

CHAPTER 17

COMPANIONS

Elder Aesop knocked on the door, and a middle-aged mustached man opened it.

—We're from the Church of Jesus Christ of Latter-day Saints, and we share a message about the gospel of Jesus Christ, Elder Aesop said.

—Come on in.

We gladly entered his house. We were walking up and down hills stretching our legs for the past couple hours with no success, no one showing the slightest interest.

—Want some water?

We pulled out our Discussion 1 The Plan of Our Heavenly Father pamphlet. Elder Aesop nodded, and I began sharing Principle 1 God Is Our Father, explaining God was the father of all of us, and he made a plan so we would be happy and grow spiritually, testifying of my belief in God's Plan of Happiness.

—How do you feel about God? I asked.

—I believe in Him.

Elder Aesop picked up with Principle 2, Jesus Christ Is Our Savior, and we alternated teaching the principles of the First Discussion to its conclusion, discussing the role of Joseph Smith as a modern prophet in God's Plan and Joseph's translation of the Book of Mormon, another testament of Jesus Christ revealed to prophets living in the ancient Americas, closing with the invitation to our host to pray and ask God to know if the teachings we shared were true. He said that he would. He also committed to read from the Book of Mormon we gave him.

—Will you allow us to return to share more about our message?

—I'd like that when my wife and daughter are here.

We set up a time to return and left elated.

That it was the first reception of its kind would be quite accurate. I had never had that experience in my first area, the only thing close was the day Elder Anselm and I spent on splits giving away a half dozen copies of the Book of Mormon to people showing an interest in reading them, but no one wanted to hear our message. With Elder Aesop we did not have a bad day, though most days no one wanted to talk to us. His positive attitude and humble disposition made working hard easier, handling gracefully all the rejection coming with the work. The key to missionary work was working through hours and hours of rejection to the few minutes of positive reception, then working tirelessly to follow up to extend that positive reception, then following up after the tireless efforts produced more rejection.

I learned from the many positive receptions with Elder Aesop that the most persuasive instrument was not the Holy Ghost, the eloquence of our presentation, our ability to create interest, resolve concerns, draw on knowledge of the scriptures, pull a shtick of charisma, or any number of skill or spiritual gift, all of which aided a missionary's efforts, but was the attitude of the missionary. He or she was the most immediate reflection of the value of the message we went on to share and testify was true. The goodness in words, gestures, and manners all communicated directly to the investigator that our message was for real, or in many cases was not. I never accepted that missionaries had success despite the shortcomings in them as messengers. It was the very explicit shortcomings combined with a sincere commitment to share their beliefs that conveyed genuine sparks of value in grocery stores, on buses, at doorsteps, and in homes, that connected sincere seekers to something outside their lives that could improve them.

I learned this early from Elder Aesop, people liked him and they did so because he was terribly likable. Over the months Elder Aesop and I were together we had many more experiences like the one with the sincere mustached man, seeing as many people join the Mormon Church in our months together as most missionaries in Georgia saw during their entire missions.

When we knocked at the gentle mustached man's house, his wife welcomed us into their home.

—Come in, Elders. Would you like some water?

—Thank you.

We sat with the parents and daughter in their living room to share Discussion 2, The Gospel of Jesus Christ. This discussion was the most important of discussions because in it, before completing the next four discussions that covered the basic tenets and commitments one would need to know and be willing to make to be a faithful member of the Mormon Church, was the invitation to be baptized. Elder Aesop and I discussed reviewing the First Discussion because neither the mother or daughter had received it, but we also didn't want to miss an opportunity to continue with the momentum from the first meeting to teach the father the second. So we did a quick review of the teachings from the first discussion and moved quickly to the second. The reception to our message was the same as the first meeting, except now the mother and daughter participated also in agreement. Elder Aesop taught the final principle and extended the invitation for baptism.

—Will you follow the example of Christ by being baptized by someone holding the *proper* priesthood authority of God?

The invitation took me by surprise because he extended it to the whole family, but we had discussed extending it to the father. Their answers startled me more.

—Yes, the daughter said.

—Yes, the parents said.

I burst with laughter, immediately converting it to a fit of coughing, begging for another glass of water. The daughter knew only a small part of what we believed, having missed the first discussion, and her willingness seemed premature, striking me over.

President Mensh stood with his chest out and his arms straight, not like a scarecrow's but not at attention like a soldier's either, like iron rods repelled by magnets, floating softly toward and away from his sides. He smiled under

his wide-rimmed square eyeglasses waiting for the new group of missionaries straight from the MTC to enter the terminal off the direct Delta flight
from Salt Lake City. We welcomed new missionaries together nearly a dozen
times.

—Missionaries arrive similar to each other but after two years depart
with great differences from each other, he said.

They walked off the airplane dazed, bright-eyed, hopeful, scared, having logged the same three weeks of intense religious instruction and skills
training, caught in a situation of surreal slow motion, believing two years of
missionary service would be a lifetime. We delivered old missionaries on the
same occasions, walking with them and extending our good wishes as we
left them at their gates. The seasoned elders wore faded suits, scuffed shoes
and fraying ties, sisters wearing ankle-length, well-kept and worn dresses. A
few boarded their departing flights certain, content, wise beyond their twenty plus one years, mixed with joy in anticipation of seeing family, friends,
and faithful girlfriends, and empty leaving a work they devoted every hour
and every day to the past two years. A few boarded departing flights bent
on getting the hell out of Dodge, miserable, depressed, still in shock at the
completion of their time served. No two years could be more markedly me-
tered than the minutes and hours adding up over daily efforts to proselytize
people through their beliefs, studying daily, praying constantly, receiving
and sending letters, recording in journals their thoughts and feelings, once a
week doing all chores, and trying always to draw upon a power bigger than
themselves.

The difference between missionaries began long before they entered a
terminal at Hartsfield-Jackson Atlanta International Airport to President
Mensh's grateful and welcoming, continent-sweeping smile, as did the differences by the time they went home. The range of difference accumulating
from eighteen years of life swamped the apparent difference seen lined on
their faces after two years of proselytizing the Mormon message of Jesus
Christ's restored gospel and one true Church. Each set of differences, those
formed before arrival and those through departure, were created and measurable in increments. Each decision shaped the person before his or her
mission, and each decision shaped him or her during it. So missionaries
arrived miles apart and the increases by the time they departed, while noticeable, were not so great as those when they began. The formula to gauge
the differences while on the mission where the many decisions in the daily grind, the steps taken to become better at proselytizing the message or

not, the most important steps being contacting everyone and following up with anyone showing interest, and the far less important steps were developing spiritual maturity and refining skills in the apartment and weekly and monthly training conferences. Steps forward or backward were measured in doing the work or not doing the work.

There was nothing mystical about success, everyone faced voluminous rejection, the most certain of certainties. The most successful missionaries faced even more of it. They had to face more to get through to the interested people. The main difference between effective and non-effective missionaries was not obedience or an abundance of the Spirit, it was the amount of time the effective missionaries put into the work to get through the tons of rejection to find interested investigators who desired to change the projection of their lives to a disciplined life full of choices filled with meaning in the Mormon Church.

The mission experience offered the opportunity for missionaries who had not focused on something other than themselves to discover the value, namely for themselves, to focus on the needs of others first. And many did and developed into able, thoughtful people for giving up me-first routines. The gleam in countenances on the last day in Atlanta in full-time missionaries was more about getting this truth than any other one. Even the most prideful, charismatic, ready-made husband, BYU-bound, returned missionary gleaned they were at their best focusing on the needs and concerns of their investigators, supporting local members, and building the strengths and helping to overcome the fears of companions. But there was no mistaking that the pre-mission routines, over a longer period of time and not carried out solely under the strictest of routines, had far more impact on the differences between missionaries.

President Mensh was right, but so was I when I answered Brother Tippin, a timid, thin, red-haired, late twenties, single, returned missionary. Brother Tippin was a dependable split in the Brockett Ward where Elder Aesop and I had been reunited. During our first president interview together President Mensh made a point of informing us good companionships did not stay together long and made good on it after our second month together, assigning me as senior companion in a rural proselytizing area centered in Cedartown, the single area of our mission extending into Alabama. For months after serving together Elder Aesop jokingly asked in president interviews when we could serve together again and before Elder Aesop's final month President Mensh assigned us to the Brockett area. During this final hurrah neither was designated the senior companion.

Brother Tippin pulled his compact car into our apartment complex beneath the shade of tall pine trees in the early night. He was pensive, calculating to take advantage of a few minutes before our curfew as he turned his engine off.

—Elder, can I ask you a question?

I became accustomed to members and missionaries asking me if they could ask me questions. I knew it wasn't because I gave profound answers because I never did, just as I didn't on this occasion. Brother Tippin had returned from a mission in Colorado, worked as a temple worker at the Atlanta Temple, an uncommon position for someone so young, and faithfully helped us whenever we asked.

—Sure.

—My mission president's wife would regularly say at zone conferences that we would never rise above the person we were as missionaries, so nothing was more important than to be the best missionary we could be, and she also said the person we were as a missionary set the course of the person we would be the rest of our lives. Do you believe that?

—No. I don't believe it. And she was wrong on both accounts. No one is wholly defined by past performance, and someone can always start putting together a run of good days that add up to a better version of him or herself.

He breathed deeply and smiled.

—Me neither, but I wasn't a good missionary, and I'm trying hard to be a good person. When I turn thirty I won't be able to work at the temple because I'm not married. I just really want to be a good person.

—And you are. Thanks for helping us.

Brother Thompson was eighteen and preparing to serve a mission, and I enjoyed taking splits with him more than any member in the Brockett Ward. I appreciated the opportunity to encourage him to serve a mission, knowing his family situation was broken with no lines of support, but I enjoyed even more just being around him. His smile disarmed everyone, not a charismatic spark on him, but one hundred percent sincere, completely open and vulnerable to everything. When he could split I took him to my favorite investigator, Sister Mary Anne Goodman. Sister Goodman was a nonmember wife of a long-time member. Most members thought she was a member because she had regularly attended church for decades, having reared her two children in it. After a split one evening a former Stake President told me that he had offered to make Sister Goodman the relief society President the day following her baptism. He shook his head confessing he had no idea why she didn't join the Church as he didn't know a better example of a Mormon.

Sister Goodman welcomed Brother Thompson and me on her deck, and we took seats on the soft chairs in the warm evening. She returned to the house and brought out lemonade and cookies, her kind routine each visit. We didn't waste time on re-teaching discussions she had already heard. Instead we talked about her beliefs and how they were formed or read our favorite passages from the Book of Mormon and the Bible. We also talked about our favorite books, and she shared one of hers, *Cry, the Beloved Country* by Alan Paton, encouraging me to read it soon upon my return. She shared her beliefs, favorite teachings, returning to recollections of a master teacher who taught a class on world religions leaving her with a continued desire and life-long pursuit to learn about all religions and the constant and cultivated impression that all religions had truths about God and offered admirable teachings about guiding their followers to improve conditions for those most in need. She didn't believe any one religion was ultimately better than any other. She smiled and complimented us repeatedly. Being with her and Brother Thompson was contagious. I didn't know I could smile so brilliantly and with such frequency as I did when reacting to them. No single person spoke my own beliefs with more accuracy than Sister Goodman. After months visiting on her porch I concluded the obvious. Sister Goodman did not need to be baptized Mormon to reach heaven. I want to remember I told her so, and if I didn't, then it was the single greatest failure of my mission.

Brother Thompson was the type of friend I looked to add, never to see or hear from him again after our last visit with Sister Goodman, remaining hopeful for years he went on the mission he wanted to serve and continued to experience a rewarding life he deserved.

My front porch visits with Sister Goodman were the beginning of a belief within myself that had been unarticulated before meeting Sister Goodman. She unlocked and gave me the confidence to embrace it. Sitting on her expansive front porch, I also felt something like a son's love for the first time in my life, uncomfortably grateful for her faith and unable to stop smiling in her presence.

Missionaries entered the room filled completely by a long table, taking seats around it. President Mensh met monthly with the zone leaders, two assistants, and two senior sisters. He met to discuss the progress and goals of the mission. I sat next to him doing what I did best, not saying anything, listening to the others in the room. Elder Whitely and I completed the assistants' training the previous month on the proper way to identify the Holy Spirit to confirm what the investigator was learning was true, neither of us unaware that our training overturned President Mensh's training on the same topic at zone conferences a couple months after we arrived in the mission, but neither of us discussed it nor did we clear our training with him. At least one zone leader was also not unaware of our corrective training.

—The assistants' training contradicted your training on identifying the spirit. Why was that?

—I believe you can answer that. President Mensh said, turning to me.

He had sat quietly through a half dozen trainings where Elder Whitely and I explained proper identification of God's confirmation through the Holy Spirit did not include a leading question, the type presupposing one correct answer, central to the skill taught in the earlier training.

—The proper way to identify the spirit can be found in at least three sources. Jesus provided an example in the New Testament; the Missionary Guide provided open-ended questions; and the suggested questions in the proselytizing discussions themselves.

—That's sufficient for me, President Mensh said turning back to the zone leader.

President Mensh and I got to know each other during monthly president interviews, but we also got to know each other during zone conferences during the last hour of president's training, which consisted of doctrinal instruction, the best part of the conference. I regularly commented and asked questions, rare participation with no precedent nor did it set one. During one of my first zone conferences in the mission, President Mensh explained the meaning of a chapter in the Book of Alma in the Book of Mormon, and towards the end when he invited questions, or didn't, I pointed out his interpretation didn't account for the previous chapter, and if it had, the chapter he discussed would have emphasized something different. He paused and almost nodded his approval. I learned during my final month under a new mission president, who was also an attorney, that President Mensh was a well-known attorney within the tight yet vast Mormon legal community. President Mensh was a former attorney general, who passed on Harvard Law School to join the charter class at the J. Reuben Clark Law School at

BYU at the request of its first dean, Rex E. Lee, the former U.S. Solicitor General, and the President of BYU that year, Dallin H. Oaks, who was later called as a Mormon apostle. President Mensh finished top of his class and clerked for a federal circuit court judge and later for the chief justice of the U.S. Supreme Court. He was not absorbed with his own sense of profundity like many LDS leaders. His lack of pretense was easily misunderstood as unfriendly, but he was engaging, asking more questions than giving answers. He chose his words carefully without wasting them, as likely to use filler as he was to affect emotion during remarks on spiritual matters. He was not lovable, and he was not fake. The highest compliment he paid was tagging one of us as a make-it-happen missionary.

Elder Whitely and I trained missionaries to appropriately identify the Holy Spirit to confront the easy flip of using skills to manipulate people into making decisions. I railed, evenhandedly and consistently, against missionaries using commitment pattern skills, drilled during the MTC and perfected each day in the missionary field, to manipulate people to fulfill commitments. I believed a fine line, very fine in the instance of earnest and charismatic missionaries, should not be crossed to get people to take steps to join the Church. On the right side of the line, I believed missionaries should help investigators follow through on commitments by developing the investigator's own motivation, and on the wrong side of the line was getting investigators to follow through for any reason other than their own motivation. What may sound too fine to parse in its explanation was not always obvious when seeing missionaries at work either, but I was convinced the difference of the motivation behind the investigator's actions correlated to their activity in the Church after the blissful early weeks of missionaries' full attention waned. And while we never discussed it, President Mensh concurred implicitly by his attempts to develop right motivation in missionaries to act and at least once explicitly at the end of the long table during our monthly zone leader meeting.

We stood facing the wall of small faces, missionary pictures on yellow industrial paper next to companions divided into districts and zones. We discussed each companionship to determine whether missionaries and the proselytizing area would benefit from a change. "Revelation is ninety percent information and ten percent inspiration." President Mensh said. We began the day of determinations with a prayer to receive the ten percent. With weekly reports of proselytizing data for each companionship—gathered by assistants each week from zone leaders, who in turn had gathered information from each district leader—and the information President Mensh gained during his monthly interview we had the other ninety percent. He smiled, pulling off the picture of Elder Allaire, who was completing his twenty-fourth month and heading home on transfer day the following week.

—The likes of us two have to get by without the charisma and good looks of Elder Allaire.

I had not thought of President Mensh as charming or handsome, but I hadn't thought of myself as not being either, but there was no one there to kid I was. And no one mistook me as having charisma. I dropped to one hundred and forty-five pounds, my wrestling weight senior year of high school, my suits and slacks draped over my thin, bony frame, scratching my dismal, uneven hairdo, a failed military cut as seemingly impossible as not being able to fold paper to fit an envelope, runs of red acne lacing my pale face, as I turned and smiled back. Elder Allaire was an ideal, dream missionary. He not only looked good, tall and athletic, spoke well, and worked hard, but he also played the piano, a most useful skill called upon at numerous monthly meetings and priceless at often poorly-planned but much-anticipated new-member baptisms. Elder Allaire had it all and no doubt after returning home would marry a beautiful girl, finish school summa cum laude and pursue an esteemed career in medicine, his smile portending the bedside manner of the best doctor with puffed baby cheeks and deep dimples drawn at a flash. He was a nice guy too.

A few missionaries made their mothers proud and learned to play the piano, capable of playing most of the hymns, making them indispensable. Then there was Elder Lamontagne. After a zone conference I walked through the hall passing the door to the sacrament meeting room, the main meeting hall in each Mormon Church building, hearing sounds coming from the piano I hadn't heard since my mother made her boys accompany her to hear the traveling concert pianist at the civic center. I opened the door and stepped inside. This music was not on The Plan, but I wouldn't be the one to point that out to the newly arrived Elder Lamontagne. If someone did, Elder Lamontagne didn't seem the type to care. He was aloof, not given to small talk and niceties. He stood apart and well above all the other missionaries, with keen flowing hair and his chest and shoulders filling out his tailored suit. He could have been a linebacker on leave from BYU's football program. He was not just playing a superior role, but he was beyond the far seconds of his peers, including the most polished Elder Allaire. Elder Lamontagne had gifts none of us had and like many talented people did not interact well with his immediate population, not necessarily from social inability to do so, rather others offered him nothing but an audience, taxing his time with no possibility of reciprocation. I treated him like I treated everyone, with respect and encouragement and indifference. I complimented him on his piano playing and told him to take advantage of working with his trainer Elder Smith, assuring him there was no one better. I knew because I served with Elder Smith for a longer period than any other missionary during my mission. He was the most successful missionary in the mission when measured in baptisms, by far. If he had been sitting with other returned missionaries sipping cold purple Kool-Aid at a county fair in a rural town in Utah and all of them disclosed how many baptisms each had on their missions, one would mistakenly assume Elder Smith served a mission in Latin America, where missionaries accumulated numbers approaching the hundreds, often exceeding three digits. He was half way there, an unbelievable feat in our mission. No one else came close. He was the best and everyone knew it.

And I'll be damned if I could hardly stand serving with him toward the end of our time together. He was perfect, and he was also the most temperamental missionary I met. One minute he was gung-ho and the other scowling over some minor decision I made, which I admit was probably wrong or not on The Plan. For example, the time an investigator showed up at our door and wanted to take us for a ride, so I accepted without consulting Elder Smith, who made his disapproval known as I looked in the rear-view mirror as the investigator sped up and turned up Bush's classic grunge ode, "Glycerine," after I commented I liked it. I concluded in our last interview together with President Mensh that Elder Smith needed to be a senior companion, he was far too good to be held back from making all the important decisions, though I had deferred to him on all the important decisions for months, which amounted to where we would go to knock on doors smiling as their owners closed them. He was dramatic with a thespian's flare, given to improvs, singing a show tune or performing fleeting dance steps as we exited the apartment, drawing on an emotional reserve none of the rest of us had, save the sisters who were fairly removed because of their small numbers and the rules barring Elders from doing splits with them.

That Elder Smith was assigned to train Elder Lamontagne spoke to the great promise President Mensh saw in Elder Lamontagne.

—You have an opportunity no one else in your group has, and few other missionaries in the mission have had to serve with the most effective missionary in the mission. It won't always be easy but learn as much as you can.

I extended my hand to Elder Smith standing next to us and he kindly took it. We had become like brothers, with no choice but to appreciate each other during our fixed service of months together, which neared the actual time served by my blood brothers, who by their good judgment probably limited time in my presence so that they accumulated only a few months around the clock over our many years. This made Elder Smith, who had no choice but continuous twenty-four-hour runs, the likely time winner. Pursing his lips and raising his eyebrows Elder Smith tossed his scarf over his neck, turned on his heels and glided to the exit with the grace of Astaire, not the physicality of Kelly. But not before he said,

—Have a very good day.

I did so many splits with missionaries that I couldn't count the number, and while I remember few of them, I remember the one with Elder Lamontagne. It proceeded like all the others: we knocked on a few doors, followed up with choice investigators, visited members in the areas of the choice investigators who were not home, talked about companions, and eventually talked about home. Elder Smith was pushing Elder Lamontagne to memorize a scripture per day along with the discussions.

—And how are you doing?

—I'm doing okay.

—Happy?

—Not a lot of the time.

—Work hard with Elder Smith and you'll appreciate it the rest of your mission. Things get better but you'll always have butterflies in your gut each time you contact someone. It doesn't mean you don't know what you're doing. It just means you care.

I pulled the car into the driveway of their apartment and could see Elder Smith and my companion through the window with Elder Smith acting out some critical scene from an episode of contacting that day, or maybe a classic Broadway play. Elder Lamontagne reached for his pocket and pulled out his wallet. He showed me a picture of a beautiful girl with long flowing curly blonde hair.

—This is my older sister. She died in a car accident a couple years ago. She was my best friend and I think about her every day. I would have liked for her to meet you. You would have gotten along well.

CHAPTER 18
MISSIONARY WORK

President Ben E. Rich was an early mission president of the Southern States Mission headquartered in Tennessee. During a civic celebration involving a parade, President Rich entered a contingent of missionaries, who were even less popular at the turn of the twentieth century than at the end of it in the Sunny South. During their march they passed Theodore Roosevelt in the crowd of spectators, and Teddy recognized his old friend Ben. Teddy entered the parade and grasped Ben.

—All boys would do well to serve one of these Mormon missions to make men of them, Teddy said.

I knew this story was true like all other stories of its kind involving famous figures and compliments to the Church, whether this one happened or not. Teddy Roosevelt was my favorite president before hearing it, because of his depiction in *The Wind and the Lion* (1975), one of the few action movies my mother relented on letting us see despite the killings, and he was forever after it.

We exited MARTA and walked the short distance to the church downtown. Trips to the city were like holidays, a break from the daily grind of sharing our message in our assigned area. We descended on the city with all the missionaries in our mission. The rare migration, happening only a couple of times during our two years of service, was no ordinary event. President Boyd K. Packer, acting president of the Quorum of the Twelve Apostles, had official business in Atlanta and took time out of his busy schedule to address us. For many missionaries the only time they heard a general authority, a living apostle or member of the Seventy, was during their missionary service. For those of us missionaries on furlough from BYU, we saw the highest leadership in the flesh every semester.

Hundreds of missionaries filled the sacrament meeting room and overflowed into the gym. I had been to see the band Live in Salt Lake City with a few guys from my floor at Deseret Towers. Weezer opened for them without their lead singer, who was backstage sick. I was stoked to see them, disappointed but impressed that they still played a couple songs. I had heard of Live, recognized a few of their songs, and overwhelmed by the night they dominated, not on the spectacular scale of U2 at Foxboro stadium the summer after my sophomore year of high school but like nothing I had experienced, as I moshed the entire set fifty feet from the stage. This meeting was nothing like that event, but I felt energy walking into the large young group, anticipating the visit of a living apostle.

Elder Packer was a heavyweight among the Twelve Apostles. He spoke his mind, and his mind was aligned to eternal truth. He was not the touchy-feely general authority who would request to shake missionaries' hands while staring deeply at them, able to make inspired judgments about their worthiness based on their countenances like the tight Marmeladov reading the troubles of Raskolnikov. The new guard of Mormon apostles could as easily pass for Tony Robbins or other inspiring life-coaches who made audiences renewed to set goals and to become better and more successful people. Again, not Elder Packer. He was sober, old school, nothing phony. He spoke gruffly, was stern and a bit obtuse. He was renowned for encouraging missionaries and members to find a testimony "in the bearing of it." Nothing reflected the depth of a Mormon's belief in God and his One True Church more than his or her testimony. Elder Packer was not encouraging missionaries and members to fake it until they make it, though he sounded awful close to that, and many missionaries and members did so. He wanted Mormons to be bold, straight-faced, and convicted followers of their shared tradition, and he knew that took time to develop, so his proclamation was more about a Pascalian perseverance to know the truth, not unlike my father's zealous and continual infusion of Jesus into the lives of his sons.

Elder Packer encouraged missionaries and members to go into their own grove of trees like Joseph Smith and receive the same witness that Mormonism's first prophet did. He encouraged missionaries and members to have all of God's revelation since Joseph had opened the heavens, but he also did not fail to point out that that very truth members would receive would be consistent with the teachings of the Church's leaders or would not be truth if it contradicted them, his corralling of his grand offer more admirable as a flare of leadership than a slip of a sound mind.

In Atlanta that day, he stroked his suspenders as he stood before us, his personal bodyguard sitting off to the side with a clear view of all the missionaries. He talked about his Presbyterian friend in Atlanta, venerating his goodness, his worthiness, his righteousness, his important work for the people of the city. But that friend didn't have God's proper priesthood, he said. The proper priesthood was contained only within the Mormon Church. We, save the dozen or so sisters in attendance, had the real priesthood, he said. We were the only followers who could trace our authority back to God himself, tracing back from whoever bestowed the Aaronic Priesthood on us at age twelve and Melchizedek Priesthood on us at nineteen, my grandfather and father, to the early leaders of the Church who received the holy priesthoods from the resurrected beings of John the Baptist and Peter, James, and John themselves. All of which we knew so he didn't need to say. With the real authority he charged us to bring the truth about the restoration of Jesus' true Church through the Prophet Joseph Smith to the people of Atlanta and the surrounding area. We had a great mission, and he gave us his blessing to succeed at it. After the closing hymn and prayer he put his suit coat back on and followed his personal bodyguard out of the building as we stood at attention.

Missionaries tried to carry out the charge by finding the elect, the chosen of God who were prepared to receive the restored gospel. The Lord commanded early elders of the Mormon Church as recorded in the Twenty-Ninth section of the Doctrine and Covenants *to bring to pass the gathering of mine elect; for mine elect hear my voice and harden not their hearts.* Elder Smith gathered the elect better than anyone, finding those willing to hear and soften their hearts. The rest of us struggled to find them. The challenge of finding the elect required missionaries to work efficiently and effectively within time limits, twelve-hour days over one hundred and one weeks, and within the limits of ways to reach them, from heartfelt television advertisements to friendly Mormon neighbors and co-workers. Given our limits, many missionaries would not follow up with a half-hearted commitment, and some would even stop teaching an investigator who did not progress fast enough through the lessons. I was not as discriminating. If anyone would visit, I did.

Office-elder companionships occasionally included a third elder who was in between hardships, in a probationary period, taking his mission one month at a time. We carried on our proselytizing efforts with three like we did with two, making a slightly more intimidating presentation at apartment doors. Once, I knocked on the door with my companion and temporary companion flanking me. A Middle Easterner with a full dark beard and thick long hair opened it.

—We share a message about how families can be together forever, I said.

—Come in, he said.

He offered his couch, and we sat. He asked if we were thirsty, and we were. I proceeded to visit with him for the next three hours. At pauses during our visit we smiled at my companions nodding off with their heads comfortably against the cushions. I had not met a Muslim in Atlanta and had only seen, not been introduced to, a couple of Muslims in Professor Tilman's class. This man provided a history of his religion, and I provided a history of mine. We talked about the importance of prophets and scriptures and devotion to religion. I drew upon what I knew from Tilman's class, masking my ignorance. After hours passed, I woke up my companions, and he saw us out.

I enjoyed visiting with people and believed strongly taking the time to have a meaningful conversation was the most important work I could do as a missionary. In most instances the people I saw join the Mormon Church had on multiple occasions met and talked to Mormons before meeting my companion and myself. I believed each meeting was as critical as any other, including the one where an investigator accepted the invitation to follow Christ to be baptized by someone with proper priesthood authority.

A thin, sickly, on-the-youthful-side, middle-aged man with a shaved head welcomed us into his home before we said anything.

—We are missionaries from The Church…

—I know who you are. I contacted you.

The window shades in the room were drawn and the dim light from a lamp in the corner strained to reach us and the other objects in the room. We sat on the nearest chairs.

—Did you respond to a commercial and order a video about the Mormon Church?

We had no record of him in the proselytizing area book.

—I've met you guys and know what you teach.

—You probably met missionaries like us. Could we share our message about living prophets and modern day scripture with you?

—I've met you before. Go ahead.

We proceeded with an abridged version of the first discussion, sure to record it as a full lesson for the purpose of our weekly report, asking questions about the various topics and moving on after his short, disjointed responses. Minutes into the visit I thought he sat like a scared cat.

I was willing to talk to anyone, except when it seemed inappropriate, which could be in any number of circumstances, including when we were in danger. I felt uncomfortable as we continued to teach the discussion. I had felt uneasy before with a few investigators. We visited an older gentleman in his tidy, well kept room in government housing, his bed neatly made in view through his open bedroom door and his kitchen clean and in order with clear counters. We visited him a few times, always being offered, and I accepting, a cold Coke, spitting on and wiping the lid before I popped it. On one occasion, our last visit, he volunteered he was abused as a young man after experiencing recurring blackouts from a fall off a fence. He needed some help, and we had reached our limit. We encouraged him to take advantage of the services the housing staff provided, assuming they did, but did not follow up with him or the staff, providing the support he needed being beyond us.

The sickly, thin, youthful-looking middle-aged man with a shaved head opened a desk drawer and pulled out a revolver. I couldn't immediately think of a graceful exit but was convinced I needed to come up with one. I tried to catch his eye.

—Our message is true and very important. Thank you for allowing us to share it with you today. I said.

He hesitated noticing the abrupt end.

—We look forward to coming back, I said.

Standing, I led my companion to the door, opening it and walked out. I wondered if the missionaries before us had removed his information so missionaries would not follow up with him. I concluded that a note with his information in large letters to stay away for our own safety would have been appropriate to leave in the area book, walking with the shivers back to the car and still feeling them as we drove back to our apartment. When we arrived home I didn't make a note in the area book either. I also failed to justify why I said we'd come back, supposing the previous missionaries likely also speedily exited upon a promise to return, possibly explaining his expectation and miffed reception.

Missionary work began early, about six ante meridian and ended at a reasonable hour, about ten post meridian. It rarely started earlier but it often went later. Once in a rare while, an emergency drew us from our apartment outside the prescribed hours. I enjoyed doing splits with other elders in their areas, taking advantage to encourage their investigators and the elders themselves, showing them it was possible to enjoy or at least positively do missionary work. And on splits, missionaries were always alert to keeping proper hours.

The phone rang after midnight, and Elder Timmons answered it. I heard it but didn't catch any of his conversation, quickly back to sleep until he turned on the lights, re-awaking me.

—A member in the ward needs our help.

—Should he call the police or someone else? We don't do emergency discussions.

—He said his son was sick and needed someone to give him a blessing.

How sick could he be? I asked, stumbling off the worn depleted mattress to the floor, standing to find my slacks, socks, white shirt and tie. Elder Timmons looked helpless.

—Should I call him back?

He knew we should not be out so late, or early, and did not want to be doing something wrong on a split with me.

—Let's go.

We dressed in a minute and stepped outside. The member, a balding older man who ran a organic holistic health food store, pulled into the parking lot in his fifty-something Ford pickup. We climbed in and he thanked us the entire ride to his house.

—My son's deathly ill.

I looked at Elder Timmons.

—Should you take him to the hospital?

—We don't do hospitals. If anyone can help him, you elders can.

The truck rolled abruptly into a driveway and stopped. We followed him into the living room to a chair set in the middle, apparently the appointed seat for the blessing. His son, a middle-aged man, sat bent over on a chair against the wall separating the room from the kitchen. He rolled slowly back and forth in immense pain.

—Who will give the blessing? the member asked.

—Will you do it? Elder Timmons asked quietly.

—Yes and we'll need first to anoint him with oil.

We both reached into the pockets of our slacks and coats, learning we failed to grab our vials of consecrated oil in our hasty departure. Missionaries carried small vials of consecrated oil, pure virgin oil consecrated by a priesthood blessing for the purpose of healing the sick, needing no more than a drop to dab on the crown of the recipient's head for these very occasions.

—We left the apartment without our consecrated oil. Do you have any on you or is there any in the house?

—I have some oil. I'll get it.

—Will this do?

He returned from the kitchen with a gallon of vegetable cooking oil about one third full. I nodded. It would have to. His son took a seat on the chair in the middle of the room.

—Since I am doing the blessing, you'll need to anoint him, and you'll also need to consecrate the oil before the anointing, I said.

Before we could take the oil and without a word, the father removed the lid and dumped the cooking oil on his son.

—Okay, he said.

The oil dripped over his son's head in thick long strands to the carpet. I placed my hands lightly on top of Elder Timmons hands on the son's head.

—Do I need to use specific language? Elder Timmons whispered.

—Say Heavenly Father I consecrate and anoint this oil by the holy Melchizedek Priesthood in the name of Jesus Christ Amen, I said, clenching my jaw.

He did. Finished he started to pull his hands away, and I gripped them keeping them there. I started the blessing, politely interrupting myself.

—Excuse me, what is your full name?

The sickly middle-aged man strained his voice to answer my request.

—Thank you.

Calling him by his full given and surname, I returned to pronouncing a blessing upon him with Heavenly Father's blessings to heal him of his current sickness and to provide him and his family with wisdom on the proper course of action for a complete cure, adding blessings of righteousness and guidance from the Holy Spirit for living the commandments and honoring the covenants he made with God. Then I released Elder Timmons hands from the son's head.

—Great blessing, elder, the father said.

—Thanks, elder, the son said.

We had a great reason for it, but we didn't sleep-in the next morning, and before we left the apartment the member called to report his son was walking around and felt much better. Anytime we could help we tried to be of service to members and investigators because doing good deeds was what we did and it also gave us a reason not to be contacting people to learn more about the Mormon Church, which amounted to continual rejection, or feeling guilty for not contacting people who continually rejected us. Day after day, weeks turning into months, we learned to make the concerns and interests of others the focus of our lives. That singular opportunity simply did not happen for us anywhere else.

PART IV

CHAPTER 19
DESTINY

Back at Brigham Young University, I sat in Professor Young's office, stretching my neck toward the single window to the north, watching the last sun rays disperse as the fall afternoon turned into evening. The office, a converted storage room, was in the northeast corner on the fourth floor of the Harold B. Lee Library, the heart of BYU's campus. I sat in the chairs lined up in front of his desk many late afternoons the semester after returning home from my Mormon mission, twenty-one years old and a sophomore at BYU.

Two years earlier, I had returned home from BYU like many other young freshman boys to make final preparations for a Mormon mission and received my mission call, the official letter from Mormon Church Headquarters, informing me I would proselytize the doctrines of the LDS Church for twenty-four months in the Georgia, Atlanta Mission. The Call had crushed me. I wanted to learn a foreign language and to live in a foreign culture far beyond the borders of my native Idaho, driven by self-interest and knowing how valuable a second language could be to a successful academic or business career, absent was any desire to expand my knowledge or to appreciate lives unknown to me. And the Deep South was not the exotic destination I had gone to in my mind. Daydreams of Europe or Russia, or somewhere in Asia, or maybe even Ireland, convinced any one single solitary foreign culture, and hopefully language, would jump-start a successful future career. The passing of two years in Northern Georgia convinced me nowhere else could have replicated my experience, and there was no better epilogue than having on numerous occasions sat in the office of Professor Young to discuss our Mormon beliefs.

I called on Professor Young weekly to discuss passages from the Book of Mormon or other sacred Mormon scriptures. We also visited about his son, his research, my classes, my dating experiences, our mutual friend, Samuel, who I met in Atlanta and who introduced me to Professor Young upon my return to BYU, and Sam's family, all told a very successful group, many of whom had also sat and discussed Mormon scriptures with Professor Young. Sam completed a Ph.D. in epidemiology at Emory and had joined the Centers for Disease Control and Prevention in Atlanta when I met him. His intelligence was exceeded only by his immeasurable decency, not a trace of spite in him.

In that converted office space, we read and discussed a single verse from the Book of Alma in the Book of Mormon for two hours and on another occasion discussed themes progressing from the beginning of the Book of Mormon to its end, paralleling the Mormon temple ceremony. Professor Young's mannerisms were consistent, always gentle and never rushed as he sat behind his desk, and frequently stood to search out a text stored in a certain pile of books or papers scattered about his office. His background was in United States history, and while he had taught courses, he was currently employed full-time at the library.

Discussions started by reading passages aloud, proceeded with Professor Young's questions, and finished with his explanations, often including physical demonstrations not separate from the act of speaking but part of it. Once he asked me to stand, to close my eyes and to follow his directions, and when I did the passage's meaning descended upon me. I had never studied scripture so deeply, with ideas emerging with such immediacy and clarity. My spiritual education extended throughout my sophomore year, halting only after his superiors addressed the growing mass of student visits. He never said to stop coming by, but brief comments and the new need to schedule appointments ahead of time were signs of mounting pressure, something he did not like, and I did not want to contribute to. I vaguely understood his job until I later sought him out to say good-bye, just before I graduated, in his new glass-enclosed office well below ground in the rare collections wing of the library. He was cordial, as always.

Our meeting this fall afternoon seared its mark pink, opening me further to infectious elements that arose later that evening. Usually, Professor Young arranged a visit by proposing a possible time to meet the following week, never a fixed appointment, but never did I miss one. For all our previous meetings, Professor Young had never double-booked a visit, although it's surprising it did not happen regularly, given the many students who sought his company. But that day, unlike every other visit another student called on Professor Young at the same time. The other student, an auburn-haired young man, a couple years my senior, was not the contemplative peer I had imagined also visited Professor Young. He was striking, broad shouldered, and charismatic. While I did not expect his company that afternoon, he was not unexpected, arriving shortly after me, taking a seat next to mine.

With the added visitor in mind, Professor Young chose the reading, a short piece edited by a future Mormon prophet, John Taylor, from the periodical, *The Mormon*, on August 29, 1857. He chose it for its topic, clearly announced in its title, "Origin, Object, and Destiny of Women" (the OODW). The author explained who we married we had chosen to marry before this life. This very idea had been denied by Zeno, as recorded in his great *Confessions*, in response to his young wife Augusta's declaration of her eternal love for him and hope of their eternal marriage. Zeno based his very denial on the same logic espoused by the author of the OODW, and that logic was the belief of eternal beginnings and ends. Zeno reasoned such beginnings and ends made marriage insignificant. Quite to the contrary, the author believed it made marriage of great importance.

But Zeno not only lacked his wife's good intentions. He also lacked the knowledge of the author of the OODW, which was based on modern revelation. Mormon eternal marriage was part of a much larger plan. It followed from the Mormon belief in a pre-mortal existence, where all people existed as spirit children of God in the presence of God before coming to Earth, a critical beginning to the Mormon Plan of Salvation. All people who have lived on Earth chose to come to Earth during the pre-mortal existence to gain physical bodies and to gain mortal experience necessary to be more like God. Their choice to come to Earth was distinct from a charted course designed by God, known as predestination. Another unique aspect of the Mormon Plan of Salvation was that Jesus also got started in the pre-mortal existence, where he volunteered to carry out God's plan. And he did so in opposition to Satan's plan. God's plan involved people choosing to follow the correct course and not pre-election, which as Calvin would point out, implies an absence of choice. Which absence of choice—for Mormons—was the key to Satan's plan, which involved the return of all God's children with no opportunity to choose for themselves the right plan. Satan offered an appealing outcome, yes, but at the cost of paltry mortal growth. All Mormons believe that real growth is contingent upon choices and making choices was the very purpose of coming to Earth in the first place.

The role of choice, central to God's Plan, corresponded to the essential element of our pre-mortal and mortal make-up, that is agency, a person's innate capacity to decide and to act according to one's volition, dare I say one's own will uncaused, albeit influenced or restrained by time and space and culture and socioeconomic and geopolitical and technological and environmental and genetic conditions. None of those factors approached the primacy of unadulterated agency in God's Plan, and this agency was, in part, preconditioned on having no memory at all of peoples' pre-mortal embrace of the aforementioned Plan, reminded of it only through Mormons' founding Prophet Joseph Smith.

Which brings me back to where I sat with the good professor and strapping young man. A consequence of some great importance in this belief of a pre-mortal existence was the role of the family, the holy arc and divine institution of historical and contemporary Mormondom—family being the very crowd one enters existence among. I understate by saying that the family is a paramount piece of God's Plan, shored up in Mormons' belief that marriage performed by Mormon authority in Mormon temples is a necessary threshold for fulfilling their highest role in God's Plan—having and rearing righteous little ones, and the more of them the better—binding children with parents for eternity. Or in other words, marriage was eternal. And according to the author of OODW, marriage had its eternal beginning in the pre-mortal life.

Deciding whom one would marry before this life not only enlarged romantic horizons but also fulfilled God's Plan with import beyond the need for repetition, but also lent itself quite appropriately to it: in summation, Mormons married who they had committed to marry before this life. This truth failed to wane in its categorical appeal; although not accepted by all Mormons before they married, it surely was universally presumed upon retrospection by all who eventually did. With no event having more significance in all of Mormondom than the union of man and wife, we can understand Mormons' unfailing fondness for Rob Reiner's *The Princess Bride* (1987) and their double certainty that true love was never threatened when, firstly, Buttercup did not say "I do," and buttressed, secondly, by the understanding that a lack of proper authority to bind man and wife ever existed in the first state, which absence insulated Westley and Buttercup's true love far beyond Prince Humperdinck's nefarious intentions. No place on Earth was more likely for souls to reunite in the meshing of true love marked by commitments of eternity, than within the hallowed webbings of BYU.

The OODW piece did not surprise me a bit. And it seemed to reaffirm the auburn-haired student's intuition that he had decided in the pre-mortal life whom he would marry. But his tone and countenance suggested he was not as sure the woman in his mortal life was the same one with whom he had made that pre-mortal decision. A pickle indeed! The consequences of either being with your eternal love or being mistaken you were with your eternal love was the difference of eternity. Eternal devastation would certainly result if one found out after this life you did not marry your *real* eternal companion, the eternal anguish of not just any garden-variety failed promise. To learn one's error even while enjoying well earned celestial glory, the Mormon's highest heaven, and exaltation (through Jesus' atonement and necessary Mormon ordinances) without one's true love seemed incompatible, almost a hellish glitch, with Heavenly Father's Plan (of ultimate happiness, no less). An eternity of pining on not what *could* have been, but on what *should*, I dare say "ought," have been, a hell of magnanimous proportions. The mere possibility caused eternal angst in the Mormon heart, its sheer piercing at the eternal unconscious the catalyst preceding the uniquely shortened Mormon engagements, commonly of a couple months, for most, young Mormon marriages. The angst only erased by the desire and the effort, mostly the effort, to get started a family—after the eternal covenant of a temple Mormon marriage—of unwieldy, perfect children, which removed any smudges of remaining angst, but possibly not forever and ever.

Professor Young told a story about a friend who believed he was meant to marry a girl he loved as a young man, but the woman rejected him. The man never married, but he never relinquished his love for the woman, and far into later life he reconnected with her after the death of her husband, and they married. The story raised all kinds of questions for me, chief among them whether the first or the second husband was the one she had committed to marry her in the pre-mortal life. And if it were the second, had she annulled her celestial temple marriage binding her to the first husband as nothing less would reward the second's faithfulness. And annulling the first sealing would have required permission from the highest Mormon authorities, for while men may be sealed (not civilly) to multiple spouses, women could not (until the dawn of the twenty-first century, creating a briarpatch of celestial bliss). Convinced of the second husband's earned reward, upon further reflection, I surmised the death of the first husband averted eternal tragedy, given my preference for the hero of the story (and assuming an annulling and new sealing).

The auburn-haired young man seemed unmoved by the story, confirming my early suspicion he was not the contemplative type I reckoned my equal. My annoyance with his presence only increased for the lack of turmoil I conjectured inside his head, a lack of torment surely matched by his inability to grasp the import of this moment. And he didn't appear a patient, long-suffering lover either. Honestly, he didn't appear the type who needed to be.

Young Mormon men had immense power over young Mormon women to decide if their feelings manifested commitments made in a pre-mortal life. This singular power of the youth next to me, in addition to his being attractive and pleasant and likely intelligent with a bright future ahead safeguarded him against the unrequited love experienced by many men. Far too many Mormon men had their pre-destined love fall on unmoved hearts of Mormon women who couldn't be brought around to remembering their earlier pre-mortal commitment. The tragedy also has included not a few non-Mormon men from the narrator's love for Gilberte in Marcel Proust's *In Search of Lost Time* to the Judge's purest hopes in Krzysztof Kieslowski's *Three Colors: Red* (1994).

Our young Mormon man sat buffered in his belief, not the least vulnerable to ruinous bitter fallouts like the Judge's, who could have avoided his whole criminal mess if he'd only known how important agency was in God's Plan, and that not everyone, including the object of his affections, was bound to choose correctly. And if they were so bound, could still have followed Satan's plan, with a cherry of determinism on top. Even the Judge would have to concede Satan's plan improper without agency despite his years of utterly bitter existence free to behave properly or nastily, having chosen the latter. Convinced I understood everything and armed with nothing, I did not want to wait for success as did the old man in Professor Young's tale, and I further hoped to avoid the bitterness of the Judge. I was, however, not the least repulsed by his redeeming good fortune through the kindness of the beautiful young Valentine, herself justification enough to mention Kieslowski's great picture show; and her significance all the more assuming that she, along with her player Irene Jacob, would no doubt be in need of an eternal companion. And I among the willing would adequately do this singular act of honor, acting as the celestial mate for endless gentiles, many of them assuredly movie stars, a burden righteous young Mormon men dutifully bore, heeding their divine call to practice true celestial marriage, the doctrinal new and everlasting covenant, and expecting God's Plan, including the pre-mortal foregoing-ons, had and would play out in my favor.

Not having made a comment during the discussion, I sat still as night poured through the window, stirring my emotions. The discussion had taken me by surprise, but the topic had not. I'd been considering the idea of eternal marriage with some fashion of eternal beginnings for some time, and now the idea was confirmed by my favorite professor, "The Mormon," present handsome company, heroic tales, and divine logic. I confess, for years eternal musings had set my expectations for my eternal companion to have the kind of devotion that Margarita had for The Master in Mikhail Bulgakov's novel by the same name. And that very same evening I just happened to have a date with a young woman I was destined to marry, Sandy, hoping to find the same devotion.

Chapter 20
Roses

Students filed into the cavernous basketball arena on the campus of Brigham Young University every week, filling seats from the floor to the ceiling. I regularly joined the throng of students who came from all corners of campus, briskly walking north to attend devotionals on Tuesday mornings at the J. Willard Marriott Center, the main indoor athletic and conference facility on campus. Attendance was convenient my freshman year because I lived in student housing at Deseret Towers, dormitories at the time located a few hundred yards directly east of the Marriott Center.

Attendance became more challenging during sophomore through senior years after I returned from my Mormon mission, when I worked part-time at the Missionary Training Center, a ten-minute walk north of the Marriott Center. Shifts at the MTC divided into morning, afternoon and evening, and I took the one that worked best with my class schedule but always tried to leave the morning open for Tuesday devotionals. The devotional speakers were prominent LDS public figures, distinguished faculty members of BYU, and leaders of The Church of Jesus Christ of Latter-day Saints, including an annual visit from the Mormon prophet, drawing the largest crowd of the year. Occasionally a forum substituted for the devotional, as in the case of the visit by Rabbi Harold Kushner my freshman year. Forum speakers were distinguished academics and conservative political and religious leaders. If my work-schedule permitted, I never missed a forum address.

One of the most memorable devotional addresses was by the Mormon Apostle Elder Richard G. Scott. I admired Elder Scott, respecting his background as a scientist, unique to the Quorum of the Twelve Apostles, and by my judgment he was the most compassionate of a very compassionate group of Church leaders. The Mormon leaders played a critical and constant role in the lives of LDS members, informing members of what was wrong and what was right and instructing them to apply the teachings of the Church to their lives. They spoke biannually at a conference that was broadcast by satellite to the far reaches of the globe. And they knew that, for Mormons, the pulpit led their world.

The pulpit is ever this earth's foremost part, all the rest comes in its rear, Ishmael observed in Herman Melville's *Moby-Dick*. What came over the pulpit at general conference had the weight of scripture but with the advantage of immediacy, even more relevant than the Holy Bible and the Book of Mormon. Ishmael's observation fit many religions, but none more than Mormonism because what authorities poured over the pulpit served to guide faithful LDS members' prows navigating the godless and hostile seas of modern life. Ishmael correctly explained the power of the pulpit but also witnessed how this power should be earned as Father Maple ascended to the pulpit in the Whalemen's Chapel by climbing a rope ladder. If only all ministers who define what is fair and foul for all others worked as hard to get there. The weekend of general conference involved marathon two-hour sessions, one on TV in the morning and another in the afternoon, Saturday and Sunday. My father granted mercy by requiring us to listen Sunday morning and to attend an additional Saturday evening Priesthood session for teen-aged boys and men, broadcast only to the stake center church building. Growing up I always hoped my favorite speakers would talk during those two sessions as they always helped time along.

In addition to hearing him speak, I enjoyed misidentifying Elder Scott in conversations with my father, intentionally referring to Elder Richard G.

Scott, the Mormon apostle, as Elder George C. Scott, the actor. George C., like my father, was a former Marine, both with seething boxed-up energy. Although it would eventually become one of my favorite films, I hadn't seen Kubrick's *Dr. Strangelove, or How I Learned To Stop Worrying and Love the Bomb* (1964) with George C.'s phenomenal chops on display. I knew the austere George C. from Franklin Schaffner's *Patton* (1970), his hardened disposition reminding me of my father at his fiercest.

Elder Richard G. had nothing in common with George C.'s disposition, and the contrast of Scotts was not lost on my father, drawing from him a mix of quick laughter and a dismissive grin, so I erred in my comparison often. Yet both men presented themselves passionately: Elder Richard G. was as conciliatory as George C. was aggressive. I believed Elder Richard G. would as readily hug his subject, friend or enemy, as certainly as George C. would wrestle his, my father being capable of doing either.

In his devotional address, Elder Scott talked about the unique environment that BYU offered its students. He startled me when he advised students who did not want to follow school guidelines to go to another school because of the many Mormons who would attend BYU if they could. I followed the rules, most if not all them, no doubt including even rules still embryonic in the minds of future BYU administrators, but I didn't agree with Elder Scott. After the talk I attempted to articulate my reaction driving north of Salt Lake City with my friend Tron, a former missionary companion, known to me in Georgia as Elder Whitely. We were headed to the wedding reception of a mutual friend, also from our mission.

—I don't agree with Elder Scott because people who don't believe they should follow all the school rules, despite the likelihood they followed most of them, added important variety to the student body. And their lack of adherence to the rules did not make them less moral than their peers who did.

Morality was a critical litmus test of measuring the value of the LDS life, competing only with economic success—synonymous in Mormondom with righteousness—for the divine standard. I learned from previous disclosures of my frustrations about my religious tradition that telling my friends and classmates I disagreed with a living Prophet ignited a charged opposition and prompted immediate suspicion. As an Apostle of the Mormon Church, Elder Scott was a Prophet like then-President Gordon B. Hinckley, only the president's authority was preeminent.

Tron was different from other Mormon peers. His belief was in lockstep with tradition, but he offered a measured response to my ideas. As venerable an LDS member as I knew, he was a rarity, not defensive against my critiques—elsewhere seen as attacks and simultaneous manifestations of my personal failings.

—Your view is right for you because you see things at a different level, Tron said.

Other sincere Mormon friends would have told me, and did tell me in similar discussions, a better (more righteous) me would agree with Elder Scott. I agreed with Tron, or my memory of Tron's comment, and still do, though I appreciate the common objection to my position. At BYU I recognized a running tension between what I believed and what Church leaders told members to believe, and this tension had begun long before I arrived on campus. I didn't question unity's requiring individual members to sacrifice personal beliefs, nor did I miss the value of a unified group, fully convinced of the many benefits from putting goals of the Church above one's own, mine included. Yet I couldn't shake the belief that the community would be stronger and still unified if it allowed for sharper thinking and better beliefs. I had always been open to the possibility I could be wrong, and was willing to sacrifice personal beliefs (even correct ones) for the ultimate sacrifice of Church unity. Hearing Elder Scott, I was no longer sure I could. I was made in my father's image—quite able to stomach horseshit on my head for the good of others but maddened as hell when someone told me it smelled like roses.

CHAPTER 21

THE DANCER

Combined, I received and sent fewer than a half dozen e-mails during my freshman year at BYU. Two years later, in my sophomore year, e-mail was the craze. Everyone was doing e-mail, and I caught the fever, checking mine a half dozen times a day, when I got to campus, between classes, and on my way home. I didn't own a computer. I wrote all my English and philosophy papers in the computer lab in the basement of the humanities building, where I also read and wrote e-mails. Within hours of returning to Provo I had two goals, get my application for employment in at the Missionary Training Center, and to find out if Sandy was still a student at BYU. Not a day passed since I first saw her three years ago that I had not thought of her, and I had been conniving how to talk to her over that same time-span. E-mail and the campus directory were a clarion call for enduring years of fear at approaching her. I found her contact information and sent her an e-mail.

The irony of applying at the MTC was obvious to me. I about drowned there and now wanted to spend four hours a day teaching newly institutionalized nineteen-year-olds. God, I was crazy but also broke, and no other part-time job paid as well. I dressed in my missionary attire, minus the black-bordered, white-stencil name tag with my name and the Church's, wearing the same soles worn down as I walked concrete and pavement around Northern Georgia. I walked to the MTC with my scriptures in my backpack at the appointed time for my interview. With other candidates, I entered a classroom and participated in a mock training session where a teacher observed me being taught and teaching from the scriptures. I received a call the next day offering me a position, and started the following week. I continued to work there for the next three years, including over the summers.

My wardrobe of Eddie Bauer pullovers, L.L. Bean button-ups, and imitation J. Crew sweaters from freshman year, did not again see the light of day, eventually was replaced by Champion block-color and Hanes crew-neck T-shirts. Because I lived off campus I did not have time to go home to change my clothes for work. Instead, in the morning I dressed for work like I was going to church all day, for three years. Making my appearance even less fashionable, I cut my own hair with clippers and scissors, a skill learned as a missionary to save money. During my tour in Georgia word of my ability had spread, and I had cut a lot of other missionaries' hair, many of them returning customers despite nicks and uneven dos, because of the alluring price of no charge. After a couple paychecks into my sophomore year I decided to pamper myself on a haircut at the BYU barbershop in the basement of the Ernest L. Wilkinson Student Center. I sat in a sturdy barber swivel chair in a huge empty room with mirror walls and a few fast minutes later stood and went straight to work. The district of missionaries I was teaching welcomed me with stares. I shrugged.

—I hope you can keep your job.

—The barber must have misunderstood you were a MTC teacher and thought you were a ROTC instructor.

—Don't worry. It will grow back in six months.

About that time I went back to cutting my own hair, using the saved money to splurge on extras like lunch.

I knew I would have to stretch the truth with Sandy, because our contact had lasted for less than a song's length with my arms lightly around her waist and her arms even more lightly atop my shoulders during the dance in the Morris center at the end of freshman year two years ago, which night

I could recall with the greatest specificity. I strategized that it would be best to recall generally we both had lived in Deseret Towers and had had a few interactions at the Morris Center, explaining I had returned to BYU after serving my mission and wanted to meet up, typing all of it in one—what I hoped—non-threatening paragraph. Congratulating myself for my bravery I hit "send." Within hours I was back checking my e-mail, and she had responded. She did not recognize my name nor did she recall our interactions. But she was willing to meet, not ruling out seeing me might help her remember, and she proposed the Creamery behind Deseret Towers. I responded that ice cream sounded great, noting that her impression on me would certainly have been greater than mine on her, a truer account never given.

E-mail's miracle of communicating with long-pined-for fair maidens came with its less redemptive side. It was a platform for the eternal recurrence of the past with friends and family. Nothing could conceivably be more stultifying than being caught in the briars of one's origins. If e-mail was not bad enough, a unified cry of "the horror" would ring around the world during the plague of "social networks" still in the kernel of the eye of technological innovators, who under the guise of connecting people, would revolutionize marketing by opening invisible doors to gushing products "suited just for you." The extended fights with my first missionary companion in East Cobb were not the first of their kind. In fact, they were of the garden-variety oral combat I had grown up accustomed to with my oldest brother, Jami. From the beginning of time to the spread of e-mail in the mid-Nineteen-nineties, generations have been shielded from revisiting the shit storms of their youth with the exception of letters, reunions and usurpations. Since e-mail, humanity has not.

Within hours of discovering the ease of finding and reaching out to Sandy, I was receiving e-mails from my third-year law student, and newly minted atheist, eldest brother. Ideas for Jami were like water rights. He clearly didn't invent them any more than the farmer did the Colorado River, but first use meant they were his. For years I always assumed arguments were about clarifying the truth by proving one idea's superiority to another even after surviving the onslaught of literary criticism's objections to superior, let alone any, truth branded on my brain freshman year. I took many years to learn arguments are mostly about having your way, accumulating power, winning, or wasting the resources and energies of your opponent.

And I only had myself to blame for my late realization. Arguments in my family were like Richard III soliloquies on repeat. Based on a distressingly large sampling of all males from both sides of the Elison and Harward divide, insecurity was the blood running through our histrionic veins. An argument no sooner began than a member of this cursed breed turned his opponents into his own personal audience. The differences from Richard III were not so obvious despite our lack of history of continual deceit and murder. The similarities could be traced in (1) the insistent desire for attention and recognition through baiting someone into a discussion and then proceeding not to consider a single goddamn counterpoint, and (2) the deluge of presuppositions for what the other was thinking for the purpose of manipulating him out of his volition. While Richard III was intent on maintaining his kingdom, my cursed breed would be intent on any of their opponents' time. They were misplaced in time and space, meant for the heights of medieval aristocratic fratricides. And resisting their very presence took the energy of fleeing a black hole. The amount of time I spent countering barrages of our sickness amounted to time spent developing projects marked by Nobel prizes. Long before I woke up to these realities, the birth of e-mail shackled me back to the family farm of madness.

Insecurity rains on peoples of all classes, colors, and creeds. Couple it with a prophet-ego and you have a common Mormon disease. Hell, I've not only witnessed its frenetic effects, but also have suffered a fair share of it. And while it was widespread, it was not the most rampant one in Mormondom. That honor was the golden contagion of manipulation by one member constantly attesting to another member that the second member's actions affected the first member's happiness. The sincerity of the first party was viewed by both members as seriously as a heart attack, though rarely did it reward the accosted second party with the first party's having one. No one could lay it on thicker than a Mormon pouring out his or her feelings from the depth of his or her pure heart, laden with fear and misery bound for the same throughout the eternities because of the actions of another. Mormons continually lathered up in these expectations as surely as the family was the touchstone for each and every one of the Church's grand eternal ideas.

In Levi Peterson's Great Comic Mormon Novel *Backslider*, the protagonist, Frank, finds himself subject to this contagion of manipulation, often interchangeable with the genuine caring woven into the fabric of Mormon culture. In Frank's case, his mother, Margaret, sees into Hell, and it can mean only one thing: Frank is headed there if he doesn't clean up his ways. Margaret wakes Frank from his sleep to share the experience she had in the fruit room, *all of a sudden I had a terrible oppression. I couldn't get my breath and*

I thought my heart was going to stop beating. I began to cry, I was ready to die because I could see into hell. God showed me damnation. I grabbed a bottle, it turned out to be apple sauce, and I got out of there. I went outdoors to make sure the sun was still shining. Now why would God do that? Why did he give me a vision of hell? Visions for and on behalf of others are about as common in Mormondom as pumpkin pie is at any Thanksgiving feast. For these diseases there are no cures, damned if I haven't tried to find them. All one can do is name them when they occur, and take all possible steps to extract oneself from them. If my family offered anything redemptive, it was our propensity toward attention and not manipulation, not for lack of trying, but as much as our skills at convincing another animate object we could love it.

Thank the few sane gods in the sky, my return to BYU also included positive, constructive conversations through the introduction to Professor Young and meeting him for talks weekly, the threesome including the auburn-haired young man the most memorable of our visits, but only one among many, and the only time I did not say anything. Our session discussing who we decided to marry in the pre-existence was hours before my date with Sandy at the Creamery, and I was aware of the electricity passing through my entire nervous system during the whole discussion. Before leaving the library I found a restroom and peed for the twelfth time that afternoon and evening. My nerves could have been telling me I was about to climb on the back of a bull or step onto a wrestling mat. Neither had adequately prepared me for the indomitable task of wooing the coed of my freshman dreams.

I cursed myself for being so scared about something as ridiculous as believing I would marry her without having spoken to her, excepting the time I mumbled some words on the dance floor, feeling sick walking north on campus to the steps leading up to the Centennial Bell Tower. I climbed them and walked the familiar path past Deseret Towers to the Creamery, and opened the door. She sat at the counter next to a giant. I stepped up, mustering a large smile, introducing myself. She offered an emerging smile in return.

—This is my brother who lives in Deseret Towers.

—Pleased to meet you.

—Go ahead and take a seat, my brother is leaving and I'm going to walk him out.

I reached to straighten my tie and looked around, not sure I had ever been to the Creamery, being not much for ice cream or, in freshman year, with extra change to spend on any. I held off ordering so I could pay for her cone. She reentered and I tried to breathe. Her hair had turned brownish blonde from elfin white, but still flowed beyond her shoulders. Her small beautiful face was as I remembered it.

—I invited him just in case you were a weirdo.

—Smart protection.

Not sure what was so smart about it, pretty sure I meant decision, god-awful glad she didn't wait to confirm her fear, and not asking if her brother played basketball for BYU because I expected everyone probably asked that predictable question, so I wisely saved it for a more natural pause later in the conversation. BYU's basketball program was atrocious my freshman year, the team winning a game or two, or maybe none. I can't remember, but I remember well learning about the coach's two sons on the team during my annual review of the *Sports Illustrated* Swimsuit Edition, our family having subscribed all my years growing up, each year my father redacting the swimsuit edition, reducing it to a few random pages with no cover. Undeterred by my father's vigilance, I purchased the splendid edition at the first gas station with a copy, entertained to find, freshman year, the article on the BYU basketball brothers between spreads of swimsuit models, sure SI's editor saw him or herself doing a greater good by tempting Mormon sports fans.

—You didn't need to dress up.

—Yeah, I work at the MTC.

—I don't remember you. Did we know any of the same people?

Having anticipated this observation I still hadn't come up with a satisfactory answer so I relented with the truth.

—We met at a Morris Center dance or party. I wouldn't expect you to remember.

—Hmmm.

—So what kind of ice cream do you like?

At any given moment, girls at BYU were caught up in boys' eternal plans, mine one among thousands, and many more that should have been were not. After learning her name in our first conversation during my dream and having it confirmed in our freshman Humanities class, smartly avoiding sharing either fact over ice cream, one day I had stepped into an aisle and took a seat a couple removed from her, having been trying to convince myself for days to introduce myself, turning my head to ask how she was doing as Professor Mitchell began class, not receiving any answer or any indication she heard my question, and not certain I'd actually asked it, catching my breath after my nerves turned the attempt to nervous laughter, an early stage of hysteria setting in during those minutes of class within reaching distance of her. Now I sat next to her with her looking at me, speaking to me, too nervous to smile.

—Yes, I'd meet up again. Send me an e-mail.

I hatched my plan, believing I couldn't lose, thanking her, stating I looked forward to seeing her again, so full of anticipation as I walked home, unable to consider what just happened, one meeting granted out of kindness or curiosity, not divine instigation to fulfill a preordained role of motherhood. On other dates, we talked about the one thing we had in common.

—She knew everything. She started speaking at the beginning of class and kept going until it ended. I spent all class taking notes, Sandy said.

—I've taken a lot of notes. She is pretty entertaining, I said.

—It's amazing someone knows that much.

—She does know a lot of stories.

Professor Sharon Western White was the first woman professor in the religion education department at BYU, and Sandy had taken her class, and I was now taking her class. No subject shared as much of our mutual admiration. And no professor at BYU got in more words during a single class than Professor White, or if someone had, it was an apocalypse I had missed, achieved by that someone's not taking a pause, and passing on even a single sip of water. She sure didn't, and if she didn't win outright for most words each week for the last three decades, she reigned supreme for most each academic year since her debut in the late Seventies with no one approaching her cumulative word production record on campus since the university's inception. That is no small feat, given the divine proclivity to verbosity of many Mormon prophets at the pulpit and their many faithful imitators in BYU classrooms. Professor White may have spoken cumulatively more words than any living or dead professor spoken on any stinking campus on Planet Earth. Professor White taught Mormon Church history in large lecture halls; her enthusiasm for the subject matter and ability to build to a climax each class, and end each class on a cliff-hanger making her immensely popular with the student body. During the class I took, I regularly sat beside a returned missionary, Melanie, who was also an English major I knew from the Humanities building. She had long curly brown hair, which struck me as odd since she was Californian. She was easy to talk to and had an attractive, long face. I was courting Sandy but got the feeling all semester that Melanie wanted me to ask her out, regularly dropping hints, which landed dully on my one-track mind.

I was a big note taker but was not sure everything Professor White said would show up on a test, so I played Russian roulette with parts of her stories, many known to me but their details not, scribbling new details into the church-history-class section of my BYU five-subject notebook, my standard resource each semester, the cover color changing from semester to semester but the notebook staying reliably the same.

Professor White revealed little about church history that stirred any incredulity in me. She spent a few minutes on the early Mormon association with Freemasons, stuff I tabled as digestible upon reflection, maybe, and fewer minutes with the Danites and their belief in Blood Atonement, carried out by one of my all-time Mormon favorites, Orrin Porter Rockwell. She didn't say it but implied that Rockwell had made an attempt to right the wrong of the anti-Mormon Governor Lilburn Boggs' extermination order of all Mormons in Missouri. What self-respecting Mormon wouldn't have tried to kill Boggs after signing it? Of course Rockwell did.

My gun-slinging education had started long before I took Professor White's class, when I consumed in their entirety Louis L'Amour classics, if that word's integrity ever had due support and educable meaning. Grandma Elison had her say with the book shelves in the basement of her home because of her stubborn persistence toward good literature, and because Grandpa Elison wasn't known to have a read a book. She had the Harvard Classics, which I rightly scorned, and scores of church books, but no run of beautiful softbounds ran longer than pert' near every paperbound of L'Amour's in print. Even Tolkien sat second chair to him in the landscape of fanciful possibilities. Who the hell wouldn't favor a Colt over a saber? Rockwell was cool, but Sackett was even cooler. I knew that the integrity of gun fighters like Rockwell required whipping authority figures like Boggs, because the Sacketts had many times. Boggs' order was driven by hatred of Mormons but also had a few straws of justification given the all-out war between Missourians and the Mormons, involving game Mormons who were the eventual losers, culminating in a massacre of their numbers at the infamous Haun's Mill and the Mormons' exodus from the state to the swamp land of western Illinois.

Civil law and divine law were fine for law-abiding citizens and faithful adherents to religions, but neither created the obligation of a higher good to fight for the poor and oppressed like the gunfighters' code, and if the Sacketts and their peers in L'Amour's classics, in sooth, made good on this highest of right actions (and they always did) I was certain Rockwell was worth his salt and did his duty as well. A gunfighter's integrity, like a knight errant's, was the universal measure for right. I could imagine Rockwell tossing in his spiritual seal like Ivanhoe before the court of the surreptitious Prince John where right action could challenge even the final judgment of the King's Court. Ivanhoe proffered his might as a test to John's judgment of witchcraft against the Jewess Rebecca. Rockwell possessed valor like Ivanhoe and, like Ivanhoe, Rockwell confronted the wrongs against the oppressed. But Boggs survived the assassination attempt, with bullets to show for it left in his skull and throat. Not enough to kill him, since he lived nearly two more decades, but Boggs wore integrity's marks from the badlands covered by L'Amour's protagonists to the realm protected by many knights, and by Rockwell in the end.

What surprised me was the article on Professor White in *Brigham Young Magazine*. The article highlighted her brilliant career in writing about the life of Joseph Smith, founder of the Mormon faith, exceeding some thousands of thousands of pages in print, and her admiration for him, including the annual celebration of his birthday with her family, none of which startled me. However, her comment that she was confident that she would recognize Joseph Smith in the next life but was not as certain that she would recognize Jesus Christ floored me. The article noted that she resolved to spend more of her studies learning about Jesus. I could not have loved her more for her unvarnished honesty, as fresh in the elite Mormon circles at BYU as it was alarming.

During my southern tour, natives of Georgia had recycled many criticisms of the Mormon religion, and among the most popular being that Mormons were not Christian. My companions and I made concerted efforts to correct that misunderstanding with as much success as convincing them that lima beans were a great source of iron. We countered that we were Christians, for one thing look at our name tags, then see the subtitle on the Blue Book of Mormon, *Another Testament of Jesus Christ*. Please allow me to share a passage from it where an ancient prophet, Nephi, who lived on the American continent hundreds of years before the birth of Christ in the Holy Land, said, *And we talk of Christ, we rejoice in Christ, we preach of Christ, we prophesy of Christ, and we write according to our prophesies, that our children may know to what source they may look for a remission of their sins.* The Blue Book fulfilled that aim, and our message was all about binding families together forever by bringing them to Christ. Many listened patiently and some not so much, all raising retorts such as that the New Testament warns against adding to it, about false prophets, etc., and we addressed each in turn. And others stated, but you worship Joseph Smith.

—I've been to your church and everyone talked about Joseph Smith, and I didn't hear mention of Jesus Christ. More than one native told me that.

They could have been right, but they also weren't listening closely because all the prayers mentioned Jesus Christ and there are not a few of them offered during the course of an LDS three-hour church service. But, their point that attention was weighed in Joseph's favor was valid. We tirelessly countered that we did not have a doctrine about Joseph Smith as a divinity, but were stuck by all the testimony about him, all the emphasis on his having restored the one true church and having the real priesthood and a singular position to speak on behalf of God, then pointing to his role in the salvation of all, which was affirmed by the leaders and members, again and again, in just one meeting. We missionaries resisted the obvious concession because, at the very least, it sounded a smidgen unchristian. The natives were not shy of a bull's-eye that many, maybe most, did worship him *in effect* by their actions, veneration, iron-clad testimonies and greatest of hopes like Professor White's. Sometime around Professor White's class, it dawned on me that the meat and potatoes of the restoration of the true Church of Christ included a lot of stuff on a par with the true understanding of Jesus. It took regular dousing at BYU to wake me from the Christ-centered focus my father instilled in his sons to the greater story about prophets' and priesthood's being central to the Church. That it did not suit me was far less of an epiphany than was putting together all the other stuff was the focus of the Church.

I thought of Sandy every day, many times during each hour, making an often interminable day. God, I couldn't help it, and if I could it was beyond my knowledge how to go about it. I took my case before one of my many BYU roommates, six of us crammed into a university-approved apartment south of campus, a ten-minute walk from campus and even shorter walk to the nearest Hogi Yogi, which always had a line I didn't have the extra change or time to join. This roommate's name was Nicholas. He was terribly atypical, so I didn't think my questions would faze him, and they never did.

—Let's wrestle.

—What?

—I want to wrestle you.

—Nick, you don't sound like you're kidding. Why would you want to wrestle me?

—You wrestled growing up. Well, I want to wrestle.

—Do you want me to teach you the basics of wrestling?

—No, let's just wrestle.

So we did. Nicholas shot right away, driving me toward the space between the sofa and television, items owned by neither of us. I under hooked his arms and threw him on the old sofa.

—How was that?

—Let's do it again.

He shot in again and I secured his arm with my left arm and ripped my right arm across his face, turning my hips into the momentum and put him on his back, tightening my grasp on his head and arm.

—How's that?

—That was rough. He said smiling through a bleeding split lip.

—Sorry about the lip. A cross-face is one of the basic defensive moves I would have shown you. Remember it for when someone tries to take you down. Your opponent's body will generally follow where his head goes.

Nicholas routinely surprised me. He broke the Mormon mold not by trying to consume all knowledge, which he and his overachieving peers tended to do, but because he was not only willing to entertain taboo questions about religion or sex, discussed more often than you'd expect or as often as you would, or whatever the subject, but he was willing to go behind them to find the answers. He was sharp, as the word connotes: you would feel the accuracy and depth of his comments. I shied from turning him into an unpaid aid for my Latin courses when we lived together, as I had my freshman dormmate in calculus. Even years removed from taking Latin, Nicholas could do better translations than I could. Despite my ability to identify correctly declensions, I was dolefully unable to make a sensible conjugation for the two years spent taking Latin to satisfy the foreign language requirement for the English degree. In our short stint as roommates, he changed from pre-medicine to various majors ending up in sociology, the stock, universal, easy undergraduate degree. But he did not make it look easy. Nicholas spearheaded thesis-like term papers I felt sick thinking about having to write. He asked me, the English major, to edit them, but he wrote like a professional academic, leaving me helpless to provide meaningful feedback. He was one of my fellow students who, I needed no reminding, was on a different intelligence plane.

His drive for physical accomplishment succeeded even his intellectual appetite. He was in great shape and surprisingly strong when we wrestled in the front room. He loved to dance and competed for dance teams at BYU, and there was one for most dance styles that come to mind, and Nicholas made one of the highly esteemed five (or however many), god-sanctioned ballroom dance teams. No university from the beginning of time has produced more ballroom dancers than BYU, the proverbial Ballroom Dance Capital of the World. The school-sanctioned dance disciplines were heavy on form and athleticism, and absent sensuous physicality. I knew a couple Mormons who had seen *Grease* (1978) but not a one who had seen *Dirty Dancing* (1987). Mormons celebrated the body in its reach for the divine, not as an end in itself. Mormon authorities repeatedly reminded the faithful that their bodies were temples for God's spirit. God could hardly dwell moving in rhythm with Johnny Castle and Baby. Any celebration of the body, for itself, was entirely unofficial. Sure, Mormons' natural desires surfaced like other humans', but somewhere in an underground scene that Fate failed to have me fall into.

Instead of progressing through the ranks on the renowned ballroom circles at BYU, Nicholas abruptly quit and started learning ballet, dropping cold all other disciplines to focus on his new love. He went from being the best dancer in the room, with the exception of other ballroom dancers—and there were always a few at any given BYU function—to being a novice of the inverse of a ballerina, or whatever rank preceded that.

His excitement for his new discipline did not border on enthusiastic. He was a fanatic. He talked about new moves and renowned dancers teaching at class on every occasion while we other roommates shared space in the kitchen preparing lunch and dinner, or sat in front of the television at the end of the day. It was ballet this and ballet that. He laughed off jokes, from the engineer/musician roommate J1 who was always extolling the supremacy of Rush over U2, about his becoming fruity. Nicholas ignored quips from the business-major roommate J2, who cried loud enough for southern Provo to hear at the end of fall semester, tears spilling from his large eyes as he slammed his hand on top of the television, which he owned, exclaiming if the deaths of Princess Diana and Mother Teresa were not enough, now we had to lose Chris Farley. These roommates offered jabs not to degrade Nicholas or the discipline of ballet, but to temper his constant proselytizing for his newfound faith. I didn't rib him, but I also didn't rise to the challenge to defend U2, knowing not a lick about music save what I liked when hearing it, nor did I open my soul weeping. No public figure's death had saddened me more than Diana's earlier in the semester, being in love with her personality, still pained over her irreplaceable loss. We cared about Nicholas, we were happy for him, but we had course work, jobs, and young coeds to try to win over. When he told all the roommates that he secured each of us a free ticket for the Nutcracker, we dutifully planned to attend.

We loaded into a coed's car and headed to a high school in the valley south of Provo. We entered unmolested, free tickets in hand as promised, and took unassigned seats directly in the middle of the auditorium before a few other people filed in. I had not seen a ballet before, and I was impressed by all the jumping and the dancers' ability to go from dynamic movement to holding still, failing to remember the names of the dancers' positions I learned freshman year in Professor Mitchell's Humanities class, and I waited anxiously to see Nicholas. Toward the end he entered with a few other male dancers dressed as if for BYU's world renowned International Folk Dance Ensemble. They were dressed in Hungarian or some former Iron Curtain state's traditional attire, doing joint routines, including a challenging number locking arms in a circle while each jumped and kicked his legs backward. All of it looked difficult as each in the group struggled to do the jumps, none seeming to begin them just—or nearing just—right, each out of sync with the others in the group, and all noticeably tired by the end of their routine. I didn't know what to expect, but I hadn't expected it to look so hard.

After the performance Nicholas was ecstatic and gushingly grateful that we came. Of course we came, we said almost in unison, his passion turning aside any potential criticism from us ignoramuses. But I couldn't believe how amateur he looked. His progress in a short time was impressive, but it was the distance he would have to go to be good that I found daunting, so much so it didn't make sense to me why he would even try.

—So Sandy doesn't seem interested in a relationship, I said.

—Have you asked her if she is? Nicholas asked.

—Not directly. But I was feeling pretty desperate yesterday, and I asked her in an e-mail if she had seen *Dumb and Dumber*, and if she had, if she recalled Lloyd's questions to the girl he was trying to help find her husband, if there was a one-in-a-million chance that she would like him.

—I haven't seen the movie. Had she seen it?

—It's good. You should. She had, and knew the reference. She answered just like the girl that there was a chance.

—That doesn't sound promising.

—But she got it. I think she was saying there's a chance.

—It sounds to me like she got the joke and that was the answer.

—What joke are you talking about?

Nicholas was not any help. I shared too much in common with the film's Lloyd to lose hope. I hadn't asked Sandy to pray and to ask God if we were meant to marry, and I don't expect I would have been the first returned missionary to extend that invitation to the coed of his wifely ambitions. Her gut response to me was more important than the doting finger of God, and I wasn't satisfied my efforts were enough to get a fair reaction. I wanted her to want me all on her own.

I also took my case for Sandy before Jared, my best friend from freshman year. Where Nicholas tried to open up reality, I knew Jared would inspire me to press on and ignore it. Few directives approached the importance of that one that BYU male students had a duty to court and marry, and Jared righteously pursued his pre-marriage priesthood responsibility of dating. During the final interview on my mission, the conclusion of my twenty-fifth month overlapping with the second month of my second-mission president, my new mission president told me that the next step in my life would be to find a wife and to raise a family. Expecting as much, assuming it to be part of a script straight from Salt Lake City, I nodded. Visiting general authorities, the bishop of my BYU ward, lessons in Priesthood meeting each Sunday, and fellow BYU students regularly reminded each other of this next step in the Plan of Salvation. Jared, like many, did not shirk his duty, actively wooing coeds by playing the guitar, making one of the tiered ballroom-dance teams, and driving a mid-size pickup truck with fat tires.

Rooming next door in Deseret Towers during my freshman year had been the aforementioned high school friends from Idaho Falls: one, Simon, the blond, thoughtful, athletic, computer-science major who encouraged me to ask Sandy to dance at the Morris Center, and the other, Brian, a brown-haired tall, handsome, cocky, accounting major. Freshman year I passed the guys in the hall and saw them at church services, but I didn't spend much time hanging out with either of them until after our missions. Then I lighted up every time I saw the cocky prick. He had become unbelievably decent, and his conspicuous, all-in, concerted efforts to fulfill his one goal of getting married cracked me up to all ends.

Brian served a mission in South Africa and taught at the MTC. One semester we taught the same schedule, and once team-taught the same district for three weeks. If I hadn't seen his transformation for myself, I would never have believed it. He returned to BYU humble and outgoing. If ever a missionary proved Teddy's observation right, Brian did. Where he had been deriding and dismissive freshman year, he was engaging and encouraging during our sophomore year two years later. He positively listened and responded, and without fail on every occasion asked if I was dating anyone seriously, even if we'd discussed dating the day before. During each visit, if a remotely attractive girl walked by us, Brian would contact her as if he were on a mission. I saw him at numerous functions, and at one preseason basketball game in Fieldhouse I cut to the chase.

—Have you seen a pretty girl to contact tonight?

—A few. There's one in the middle of that section. She's olive-skinned with long dark hair. See her, he pointed.

—Maybe.

—She came with a friend. Let's go stand by them.

—There's no room.

—Come on, no space is going to stop us. She might be the one.

I passed, not unbelieving, as he made his way to the girl, eventually talking to her in the midst of screaming fans watching the game. Later she left with a guy about her height that I recognized from the weight room, ensuring that she wasn't the one. After Brian's stint at the MTC ended I saw less of him, and then we saw each other in the entrance of the new addition of the library towards the end of our BYU tenures. He greeted me as excitedly as he had at the game two years before.

—How are you doing? Still teaching at the MTC? Engaged yet?

—Great, yes, and no.

—Me neither, but the right one is out there, just got to keep looking. His eyes followed each girl passing us into and out of the library.

—And there's a new batch to find her in every year.

I rocked back at his brilliant resolve before he spoke, wishing him success at his play, while my own beating heart slowed with rarely a flutter, having largely pieced together the absurdity of my own dating life.

—Just take my truck; chicks dig trucks, Jared said.

—She'll know it's not mine.

—But she's gonna dig you when you're driving it.

—This weekend?

—Whenever.

—She said she hadn't been to a professional basketball game before, so I'll take her to see the Jazz in Salt Lake.

—You like basketball?

—An hour there, three hours, at least, there, and an hour back. That's a lot of quality time.

—Don't wreck my truck.

Game night, a blizzard hit. Having spent all my extra money on nose-bleed seats, I convinced Sandy a little snow was no big thing for a kid from Idaho. We'd be fine if she still wanted to go, and against both our better judgment she said okay, and I picked her up.

I did not follow basketball in college as I had as a kid, but I still venerated Larry Bird, and the Jazz were playing the Pacers, and Larry was coaching the Pacers. I wanted to see him, and by the time we found our seats I made out his antlike features, relying on a competitive game to fill in the long pauses. Sandy didn't carry on a great conversation, but I didn't blame her; heavens, neither did I. She had humored me with a few dates, and each seemed a little more promising than its predecessor. During each I looked for the kind of tell that a girl liked you, as Sonny LoSpecchio explained to C in *A Bronx Tale* (1993), sure that that night I'd get one.

They threw Larry out, and the Jazz won the game. Dumbfounded in my luck, I cried bollocks the remainder of the game, randomly cursing the referees and Jazz fans. In lightly falling snow hours later, I unlocked the passenger door and, walking behind the bed of the truck, I watched Sandy through the back window. She didn't reach across the seat to unlock my door. I could barely see Larry during the time he walked the court coaching his losing squad, but I could see clearly that Sandy was not going to take. I didn't regret borrowing Jared's truck to learn whether she would, because I enjoyed being in her presence so darn much, however uncomfortable it was for me and boring for her.

We left the Delta Center and headed south on Interstate 15 in a whiteout storm. I couldn't tell if my headlights were on, switching them on and off every few minutes, driving in four-wheel drive, passing slower cars in the right lane and many that had slid off the road.

CHAPTER 22
THE POET

My brother Jacob attended BYU his freshman year during my mission, and vowed not to return. He made one friend and hated everyone else and his classes, over two semesters of next to no fun. The only havens were a few exclusive kegger parties in the Orem River bottoms with our childhood next-door neighbor, who was a defensive lineman on the football team. After Jacob's mission he attended Idaho State University in Pocatello, twenty minutes south of Blackfoot. During visits home on holidays, I learned he was taking and enjoying a literature class, leaning towards changing his major from biology and pre-medicine to English. I told him he should return to BYU to study with the poet Leslie Norris.

Over my tenure as an English major I stuck to literature and language courses, but I sent e-mails to creative writing teachers requesting to audit their courses. All rejected my request but each invited me to enroll in his, three of them, or her, one of her, course. I planned to attend graduate school and could ill afford a low grade in a writing course. I did not accept their offers, but I suckered one into letting me attend off the roll.

I learned a fiction writer taught my Uncle Jeff twenty years earlier, and I armed myself with a copy of the made-for-TV movie he wrote, *The Hired Heart* (1997). I knocked on his former writing teacher's door and introduced myself. I peppered the professor with my uncle's praise, asking if he'd be interested in a copy of his movie. He was. Not a fool, I told him I'd bring him a copy, leaving mine secure in my backpack. I concluded our visit by explaining my interest in auditing, not enrolling, in a creative writing course, asking if I could sit in on his class. He waffled in his chair and said to come the first day and he'd see, and I did. The first day of class I brought a copy of my uncle's movie that was about the death of a guy on a wild bucking bull and his widow's subsequent struggle to fall back into love, climaxing with a bull ride by the widow's new love interest. It was fun, though the bull ride was pathetic.

I made the same request to Professor Norris after taking his class on the Romantic Period. He welcomed me into his graduate level writing course, knowing I had no background in creative writing, but stated he would be taking leave, as BYU worked to complete a film about his life in his home town of Merthyr Tydfil, South Wales. To my lack of fortune I discovered him too late and would graduate before he taught his writing course again. I told Jacob if he loved to read and to write, he would not do better than to study with Professor Norris, the only sound, let alone kind, advice I had ever given him. He recognized the departure from my regular contributions and returned to BYU during what was my final year.

Josh also moved to Provo the same year. He and Jacob worked as cooks at a restaurant at night, and Josh worked as a janitor during the day, taking weekend trips to rodeos and bull-riding events around the West. We found an attic in a large house south of campus to rent together. With no furniture, a mattress, and blankets for beds, we moved into the two-bedroom space with wooden floors, a sloping kitchen, low ceilings, and a five-by-ten foot front living room. I took the blankets, convinced the floor would help my back. None of us had extra money but someone acquired two white lawn chairs and a used television for the front space. We agreed to split the cable bill, motivated by a promotional six-month free-movie-channel package, which we intended to cancel upon the promo's end after thorough and routine viewing.

Professor Norris often lectured beyond the bell, which rang on the hour, or ten minutes before it, to break up classes throughout campus. He stood small before the rising rows of seats in front of him, his Welsh accent holding our attention, supporting the credibility of his poignant explanations of the romantic visions of Wordsworth and Coleridge and company. Everyone's refusal to rustle in their seats was a uniform blend of respect and admiration. No other classroom of students responded in kind, even remotely. No other audience did either during the dozens and dozens of devotionals I attended in the Marriott Center, where students regularly stood and climbed up and stepped down flights of stairs to exit before general authorities, including apostles, finished their talks.

—As my friend pointed out, Keats explained in a letter to his brother not reaching after facts and reason can be a virtue, Professor Norris said.

I hadn't thought much of Keats' letter when I used it as an excuse to visit Professor Norris during office hours. Heavens, I could not recognize negative capability in Shakespeare from an unreliable narrator in the Dostoyevsky or solipsistic certitude in Rousseau. I visited him like all my professors a couple times over each semester, believing an earnest face associated with my name would prove beneficial when they recorded final grades. And I certainly hadn't expected my practice qualified me as a friend, but I couldn't fail to wear his compliment with a surprised smile, turning to Melanie 2, who I sat next to each class, in case she missed who Professor Norris's friend on the back row was. Melanie 2 was an English major I knew, from overlapping schedules in the Humanities building. We talked regularly and, while she was not striking looking, she was coolly reserved and full of smart observations. Toward the end of the semester I mustered the confidence to ask her out when she unknowingly preempted my invitation with the information she had received her mission call. A couple weeks later I followed up.

—How is your preparation coming along for your mission?

—Kind of on hold. I met someone.

—Really, congratulations.

—Well, it wasn't that fast. We met before I received my call, but it's getting more serious, so I might postpone going after the semester to see how things go.

—I hope they go well. The mission isn't going anywhere. Neither is the MTC, I can assure you.

I took notes in the margins of my Romanticism Anthology, not my common practice, but I figured to keep it in memoriam of the first class where

I experienced a free distribution of ideas, then in an equally enthusiastic transference arranged them into the three term papers. I wrote each paper on a Sunday afternoon, stating what I thought about the work, scattering supporting quotations from its text, and not what some critical theory suggested I should think about it, the standard approach to interpreting a text. I wrote the papers in the spirit of Norris's class, as one captivated by ideas, bent on explaining and engaging them. I later handed off the Romanticism Anthology to Jacob, encouraging him to use my notes, as many were near word-for-word renditions from Professor Norris.

At the beginning of each shift at the Missionary Training Center, I read the teacher log on the district's classes earlier that day. Teachers described the attitude of the district and singled out missionaries who were struggling, or improving. According to the teachers' notes, districts had a lot of bad classes. The missionaries were prone to insubordination, often refusing to practice, and more commonly failing to put forth the effort the teachers expected of them. I had entered class for three years running, going into welcoming districts, not a single disappointing group and not a single disappointing missionary, many of them frustrated, exhausted or bummed. My key to success was not having a one-size-fits-all type for the happy group or happy missionary, which I easily applied—not believing in the goal of happiness. The missionaries could talk over each other about Brother So-and-so or Sister So-and-so's being upset with their performance, and I would listen and begin class.

—We pitched in and got this for you, the district leader of a group my first year teaching said to me. I half expected it would be a sweater for their El Guapo, but the district leader did not resemble Dusty Bottoms.

I took the leatherbound Book of Mormon with my name imprinted in gold cursive on the front. I taught the set of scriptures I had had since seminary in high school and used during my two-year mission in Atlanta, cheap plastic-bound books, the edges frayed and the pages bloated and heavily marked. I didn't tear up at their gift.

—Thank you—I looked around the room, smiling—Thank you.

—Can I ask you a question? a timid missionary once asked me, as a district I had been teaching for a couple weeks exited to go to a meeting in another building.

—Shoot.

—I have a personal question I've wanted to ask you.

—How personal?

—It's about my dad. He was excommunicated, and I've always wondered how being sealed to my parents will work out since they were married in the temple and now they're not married anymore. My dad is a great guy, and I worry about not being with him.

—There are a lot of people in the church who feel competent to judge your dad but judgment is up to God. If your dad believes in Christ, you don't have anything to worry about. You'll see him plenty.

—I thought so, he smiled.

Midway through my tenure at the MTC, all districts were assigned duty in the Telecenter, a building in the middle of campus where missionaries took telephone calls from people responding to television advertisements. Many calls went to a larger center somewhere in Colorado or Arizona, probably not California or certainly not India in those pre-outsourcing days. During waking hours most calls came through Provo. Missionaries followed the prompts and practiced the commitment patterns skills they learned in the classroom, focusing on finding out what impressed the caller and inviting them to learn more by receiving a message about the Church from missionaries in the caller's area. Most callers just wanted the video and were not interested in hearing more, a few accepted the invitation to have the missionaries stop by, and infrequently someone called to harass or mock the offer.

A missionary waved me over, a common distress signal for help from a challenging caller.

—He has a problem with sinning and asked if the Book of Mormon will help him quit sinning, he whispered, having muted the call. His swinging arms had drawn the attention of other missionaries not currently on calls.

—So what does he want? We'll send him the Book of Mormon.

—He said he's addicted to masturbation and needs help right now. I figured you'd have more experience and could take over the call.

I laughed, and other missionaries listening in nearby cubicles laughed too.

—I didn't mean it like that, he blushed.

—I'm sure I do. Let me have the headset.

I remember hundreds of faces and no names except one over three years. This Elder had the most distinct face too. He was pale, not ghostly white pale but sickly yellow pale, with puffy cheeks and a sharp, long nose, with neatly combed and parted black hair. He name was Elder Joyce. He was timid, not one to engage in conversation, but he was polite and unassuming. A couple weeks into teaching his district I popped the question.

—Are you related to James?

—Yes.

—You are absolutely kidding me?

—No.

—I've never been more impressed.

I had taught grandchildren of general authorities, including the great-grandson of a living apostle, who with noticeable pride told me he was the first in the family not to attend BYU, not to mention a lot of lesser sorts like athletes on leave from BYU, and had met at some time or another higher sorts like World and Texas Champion bull riders and Olympic champion wrestlers. But no encounter prepared me for this moment.

—So did your family religiously read *Ulysses* growing up?

—We have a first edition.

—I'd like to buy it.

He cracked a grin. And that was it. I felt like talking more about James Joyce would be pestering a celebrity. My one sole solitary and singular regret during my half-decade in Provo was not badgering him for more, like asking him to be a life-long pen pal.

Team teaching was not as common as teaching solo, but over the winter fewer missionaries entered the MTC, so teachers were often paired together. I didn't mind at all, happy to have an inspired presence to balance mine.

One teacher took the opportunity to use the example of a prominent Mormon's opting not to appear in Farrelly brothers' *There's Something About Mary* (1998) in the final scene when this person's replacement, Brett Favre, shows up as the brother—the kind of rumor that would run its course through Provo whether it had a basis or not—to show the importance of following the direction of Church leaders, in this case avoiding R-rated films.

I remembered my brother Jami, who at BYU resembled singer Richard Marx, with chiseled features, long flowing hair, strapping shoulders, riding a motorcycle to boot, with BYU coeds swooning over him, and dated a girl who had dated the prominent Mormon who opted out of *Mary*. The girl was the kind of girl who would have mistaken Jami as hard and dangerous—how could she not have with him riding his motorbike around Provo each fricking day?—as someone with the experience she took to. She proudly related to Jami she attended the NBA all-star game in Salt Lake with this prominent Mormon, and later quickly dumped Jami when she learned he was more straitlaced than he appeared to be, but I did not offer her, though I could have, as a counterexample to abstaining from the Farrellys' movie.

—That was a hilarious movie, one elder said. Others agreed.

—Did you see it? An elder turned to me. He was the spitting image of Kirk Douglas and could have just left a set remaking *Paths of Glory* (1957), one of the finest war movies ever made, to enter the MTC. Instead he had been an extra in *SLC Punk* (1998), filmed on location in Salt Lake.

—Very funny movie, I said.

—But [the prominent Mormon] passed on being in the movie because it was rated R. And the prophets have counseled us numerous times to not watch rated R movies. Flustered, the other teacher protested.

—But it was good, the Douglas elder said.

I never told the missionaries anything special because I never had anything special to tell them. I told them missions were hard and to be successful they would have to work hard. I also tried to convince them not to be fake, not to pretend, and not to manipulate investigators when they became proficient with commitment pattern skills.

A teacher I taught a number of districts with routinely emphasized the importance of loving the people. He emphasized loving others during the conclusion of one lesson, stressing its importance by demonstrating it.

—Elder, this message is true and it's about Jesus Christ's love for all people. I love to share it, and I love how it changes peoples' lives. And elder, I know God loves you and wants you to be happy. Elder, I love you. I want you to be successful and happy.

The district quieted and everyone stared at the teacher. The teacher paused waiting for the elder to respond. He stared, befuddled, unsure of the proper response. Then his face lit up.

—I love you too, man. He didn't say he wouldn't give up his beer, though all of us familiar with the commercial thought it and laughed out loud.

Work hard and don't pretend, and you'll have success. I may never have recommended orally either practice or made the promise, but I tried to demonstrate their value and their link to meaningful results during each class with each district.

After his second trip to the National High School Finals in Gillette, Wyoming, Josh was offered a scholarship at a college in southwestern Oklahoma. He accepted and planned to move to join the rodeo team after the summer. Before school began, he assessed his financial condition, noting he had next to no money, little in the bank and not much in his pockets from his rodeo winnings that summer. He did not approach our father about rodeoing at college, and our father did not approach him. Where my father had zealously supported Josh and Jeremy in high school, after graduation his enthusiasm took a precipitous dive. Josh knew our father wanted him to serve an LDS mission, so he chalked up our father's indifference to believing that if Josh went to Oklahoma he would not go on a mission. Riding bulls in Oklahoma was ideal for developing skills in an elite environment, including for the first time having a coach, and incomparable practice and competition throughout the bull riding belt of the South. After school began, the rodeo coach called Josh and asked where he was, and Josh said he wouldn't be coming. A few months later he began a two-year, Lao-speaking mission in Dallas, Texas, speaking nary a word of its biting irony or showing any semblance of regret.

The years after his mission involved more rodeoing, which required a lot of working as a cook and janitor during the week to pay for entry fees and traveling expenses on the weekends. These costs were piled onto his generosity, as he often paid more than his share when he travelled with Jeremy and other companions, so Josh was hardly able to get ahead.

Jeremy called and asked if he could leave his friend's van on the street outside our attic apartment in Provo. We were relatively close to Salt Lake by Idaho airport standards, so I didn't question the wisdom of his plan to leave the van in Provo to catch a flight out of Salt Lake, though I didn't ask how he was getting to Salt Lake either.

—I'm coming with a friend who is a big Christian, so have your Bible ready, he said.

—Shoot. I'm happy to teach him what's in it, I said back.

—He really knows it. He's into it.

—He won't be the first Christian I've discussed the good book with.

Georgians knew their Bible. My best approach to garnering interest among them during my mission tour was to know it too. I read and reread the New Testament, familiarizing myself with the passages used to oppose our message about a new testament of Jesus Christ and modern prophets who lead his true Church, but mitigating those controversies was not my focus. I paid attention to the teachings of Jesus and his parables and routinely drew upon them to support our attempts to teach more. Citing Jesus' teachings did not usually get us in the door, but focusing on his recorded words almost always changed the tone of the conversation from confrontational to one of mutual interest in what ideas were worth believing and trying to live in concert with. And it helped that Jesus' New Testament teachings, drilled by my father for all my teenage years at home, were the main part of the missionary message I believed.

—He's a young bull rider named Wiley—Jeremy continued—and he loves talking about Christ, so be ready. I told him you teach at the MTC and know the Bible like the back of your hand.

—I'm ready.

They didn't spend more than ten minutes at our apartment between dropping Wiley's van off and picking it up on their way to and back from Miami. Miami was Wiley Peterson's first PBR event, a Touring Pro show, where he placed and won his first PBR paycheck, the first of many over one of the most successful PBR careers, among its ten-highest career-earning leaders, including winning the PBR finals. He may have had other firsts in Miami. With time to kill, Jeremy and Wiley ventured to South Beach, a test for the most ardent of Christians to avert one's eyes from God's beautiful naked creations sun bathing on one of God's many impressive feats, the beach, all attested as true by Jeremy's firsthand account, admittedly failing in his own ability not to look.

Josh also went to a dozen Touring Pro events with Wiley, including a couple events where they traveled in Wiley's van with Brock and Judd Mortensen debating the Book of Mormon. While Wiley was outnumbered by the Mormons, he held his own with his superior knowledge of the New Testament, and benefited from one other sober driver, Josh, to split driving duties on straight runs over a few nights to make the events through various states. Over those touring shows, Josh's riding percentage bested his traveling partners, including Wiley's, but he didn't win money and fell back into work for paychecks until the next show routine, pacing out his participation, no surer way not to break in, spanning the period of his mid-twenties, the height of a bull rider's ability and the time for the greatest achievements.

There was no question whether he had the ability. Before the Canadian Daryl Mills won the PRCA Bull Riding World Title in 1994, beating the greatest rodeo cowboy of all-time, Ty Murray, having lost barely to Ty the year before, he rode at the Bull Riders Only events like other bull riders, looking for a trip to the highest paying pay-window. In Ninety-two, Mills traveled to the Bull Riders Only show at Ogden Utah with his Canadian traveling partner Glen Kelley. Daryl drew the bull Wanna Be and Glen drew Tressbraker. Both bulls were owned by the Pearsons out of Darlington, Idaho, about ten miles north of Arco, which was the first town ever lighted by nuclear power. (That power came from a reactor at the Idaho National Laboratory, which housed more reactors in the high desert of eastern Idaho than any other cluster in the world.) Whatever the cause, Pearsons had bulls that bucked. Jimmy and Dustin Young drew at the Ogden show, and Jimmy assured Daryl he could ride Wanna Be. Jimmy knew Pearson's bulls well and knew as well that Daryl was among the best riders anywhere. Daryl and Glenn both bucked off. Pearson's bulls won big in Ogden, with only the staple finalist Aaron Semas riding one of theirs that day, and Jimmy could only shrug.

Josh had ridden Wanna Be for eighty-seven points in Montpelier, Idaho, minutes from the Wyoming border, earlier in the year and later rode Tress-braker for eight-five points in Pocatello, when scoring bullrides was tempered by judges' best judgment more than by the PBR's television deal, a relationship resulting in the inevitable increase of scores, by any conservative estimate, of a half to a dozen points. Yes, ridiculous for a bull-riding fan born watching Denny Flynn cover the rankest bulls to clip hoofs on terra firma, but hell-a-glad for bull riders to finally get their just reward of high paydays, propped up by the new PBR inflated scores and TV deals. Josh continued to ride but not with the consistency necessary for financial strength to travel throughout the states, and he was just a couple of sponsors, or something near a trust fund, shy of making a run at making the finals. But what Josh did do was never demean the abilities of those he knew and those he didn't, and he never begrudged them for their successes.

CHAPTER 23

THE PHILOSOPHER

President Mensh moved his family to Provo after leaving Georgia. I called on him a couple months later when I returned to BYU, and he welcomed me with his enormous smile and characteristic bear hug. During his last few months as mission president, the mission set monthly goals, culminating with all companionships having a baptism the last month and nearly a hundred companionships reached that. He requested all his missionaries send him stories of their experiences during the final month to compile into a book, and I did.

Before instituting the mission goals, the mission leaders attended a monthly leadership meeting where President Mensh invited them to kneel around a long table to join him in prayer, asking God to know if the missionaries should participate in the proposed plan leading up to all the companionships having a baptism. After his prayer we took our seats, and he invited the missionaries to share their feelings about what we would forever after reference as The Plan. He turned to me to begin, and I said let's get to work. The group unanimously felt The Plan was right.

One of the months focused on repentance. Other than the final one, the repentance month was easily the most memorable. President Mensh made his call to repentance as broad and deep as the Grand Canyon. He laid it on the missionaries pretty thick at all the zone conferences throughout the mission. As a result, everyone confessed each and every sin they had ever committed and, not surprisingly, a half dozen confessed serious enough sins to be sent home. After hearing the lesson repeated at each zone conference, I questioned my own worthiness to be on a mission. I had been one of his assistants for many months and felt an enormous amount of anxiety the days leading up to our monthly interview. I entered sick, forcing a weak smile. He asked me if I had anything to repent of and I answered him that I did. One of his defining characteristics was holding a seasoned poker face, a prominent lawyer in his previous life, and I don't recall him being the least fazed by my response. I proceeded to tell him I hadn't always repented for drinking beer. He asked was that all? I said no, that I also hadn't always answered my bishop truthfully when he asked if I had a problem with masturbation, denying that I did when in fact I did. He didn't ask me if I only had one bishop growing up and I didn't volunteer that I'd had many, including my most recent passing as the grand inquisitor at BYU. Still smiling the same smile he wore when I had entered the room and during every other interview over the course of my mission, he told me to write my old bishop and tell him I had lied and then to consider myself having repented of my sins. I was relieved he didn't ask if I felt bad because I didn't want to lie to him that I did, believing my anxiety was wholly something other than guilt. I wrote the letter to my old bishop, memorializing only the second time I confessed my sins and also the last.

—How is your book coming along? I asked.

—It's coming along well and thank you for providing a copy of your experience. But you didn't share anything special, he smiled.

I had shared a redacted version of the experiences of the last month, but even if it hadn't been, there was nothing special to share. We did that month what we did every month, talked to and taught as many people as were willing to listen to us. Within the first couple weeks of the month we welcomed a new member through the ordinance of baptism for the remission of sins and the ordinance of confirmation into the Church, including the bestowal of the gift of Holy Ghost. President Mensh pulled me into his office and asked what I thought about going into another area to help the companionship reach their goal of getting a baptism. It sounded good to me. He did the same with other missionaries. I expect he sent Elder Smith into a new area every day.

He assigned me to a young duo in an affluent area north of Atlanta. The senior companion had not been out long, and the junior companion towered over him and had not been out long either. They timidly received me, holding my small suitcase with a few days' changes of clean underclothes. Curious about how long I planned to stay, they jumped each time I addressed them. I assured them, just as long as it took. They were even more sheepish about their pool of investigators as we identified their best candidates my first evening. During the next few days we followed up with each investigator. One night I struggled to sleep on their floor and dreamed of a woman on their short list. She told me the name of someone important to her, and I immediately woke and wrote the name in the margin of my blue weekly planner, not positive but pretty sure I remembered it close to correct.

We invited her to meet us at church and she accepted. A split—a middle-aged gentlemen in the ward—the senior companion, and I met her in a small classroom. The senior companion had been resisting my efforts for days with a scowl on his face, and shortly into our visit he broke from our script, taking the lead of the discussion by asking pointed questions about the woman's desire to be baptized. He was awkward and defensive and in a shaking voice asked as relevant questions as I would eventually gotten around to. I watched them interact, asking her and the split questions to move the discussion along for about an hour. She attended church and had on and off for years, but wasn't interested in joining at this time. She was polite, confidently above us, not condescending but climbing. We walked with her out of the building, and as she opened her car door I thought to ask if I could sit in the passenger seat for minute to visit, looking for a way to bring up the name on my blue weekly planner.

She was beautiful, with dark curly shoulder-length hair, thin, nearing if not securely in her fifties. She demonstrated no interest in joining the Mormon Church, and I hesitated to provide a reason she should, assuming I had correctly scribbled one down, not disposed to force another's choice. But that is not why I did not say anything. I just did not say anything, watching her drive away. The next day the short and tall duo received a call from a set of elders in a bordering area, informing them that they, the other set of elders, had been teaching a man who turned out to be living in their area and the man committed to be baptized the coming Sunday. These other missionaries gladly turned him over to be baptized in his proper ward. I congratulated them on reaching their goal, and left during the final week for one of the remaining areas that hadn't reached their goal of a baptism. The area was in east Atlanta, part of a ward I had worked in for a couple of months. I joined the companionship to attend church on the last day of the month, expecting a baptismal candidate to show up, and one did.

The elders pointed out a balding, thin, middle-aged man with glasses sitting in the back during Sunday School class. They knew him but had not taught him any discussions. During a break between classes I stopped him in the hall and introduced myself, asking him if he'd like to meet with us after church. He hemmed and hawed, and I backed off, leaving it that we'd be around all day if he wanted to meet after church or come back late that afternoon. Our stay at the church extended from the three-hour service into afternoon and evening. He came back.

We visited about the history of the Mormon Church and asked him many questions regarding his beliefs and feelings about being a member, covering the principles of all six discussions, inviting him to join that evening. Our visit went on for hours, and we called another missionary to come interview him to ensure he qualified for baptism, despite his not yet committing. We intended to satisfy all the formalities by the time he did. Earlier in the day, one elder in the area informed me that the man had a shady past, rumors of criminal record and child molestation, and the bishop had asked them not to teach him the discussions. I undeniably had a creepy feeling sitting across from him. He wouldn't make eye contact and did not share much. I responded to the bishop's warning no differently than with any other investigator. We needed to find out if he desired and was qualified to join, and if he did and was, then denying him the blessings of dying and rising in Christ were not ours to decide. They were ours to offer. The missionary we called to interview him was Tron, Elder Whitely. The interview went long, and the elders were anxious whether he would be the fulfillment of their goal.

—Should we fill the baptismal font? one elder asked me.

—We're running out of day, another elder pointed out.

—We'll have to open the spouts full to get it filled, an elder said.

—And we'll need it full if our aim is to immerse him as we're required to do, I said.

When we called Elder Whitely, it was still a couple of hours before midnight, and when he finally finished the interview it was about thirty minutes to midnight. He came over and sat down on the floor against the wall next to me.

—I don't think he's the one for this companionship. He's got issues.

The middle-aged gentleman exited the room without looking in our direction, and he walked toward the back glass doors. He opened them and left a half dozen of us in the hall looking on.

—You can stop filling the font, one elder said.

—We were close, another elder said.

—At least the Bishop won't want to kill us, an elder said.

—It's late. Let's go home, I said.

The Karl G. Maeser Building, center of the Honors Department, stately well-hewn granite blocks, sat on the southwest corner of BYU, facing modern characterless buildings many times its size that spread over campus, propped high above the city of Provo, a half moon lining its background. Maeser, one of the founding principals of Brigham Young Academy during the second half of the nineteenth century and considered the universities' educational spiritual father, joined the Mormon religion as a young married man in Dresden, Germany, and immigrated with his young family to Salt Lake City. The building bearing his name was the most ornate and esteemed on campus, with halls, stairs, and classrooms finished in wood of the highest craftsmanship. I entered the building twice a week the semester of sophomore year after returning from my mission in Georgia, feeling I was in a building fit for higher learning, to attend lectures for a survey course on modern philosophy taught by a tall, gangly professor who never seemed comfortable with his massive hands, routinely holding them behind his back, releasing them to open a book, turn a page, or to write on the board, and whose repertoire of courses I exhausted over the next few years. His modus operandi was accuracy. He broke down each philosopher's arguments to its building blocks, and his tests were notoriously challenging, one- or two-sentence questions with three short multiple choices, the most precise answer being the correct one.

Part of the building's mystique involved sitting in small wooden desks, which linked the motivated classes to past generations and simultaneously wore out soft derrières. I liked going to class and never minded leaving it, not having been as saddle-sore since last volunteering to ride flank when pushing cattle to the hills in the spring. I recognized one classmate who must have been more uncomfortable than me. He was no more than an inch taller, but his frame doubled the next-biggest in class, with square shoulders fit for the NHL, his Nordic jaw and Viking neck unmistakably the same as a new teacher in my rotation at the MTC. His name was Ken.

—Are you a philosophy major? I asked, exiting the Maeser building.

—Math, but I'm thinking about changing majors to philosophy. How about you?

—English major, philosophy minor. I prefer easier reading but feel like I should know some of the harder stuff.

Our survey course started with Descartes and, after the first assigned reading, I bagged reading the assignments until the next philosopher, and then I found Locke and, again, Bishop Berkeley and their modernist cohorts were no more accessible. I resigned myself to a semester of seconds spent turning pages a few minutes before class, spot-reading sentences, circling words I recognized, filling my notebook during lectures until the final section on John Stuart Mill. By then my routine of pre-class skimming the text and in-class rigorous note-taking was so engrained that I didn't read many of Mill's intelligible sentences, but at least one more in his work than in that of all the previous philosophers. My introduction to philosophy could not have been more stultifying.

During the middle of high school, one Sunday afternoon in my home ward of Riverton after priesthood meeting, a recently re-activated member assigned to the priest quorum, Nick, walked next to me as we filed into the hall toward the chapel for sacrament meeting. He asked if I had read Descartes. I hadn't even heard of him. Nick said that, from my comments in class, he thought I'd enjoy reading him. I did not get around to taking Nick up on his recommendation, and when I finally read, or tried to, Descartes in the survey course, I churned inside remembering Nick could have thought so highly of me, knowing he wasn't the only one who had been or would be fooled by the apparent depth of my comments.

Ken and I talked about every Mormon doctrinal issue raised under the sun over the next few years, ripping into many of them at the MTC. We team-taught a few districts, which afforded us abundances of minutes to riff about one spiritual thing and another, our conversations running one day into the next. Ken served his mission in Detroit, and like me, most of the converts to the LDS Church he taught were African American. Mormonism's relationship with African Americans most notably turned for the better in 1978, when then-president of the Church Spencer W. Kimball announced to the Church by official declaration and to the Associated Press by press release that he received a revelation from God to afford black men the right to have the Mormon Priesthood. During his mission, Ken heard rumors that Joseph Smith had conferred the priesthood on black men within the first decade of the Church's inception, but his mission president quickly dismissed them as false.

—No, you heard the rumors right. Joseph Smith gave the priesthood to Elijah Abel. In fact, he made him part of the leadership of the church, I said.

—That can't be right. I specifically asked my mission president about Abel, and he said that didn't happen.

—Did too.

—Are you sure?

—Look it up. In fact, not only look up Abel, but you can look up Brigham Young's reason for revoking his priesthood and putting an end to giving it to black men, in his Discourses. You can pretty much find Brigham's opinions on every matter that crossed through his brain as he never failed to voice them and he either wrote them or they were recorded in his Discourses, if you're so inclined to know them. He was not as discriminating in his thinking as he was in his beliefs.

—Have you read them?

—Not in this lifetime nor will I in the next, only a few excerpts, enough to count on my left hand, not including my trigger finger.

The very next day I walked into the MTC to team-teach with Ken.

—You're right. I went to the library and read about Abel receiving the priesthood from Joseph. Then why on earth did Brigham revoke the practice of giving black men the priesthood?

—Brigham could excuse Joseph's financial irresponsibility in Ohio because he wouldn't question God's anointed, but he couldn't condone his mistaken views of racial equality despite his being God's anointed. Joseph wasn't prejudiced against blacks but Brigham was. No other justifiable inference lends itself.

—At least they agreed on polygamy.

—Inspired bastards.

—What happened in Ohio?

—I don't know, some kind of Ponzi scheme, you know, give me ten dollars and I'll turn it into twenty by this time next month. It's all cool.

I never had to explain Joseph's banking scheme in Ohio, but I regularly explained Joseph's view of African Americans during my efforts to convert the citizens of Atlanta. I didn't, however, mention those of his successor

Brigham. And the issue about Mormons' relationship to black people always came up during our discussions with African Americans. Always. Black immigrants, not always or hardly ever, if my memory is not mistaken. And most of the discussions we taught were to African Americans.

I did not have a strong witness of Joseph's divine role in God's Plan of Salvation, so I did not offer the standard missionary testimony of his calling as a modern prophet during the first discussion and subsequent discussions. I admitted the same to a returned missionary a decade later, and he was incredulous. Impossible to teach for two years trying to get people to join the LDS Church and not bear witness of Joseph Smith as a modern prophet! he responded. I couldn't blame him for not believing me, but it was true. What I did repeatedly emphasize about Joseph was his absence of prejudice against minorities and his early followers' abolitionist reputation in the territory of Missouri, one reason their neighbors drove them into the swamp lands of Illinois. I didn't mention the abolitionist reputation was not likely true but was more likely a creation by anti-Mormons to increase indignation against the Mormons in that slave state, because I didn't know it myself until years later. It was sufficient that I really wanted the rumor that Mormons were abolitionists to be true. Hearing these historical facts often assuaged concerns of our African American investigators, once they knew that Mormons' founding father and the pre-westbound pioneers respected their race decades and even more than a century before many American Christian churches.

What I eventually, and sheepishly, confessed was that not all Mormon leaders who followed Joseph felt the same way and, as a result, Joseph's revolutionary perspective on equality was not again accepted until a brazen and fearless prophet, Spencer Kimball, affirmed officially what Joseph had practiced over a century before, when he announced his Declaration permitting all black LDS men the opportunity to hold the priesthood. Yes, this was shortly after numerous universities boycotted intercollegiate competition with BYU, and the explosion of South Americans of African descent joining the Mormon Church in Latin America, but it marked the end of a protracted history of official bigotry. I could say what missionaries just a couple decades before me could not, that all black men can fulfill leadership roles in local churches and can officiate in the Church's most sacred saving ordinances in holy temples.

We cycled our Schwinns on busy streets throughout South DeKalb County, just inside its perimeter, veering into apartment complexes looking for people to hear our message about the restoration of the true Church of

Jesus Christ. We were not only minorities, the only two white people we saw all day, some days we were the only two males walking around the complexes during the day. Because we could not enter the home of single women without an adult male present, we taught many modified discussions on doorsteps or park benches in small common areas.

One hot afternoon we met a middle-aged woman who invited us into her home to visit about our message. Upon learning that her boyfriend was at home, we gladly entered. He introduced himself and shortly after our greetings he departed. I looked at my companion, Elder Young, who was my senior by many, many months but had the subordinate role, as the junior companion, in our companionship. So he deferred to me, and I shrugged and we stayed and taught one of the best first discussions I taught as a missionary. J, the heroine of this story, was the mother of two children at home, single, working full-time, and smart as a whip. She responded positively to our invitation to read the Book of Mormon and to meet us again to discuss more of our beliefs.

We went back, and on the return visit I explained if her boyfriend was not home, we'd have to visit outside. She was fine with the arrangement and brought a couple chairs onto the front porch. We taught all the remaining discussions sitting in the doorway. She voluntarily engaged us on the principles of the gospel, a sure sign of the elect, always alert, asking questions, processing each new piece of information. She agreed to attend church and asked if there would be other black people. Of course, we assured her. And, almighty heaven, were we relieved there were on the Sunday she came. She committed to be baptized a few weeks after our initial meeting and was baptized and confirmed a member of The Church of Jesus Christ of Latter-day Saints. J's children eventually followed her decision to join the Mormon Church after we left the area.

In a different area with a different companion, Elder Hill, we tracked into a "golden" family, the prayed-for investigators all missionaries hope to find, a family who wanted to hear the message about the One True Church of Christ, as rare a find as its elemental signifier. They gladly welcomed our visits, one followup visit ending with us standing before an apologetic father after his wife Sister G had voiced her intention to attend church services. Far into the visit with the entire family, two parents and three children, sitting attentively in the front room, the father threw up his arms voicing his displeasure at his wife and children being interested in a church run by white devils. We demurred for a few penetrating silent moments until his wife strongly encouraged us to continue with our presentation. The father didn't throw us out of his apartment. He just left the front room, and after we finished our meeting we stood and walked into the night. Sister G closed the door behind us, and he opened it and called us back.

—I have nothing against you two. As far as I'm concerned you two are great guys. But I can't believe my wife is making this decision.

—We're sorry.

—White people haven't all been bad. I grew up in Brooklyn, and one time a white friend stood up for me when I needed it. I've taken the prejudice against me knowing not all white people are bad.

—If you don't want us to come back, we'll respect that and quit teaching your family.

—It's her decision but don't expect me to be around when you come back.

He was not around again, and his children followed the wife's decision to join the Mormon Church after we left the area. Ken told me similar stories involving tension toward white missionaries in black communities where he served, but our experiences were, by far, positive receptions, whether our introduction on doorsteps prompted an interest to visit further or not, most respecting our efforts to hit the pavement inviting folks to learn about our message. African Americans were always insistent hosts, offering us refreshments and shade from the heat. Sure the youth consistently slung slanders our way, but that might have been for our appearance of white shirts, flowing ties and backpacks over our dress shirts, topped with shining helmets, pedaling furiously on the road's shoulder, more than for the color of our skin; heavens if the white kids in the suburbs weren't saying the same thing as they roared pass us in their parents' SUVs. Teenagers were smart and angry for a thousand reasons, all immediately apparent to themselves, while histories and institutions were far-removed concerns that only later served as ex post facto justifications of complaints about life's misdirections and glaring rejections of effort—those timeless excuses that infect lives indiscriminant of color, gender, and creed. But the unfair cards dealt young kids showed in many hands that we encountered every day.

When I could bum a lift, I enjoyed riding up the mountain to visit President Mensh for Sunday dinner. While I enjoyed his family, my lofty motivations to remain in good standing with my mission president carried impurities, as I was hard pressed to pass on a home-cooked meal. Sister

Mensh maintained the practice of cooking her exquisitely tasty and filling chicken casserole into post-mission life, and while short on fine manners, I wasn't completely without some and could resist a heap of second helpings, despite nothing being more on my mind during dinner. They encouraged more helpings at every meal, but I fought them off, breaking down only a few times for more, maybe the majority of dinners, but I never kept count. It was a new battle to develop manners on each new occasion, be it dinner or something else, it was one more battle in an ongoing war to behave well, one with more defeats than victories.

One Sunday afternoon, to my surprise, another guest, the Mormon philosopher WT, sat across the dinner table from me. President Mensh impressed me with all his success and reputation but nothing approached his knowing Professor T, who I learned upon introductions was a brother-in-law, having married Sister Mensh's sister. Upon good sources among philosophy majors, I had heard that Professor T studied and taught at Oxford. He hadn't published, but few Mormon philosophers did. Upon good information from philosophy majors, the faculty didn't encourage publishing. What they did was teach and impress the heavens out of undergraduates, and Professor T's reputation as a masterful teacher was unanimous. When I inquired who the best philosophy teachers were, his name always came up, setting the gold standard. We looked at each other and nodded our acknowledgments. I caught his momentary, stumped look, which faded with our immediate lack of conversation. He may have recognized me. I recognized him. I audited his class on Kierkegaard for a few weeks shy of half a semester.

I didn't know Soren Kierkegaard, who I warmly refer to as "K," from Immanuel Kant, and I didn't know Kant from anyone on campus named Young, but it was the only class Professor T taught that semester, and upon good information from philosophy majors, Professor T did not teach each semester. I didn't register for the class, deciding to review it the first week before making a commitment. And while I decided not to enroll after the first day of being spun in total confusion, it was informal so I kept going until my other classes required my undivided intellectual attention, all two feathers' worth, during some inconspicuous week leading up to midterms.

Professor T ran his class like no others I had attended. He sat on a chair in the front, leading discussions about the reading, occasionally writing terms and their corresponding definitions on the board. And his students responded, unlike other students in classes I had taken—many, if not most, having something to say about the material, all appearing to enjoy a familiarity with Professor T, either having taken a course from him before or chatted musings over a caffeine-free soda in the student center. I took a seat in the back each time, as it was always open. There were usually a few seats open between my back seat and the next filled one. I never said a thing, not out of fear or indifference as in other classes, but my thoughts were too jumbled to produce a coherent comment. The format confused the dickens out of me. I couldn't follow students' comments and would have made as much sense if they were speaking in the Adamic tongue, the perfect language spoken by the descendants of Adam before the Tower of Babel episode led to the confusion of all humans upon earth forever after forced to speak different languages, a plight commiserated with no groups more than immigrants and philosophy students.

And yet, few books captured my attention like K's *The Sickness unto Death*, the class's primary text. I attended class under the impression I understood some of what K wrote, only to have my impressions corrected by the comments of my peers, whom I wasn't sure Professor T agreed with but whom he always seemed able to understand well enough to respond to their points and move the discussion along. Despite class's being a chaotic run of voices on the days I sat in, the book cracked a wall I had been uncomfortably atop for all the years I'd been sitting on it.

My intellectual development ran on a continuing *tabula rasa*. Everything was new, and not just new information. The processes and concepts needed to understand the information were new. Nor dare I fail to mention the recurring, new awareness of my mind's inherent capacity, which needed first to be discovered and then to be nurtured. I seemed to rediscover it through each class and day, as it developed from infinitesimally small to slightly grander. The philosophical cards were not merely stacked against me, they were waves in a sea I have continued to tread.

K's writing showed passion for ideas as much as it did brilliance in expounding them. For him, incorrect arguments had consequences. And while I had a hint of passion and was short on brilliance, I agreed completely that everything was at stake if I lived my life according to incorrect beliefs. And I believed I was responsible for what I believed and nothing—and I mean no iota of a thing, monadic or atomic—repulsed me or fired my guts more than folks who proposed that they believed correctly and I should believe them, all too commonly oblivious to their duty to provide support for the belief they thought I should have. If their audacity didn't stink the whole room they instinctively, and unpardonably, shifted the burden to me to justify not believing. Nothing seemed more evil or more disrespectful or more pessimistic or more doubting of my potential, even my freedom, to know what was true.

K's style was responsible, accounting for his propositions with reasoned explanations. He also was earnest, and while I admired him for it, I was fool enough to know that, time and again, feeling strongly about something or affecting certainty had no necessary connection to truth, usually did not have a connection to truth. Showing certainty had more to do with having consumed three square meals, bedded upon a soft pillow, and accessing other reinforcing, supportive resources, rather than the self-affirming opposite extreme of absences, or in my instance living off fast-food dollar menus and resting each night on a stained thin sorry excuse of a head prop in sync with an obdurate personality.

K claimed everyone was in despair, and you had to be a Christian to be aware of this despair, which he called sickness to death, not the greatest sell for non-Christians to pay him much heed. While he included all people in need of becoming aware of one's despair, his message was directed at Christians for failing to live up to the ideal of Jesus Christ. He derided the theoretical approach to Christianity in vogue during his day, the first half of the nineteenth century. To be fair to his contemporaries, they were dealing with a new deck of cards after the writings of the greatest philosophers of the major philosophical traditions changed the landscape of how theologians and philosophers talked about ultimate realities like God. The best agreed there were limits to what humans could know by reason, and one of the acknowledged limits was knowing God by reason alone—so fashionable during the Middle Ages and at the beginning of the Enlightenment. For example, the father of the Enlightenment, Rene Descartes, stated his idea of a perfect God included existence, the same Descartes who coined possibly the most famous phrase in the history of philosophy: *I think, therefore I am* (properly understood as a method to gain knowledge and not as the oft marshaled proof of existence). Kant, the last of the Enlightenment pantheon of thinkers, pointed out that existence was not a property of the idea of God. Having an idea of a thing and adding the property of existence doesn't make it exist. That is to say if existence is not a predicate for every idea you can think of, say a liger bred for its skills and magic, then it's not proof of the idea that God exists. While Kant might be right, I'm far more like Descartes persuaded by the power of my own ideas, convinced if they were thought by me, then by John they have reality sufficient for lots of other ne'er-do-wells like me, not to mention my eternal aversion to capping the dynamite imaginations that come up with this stuff.

Ideas fashioned together as arguments also used to prove God came under heightened scrutiny. Logical arguments for God about His *unconditioned* and *immutable* qualities often sound persuasive because the conclusion follows from the premises, but the assumed connections between the premises and subsequently to the conclusion show the *validity* of the argument and are not *proof* of the conclusion. For example, change is one state passing into another; a perfect being does not change; thus God, being a perfect being, does not change. That's a valid argument. It's certainly not proof of a characteristic of God. Honestly I have never had much invested in a practice that took to rigorous analytical reasoning, lazy as I am by nature, so the Enlightenment philosophers' assault on various forms of logical proofs for God didn't remove the seat of my God-fearing pants.

The limits of knowledge were acknowledged not just by the thinkers like David Hume in the tradition that emphasized knowledge came from experience through our senses and impressions (which left no room for theoretical proofs about God), but also by the thinkers like Kant and Georg Hegel, the two most famous of Idealists, guys in the tradition that emphasized the mind (not experience) accounted for knowledge. Both Kant and, to a greater extent Hegel, explained how truths could be known even not from experience, that is to say from abstract reason alone, but their explanations were keenly tuned to the widely accepted limits of human knowledge demonstrated by Hume; in fact, they fashioned their justifications with respect to them.

So then shortly thereafter along came K, who found himself in a bit of pickle. He didn't care much for Hegel or his followers who made *speculative* arguments to justify claims about knowing absolute truths about reality, which arguments religious thinkers immediately converted to absolute truths about the supernatural, or in other words making the speculators' ultimate claims synonymous with God. K's disgust with Hegelians didn't put him in the pickle, though, but acknowledging skeptics' arguments showing limits of knowledge did. The limits on knowledge about God were not more cogently presented than in Hume's classic *Dialogues Concerning Religion*, and Hume patterned his classic on another classic, Cicero's *The Nature of the Gods*, bounded timeless personalities as much as their works were pointed critiques of traditional theoretical arguments of the idea of God worthy of a few summary paragraphs.

Among the many critiques about the limits of knowledge on the proofs of God marshaled from the characters in Hume and Cicero's books was one against the argument from design, one of the most popular arguments for God's existence today: that is the argument that the supreme effects of orderliness and direction in the natural world prove a designer, a God. Taking just one aspect that the sheer perfection of the conditions on Earth and in our solar system make life possible; and if the conditions were slightly altered, the result would be no life, which showed an immensely persuasive cache of purposefulness for ultimate-minded individuals.

In Book II of Cicero's *Gods*, the stoic Balbus presented a version of the design argument, among his plethora of points—one highlighting the harmony of all parts of the universe—asking who cannot wonder at the *symphony of nature*, noting *everywhere similar signs of purposive intelligence.* While noting nature's purposive intelligence, he included the preservation of all different kinds of animals and their roles, such as asses clearly meant to serve man, which to my knowledge is a piece of evidence yet to be disproved to this very day (finding its greatest support in Apuleius' *The Golden Ass*). He concluded *From all these arguments we must conclude that everything in the world is marvelously ordered by divine providence and wisdom for the safety and protection of us all.* He made other arguments for God that preceded the rational (abstract) arguments (not from experience) so loved during the Middle Ages, surmising, *Yet beyond there is nothing superior to the universe, there is nothing more excellent or more beautiful. Not only is there nothing better, but nothing better can even be imagined.*

In Book III, Cotta, the skeptic and widely recognized voice of Cicero, responded against the rational argument that the universe was the best possible universe by stating that he could rightly assert that Rome was the greatest city but that didn't mean he couldn't conceive of one better, so claiming something was the best was not proof that it was. He warned against abstract arguments proposing something being *superior* then relating the superior aspect to God's super *superiority* because those arguments perpetuated a fallacy, not a proof. He quoted Stoicism's founder Zeno's syllogistic, or logical, argument that any being which reasons is superior to *any being which does not. But there is nothing superior to the universe as a whole. Therefore the universe is a reasoning being.* He extended this logic to its absurd implication by replacing reasoning with reading, concluding the universe as a whole could read.

He attacked a specific aspect of the Stoic version of the design argument, which emphasized the rational component of all parts of the universe noted in Zeno's syllogism above, also known as the infamous pantheistic fancy pants worn—but not always comfortably—by all those who subscribe to a universal, perfect, unconditioned, ultimate, necessary, infinite, simple single substance, first cause (assertions overlapping other classical proofs of God). He explained the wondrous features of the world do not need a God to explain them.

Then he berated the stock Epicurean Velleius' nonsensical notions about atoms that didn't exist and theories of the heavens being created by accidental collisions, reminding us, fair reader, that the measure of the best philosophy is not that its claims fall short after the test of time but that it measures the length of the knowledge of its day.

In Hume's *Dialogues*, a trio of acquaintances also argue about the nature of God. The first half of their insightful exchange deals with the argument of design, their version a thorough extension, not repetition, of Cicero's orators' ideas. In Book II, a theist, Cleanthes, introduces the argument, making its strongest defense by claiming that when one looked around, one could find nothing but evidence of a great machine, the world, and other smaller great machines. He argues there was evidence from experience, and not exclusively from rational arguments (which, we might expect, everyone of Hume's creation would have summarily agreed because of the deficiency of abstract reasoning), that the minute parts of the machines in nature, including humans, show the intelligence of a human designer. He concludes one may reason by analogy an intelligent divine designer of the universe.

Hume's own voice in the text, Philo, counters that *a stone will fall, that fire will burn, that the earth has solidity, we have observed a thousand and a thousand times; and when any new instance of this nature is presented, we draw without hesitation the accustomed inference.* He explains that humans are limited to draw inferences about causes from the effects they regularly perceive, not ever able to identify those causes. That is to say, humans cannot prove causes in the natural world but become accustomed to making inferences about causes. Humans infer causes when the similarities of the new circumstances resemble those from familiar circumstances, and, with less certainty, when new instances in nature present themselves without similarities. Humans don't fare well to infer the causes, let alone ever prove them. Philo demonstrates that it is impossible to assign any one cause to an event, and if we cannot identify causes in nature, then we can hardly by analogy identify the origin of the whole universe. So a proof of God as designer from experience fails.

In Book IX, the third friend, Demea, proposes that, where arguments from experience are deficient, a rational argument could prove God's infinite qualities, proffering the argument that whatever exists must have a cause or reason for its existence, so there must be recourse to an ultimate cause that *necessarily exists*, his expression of the cosmological proof of God. This proof aligns to the abstract reasoning of Balbus and the various attempts of Descartes. Here Cleanthes the theist, and not the skeptic Philo, counters that rational arguments are meaningful only if the contrary implies a contradiction. That is to say, we can prove by abstract reasoning if its negation is inconceivable. For example, the *Dialogues* claim it's impossible for twice two not to be four. Its contrary of "twice two is five" is a contradiction or is inconceivable, so it's a fair rational proof. Cleanthes continues, *whatever we conceive as existent, we can also conceive as non-existent. There is no being, therefore, whose non-existence implies a contradiction. Consequently there is no being, whose existence is demonstrable.* That is to say a non-existing God is not a contradiction, or inconceivable. Take Thor, for example. It's actually conceivable Thor does not exist, so it's not a rational proof that he does exist based on my being able to think that he does.

This clearer picture of K's fix, to wit the limits of knowledge, to explain a viable relation for humans to have to God, provides a clearer focus on his herculean attempt to justify such a relation in his complicated explanation of true Christianity. K begins his view of true Christianity by explaining that humans were a combination, or his term *synthesis*, of polar aspects of finite and infinite, temporal and eternal, and freedom and necessity. These aspects were in constant relation, and the aspects relating to each other caused despair, whether one was aware of the despair or not. People experienced two kinds of despair: first, not wanting to be yourself; and second, wanting to be yourself (by your own standard, not in relation to God). The Self, or what K also called Spirit, was this relation (synthesis of the aspects) that related to itself. That is to say, in K's words, *The Self is not the relation but the relation's relating to itself,* or in other words, self is the muddling of opposing forces (if I might rightly add indolence and initiative) in motion, acting on and reacting to each other, and in the interactions' combustion (my form of the relations relating) enters chaos, or as K prefers, despair. K's aim of a human is to become a Self through the process of discovering and overcoming the sickness of despair by relating and wanting to become itself grounded transparently in the power that established it. That power being God. Despite his dislike for Hegel, K sure warmed mightily to Hegel's dialectic of thesis (an independent concept), antithesis (the first concept being dependent upon another concept), new thesis (reinterpreting the independence of the concept to include both concepts) and one thing and another.

A few of K's comments persuaded me that his project offers more than just evidence of an incisive intellect, despite a pocketful of incredulity poking me as I sat in Professor T's class and sit today. His *project of self-awareness toward a higher truth*, this whole dialectic of one's relations relating to itself to become a Self grounded in God, cemented its foundation in a few bracingly intelligible ideas. For one, the presence of *possibility*, which K connects to moments of actual despair, bridges our temporal circumstances as we remember them in the past and experience them in the moment, to reaching for what may be possible tomorrow on the tail of eternity. K seems correct to assert that each human at some moment has thought *is this possible*, having some notion of the eternal, and doggone if he isn't also correct that during those moments, despair is one of the first uninvited guests to arrive. But it doesn't just arrive for K, it's constitutive of our relations in flux or, if we're lucky, when they're relating. While K presumed the goal was to overcome despair, not all through the ages have agreed. Dostoyevsky's Underground man, revealed he was sick with a bad liver, and at times a toothache, and a healthy dose of despair, the spiteful kind. Like K, the Big U believed everyone who was conscious was ill, an illness stemming from competing opposites, too, in his own words a *fever of oscillations, of resolutions determined for ever and repented of again a minute later*, including a large batch of hopelessness, the other side of the possibility coin. Acknowledging the same predicament, the Big U opted as willfully and faithfully for vengeful self-preservation.

Next, K identified the necessity of the faculty of the imagination as the medium *of infinitization*. I don't even know what that word means, and couldn't be helped even if it describes the kit and kaboodle topped by the bow of an *ism* but no one can successfully brace him or herself against the force of truth. When a human transcends the finite confines of his or her abilities and circumstances, it is always by aid of the imagination—or call it vision or new perspective or a breath of fresh air. Yes, I'm biased for the role of imagination in successfully understanding, imbibing, and animating philosophy as much now as I was then, so I warmed forever to K.

Within a semester of auditing weeks of professor W's class, I was back in another one of my favorite gangly philosophy professor's courses arguing that Arthur Schopenhauer's best insight in his *The World as Will and Representation* is *The high value of imagination as an indispensable instrument of genius.* Making not only a most daring thesis, but also following it with my best reasoned argument, that paper confirmed how spot-on I was when my favorite professor rewarded its merit with a B, not warm to the proposal that imagination breathed life into philosophy, no doubt seeing it simultaneously as a threat to soften philosophy's infallibly rational spine, a rare sting for me but sorely not for lady Wisdom. How could he of all my great teachers miss imagination's value? K hadn't shirked when, without shame, he deferred to the power of humans' fancies to reach the infinite, neither had Big U when he blamed the self's imaginings for adding details to one's injuries over the years of one's life.

Finally, K establishes the foundation for his project by describing where the tug-of-wars between polarities like freedom and necessity take place. *Becoming oneself is a movement one makes just where one is. Becoming is a movement from some place, but becoming oneself is a movement at that place.* This discovery was made independently by others before K, as it was after him. At least one example, a couple years later half across the world, will suffice: Captain Peleg's tour of the *Pequod* before it sails. Captain Peleg asks why Ishmael wanted to go whaling, and Ishmael replies, *I want to see the world.* Captain Peleg instructs him, *Well then, just step forward there, and take a peep over the weatherbow, and then back to me and tell me what you see there.* Ishmael recounts:

> For a moment I stood a little puzzled by this curious request, not knowing exactly how to take it, whether humorously or in earnest. But concentrating all his crow's feet into one scowl, Captain Peleg started me on the errand.
>
> Going forward and glancing over the weather bow, I perceived that the ship swinging to her anchor with the floodtide, was now obliquely pointed toward the open ocean. The prospect was unlimited, but exceedingly monotonous and forbidding; not the slightest variety that I could see.
>
> "Well what's the report?" said Peleg when I came back; "what did ye see?"
>
> "Not much," I replied—nothing but water; considerable horizon though, and there's a small squall coming up, I think."
>
> "Well, what does thou think of seeing the world? Do you wish to go round Cape Horn to see any more of it, eh? Can't ye see the world where you stand?"

Suffering another example, though no self-actualization process is advanced, the Big U concurs that there's nowhere to go to become one thing (a thesis) or another (to wit, its antithesis) because you stay the same in the corner you inhabit (nothing to reinterpret), even balefully dropped out of context:

> It was not only that I could not become spiteful, I did not know how to become anything; neither spiteful nor kind, neither a rascal nor an honest man, neither a hero nor an insect. Now, I am living out my life in my corner, taunting myself with the spiteful and useless consolation that an intelligent man cannot become anything seriously, and it is only the fool who becomes anything.

The Big U's place and philosophy of change merely embellished its forefather, Milton's Satan chained to a burning lake in hell:

> The dismal situation waste and wild
> A dungeon horrible, on all sides round
> As one great furnace flamed, yet from those flames
> No light, but rather darkness visible
> Served only to discover sights of woe
> Regions of sorrow, doleful shades, where peace
> And rest can never dwell.

Satan broke his chains, expanded his wings and flew to dry land, proclaiming,

> Farewell happy fields
> Where joy for ever dwells: hail horrors, hail
> Infernal world, and thou profoundest hell
> Receive thy new possessor: one who brings
> A mind not to be changed by place or time.
> The mind is its own place, and in itself
> Can make a heav'n of hell, a hell of heav'n.
> What matter where, if I be still the same...

Ishmael, the Big U, and Satan became, or didn't, who *they were where they were*, though the *where* of Ishmael involved one hell of an adventure

chasing the white leviathan with the mad Captain Ahab, as surely as K did
the same at his writing desk in Copenhagen, laying the foundation for his
project of self-actualization.

Then K sets the cornerstone piece of his project, the struggle of *faith*
for possibility. Or maybe he had set it first and waited to mention it as the
climax in *The Sickness unto Death*. Regardless, he describes having *faith* as
precisely to lose one's mind so as to win God, as the truest way to become one's
Self. And is reaching for the possible perceived as anything but the art of the
crazy? Although his prize was not God, the Big U describes a similar crazy
act of the will against the laws of nature and rationality, *jesting against the
grain*, to preserve one's personality and individuality. He describes acting in
opposition to all laws as *advantageous advantages*, illustrating such absurdity by claiming, *twice two makes five is sometimes a very charming thing too*.

Faith in the eternal is crazy and absurd, or in K's words a *paradox*, made
possible by the atonement of Jesus Christ; hence, providing the justification
for the central role of Christianity in curing the sickness to death, or despair.
In and out of Professor T's class, the wall to reach the eternal came crum-
bling down, or appeared to as I noticed for the first time falling off onto my
head a new Christianity while I wondered whether I could ever be put back
together again, this new look requiring a leap of faith, not a sure wall of abstract rational arguments and physical evidence in the natural world.

K's Christianity provides a person the opportunity to become aware
of the despair and to cure its sickness. But how the hell how? Professor T
knew as well as his students, including itinerant auditors, all presumably
well-informed Mormons, that the Christianity of K's day, both the one he
idealized and certainly the one he criticized, were not the Christianity of
Jesus' day. That had been lost, and the true Christianity was being restored
across the Atlantic in Vermont, New York, Ohio, Missouri, and Illinois as
Joseph Smith migrated from one hostile place to a hoped-for oasis. Did K
merely describe a venerable process, the actualization of the Self by overcoming despair by embracing the greatest possibilities? His project seems
no more defeated by his misunderstanding of what is the true Christian
religion than it is by requiring that the true Christian religion necessarily
be the highest possibility. Or in other words, K's explanation doesn't appear
any more defeated by not having the right Christianity before him than the
truth of God loses its hold over so much of humankind by the ubiquitous
failure to agree on who God is, let alone requiring all those who believe
in God to subscribe to some concrete understanding for the belief's full

benefit. Writing his masterpiece, *The Sickness unto Death*, under the pseudonym Anti-Climacus, whose personality K distanced himself from, permits a tempered appreciation of Christianity as the highest possibility, whether the admiration be from a Mormon in the know of the true Christianity restored in these latter days, or from those adhering to other Christian sects with parts of truth and non-Christian religions like Judaism and Islam and a whole plethora of non-Abrahamic traditions, or from those belonging to nary a religion at all but still committed to reach and be grounded in life's greatest possibilities.

The same aim can be advanced for the Big U when Dostoyevsky's satire reveals an agent defying reason as an ultimate expression of the will, the last bastion of authentic individuality, an outright absurdity but blindingly in concert with Anti-Climacus. Consider the Big U's solution, at this point in his diary the clear voice of Dostoyevsky, to his spitefully miserable condition was *faith in Christ*, no small proposition in the penultimate chapter excised by the censors before its publication. At the minimal risk of overstating, Anti-Climacus and U, like K and D, were suffering soul mates.

The wall I tumbled off was not made of rational arguments, outside of experience, nor was it made of the many bounteous physical proofs in the natural world by a divine designer. From time to time I tried to repair it with both. When I was a sophomore at BYU, the wall supporting my idea of God was made of bricks of revelation. God speaks directly to his chosen Mormon prophet and directly to his chosen Mormon people. Mormons' relationship to God is not dependent upon rational defenses or perfectly balanced ecosystems observed in nature. God spoke to Mormons' first prophet and has been speaking to Mormons since.

The role revelation has played in explaining God didn't start with the Mormons, but few groups in history have embraced it more heartily and unabashedly. Hume and Kant acknowledge it as a form of knowledge, but both argued revelation would be consistent with reason, and Hume argued that revelation, including miracles, was not different from nature; that is they contained nothing really miraculous. K did not rule out revelation but claimed it involved God's acting in history, which was rare in deed: for example, the singular atonement by Christ the Son of God. K noted when God did act in history, accessing that history was a doubtful proposition at its best and, more commonly, quite misleading at its worst. K pointed out getting your own facts straight was hard enough, let alone historical facts, so basing a belief in God on facts was a dicey enterprise.

Revelation for Mormons is not just a record of God's dealings with humankind in Christian scriptures of the Old and New Testaments and numerous modern Mormon scriptures. God's revelation was a meteor shower for those under his new and everlasting covenant of priesthood restored to Joseph Smith in these the latter days. Mormons' relationship to the divine was not encapsulated in subjectivity, the purely personal reality of God insulated from secular and natural vagaries that obliterate historical and rational load-bearing beams for communal beliefs in God. No, Mormons' connection to God has a two-way street, the believer's efforts to God and God's reach back to him or her. Capital Revelation comes through Mormon prophets and, lower case, directly to individuals, at all times of the day. In sum, God directs each Mormon's every righteous step, from the Prophet to the most newly minted eight-year-old.

No steps were directed more than a Mormon husband and wife's toward each other to determine how big to make their family. Should they stop at five or go for seven? Each attempt at conception involved asking God if they were meant to bring another of God's children into the world and God's response confirming their righteous desires or creating doubts sufficient to convince them to toe the line with their current brood. That line was the health of the mother, physical and mental, and most couples shirked off their doubts and went beyond it. And how could they not, under the pressure of capital R and lower case "r"s from everyone else they knew caught up in their multiplying efforts, directly and always indirectly encouraging them to increase God's bounty with one more of his children intended for their mortal care? The power of this revelation—to fill the earth with children— colored all other revelations.

The revelatory call to honor God's directive of continuous conception, repeated through the decades by his chosen prophets, was the incubator, if not a contributing cause, to the decimation of my mother's health, destroyed not so much by the birthing as by the fallout of raising her six boys, demoralizing work cultivating weeds when you hoped for poinsettias. She should have stopped at three or maybe two. Heavens, maybe one son could have done her in. Her only hope would have been to renounce Mormonism, join Catholicism and become a nun. The wall of revelation to God I had been teetering upon crumbled further with each connection to my embittered reaction to my mother's demise, but I first noticed it only when I encountered an alternative to believing in God, as explained by K.

Then there was Angel Moroni's trumpet blaring the greatest inanity of mortal existence! If life was a test, then why did God reveal all the answers through his chosen prophets? Did God give humans their agency, or free will, only to choose the right answers? Of course! He didn't give agency to choose the wrong answers! But this is not a paradox like Christ's atonement. It's more like a sting. It's wrenching to stomach the idea of life as a test, and a test with all the answers is nothing less than cheating. Or, it is really not a test. Unless God cheats. And isn't agency on the yellow brick road of correct stepping stones something less than agency?

During my freshman year, in Deseret Towers, the roommates next to me and my flat-mate included two blond cousins, one full of bravado. One morning we argued through the cement walls to the surprise of both of our roommates, surely a result of how loudly our voices carried as much as my position. He insisted that Mormon prophets spoke to God face to face; I countered there was no chance. A great friend and roommate after my mission advocated similarly that no one could get to God but through Mormon prophets. I countered, bollocks. Both were blond grade-A students on scholarship and fair representative cross-sections of Mormon membership, the first a Caucasian westerner descended from a line of Mormons and the second a multi-ethnic easterner with a first-generation Mormon parent. Both nailed the hallmark of Mormonism, that God revealed himself to Mormon prophets. The modern Mormon prophets' brazen affront to the access of the good news of Christ paled against its pernicious affect on young Mormon couples, all their perilous consequences measured by one, the death of my mother. Not to mention the merits crisis caused by the answers from revelation. The gust of K's *wind of the struggle of faith* in the eternally possible pushed me onto my head, cracking its density open to a viable relation to God.

CHAPTER 24
GOD

Grammie slowly stepped through her living room toward the doorway into her kitchen. Neatly brushed white hair, long since having its last dye, crystal strands thinning and springing over the crown of her head, she turned toward me and grasped my arm.

—Do you want a Coke?

—No thanks. I'm fine, thank you.

—An ice cream bar?

—I'm good, thanks.

—On your way out maybe.

She turned to the stairs descending into the basement, gripping the rail on the wall with her left hand, lifting each foot to the step before moving down to the next one until she reached the green-carpeted concrete floor. She waived her hand in a half circle.

332   MY BEST MORMON LIFE

—Take anything you want.

Hundreds of books authored by Mormon prophets, apostles, and Church educators lined shelves on the far wall. For years Grammie and Grandpa Bob operated M&H (Moldenhauer and Harward) Office Supply, in rented space next to the post office in old downtown Blackfoot, a couple blocks west of Main Street. When they sold it to my uncle Rocky, he moved it two blocks south to a larger space in the banking district, a few hop-skips from the Potato Museum. My mother carted us to the store near the post office when she needed to make copies of selected readings for seniors in her weekly literacy classes. Bob and Bernie, as Grammie was known to her friends, had the only copy machine in town or, if not the only one, certainly the first we saw in the flesh.

Mom made copies, and we went back to the office to find Grandpa Bob sitting at his desk under mounted heads of elk and black bear, hoping he had something to give us, hard candy or a dollar but not the hundred dollar bill he pulled from his cowboy boot, which I reached flat footed, where he returned it before he stood to walk with us out of the building when my mother gathered us. Grandpa Bob was large, with broad shoulders and a thick belly from my earliest memories at his store to later visits in Provo on their way to winter at Lake Havasu, Arizona, and on their return to summer back in Idaho. Grammie was attractive far into her golden years, with her mother Stella Jones' edge, not mean but strict, no nonsense, don't get in the way or into something you shouldn't be.

M&H had a small religious book section, and the Mormon publishers in Salt Lake City sent free copies of new books year after year, and Grammie took many home, creating the impressive collection of Mormon Church classics on the north wall of the basement television room. I scanned spines, pulling out books, turning pages, many for the first time. I struck the mother lode of Mormon thought. The shining nugget was the founding Prophet Joseph Smith's clearly- and pugnaciously-argued discourse on the character of God and man's relationship to Him.

The production of works by Joseph Smith bewilders anyone who has put finger to keypad. We are not talking about Thomas Aquinas or the early Christian father Origen, undisputed geniuses responsible for thousands of pages of brilliant discourses with scribes following them everywhere they sat to think upon all matters eternal. Joseph lacked a proper education, yet he produced many works, translating Mormons' seminal scripture, the BOM, or the Book of Mormon, dictating God's very own words in the Doctrine and Covenants, its closest parallel being Islam's Quran, and also making minor "translations" of the Books of Moses and Abraham, which you may not have known were extant, let alone in English, and selections of the Holy Bible, Old and New, along with his disparate teachings as compiled by Joseph Fielding Smith, all demonstrating a varied stylist, defined by form as well as by content.

But no single work can be as directly attributed to him, unmitigated and transcribed without an editor, as his King Follett sermon, delivered months before his assassination, at the funeral of one King Follett. The KFS marked an insistent man doubly convicted of his divine role and the truthfulness of his message. The KFS is a highbrow source referenced by Mormon intelligentsia, themselves lay members, rarely cited, if at all, by the members constituting the majority of the attendees at Sunday services, and never even sneezed at by modern leaders of the Mormon Church. The sermon must have been reprinted more than any other, during the golden age of Mormon doctrine publication following the Second Great War, until the Church's correlation committee tamped down on unorthodox treatises on God. But a fair sampling in the multiple volumes containing KFS tightly nestled into my grandparent's north wall.

In it Joseph unapologetically declared eternal life depended upon *correctly* knowing God. He explained the first principle of the gospel was to know the character of God. The centerpiece of correctly knowing the character of God was man's ability *to converse* with him as one man converses with another. God was nothing if he was not the anthropomorphic God of the Holy Bible, the God in whose image man was created (Genesis 1: 27, the great scandal of the Christian tradition), with passions like love and hate, and who did a lot of stuff, good and bad, to the Israelites. None of this is shocking, really, but what followed tended to be. However, none of what followed ran inconsistent to the anthropomorphic God, a limited divinity located in time and space.

Joseph declared *if men do not comprehend the character of God, they do not comprehend themselves,* supporting his claim by citing the Gospel of John, 17: 3, *This is life eternal, that they might know thee the only true God, and Jesus Christ, whom thou hast sent.* Joseph stated God was exalted man, still not wholly shocking part and parcel of the anthropomorphic God of the Holy Bible but followed with *that he was once a man like us; yea, that God himself, the Father of us all, dwelt on an earth, the same Jesus Christ himself did; and I will show it from the Bible.* Unpacking this doctrine, he continued,

you have to learn how to be Gods yourselves, and to be kings and priests to
God, the same as all Gods have done before you, namely, by going from one
small degree to another, and from a small capacity to a great one: from grace
to grace, from exaltation to exaltation, until you attain to the resurrection of
the dead, and are able to dwell in everlasting burnings, and to sit in glory, as
do those who sit enthroned in everlasting power.

This great *secret*, Joseph's word, has caused some consternation among
Mormons and non-Mormons and in it lies the crowning jewel of Mormonism, that is *eternal progression* defined *from one small degree to another, and*
from a small capacity to a great one. Nothing more audacious about the potential of humans could be said.

I would like to think that the lack of attention to the KFS within the
Mormon Church derives from Joseph's informal delivery, not its ambitious
claims about God and man's true potential. But given the Church's concerted efforts, during the last couple of decades, to be considered within the
Christian tradition, I know that I'm wrong. The sermon's loose style, both
in content as he moved from one idea to another and back again, and in
form as he jumped around dipping into rambling diatribes, removed layers
of decorum that would otherwise have obstructed the prophet's personality.
Multiple Church leaders independently recorded it, so fidelity to his words
ensured as authentic an image of him as any ever taken.

Joseph spoke honestly with his mind and heart, not polished with sincerity and with certainty so typical among his modern descendants. He explained God's Plan of Salvation from the beginning, requesting his audience's confidence and laying bare his integrity for all to judge him. He roared
as a man besieged, striking at his critics who made numerous attempts to
expose him as a false prophet, and the not a few who wanted to pike his
head outside their places of worship. Like any good fight, the KFS was not
choreographed and was full of vulnerabilities, showing Joseph's tiger spirit,
not merely his prophetic one. While he claimed that the truthfulness of his
message could be tested by the vanquishing of his foes or its falsehood by his
demise, his words measured his mettle to press on against them, not a test of
his legitimacy to speak for God.

He stood before his followers justifying the value of King Follett and
their commitments to live faithfully in Christ's restored religion, all of them,
him foremost, in the face of continuous threats to their lives. Standing for
them he affirmed life and their reach for its highest significance imaginable.
They were meant to be Gods. In the end, Joseph's punchy rhetoric may prove

too unprophetic for modern Mormon leaders who want to relegate this gearing up for a fight he did not win to history. The lack of interest has the cost of missing Joseph brimming with emotion more than clear explication, spouting challenges in-hand with Mormonism's most secret ideas. By god he was brilliantly game. KFS came from a man not resigned to be a martyr. It came from a man ready to rumble with one aim of winning.

In the decades following Joseph's life, the doctrines of the Church went through a public maturation process, reaching its zenith after the turn of the twentieth century on the backs of a trio of Europeans, demonstrably the most intelligent and prolific theologians in Mormonism's history. There could not have been more able advocates of what Joseph started, as they provided the foundation of rational arguments to support Mormonism, their projects commensurate with the contributions of intellectual fathers of any religious tradition, but more importantly they provided shining examples of humans' potential. The most celebrated of them added footnotes to the KFS, fitting attribution for his preeminence within the Mormon tradition to have his words securely part of that watershed document, marking Mormonism's coming out brazenly with humans' potential. His name was Brigham Henry Roberts.

B.H. Roberts grew up in northern England, immigrated to America as a young man, and walked across the states to join the Mormons in Utah. His fame outside Mormonism largely came from being the Utah congressman denied his seat for practicing polygamy about a decade before Reed O. Smoot began to spend years overcoming the challenge to his seat in the U.S. Senate. Smoot didn't even get to practice polygamy! If Roberts is known within Mormonism today, it's because of his six-volume *Comprehensive History of the Church of Jesus Christ of Latter-Day Saints*. During his day, he was known for his formidable intellectual contributions to explain the defining principles of Mormonism. Amid exhorting those principles, Roberts enthusiastically defended Joseph's doctrine of God, which marked a clear divergence from traditional Christianity. In his little classic *Mormon Doctrine of Deity*, building upon Joseph's KFS, Roberts carries on a hearty polemic explaining Mormonism's idea of God more clearly than had any Mormon theologian before him. Mormons' God, as noted above, was an embodied God of the Holy Bible subject to all the criticism that anthropomorphism has received from Cicero's day to Hume's, but with the fillip of the possibility for humans to become like him. And Mormons' God was importantly *not* Plato's Idea, the God's God, immutable, unchanging, immaterial, unconditioned, necessary, absolute, simple, single substance fixed as the cornerstone of historical Christianities, traditional and protestant; Roberts quoted from Plato's *Timaeus*:

> We must acknowledge that there is one kind of being which is always the same, uncreated and indestructible, never receiving anything into itself from without, nor itself giving out to any other, but invisible and imperceptible by any sense, and of which the sight is granted to intelligence only, and later, what is that which always is and has no becoming; and what is that which is always becoming and has never any being? That which is apprehended by reflection and reason always is; and is the same; that on the other hand which is conceived by opinion, with the help of sensation without reason, is in process of becoming and perishing but never really is.

Plato hardly had a human-like God in mind, any more than he had in mind any God, but the formers of early Christianity during the first half dozen centuries after the life of Jesus and of his disciples were heavily influenced by Hellenistic thought, an angel-food cake of Plato with homemade whipped cream of Aristotle and strawberries of Plotinus on top. This is understandable because all the bright people had been Greeks, and even the Romans, who were terribly successful conquering a large portion of the known world, envied them. The new Christian religion rightly reached for the best ideas on the Ultimate Reality Ideas Market, having their roots in Plato. Those in power put their heads together to develop creeds to unify believers, and the process within their heads that we call reasoning measured their beliefs against Plato and Plato's intellectual heirs' writings more than anything else on the market, including what the disciples of Jesus had written.

In the early centuries of traditional Christianity, Church fathers developed the Nicene Creed in large part to quiet the doctrine that God had created Jesus, later Church fathers developed the Athanasian Creed to quiet notions that God and Jesus were not one, and yet others developed the Creed of Chalcedon to put to rest any doubts about Jesus being fully God and fully man. It is not terribly controversial to acknowledge that these creeds succeeded brilliantly to unify those who called themselves Christian, nor that they showed fidelity to Plato and his heirs' descriptions of ultimate reality. Roberts points out that the creeds also had the effect of privileging an abstract idea of God over the revealed God of the Holy Bible, by a Mormon's wager at the cost of everything, including eternity. Regardless of Roberts' winning outright, more importantly he clearly defined Mormonism's stake in a knowable, embodied God, like the descriptions of the divine in the Old and New Testaments.

B.H. Roberts did not discriminate against his opponents. He took them on outside and inside the Mormon tradition; anyone purporting to be embarked on a quest involving truth about ultimate reality—the realm of Gods—was within his purview. Roberts advocated that Mormons must include knowledge from science as part of their discussions on the truth about God. For example, he took seriously scientists' proposals for the age of Earth, billions and some years, far exceeding the chronology of the Holy Bible. This kind of accountability has its theological risks, as reference to the science of one's day tends to create a ceiling for the theologian not unlike for all those who have advocated similar accountability before Roberts. Take the gifted orators in Cicero's *Gods* and Hume's *Dialogues*: their descriptions of the earth are filled with dated potholes: one from Balbus's many stating *stars have their being in the aether*; and another from Philo stating, *what if I should receive the old Epicurean hypothesis? This is commonly, and I believe, justly, esteemed the most absurd system, that has yet been proposed; yet, I know not, whether, with a few alterations, it might not be brought to bear a faint appearance of probability. Instead of supposing matter infinite, as Epicurus did; let us suppose it finite.*

Toward the end of his life Roberts composed his magnum opus, *The Truth, The Way, The Life* and sought Mormon leadership's endorsement, himself near the top as the President of the Quorum of the Seventy, the layer just beneath the Twelve Apostles, which is one layer from the First Presidency that includes the President and Prophet, Mormon's chief voice of God. One of the junior Apostles raised spirited objections to Roberts' book. That apostle was Joseph Fielding Smith, the aforementioned editor of Joseph Smith's *Teachings* and father-in-law to the most significant codifier of Mormon belief in the religion's almost two-hundred-year history, Bruce R. McConkie. Smith objected to Roberts' explanation of the billion-year-old Earth, and vehemently opposed Roberts' advocacy of evolution. After each man presented his case to the leadership, Smith's objections were not endorsed, but he won out because Roberts' work wasn't either, a blow to the Church's most renowned intellectual just years before his death.

It would take events worthy of a blockbuster film written by Aaron Sorkin and directed by Paul Haggis to ensure its publication a half century later on the initiative of a young Roberts admirer and eventual member of the First Presidency, a bold Canadian by the name of Hugh Brown Brown, who preserved Roberts' manuscript and directed his heirs see that it was published.

During the controversy over Roberts' book, the Mormon leadership turned to the most revered thinker within Mormonism, the scientist James E. Talmage, the second of the trio of Europeans who anchored the intellectual tradition of Mormonism. Talmage met Albert Einstein, the guy most polls rank at the top of lists of the smartest blokes of the twentieth century, who reputedly, according to persuasive rumors, commented that Talmage was the most brilliant man he had ever met. Heavens, I could have told you that because I have no reservation speaking on behalf of other people, especially really smart dead people, but it just wouldn't taste the same as you spit.

Talmage grew up in southern England and immigrated to the United States as a young man. He obtained a Ph.D. and taught geology at university for years. During the Roberts vs. Smith match, Talmage was an apostle with an impressive bibliography to his credit. While Roberts' works have faded into obscurity, Talmage's still serve as the seminal Mormon works on their topics, among them *The Articles of Faith*, *The Great Apostasy*, and *Jesus the Christ* (all approved reading for missionaries). If there was any doubt the Church considered this Brit their Noblest Knight of Intelligence, consider his assignment to represent the Mormon Church during the Reed O. Smoot hearings. Under oath, Talmage answered the committee's questions decisively. I imagine his support for Roberts' view of Earth and evolution was as definitive.

Both Talmage and Roberts died a few years into the Great Depression, but not before then never-having-practiced-polygamy Mormon Senator Smoot co-sponsored the Smoot-Hawley Tariff Act, sending the country deeper into it. A couple years before Talmage died, he presented a paper advocating for the scientific method, which Joseph Fielding Smith also took it upon himself to denounce. And our third European entered the stage to declare a winner.

John A. Widtsoe was born somewhere in Norway, and as young man also immigrated to the United States. He was a Harvard man, Ph.D., a scientist, actively involved in the development of Utah's farmland, and he published multiple academic works in the field of agriculture. His contribution professionally outside the Mormon tradition was Mormonism's inaugural, or at the least then most prominent, dual threat as he also published extensively on Mormonism. The Talmage vs. Smith face-off risked being a stalemate like the earlier match between Roberts and Smith, but the leadership sought Widtsoe's opinion, whose endorsement of Talmage led to a clear winner and to the publication of Talmage's work on evolution.

Outliving the Englishmen and Norwegian, Smith got the final say two decades after their debates when he published his watershed work in the 1950s, *Man: His Origin and Destiny*, defending his thesis that Revelation to God's prophets provided truth about God and not scientific theories, indefinitely setting Mormonism against science, a sad state of affairs the Church has yet to recover from. The most embarrassing blight of condemning scientific (synonymous with secular) standards has been long, and thankfully, forgotten during the shameful tenure of Brigham Young University's longest serving President, Ernest L. Wilkinson. Wilkinson organized a spy ring of students to report on liberal economic professors, and then he denied doing it. The plot and the characters provide drama, intrigue, and prevarication sufficient for David Fincher to turn into a film classic.

Smith's infamous son-in-law, Bruce R. McConkie capped any remaining opening of the intellectualism well, forever making "intellectual" a dirty word, with his aforementioned work, *Mormon Doctrine,* its second edition published in the mid-1960s as endorsed by the Church. Subsequent leadership applied the dogmatic temper of both works to create the efficient and uniform doctrinal instruction informing and policing the intellectual development and discourse of the modern Church. Despite the spiral downward, consider the miracle there could even be a downward spiral made possible on the backs of the lions of Europe. Their emergence was miraculous. They came from Mormon stock in its first decades when there were more Mormons in England than in America. Imagine that while we're on the topic of miracles.

During the calcification period of anti-intellectualism, the two most famous Mormon philosophers entered the stage, one from the left and the other from the right, both enjoying insulation for at least two reasons from the Smith-McConkie mind-numbing tsunami embraced by Church leadership. First, they were not leaders in the Church. And second, their razor-sharp analytical reputations shielded the leadership from prudently choosing not to engage them, despite them being on very different projections. If there are intellectual Mormon honorable-mentions for the rational support of Mormonism, then they go to these two Utahans.

Sterling M. McMurrin and Truman G. Madsen had opposite philosophical styles, took different postures defining Mormonism, and were widely admired for their generous and genuine personalities. McMurrin started his educator's career in the famed Church Education System or CES, deciding to forge ahead into academia after years earning his stripes as a religious instructor. He was a life-long advocate and expert of education. During his life he emerged as the leading Mormon philosopher, spending his career at the University of Utah in the shadows of the Church's headquarters in Salt Lake City. Ironically, a career at the "U" was the only place a Mormon intellectual could remain outside the grasp of the Church's control, which may have been headquartered in SLC but was centered in Provo, Utah, home to BYU. The Church held McMurrin in suspicion, marking him as a skeptic, which McMurrin conceded at times, stating that his belief in God had more in common with Bertrand Russell than Joseph Fielding Smith (okay, he only said more in common with Russell; I added on his behalf Smith). And during its history, the Mormon Church has not received a more persuasive and reasoned exposition of its theology than McMurrin's *The Theological Foundations of the Mormon Religion*. In conversation with the history of religious thought, McMurrin defined Mormonism on a par with its greatest thinkers. He could not have been more generous in doing what none of the faithful could.

The Theological Foundations of the Mormon Religion was not the customary litany of Mormon beliefs. It was a reasoned exposition. McMurrin compared the theological underpinnings of Mormonism to Catholicism and Protestantism and non-Christian world religions. I honestly did not know a Mormon mind was capable of doing what he did, until I read his book. There is not a shortage of brilliant Mormon minds, but they wrongly underestimate having a sound theology. The work argued the value of Mormonism's conception of a finite, non-absolute God, in keeping with Joseph's and B.H. Roberts'. McMurrin readily admitted that Mormon theology was not systematic or even widely upheld by professions of belief by lay members and its leaders, but he ably demonstrated the importance of Mormonism's theological meanings with ample support from Mormon teachings. He showed Mormonism's unique contribution of an optimistic view of God's plan, providing the tradition he loved with its most secure foundation to date.

Madsen was cool as ice, a real Cool Hand Luke, not as real as Mr. Newman but with the same restraint that generations of cool mimicked until the long-haired eighties or some other cosmic divergence to whatever cool has become not to mean today. Madsen still exuded a mix of warmth and confidence as an older man during the short time I attended his stake conferences as a student at BYU. I admit that I loved the man, not love love, Walt Whitman-style. Although, I confess having the guy-love shown between characters in Shakespeare that raises modern proponents of identity politics to a fever pitch: the sentimental, pre-Freud man-love when a cigar could still just be a cigar.

Madsen enjoyed a larger-than-life persona within the Mormon imagination, largely introduced through *The Life and Teachings of the Prophet Joseph Smith* series on audiotape, listened to and thoroughly enjoyed by missionaries the world over. The tapes were off The Mission Plan in the Georgia Atlanta Mission, but some contraband got through, or just couldn't be kept out. Madsen's Joseph Smith took on the life of a comic-book hero with super powers fighting the evil of his day, and we ate it up. Madsen also wrote a biography of B.H. Roberts, providing many members their introduction to the Church's greatest theologian.

Early in his career he wrote more philosophical and theological works like *Eternal Man*, his debut into Mormon thought, and *Christ and the Inner Life*, which didn't spark McConkie's ire like George W. Pace's book on Jesus Christ, despite Madsen's advocating the same role of Jesus in LDS prayers, We pray *"in his name" as we pray through him, and with him*. Madsen had a conversational style, even a dialectic similar to Dostoyevsky's Underground Man, posing questions, providing the rebuttals and solutions, minus any intended irony. The more serious the philosophical inquiry, the more his writing becomes cryptic. Instead of unpacking philosophical concepts like McMurrin, Madsen mentioned concepts as flies that needed swatting, failing to treat them with more than a passing reference to show the significance of his thesis, that Mormonism had all the truth. But he cannot be faulted for writing aware of his audience, clearly assuming it was only Mormons who did not expect him to support his position, happy as larks to see how their shared belief passed over the many "Great" ideas outside the Church, including references to nascent psychology concepts from William James, "the real me," to stock pickings of existential crises from Shakespeare, "to be or not to be," all mere popcorn popping on the apricot tree, and all the while evidencing a sharp mind capable of so much better.

I admit a proclivity to pattern myself on passing references, ripe and ready to abuse others' ideas outside their uses as in James's scientific work and Shakespeare's existential drama for my own purposes, but I don't leave any inference I could do better. To say Madsen's lack of accountability disappoints, understates when he wore the crown of philosopher among the Mormons with nary a hint of responsibility for the title despite the headband with his name in capital letters over it. These early works showed his life-long projection as chief apologist, which he refreshingly did not fulfill primarily *defensively* with victim rhetoric like his apologist peers. He simply did it coolly, consistently implying his point in all of his works that he had the right answer before he proceeded to fail to defend it. He presumed its proof and in his characteristic eclectic approach showed how everything else related to it. And this presumption defined the Mormon religious epistemology.

Mormons don't have to seek outside Mormonism for what is true. They already have it through Mormon revelation. When Mormons seek they do so within the boundaries of the Church's teachings, and when Mormons study, they study whatever it is they study to determine how it pairs to the teachings of the Church. If there are questions, apparent contradictions, or outright opposition, then those are settled by thoughtful prayer to God, not by weighing the evidence or scrutinizing the argument, mere diversions. Madsen is the shining example of how a Mormon knows the truth and swims in the sea of historical questions and ideas, pointing out how they confirm what he already knows.

The Mormon philosopher who took the opposite approach, fulfilling the duty to prove his position with reasoned arguments was consequently the Mormon philosopher that Mormons have wiped from memory—on my honor the most competent Mormon thinker of its short history has been buried for a century, so that even its brightest minds, let alone its leaders, have no knowledge of him. But his work had not disappeared from Grandpa Bob and Grammie's basement wall.

—There are plenty of boxes, so take them all if you want.
—I'll take this stack. Thanks. I'll come back.
I placed the book I held onto two dozen piled on the couch. My selection had been on the wall since I first toddled into the basement a decade ago. I was confident I scanned a few gold veins but did not identify the fancy diamond among them until later, digging into these pristine volumes of Mormon doctrine, boxed and carried out of Grammie's basement to the trunk of my car, eventually added to my portable library as I moved from state to state. How did I know when I found it? You really should ask. You have to know how to judge a rock of value when you see it.

There is often a relationship between good writing and good thinking, but not a necessary one. Technical writing in various disciplines from anatomy to aeronautics often falls into a lot of smart readers' category of bad writing but involves some of our best thinking. Philosophical writing tends to suffer the same. And what often gets the nod as clear writing—considered by many smart readers as good writing—is not necessarily tied to our best thinking. Judging writing in less moral terms may prove helpful, maybe even liberating. And we must judge writing if we read with a purpose, and we do read with one, any from entertainment to finding new ways of thinking.

Judgment is the value that sharp readers apply to a work after combining or reflecting upon parts of sentences and their combinations with other sentences until they complete parts and eventually the work as a whole (or hole, depending upon how they combine). Putting value is constitutive of a brain working from the cognitive process of making sense of the words, to the epiphany of grasping the newly minted idea running with or confronting preceding ideas, both in what you're reading, if you're paying attention, and in your brain, whether you are or not.

Setting aside the moral barometer, writing can be more and less successful based on its own expectations and on what it does. No doubt a writer is aware of external expectations, but he or she is likely involved in fashioning and trying to reach his or her own. We, the readers, may judge on some of the same external criteria, but if we read closely enough we may also judge writing on what the writer promises to do and how well he or she does it. Following the writer's aim is by far the more challenging and rewarding task, the work largely a picture we have to piece together, with the most successful writers having provided all the pieces so we eventually can.

We readers hold the judgment card, not the writer. We decide if the writer is successful. There's a lot at stake, our time and the digital fee mere beginnings. Our efforts garner the benefits or lack of them precipitates the losses. But the range of the benefits and losses come from the writer. We're in it together. The writer decides if a sentence contracts or expands, moves a narrative forward, builds or reflects on previous ideas, focuses or blurs an object or action, treats accurately or exaggerates facts, invokes unfamiliar images or makes unexpected twists, and many more moves to reach his or her aim. And all he or she does points the reader toward that aim. And we decide if it worked or not. And *the work we readers do* determines if we decide accurately or not. A successful writer transfers the work to us, and needs us to be as successful receiving it, the degree of success depending on both parties' actions, but the quality of our judgment remains all our own responsibility.

Allow me to propose that we call a pear a pear, and that pear is the sentence. Sentences not only produce ideas but also rely upon them, the abstract stuff the writer consciously or not includes. For example, the second clause in the preceding sentence suggests there are at least two levels of ideas, one coming from the sentence and one beneath. The second level contains ideas we call propositions, just as *sentences* contain a subject and predicate; the combination of the subject and predicate is a process that *produces* something, this combination resulting in *ideas*. The combination *relies* on supporting but unstated ideas (all that stuff is the second level). The unstated propositions could be broken down even further into self-contained parts like what a subject is, etc. The arrangement of a sentence's levels, where parts go and how many there are, determines its success, both standing alone and in relation to the sentences preceding and following it. That is to say, there is a relationship between arrangement and content; or in more words, the topic and how the topic are discussed are keys to a sentence's success.

That is the pear then, dressed with sounds and cadences, creating a rhythm and lucidity in units of words, clauses, sentences, paragraphs, sections and heretofore unnamed and yet to discover parts of the whole work. We readers have nothing primarily to do with its look or flavor, any more than we do with its encounters with others, but we have everything to do with our reception of it, as our developed taste tests it as it passes through our lips, our teeth break its skin and with our jaws we crunch its core, then our tongues savor it and if we don't like it we stop crunching and spit but if we do we swallow, our gastric juices break it down until it's absorbed into our bloodstream, running to the well-deserving cells throughout our body.

I noticed the fancy gem, just short of singing, from the successful writing of Mormonism's finest philosopher, and I kept reading and realized I had also found a great thinker, the double of all whammies of persuasive discourse. His was a great mind based on the combination of demonstrable characteristics including analytical capability, breadth of knowledge, and originality. And I was incredulous at the heaps of rubbish burying his voice. I had found N. L. Nelson.

Nels Lars Nelson's works demonstrated a consciousness apparently without bounds, as with great writers before and since him. The inference amounts to an illusionary omniscience that is not supported by the writer, showing expansive breadth of knowledge (though that tends to impress), rather the illusion is created by how he or she treats knowledge with precision and accountability. Precision is a plane, not a point, from stating a thing accurately to addressing it by an entirely new idea with a head-toppling metaphor (though some ideas' planes might amount to mere points). A great writer knows the plane and moves effortlessly on it or may expand its ends. Accountability is everything else, because how a writer develops momentum and represents ideas always is either establishing credibility or losing it. We're at the writer's side for the story or argument, or along at some lesser degree. Nelson moved on the plane of his ideas from many angles, showing versatility beyond his peers, and his treatment of subjects always showed fidelity to accountability. Make no mistake, writers who put a premium on both values leave themselves vulnerable to falling short, as all the great ones, in their momentous leaps, have done.

For practical purposes, writing's utility lands into various cultural tiers from a text message to a novel, but writings can be as diverse as the catches of the sea. Many writers expect to report information and that's the bar by which we can measure their success. Some writers intend to analyze the information they present. Even a few writers want to report, analyze and persuade their readers (too many writers are indifferent to carrying their burden of persuasion, marked by their style, most noticeably in the form and unmistakably in their content).

Then there are philosophers who intend to do all that, while fulfilling the responsibility to locate their position in the history of ideas and their conditions with a reasoned projection of the ride they take us on, "reasoned" defined broadly as writing with support, not defined narrowly as abstract argumentation, though some of us may have a hankering for the latter on occasion. Historical and contemporaneous philosophers have dealt and deal with all subjects. We find them in all media, old textbooks, newspaper editorials, magazines, blogs, TV blips, some professional journals, and even a few academic departments in both the sciences and humanities. They are minority voices that break the clouds of expedient discourse in vogue among those of all partisan stripes. They demolish old and construct new ceilings of our thought, stir dormant emotions and expand the range of our emotions, and enhance our ability to understand more concretely and often anew. All the necessary qualifications come under one spine of passion for and competence of their subjects.

Their chief attribute, the cord connecting their nervous systems to ours, is their overflowing generosity to tirelessly articulate sound reasoning, to inquire, to refine, and to challenge how we know the world we experience in order to move us toward experiencing it more meaningfully, and more completely. Then there are writers who entertain the heavens to our cheers, who may or may not dabble in any or all of the above. The most effective writers make us feel their message, plunging into the depths, say Fyodor Mikhaylovich Dostoyevsky.

Nelson's first book fit into the discipline of the deadly-to-abuse category of rhetoric, the skill of using language to communicate. He spent hundreds of pages constructing an apparatus of principles but not before spending the first fifty pages skewering Mormons over their epidemic of mindlessness. He focused on Mormons who relied on the scripture, *take no thought about what ye shall say* while forgetting what followed: *but treasure up in your minds continually the words of life* from Section Eighty-Four of the Doctrine and Covenants. Nelson's targets would have likely championed Folly in Desiderius Erasmus' work of the same name, as she exercised a similar method *to blurt out whatever pops into my head.* Nelson criticized Mormons for providing no thoughts for the Lord to work through, and his project covered his explanation of how they might develop into a thinking people, and subsequently preach more effectively.

Preaching and Public Speaking: a Manual for the Use of Preachers of the Gospel and Public Speakers in General first hit shelves throughout Utah in 1898. Its second edition, renamed *Preaching and Public Speaking Among Latterday Saints: A Protest Against Abuses and a Course of Instruction Whereby They May be Overcome*, landed in 1910. In the second edition's preface, Nelson explained he nearly excised the first fifty pages addressing Mormons' abuses, but felt his admonishment still had value, apparently enough to note its prominence in the new title. The second edition's gain came with the loss of acknowledging its *general* application beyond Mormons. The second edition also contained an endorsement from the leadership of the Church, the *sine qua non* for authoritative Mormon letters.

Nelson's writing had vitality, using apt metaphors and providing reasoned support intermixed with his commanding expositions of Mormon doctrines. This extended passage from the section "Non-Preparation Tested by Scripture," which I unapologetically share, shows all three.

> Seriously, I profess no charity for the Latterday Saint who has ceased to grow, especially if he be an Elder. Eternal progress—this

grand device is not alone emblazoned on our banner; it is the very genius that carries the banner. It is not a time to bury our talents. Thought today must breed fast, talents must duplicate themselves daily, hourly. For us that have the whole world to move, it is a crime to stand still, or merely beat time.

Mormon theology embraces such a variety of truths that nothing which affects the temporal or the spiritual welfare of man, can come amiss on Sundays if selected by the Spirit of inspiration. Indeed, anything that arouses attention and stimulates thought—be it Gospel principle or advice about husbanding crops—will be not only listened to but relished by Latterday Saints, such is our boundless respect for all God's truths.

But it requires thought to arouse thought. What then can be expected from men that never think themselves? What can the Spirit find there to edify the people? Often there is but a very scant store to draw from, even of the ideas of others. Such minds resemble second-hand junk-shops. The sermons drawn therefrom are a wearisome patchwork, made up of thoughts and ideas disconnected; aged but not venerable; worn out by having been said a thousand times before; dressed in a garb of insufferable phrases, old and hackneyed; platitudes with the green mould clinging to them.

And one more from two sections later, "Non-Preparation Tested by Results at Home,"

I cannot think of a more profitless hour than that spent in listening to an aimless speaker; whose 'remarks' are spread out from Dan to Beersheba, and actually touch nothing but the peaks of thought; whose worn-out generalities one sees with dread afar off, as one by one they come, each caused by the speaker's stumbling upon some familiar word, which like a stone in the road, bobs up in the distance and throws the discourse into a rut.

The weary length of these ruts must be painfully familiar to Latterday Saints. Occasionally one is beguiled into an idle curiosity as to whether there will be a variation this time. But generally one is doomed to be disappointed; for the man that can inflict platitude after platitude upon a congregation, is not the man of sufficient mind-activity to draw new applications from old truths.

What is my duty, then? May I stay away from meeting? No; I will go, even though I know such a rambling talk is coming. The real blessing of a Sabbath meeting—the strengthening of one's determination and the renewal of one's covenant, which come from thoughtfully and prayerfully partaking of the sacrament—no preacher can take away. This blessing received, I can sit back to an hour's punishment, if need be, and count it among the blessings of adversity. Such, at least, is the conclusion I have had occasion to reach many a time in this matter.

Amid the first fifty pages of chastisement, Nelson provided a personal experience in the mission field illustrating the need for humility when he delivered his first missionary sermon creating unanimity of rejection in the community against him and his companion. He followed this experience with an incisive criticism of Mormons' love of "glittering generalities." Nelson argued that Mormons' recycling "all the truths of history" in their possession led to complacency, an impediment to progress. He urged those in possession of "all the truths" to offer *one specific idea*!

And over the next four hundred pages, he showed how Mormons could develop the skills to be effective preachers, mildly criticizing along the way, always drawing upon truths in their tradition for support. While his book faithfully conforms to the revised title that excised the reference to public speakers in general, he provided ample support without religious draping that promises to please all thoughtful readers.

Among the highlights, he argued for the role of thinking to develop better preaching. A thinking person was not one with *a splendid memory, vivacious mind,* with *the graces of rhetoric and elocution.* A thinking person had *a virile power of the mind* whose virility had not been *altered or diverted to channels of uncreative activity.* Nelson emphasized the cognitive process in improving one's thinking process. He argued sharp perception was the first step to one's best thinking. After one perceived, the next and critical step was to apperceive, or to consciously process the thoughts, impressions, hearing, tasting, smelling, and feeling so it became part of one's existence. One bent on thinking better could not repeat a process too much or concentrate on a subject hard enough.

He repeatedly explained that a concerted effort to break ideas and facts down to their particulars laid the ground for thinking correctly, insisting that God needed specific ideas in the minds he worked through. Nelson introduced his theory of education based on vigorous inquiry, tireless questioning and painstaking attention, urging those in his tradition to never stop asking how and why. He also introduced his theory of art as measured by its unifying power, largely through the fulfillment of purpose marked by its power of suggestion. The master of a suggesting style being Shakespeare, for not so much what he said *as what he makes us think.*

Nelson chided those who credited the devil to explain others' success or one's own blunderers. And he decried the sermon of exhortation for its *running series of "shoulds" and "oughts," and "behooves"—covering duty in the catalogue without break or breathing spell between, and with no other order than as they happen to strike the speaker's memory—it is then that good advice becomes as cheap as oyster cans by the road side.*

He decried further,

> [C]an we say to a man: 'Be sad—be merry—now laugh—now cry'—and expect these emotions to respond? Then why should we look for results when we say to other emotions: 'Be humble—be prayerful—be chaste?' And if we repeat these commands or entreaties for an hour together will our hearers be better or worse for it? Are the doors to the emotions so flimsy that they may be battered down by much knocking? The fact is, we seek to reap where we have not sown. We look for effects when there are no causes. We must bear in mind that if we would stir up a feeling in the human heart, we must present an adequate cause for that feeling and present it skillfully. If the feeling seems to be stirred without an adequate cause, depend upon it, it is sheer hypocrisy, or perhaps self-stultification.

Nelson not only explained the necessary skills to improve Mormon preaching, he provided the measure of its success.

Quite at home discussing Mormon doctrine, as any Mormon intellectual must be, Nelson had few Mormon peers on thinking well and writing and preaching effectively, he himself being a professor of rhetoric and an early president of Brigham Young Academy. To many late twentieth-century Mormons, at least one Mormon used language as vividly as Nelson, with a venerable intellect of his own. Neal A. Maxwell wrote on topics covering the forms of true Christian discipleship as well as any Mormon, with a clear and intelligent style akin to C.S. Lewis and G.K. Chesterton, British subjects whom Maxwell repeatedly relied upon, and of whom Nelson would have surely approved. (Grammie's north wall also included a sampling of Maxwell's books, *A Time To Choose, Deposition of a Disciple*, and *Notwithstanding My Weakness*).

Nelson's arguments are as relevant for Mormon thinking and preaching today as they were in his own time. If you need confirmation, ask your Mormon friend over a diet caffeine-free cola in the milky-walled break room whether Nelson's descriptions of Sunday sermons and titillating exhortations given biannually are not true every jot and tittle, or one Sunday venture into a meeting to see for yourself. No manual for Mormons has ever been more thoughtfully on the mark.

In these confessions, Nelson lamented the absence of a profound study of the Gospel and the Church. He met the first half of his implicit challenge with his next book, *The Scientific Aspects of Mormonism*, in 1904. If a half century later McMurrin's *Theological Foundations* provided the best exposition of Mormon theology in the history of western thought, then Nelson's *Scientific Aspects* provided Mormonism's first rational defense in the same history.

Nelson's *Scientific Aspects* is a treatise on Mormonism's compatibility with science. I've already presented the central role of revelation to Mormons, the past kind in Holy Scripture and, more importantly, the modern kind continuing through Latter-day Prophets, so it will not come as a surprise that fidelity to how truth develops in science does not threaten Mormon theology. That is to say the development of knowledge of all kinds, including science, is consistent with Mormon theology that endorses eternal progression. For Mormons, humankind's views are never complete and always have a component of potentiality to them, because truth is always becoming revealed: so of course the unifying theory of all matter, string theory; and multiple universes, something Mormons have been saying since their beginning.

Nelson made striking observations in his introductory comments that were blisteringly prescient, if you'll indulge a slight exaggeration. He opened his work with strong words for Mormonism's critics (and what would a classic work of Mormonism be without a few solid punches to the enemy!), but he quickly moved on to defining God. He described a form of the argument previously designated as the design argument for the proof of God made by the characters of Cicero and Hume, but Nelson provided it not as proof of God but as the *largest truth of which human kind is capable* about the physical universe.

Then he went and said this,

[O]ther aspects, though dependent upon perception and inference, are almost as self-evident. One of these is the fact that the universe is not empty, but full. Full of what? Ah, there we come face to face with the Mystery. We call it ether—quite as if that signified something. Let us rather say, full of power, static, quiescent,—a dark, silent ocean of energy out of which forces rise, and into which they sink, after they have played their transitory parts before the mimic stage of our senses; say rather that the universe is full of the mother-essence of creation, out of which Invention has formed worlds without number, and the resources of which Invention shall never exhaust.

Poetic and full of creative conjecturing, nestling insights the universe is not full of ether but full of a dark silent ocean of energy and the source of its own creation showed either a man faithfully reading *Scientific American* or given to expanding visions of a universe no one really knew. And isn't he correct that the knowledge essential to the argument of design, the knowledge about harmony and order, plays before the *mimic stage of our senses*?

A year *after* The Knickerbocker Press published *Scientific Aspects*, some bloke named Einstein published a paper "On the Electrodynamics of Moving Bodies," affirming Galileo and Newton's theories that all physical laws, including electromagnetism, applied to humans in uniform motion, all kinds we experience on Earth and would experience racing around our solar system. He confirmed the general application of physical laws a decade later in his generalized theory of relativity, explaining the property of gravity as geometrical space-time, justifying much speculation including *curvature* in outer space. When he wrote these papers, he respectively obliterated the idea of ether and concurrently established the cosmic structure of the universe, much later called *dark energy*, properly named only years after *Cheers* quit running on the National Broadcasting Company.

Where did Nelson come up with these ideas? Sure, he thought the universe was static but so did Hume, Einstein and a lot of other smart blokes. Heavens, no one knew the Epicureans had been improperly labeled as stupid for two thousand years until scientists proved the universe was expanding after Edwin Hubble confirmed the Milky Way was just one of many galaxies.

I do not know if Nelson subscribed to *Scientific American*, whose writers' love affair with humans' finest thinking—coming on two centuries—likely debunked ether and proposed cosmic structures of energy. What I do know is that in *Scientific Aspects*, Nelson used the unknown universe as the basis, or justification, for the role of religion as the means *to provide form to the unknown*, and that he went on gallantly to show how Mormonism did it. His idea of a *dark silent ocean of energy* did not foretell Hubble and Michael Turner's theories, and those of all their physicist cohorts who have explained the cosmos, but it showed a virile intellect. If the Scott Patrick Matthew gets credited for articulating natural selection first, then by John, the Mormon N.L. Nelson has earned a toast for describing the fabric of the universe.

It might not come as a surprise that the underlying scientific theory of Nelson's project was evolution. What might come as a surprise is his keen understanding of competing understandings (and uses) of evolution of his day and his fidelity to, not abuse of, components of Darwin's explanation. Although you would correctly guess he advances a transcendental evolution, as did thinkers like Johann Wolfgang von Goethe before him, and he does, Nelson does not deride the historical transmutation of species nor does he neglect the effects of species-change through the mechanism of natural selection. To the contrary, he does not dispute them as any Mormon would not, any who believe God has all the knowledge and humans who tirelessly and endlessly strive to gain all knowledge can eventually have it all too. This tireless progression embraces all scientific knowledge as pieces of the unknown, not unknowable, universe puzzle. In other words, for Nelson *evolution* was interchangeable with *eternal progression*.

Nelson's evolution was not merely the progressive kind of Herbert Spencer, it was also the random variation of Darwin. To appreciate Nelson's use of biological evolution to explain his religious propositions about humans' ascension toward divinity, both their God and their own, allow me to refresh your memory of Darwin's theory in a handful of sentences or less. Remember that Darwin popularized evolution but broke new ground by arguing the main mechanism of evolution was natural selection: *a principle of preservation* that initiated species-change when certain conditions were met. Those conditions were a variation among the species, a struggle among the species, and a correlation between those two causing *an infinite diversity in structure, constitution, and habits, to be advantageous to them*. He proposed the advantageous characteristics were passed through birth, but the kicker of heredity was a mystery except to a monk living around the time of Darwin named Gregor Johann Mendel, who no one knew anything about but who introduced the study of genetics, and whose theories were not discovered until long after Mendel's death.

Only after undergoing healthy doses of refinement do we get to the modern studies of genetics we read so much and know so little about to-day in magazines like *Scientific American*. Remember the discussion about the descent of humans through modification, around before Darwin, has a larger scope and stirs up far more people and controversy than natural selection, if for no other reason natural selection is ignored or mistaken as synonymous with evolution. The descent of humans was a subject Nelson did not happen to miss but also did not permit to warp his reading of Darwin.

There could not have been a more suitable marriage of Science and Religion than that of Evolution and Mormonism. Or in other words, Nelson's, *Mormonism accepts all the facts of evolution, but has its own way of accounting for those facts*. His fidelity to both horns of the dilemma proved true: he explained the modification of species occurred under intelligent supervision, consistent with theologians of his day who embraced Darwin's ideas; and he argued the fact of gradual adaptation accounted for the beautiful variety in nature.

Nelson's systematic defense of Mormonism included layers of support to show the psychic evolution of humans, or what he explained as the development of faith in God for the benefit of humans, not for the glory of God. He used the term psychic not quite to our modern fancy. He introduced his psychic theme back in *Preaching and Public Speaking* in connection to the physical attributes needed for successful preaching, advocating for proper posture, attitude (that which is projected physically through speech and nonverbal gestures), and breathing to support the best thinking of a proper mind and personality fit for preaching. Dare I venture to claim that he identified characteristics, or phenotypes, that could change to make an individual more fit? In *Scientific Aspects*, the psychic theme became the focus of a person's development of Spirit, the conduit to all things divine. A person's Spirit served as the window into God's view of the world, and the further along in one's development the more complete one's view became.

Nelson embraced the notion of indirect forces, the randomness or chance of natural selection. He stated such forces would continue until the end of time, and he used them as a metaphor to mark the various stages of faith, repentance, and baptism so often inexplicable in their occurrences but necessary for coming to God. That is to say, he understood the forces to be akin to divine organizing principles. For Nelson, chance had a meaning more aligned with Darwin than with modern-day Darwinists. Darwin purported that chance was a category for laws we did not know, not the accidental combinations we assume it is today. The major difference for Darwin was that accidents did not have an intelligent cause. In *Preaching and Public Speaking* Nelson relied upon the accidental aspects of life but lamented evolutionists' failure to recognize the Spirit at work during those accidents. His praise for Darwin survived into its second edition, appropriately in the section on the art of thinking where Nelson wrote, *Darwin, the profoundest thinker on natural science of this or any other age, was it is said, a most stupid school-boy.*

While Darwin's influence on Nelson did not subvert Nelson's overall project, and only paltry apologists would suggest it did, Nelson acknowledged that if he had studied Darwin a decade earlier, the potency of Darwin's ideas might have changed the course of his faith, a clear indication he appreciated the consequences of Darwin's thought. He was not admitting a possible corrupting influence but rather was offering honest deference consistent with his overall project to continue learning and embracing all truth, a process of progression mapped by struggle not bliss, development contingent upon one's fidelity to the facts, not unexamined acceptance of orthodox beliefs. Nelson did not misconstrue Darwin's theories, so he did not miss their significance. Make no mistake, the cost of the knee-jerk derision for those who propose something inconsistent with our beliefs is not the lack of their due praise but is truth we miss.

John A. Widtsoe, one of Mormonism's aforementioned early great thinkers, wrote his own treatise on Mormonism and science, publishing *Joseph Smith as Scientist* in 1908, a compilation of essays he had written years before. In the chapter, "The Law of Evolution," Widtsoe showered praise on the philosopher Herbert Spencer for producing *the only philosophy that harmonizes with knowledge of today.* Evolution made for unexpected bedfellows, as Spencer was no theist, which explained why Widtsoe was not short on providing disclaimers about him. In that chapter, Widtsoe discussed evolution: *[i]n 1859, Mr. Charles Darwin published a theory to account for such variation, in which he assumed that there is a tendency on the part of all organisms to adapt themselves to their surroundings, and to change their characteristics, if necessary, in this attempt.* This description was faithful to Jean-Baptiste Lamarck's explanation of acquired characteristics through habit (and Darwin's grandfather Erasmus' notion of adaptation), or use or disuse (which Darwin acknowledged). Later Widtsoe accurately emphasized the key to Darwin's theory by highlighting natural selection, but also concluded there was still not enough support for natural selection, mentioning that even Darwin had noted it was only one of the means of species' change.

Despite not being persuaded by Darwin's idea of natural selection, Widtsoe ably discussed evolution's many implications, one of which was organisms' development as an exception to the law of entropy, or the fact that energy moves to a state of disorder. As you would expect, he discussed the topic to show the distinction between material and spiritual realities, the former ultimately in decline and finite, and the latter full of potential and eternal. Widtsoe acknowledged the evidence of evolution and championed it throughout his life.

I mention his obscure work (a fair characterization of all the great Mormon thinkers' writings) because, like Nelson, Widtsoe placed a premium on fidelity to facts, in this instance including what Darwin actually proposed. Treating available facts sympathetically, that is accurately and in accordance with the best knowledge of one's day, is a fair measure of the quality of one's faith. It's not the only measure, but a most significant one.

Our faiths, our beliefs, our hopes, our aspirations and our dreams are composite pieces of endless bits of information, emotions, and recollections in snapshots and always intertwined with the histories and developments surrounding them. If we misconstrue the facts, likely despite genuine best efforts, the trade-off is a faith built on and made of as many corresponding impurities. And examining the evolution of those facts requires the utmost care. And those are facts the likes of Widtsoe and Nelson were not willing to ignore, because their eternal progression from a small capacity to a great one, from grace to grace, depended upon it. Nelson's appeal to the popular Mormon notion that humans were Gods in embryo emphasized the long, arduous, and mistake-laden and accidental process of maturation. No wonder Darwin offered support and not offense.

Aunt Mary laid a pad of paper and pencil near the two decks of playing cards sitting in the middle of the kitchen table. Grammie picked up the cards and sorted them, passing one at a time until each of us had ten. Grandpa Bob sat a few feet away in the living room, watching television. Mary lived on the south end of Provo in a small trailer park fifty feet from the noise wall separating park and interstate, and Grammie and Grandpa Bob stopped to see her each fall on their way to Lake Havasu and each spring on their way back to Blackfoot. When they did, the cousins attending BYU made a point to visit Mary to see the grandparents and enjoy Mary's homemade brownies and chocolate chip and oatmeal cookies. Between rounds of "May I," Mary rose to check on the pastries emitting their aromas from the oven through the entire sixty feet of her trailer.

Mary inherited the trailer from her grandmother years before my freshman year, when I learned the shortest route to it from north of campus where I lived in Deseret Towers, shouldering my dirty laundry miles to her place. I spent many Saturday nights washing mixed loads and watching *The Godfather* trilogy and other epics. I did not have money to go out on weekends, and I didn't care for attending church Sunday mornings, so if there was a more suitable time to do laundry God had yet to reveal it to me. Grammie and Grandpa Bob seemed the same age all my years growing up with them in Blackfoot. Only when they made those visits passing through Provo did I notice how they changed. The many years they had it, they left their fifth-wheel RV at the KOA campground west of the interstate, fifteen minutes from Mary's. The cousins met for many a round of "May I?" at the small table in the RV, but I guess most of them favored Mary's place because they knew they would enjoy fresh and still-warm brownies while they played.

I didn't care for card games, too competitive maybe. If I could cheat I usually did, not to win but to ignite an attentive competitor's ire. But I did like Mary's brownies, consuming more than a fair share each visit. I did not fear gaining the freshman fifteen because I had plenty of weight to add before returning to where I was before my final wrestling season when I cut twenty pounds from 165 lbs. to wrestle at 145. For years running into decades, I dreamed I had quit wrestling before my senior year, in those dreams feeling awkward in halls and classrooms passing teammates, often contemplating a comeback. In the dreams regret saturated me, then I awoke and minutes later I had even more regret for not quitting well before my senior season. The only dream recurring more often was missing a due date on a paper or forgetting to take a test. During each visit with Grammie and Grandpa Bob, pending assignments and looming tests bombarded my mind. When school was in session, since my first day of high school, I never had complete ownership over a single thought, and that might be why I willingly gave them to the directors of the many films, good and some really bad. No dreams felt more real than quitting wrestling and missing deadlines, the sick feelings in the pit of my gut making many a return visit. Few places calmed my mind like Mary's, visiting with Grandpa Bob and Grammie.

Grammie placed her marble hand over mine, thick blue veins branching over smooth white skin, her fingers sliding inside my palm, lightly squeezing. A moment inspiring me to write a poem, my single attempt among the lyrical heights of our creation, lost among college notebooks but not before I sent a copy to her. She did not probe into personal matters, not because she did not care, but out of respect for privacy. She engaged as far as her conversant wanted to, and for me it wasn't far. For her it was merely enough to be together, there was nothing else besides spending time together. She didn't need your undivided attention nor did she thoughtlessly bombard you with herself, never unlocking the floodgates of regrets and insecurities. She didn't make worthless attempts to affect your behavior. And she never reeked of the familiarity often assumed by family members, the kind that replaces respecting others' rights to think their own thoughts and make their own decisions, the kind that gets so putrid and sticky it's impossible to extricate yourself by any other means than ending any contact at all. She sent one message, that she loved her grandchildren. She did not love everyone and she was far from perfect. But what fool imagines God indiscriminately loves everyone and how could one who was perfect ever be worthy of genuine worship?

A jealous, spiteful, partisan God appeals to those it favors, but even those select few rarely exhibit a life having been the better for having worshiped it. Surely my mother told me she loved me, cuddling me my first months of life, but I do not recall her saying she loved me during the next eleven years of it. If either of my parents had, I would have recognized the lie even then. The only person to express love towards me and mean it was Grammie. Every other utterance has been burdened with offense in comparison. Give me a God who respects individual life as much as it demands respect from it, and that's one worth worship, worship of the individual and communal stripe. A greater lie has not been introduced into the genealogy of our thought than that saying unity of a group is not compatible with respect of the individual, itself perhaps the oldest lie of all. That lie is as demonic as the modern contradiction between rules and liberty, each of which is necessary for the full development of the other. No greater love hath a God for her creation than one who means it, and Grammie was one of that select class, grandparents, of qualified beings to prove it.

PART V

CHAPTER 25
STEELMAKERS

—Here's our summer jobs, I said.

I handed the newspaper to Jacob, pointing out the advertisement for employment at Geneva Steel.

—Good money, Jacob said.

—The best we'll find in the valley.

—Yeah, but it will be hotter than hell.

Graduation was in a couple days, but I didn't plan to walk. Wearing a gown didn't bother me as much as sitting through interminable platitudes. I had to quit teaching at the MTC when I was no longer a student at BYU, ending a three-and-a-half-year run, and Jacob was tired of cooking at Red Robin at the new mall in south Provo. Both of us had money in our pockets, but it wasn't much and Geneva would make us richer than we had ever been.

We drove out to the mill, which sat on the west side of Interstate 15 directly across from Orem. You couldn't miss it, covering hundreds of acres with dark rusted buildings straight out of a Kevin Costner post-apocalyptic epic. We located a few buildings set apart from the gated metropolis and parked the car. We entered a building and someone pointed us to a building farther down the road where we successfully found and completed applications.

—We'll call if you're chosen to the next phase to take some tests, the blonde, rotund and helpful woman who took our applications said.

We were at Utah Valley Community College within days, taking tests in basic grammar and math. The first cut included about twenty other blokes sitting there with us. The next day a woman called, offering positions on the blast furnace, and we accepted. Geneva Steel was a one-stop shop, processing natural resources into finished steel products. The mill turned ore and coal into pellets and coke at facilities on site. Mixed together with other chemicals, the smelting process within the blast furnace turned the ore into molten lava, molten iron really but it looked like streams of fire running down Mount Kilimanjaro or whatever the landscape was in *One Million Years B.C.* (1966) creating havoc on Loana and the blond- and brown-haired tribes.

Jacob and I dressed in our fire-retardant green pants and jackets. Then we laced our steel-toe boots to our tibiae. We grabbed our lunch and helmets with their tinted visors where we had stuffed our gloves inside their rims. About fifty paces away we climbed the ladder to the floor of the south blast furnace. Then we got our orientation.

—The furnaces are down so we need two of you to clean these three drill bits. I'll take the other one to do some cleaning on the north furnace, the crew boss said.

The bits were massive, about half the length of my leg and twice as big round. Another fresh hire started the same day as us. He was as green and volunteered. I hesitated, and Jacob volunteered too.

—Okay, come with me, the boss said.

Shortly after starting me on a task he disappeared and another member of the crew stopped me.

—You a new guy?

—Yeah.

—Come on. I'll show you around.

I thought he meant to see more of the blast furnace, but he didn't. We left the blast furnace and climbed some stairs above it with a view of the mill.

—Should we be up here? I asked.

—It's my last day. They can't do anything to me.

—What about to me?

—You're new so they'll let it go. Come on. I'll show you how the coke comes along the rail to dump into the furnaces.

I followed him into a lift.

—Do you know what you're doing?

—I worked this for years.

We rode it to another building and exited onto a platform.

—See the building there? That's where they turn the ore into pellets. He pointed to the south.

He turned to his left and pointed at another building.

—That's where they turn the coal into coke. I used to transfer the coke to the furnace with this tram. You and your brother should be glad you didn't get jobs over there. People get hurt there all the time, some guys got burned up real bad the other day.

We climbed around the building and looked at the complex. The mill was built during World War II, and the technology had not been updated. It was inefficient and there was widespread doubt whether the most recent emergence from bankruptcy would last long. We were gone for what seemed like hours and I was not nervous; in fact, it was the first time I knew I was doing something I should not be and I didn't feel bad about doing it, swimming in the largeness of the mill around me.

—Let's head back. They'll be worried about you.

—Thanks for the tour.

—Sure. You and your brother have the hardest job in the mill on the floor. It's safe though, but it sucks.

The crew boss welcomed us shaking his head. Since I didn't know any better he didn't reprimand me, unless telling me I didn't know any better counted. He offered no reproach to my guide. I found Jacob and the other new hire exhausted in the enclosed break room on the floor.

—How was it?

—It was pretty amazing. He took me all over.

—We had to clean mud off the drill bits with a jack hammer. My arms feel like jelly. I couldn't do it for more than ten minutes at a time. Fortunately we only had one jack hammer between us so we took turns.

—You've been doing that all day?

—Since you left.

Jacob and I worked our first twelve-hour shift together, that is he worked and I toured the complex—we got paid the same, but we hardly saw each other the rest of the summer except when relieving one another's crew on the floor, or on overlapping days off passing by in the kitchen as he would be getting up from bed in the afternoon and I would be heading there, or vice versa.

Nothing at BYU prepared me for work at Geneva Steel, although all my life growing up shoveling ditches and moving pipe had. But BYU had enriched my life by being the experience advertised by Church leaders at every devotional I attended. I learned a bundle. My learning experience had been a walk among a constellation of varying shapes and bright stars and none affected me more than witnessing the slow death of BYU's strongest.

Professor Tilman's aforementioned life-altering course on world religions had been in the Joseph Smith Building (JSB) at the southern border of campus, the location for most of the religious instruction courses ranging from church history to courses on the Bible. But the high volume of religious hours required to graduate, combined with the sheer mass of the student body, forced courses to be held throughout most buildings on campus, spreading religious instruction into the corners of engineering and physics halls, most assuredly by design. Due north of the JSB sat the Spencer W. Kimball Tower, the lone steeple on campus, and directly west of the JSB sat the testing center. Farther south behind the JSB and the Testing Center, the campus precipitously dropped to the community of Provo surrounding it, accessible by a set of hundreds of concrete steps.

Around the southwestern corner, campus continued with athletic facilities and fields, the George Albert Smith Fieldhouse, known as "the Fieldhouse"; the site for much of campus's activities at one time, including devotionals, it also acted as the hub of extracurricular activities during my time on campus. BYU students entered the Fieldhouse just as generations of other students of other universities had entered their fieldhouses before the emergence of large athletic facilities, marking the birth of big-business universities. The Fieldhouse shared an intimacy with its audience, something absent in the larger athletic centers like the Marriott Center. Student athletes and students playing intramurals mostly used the Fieldhouse. I trekked from the northeastern tip of campus from my freshman dorm to the Fieldhouse on the far outskirt of campus's southwestern tip, and regularly made similar trips the next three years from various starting points bordering campus—to use the weight room and to watch volleyball, men's gymnastics (the women often competed in the Marriott Center) and wrestling.

My treks typically led to the first of three entrances on the north side of the building. The one-door entrance opened into a hall with offices of football coaches. Fifty steps down the hall stairs appeared, ascending back north to the second floor where, after turning back around, a few strides down the hall on the right was the weight room, policed by student employees checking for student identification and appropriate BYU-issued shirts and shorts, uniform garb required for admittance.

Farther west down the north side of the Fieldhouse were two other larger, multiple-door entrances that led into the main open space for volleyball and wrestling matches. Stairs led to bleachers on the balcony that extended above the room down the south and north sides, and bleachers leading up to the ceiling on the east end. The large open space was often separated, by partitions, into multiple basketball courts. I was a four-year intramural basketball veteran of the moderate-level leagues. BYU's intramural programs were widely popular throughout campus, supporting multiple leagues from novice to expert skill levels. BYU was reputed to have a higher percentage of student body participating in intramural sports than did any other university in the nation. I played many basketball games in the Fieldhouse and its sister facility to the north, the Stephen L. Richards Building. The stairs leading up to the balcony in the Fieldhouse led to other coaches' offices toward the east end of the building, back toward the weight-rooms, the coaches of gymnastics and volleyball, including the men's renowned coach, Carl McGowan. One of the doors was marked by the unassuming label of Mark Schultz, Head Wrestling Coach.

I was an eight-year-old freestyle wrestler the summer of 1984, and I avidly leafed through my free subscription of *USA Wrestling News* that came with my membership in the local freestyle club. I didn't see any of the Olympic matches the summer of 1984, but the spring after the 1984 Olympics I got a free poster of all USA Wrestling Gold Medalists at a tournament somewhere in Eastern Idaho, and hung it in my bedroom where it stayed for the next decade. It shared the short walls in the converted attic space of my teenage years with posters of a dribbling, short-shorts Larry "The Legend" Bird and my favorite professional athlete, Walter Payton, in his Walter's Run, a staged shot where he eluded opponents falling in his tracks. Two of the USA Gold Medalists on the poster were brothers, Dave and Mark Schultz, the few Americans to regularly beat their Russian counterparts, feats worthy of accolades no medals could mark. In my young selective memory, Dan Gable before them and their contemporary Bruce Baumgartner were the only other American wrestlers to have success against their Iron Curtain foes, though I'd come to learn of many other names who did, and followed some of them after the Curtain fell. *Sports Illustrated* ran a piece on the Schultz brothers after their 1984 Olympics success, where Russia did not compete, and those pages were also posted to my wall.

Dumbfounded at the idea of this champion's working in proximity to where I was living, my life went beyond my constant state of not understanding the world I lived in, as I walked east down the balcony past the offices until arriving at the one with the name Mark Schultz, hoping for a sighting of this wrestling legend, wondering if Schultz was Mormon and if he was not, how in *thee sam hill* he ended up at BYU. Joseph Smith was reputed to possess and to exercise on occasion great physical strength. He once challenged a friend to a wrestling match and broke the man's leg. His physical nature seemed to set him apart from many of the Prophets in the Bible with whose roles Joseph and his followers identified him. I warmed to the idea that Joseph was not a prophet suffering from a physical ailment. I expected in the pre-mortal existence Joseph spent his time among fellow wrestlers as much as he did among fellow prophets. No doubt he knew all the Mormon wrestlers, including Schultz.

According to Mormon theology, all people come to earth to gain a physical body and to gain experience available only to the embodied, a belief supported by the central event of Christ's resurrection where he not only conquered death but did it in the flesh. The presumption that the body is a condition for possessing certain knowledge is necessary for the Mormon argument that God himself is with a body. Having families—made possible by the flesh—naturally followed as the preeminent experience of mortal life. But all things, not just procreating and rearing children, experienced in physical form furthered the purpose of gaining knowledge and becoming more like God, ranging from mental and physical suffering to triumphs of athletic feats, all made possible by having bodies.

Joseph Smith experienced physical challenges as a youth and adult, and by all accounts, even his own, benefited from life's physical challenges. If Schultz was a Mormon—the truth of rumor often indistinguishable from the truth of doctrine within Mormonism—then he had to have been part of the small Mormon contingency of wrestlers in the pre-mortal life, the good and the not so good, including yours most truly, and he would have been known to Joseph Smith. Presumably I may have drilled some with the man himself, the prophet, not Schultz, not so foolish to grapple with him even without a body. And if my logic is as valid as a pre-mortal existence was existent, then it's sufficient to rest my case on the similarities of Joseph's and Schultz's having grappled with their peers during their lives. Neither was the only famous historical figure to have done so, as Abraham Lincoln—and to no one's surprise—Theodore Roosevelt grappled with theirs.

And great authors throughout the world have memorialized wrestling. Someone important recorded Zeus besting Kronos to win dominion over the earth; Homer described a draw between indomitable legends Odysseus and Ajax in *The Iliad*; The host may have cut off Geoffrey Chaucer's own Canterbury tale of "Sir Topaz," but not before hearing of Sir Topaz's renown as a wrestler with no peer; Shakespeare established his hero Orlando by his victorious wrestling matches in *As You Like It*; and Chinua Achebe's warrior Okonkwo gained fame as the greatest wrestler of all villages, a universal valor recognized throughout the African continent, the very cradle of civilization, in *Things Fall Apart*. I regularly passed Schultz's office to round the corner for a glimpse into the wrestling room, covered by blue wrestling mats, the space not much larger than the room I practiced in covered by green mats during high school, looking for him. If Schultz would be somewhere, it wouldn't be at a desk.

I was exhausted, and I could not lie still. My head was on fire, and my arms and legs ached. I rolled from one shoulder to the other. I tried to breathe slowly. I fell into a sleep and out again. I could not find any rest. I was becoming more tired. I tried counting. I turned over to lie on my twitching chest. My consciousness was scrambled. I got up to shower for another day of my first week on the floor.

My stomach hurt, and I did not want to go back to work at the mill. And I felt sick thinking about trying to fight for sleep when I got back home. There wouldn't be any peace for the following days as I became accustomed to climbing the web-grated stairs from the parking lot into the mill and back again twelve hours later.

The goal on the floor of a blast furnace was to complete an error-free cast. Each cast ran for thirty or so minutes from the start of drilling into the furnace to release the molten iron to filling a half dozen ladles sitting on tracks running next to the facility. The ladles were pulled to another facility for the next part of the process where the iron was heated up more to make steel. The final step rolled the steel into the products the company could never competitively place into the market for a profit over its last decades in existence. I spent my summer there during its final throes.

Members of a crew each had a specific role to ensure a successful cast. The crew boss hung out in the control room where the controller monitored the furnace. Level One drilled into the furnace to release the molten iron into the trough and operated the mud gun to close the hole after the last ladle filled. Level Two monitored the slag halfway through the cast. Level Three filled the ladles.

—You have too much dirt.

Level One jumped into the iron-side runner where the liquid iron would flow during a cast, to shuffle out dirt I'd thrown on the gate. The iron side consisted of a straight runner with four, maybe five gates diverting the hot iron to a short runner overhanging a ladle below. After each ladle filled the next gate was pulled to fill the next ladle.

—You just got to pack it. It'll work with less dirt.

He beat it with the back of the shovel and smoothed the top of the dirt. He stepped out and handed the shovel back to me. Casting was a test of patience in unimaginable heat, hell of a crucible on your body and your mind. Timing was critical for Level Three, as he ensured the ladles filled but not too much, to avoid spilling on the track all the way to the next furnace. Before filling the ladle, Level Three had to set strong but not overly fortified gates to withstand the iron flow. Too fortified would take more effort than one had in the heat of a cast to bust it up and a partial gate could continue, for a few unexpected seconds, to divert more iron than desired into the already sufficiently full ladle. If a gate broke, and one occasionally did, then one less ladle would be transported and management would know it. Level Three might be the only one working during the cast, as Level One stood near the trough with the crew boss—if he stepped out of the control room—admiring the hot iron, and Level Two took samples from the trough as each ladle filled, managing the slag when it began to run near the end of the cast.

The cast was often cake. The real challenge came between casts to keep the floor clean. On a good cast, when the iron flowed smoothly, not a lot was left behind in the runners. Typically a crew would pitch in to clean the iron side after a normal cast. During a bad cast, the iron could run so clumpy that slag started before the first ladle filled. As that undesirable scenario unfolded, how much cleanup would be needed depended upon how fast the mud-gun could plug up the furnace. If it didn't plug quickly, the slag could pour all over, so we'd not only be busting up the hardened iron in what was once the slag runner, but also the cooled iron on the floor. No cleanups could be more brutal than a fucked-up slag-side save one, the routine cleaning of the trough that was so hot each person took his turn of far less than a minute to bust up the iron or shovel it out.

—You should bring two shirts and change between casts so you can start with a dry shirt, Level One suggested.

And I did the second day and spent the first few minutes after each cast, no matter how bad the clean-up ahead of us, directly in front of the air conditioner. One single solitary air conditioner blew nonstop for the crew's morale. Between each cast I put on the dry shirt after drying my torso and hung the wet one on the conditioner.

One hot shift, the last ladle filled near the top and I signaled to Level One to plug the hole. The noise during a cast was deafening, so loud you couldn't hear someone shout so I did my best to read lips. I did not fail to wear earplugs or bring an extra pair. I acclimated to the hot iron bursting out of the runner onto my jacket and into gloves and within weeks only noticing the popcorn burns for a few seconds, but the noise at the beginning of cast always caught my attention.

My signal to Level One spurred him into swinging the mud gun in place to plug up the hole, which typically ended the cast and sent me to the break room via the air conditioner to cool off and change shirts, but he swung the gun back. The gun was not plugging the hole. I didn't worry much because it didn't mean a mess on the floor. But it meant a hell of one on the tracks below near the overflowing ladle. Level One grabbed a steel pole, a couple of inches in diameter and about ten feet long. It was one of two necessary tools for clean-up. A worker used the pole to bust up the cooled iron in the runner; then another stepped into it with a shovel to remove the pieces. He furiously stood over the trough knocking mud away from the hole. He kept over the trough for the longest minute until the crew boss yelled him off, swinging the gun back over the trough for a second try that was successful.

Jacob and I worked on all the different crews on both furnaces as we floated that summer. This Level One had two distinguishing habits. He didn't button up his fire-retardant green jacket, nor did he button up his shirt. I always considered that one and the same, that he did his job with a bare chest. Second, he was always reading different books about Custer's Last Stand.

—How is it? I asked between casts.

—It's good. I've read ten about Custer and Crazy Horse.

—How does that one measure up?

—They all have different points of view, the ones I've read. There's a dozen more with more points of view I haven't.

This Level One may have been the most influential coworker I ever had. Any topic I've a hankering to comprehend requires multiple sources for their competing points of view and by the end of that long, hot summer I didn't button up my coat or shirt either.

I had not craved water as much as I did on the floor since my days cutting weight during high school wrestling. I went for water even when it was someone else's turn to go fetch it, because I was always thirsty. Someone had to beat me to it or between casts I climbed down the ladder on the back of the furnace in hunt of its priceless return for my extra labors. I packed bottles on my shoulder back up to welcomes by management and members of the crew warning me about drinking too much water. I looked at them wide-eyed, not saying a word and helped myself to another drink. You'll get cramps they said, but I never did.

During my junior year, a student from Pennsylvania wrote in the opinion pages of the BYU student newspaper, *The Daily Universe*, that he disapproved of BYU's cutting its wrestling program. His disappointment was shared by a few of us on campus, including the Athletic Director, Rondo Fehlberg. Fehlberg had been an All-American wrestler at BYU who loved the school enough to leave his high-paying job as a corporate lawyer to take less money as BYU's athletic director. He and his brothers grew up in Wyoming and were among the most storied BYU wrestlers, and only the Hansen brothers from Idaho held a comparable part in its history. Fehlberg fought to keep the program but lost, and resigned in the summer of 1999.

The school's official position for dropping wrestling (and men's gymnastics) was to comply with Title IX's proportionality standard. Since the late 1970s, the federal statute prohibiting sex discrimination in colleges, forever after known as Title IX, has ensured that women student athletes were included in college sports. No one could argue it hasn't been a smashing success for women student athletes. One need only follow the most dramatic of all sports, that of women's soccer (futbol) during the World Cup to see its fruits. If we were serious about children's deriving the benefit of sport, then we would mandate participation of girls to play soccer with the goal of the Women's World Cup, and for boys too. A university can comply with Title IX by satisfying the proportionality standard in allotting athletic scholarships to men and to women in proportion to their enrollment. When I was at BYU or shortly thereafter, there were more women than men students. However, the proportionality standard was *one of three* ways to comply with the federal law; the other two were to demonstrate an expansion of the underrepresented sex's sports, or to accommodate the underrepresented sex's interests. Complying with either of the latter two options did not require cutting men's programs (neither did the proportionality standard, necessarily, if the university matched scholarships to increases in enrollment), but BYU followed far too many universities before and since, using Title IX as an excuse to cut unprofitable, less popular and poorly attended men's sports.

The same year the fellow student wrote to the paper, concerned alumni ran a campaign to save the wrestling program. It included a special dual meet between BYU and the University of Iowa at the Delta Center in Salt Lake City. Iowa had dominated college wrestling for decades, and only one other school, Oklahoma State, had a comparable college wrestling tradition. Dan Gable, one of the United States' most celebrated wrestlers, had retired as Iowa's head coach a couple years earlier. He attended the event, giving a short speech to encourage supporters' fight to save the program. He emphasized Utah's great amateur wrestling tradition, with more high school wrestlers per capita than anywhere in the United States. He also pointed out Utah's production of the young freshman wrestler at Iowa State, Cael Sanderson, who hailed with his brothers Cody and Cole, also Iowa State wrestlers, from Heber City, Utah. Gable had the foresight to highlight Cael at the beginning of Cael's improbable run of an undefeated college wrestling career over the next four years. Cael's run was unprecedented except for a few of college wrestlers' greats, including Gable's own college career, which ended in only one loss, his final match. After Gable's speech, Iowa trounced BYU but not without making a thoughtful gesture unknown to many BYU fans in attendance by sitting starters at the weight classes of BYU's best wrestlers, Rangi and Rocky Smart. The Smart brothers were homegrown from Lehi, Utah, and they won close matches against Iowa's backups. The foresight of Iowa's coach allowed BYU's big event to save the team everyone was there to support from being shut out.

The campaign to save the program faced the challenge of raising enough money to support the program, plus the impossible task of convincing BYU leadership of wrestling's value. It was doomed from the start. For one, President Merrill J. Bateman and Vice President Fred Skousen had already explained why they cut wrestling before the campaign got underway, and the reason was not money. Or, it was not explicitly money. It was to comply with

Title IX's proportionality standard. The more obvious wall that supporters could not climb was to convince BYU leadership of something they did not value.

Has there ever been a more impossible pursuit to convince someone of something's value when the person you intend to convince doesn't share the same value? The task is impossible because value isn't transferred to someone by eloquent explanation of it. Value comes from experience. To value something draws upon one's past connection to that something. If one doesn't have a direct connection, then one is not without hope. He or she can still have a semblance of something's value by drawing upon past connections to something similar. Hence proselytizing values is as productive as convincing you of the fine taste of hops. The only way to appreciate it is to taste it. Gaining value always takes steps and recognition of those steps. BYU leadership had no particular connection to draw upon to value wrestling. Or, like ancient Israel, they had entered a prolonged cycle of having forgotten.

Then why blather on about something's value? There are many reasons that fall within at least two large ones. And your being the beneficiary from making the effort to explain what it is you value is not one, but those rewards are rich because you should be an expert on your own values. For one, a spirited attempt to explain one's values—aided by propitious circumstances—may motivate the other to consider and eventually put your claims to the test. That is to say, if you are lucky to connect on touch points bolstered by emotional cache in the other, then there's a chance he or she will dip a toe into your value, gaining his or her own experience of it. For two—but harder to track a causal relation to your dashing eloquence—your assertions vie for space among the personal constellation of the other. Regardless who we are, if we value, then we rely upon those experiences that form our values and, as soon as we share them with another, we ascribe the weight of the experience to the value. In time, what we shared and how we remember the experience replaces the experience. That just is. The constellation is of explanations and memories, not our limited experiences.

The space of one's constellation sets the limits and structures for how we make meaning. The aligning and realigning of our big and small dippers are in flux in real time, not measured in eons. Your proffering of values sends them into my outer space. Now whether it was a successful launch depends upon how much practice you had put in before you battered my time away. But it is up there with everything else previously launched, all for me to consider, maybe not right away but by god I will have to account for its exposure eventually. I may always rightly dismiss it based on my certainties of faith, logic, and preference, but it wouldn't be there for me to dismiss if you hadn't launched it.

Title IX is complicated by the pink elephant sitting on the three compliance tests. Parties using or decrying Title IX to further gender equality or to emphasize pernicious effects must substantially account for the separate classification of football scholarships but rarely do. Football is unlike all other college sports in all material respects, one being that it does not have a female counterpart. It's a black hole consuming all vulnerable male sports that administrators are beside themselves to cut to save costs. To football's credit, no other sport accomplishes the branding it does for a university, with the exception of a few men's basketball programs, namely the ACC, maybe the SEC and Big East, too. And nothing with the same exception is quite as much fun to watch. Its marketing potential separates it from all other sports, and nothing could be more material to big-business universities of the twenty-first century.

If parties were concerned about fairness, there would be a proportionality standard solely for football, to ensure an equitable return on young men's one- to four-year investments into generating the university's main source of revenue, next to the persistent tuition bubble. No one is fooled that free tuition and books compensate players for the physical tolls on their bodies, or that the time and emotion committed to the gridiron allow for a reasonable shot at success in the classroom.

Title IX does not account for football's distinctness and incomparable market value to universities. Some folks would point out that all collegiate athletes face the same challenge to find time to excel in the classroom. Those folks overwhelmingly buckled down and did well in school without having any fun. Consider what assuming "every student athlete has it tough" ignores. Football players provide immediate monetary return others generally do not, and generating money attracts just as immediate, culturally-induced distractions. The type of life most of us wish we'd had in college, footballers actually do. As significantly, football scholarships *primarily* support professional ambitions in the same sport, and this is not the case with other college sports. In academic parlance, presuppositions actuate consequences. In my words, a football player's aspirations affect his efforts. No other college sport serves as an *exclusive professional minor league*. The football player is aware of it. Rabid alumni and driven administrators aid and abet it. Subsequently, the billion-dollar college football industry is a major cause of the death of men's college sports. Title IX *as applied* has a disparate impact on a protected class of sex, *men's* sports, which is a violation of equal protection. Rebutting that it does no such thing simply ignores the elephant or, with eyes pinched, describes how it is similar to the other mice as it stamps them out.

But who cares about wrestling? Having read how I regularly got beat to hell doing it, I may shock you confessing that I do. However, if you know anything about how Mormons locate their purpose as Mormons, with reference to every great truth recorded throughout the ages, you would be far more shocked that their leadership did not care too.

I felt about wrestling as Ishmael did about whaling. People did not understand it; therefore they could not appreciate it. And if I failed to defend it, I would be as blameworthy as he would have been had he failed to defend whaling.

First of all wrestling does not produce the celebrity athlete. If a wrestler were introduced among sports entertainment regalia, no one would probably hear what followed *wres*, mistakenly concluding they just met *Wes*, and the couple who appeared to hear would only be hesitating as they reached to check messages on their sleek new smartphones. And no wrestler would expect anyone had learned more than his new name.

Regrettably the reason people widely do not venerate wrestling is that it is antithetical to spectacle. There are no fireworks and no monster big screens, no fans gyrating to blaring popular tunes, with no dances after scoring and no chest bumps after each executed play. There is no show. It's raw action. Movements are directed toward the purpose with no tint of theatrics; when fans react, their movements are mimetic contortions, and silence backstops with intermittent hollers and Hawkeye roars. Wrestling is the preeminent exhibition of motion, not poetic and not graceful but unvarnished and pure.

Preeminent exhibition of motion? Name in your head another sport that demonstrates unaided human motion? Sprints, marathons, combat, dance, keep going. Wrestling does not depend upon additional fixtures to exaggerate motion, and no other propless sport involves as many possible changes in direction or forces acting on each other than two bodies grappling.

But still, an incomparable display of motion? Bodies at rest stay at rest unless acted upon by another body; force acting on a body causes that body to accelerate in proportion to that force; and the forces acting on a body and the body's reaction are mutual, or "every action has an opposite and equal reaction," the one law we all remember. And where might these laws of motion be better observed than two bodies exerting force on each other?

And where could this display be more depreciated than under today's professional lights? The shame of our nation. Wrestling is dynamic motion blotted out by the fantasy of World Wrestling Entertainment personas imbibed by every professional sport where bigger and louder is always better since Dennis Rodman birthed its market value. Outside the bombast and egos of the monetary sports circus, skilled and powerful grapplers display forces where advantages are gained in milliseconds during nonstop motion. Want a warrant? Check out Cael Sanderson, the greatest of all time, on YouTube. No small claim among wrestling intelligentsia, but irrefutable based on the presumption that wrestling is the finest display of unaided motion. Counters only lower the bar. An informed but misplaced counter would be that Bouvaisa Saitiev was the sport's greatest. Saitiev was the greatest international *freestyle* (the style of Olympic wrestling) wrestler of all time. Watch him on Youtube, too. This counter is based on a different presumption. By its rules, freestyle wrestling handicaps a full display of forces by largely removing motivation for motion. (You don't have to know anything about wrestling to understand this point. You only have to know how to think.) For example, the bottom wrestler in par terre position (action on the mat as opposed to action standing up) has no motivation to move. The top wrestler in par terre position has the motivation to turn the bottom wrestler so his back is exposed to the mat. Exposure? Really, slight turns—not controlling an opponent for seconds of exposure or for a pin—decide who wins in freestyle. Freestyle wrestling is a technical brute ballet aimed at spinning your opponent as high as one can. It's too prohibitory: rules—not competition—dictate the outcome, and it shackles itself from displaying the full range of possible motion.

And a wrestling match ought to allow for, and the rules ought to encourage, all possibilities of motion if it is to be the supreme example of its laws. The full range of motion stems from encouraging forces at all times; whether a wrestler has control or is being controlled, he ought to have the motivation to move. The pinnacle of motion is the scramble, where either wrestler can come out in control, but a scramble is rarely, if ever, seen in freestyle because scrambles involve both wrestlers being vulnerable to potentially exposing their backs. And where there is a scramble, often the wrestler who gains control has exposed his back and comes out behind on points—an appalling contradiction of action.

One of the most blatant absurdities in freestyle wrestling is rewarding a wrestler who gains control with more advantages. In freestyle, the wrestler who obtains a take-down from the starting position has a superior position and clear advantage just as in other disciplines. But the rules of freestyle then give him further advantage because the bottom wrestler's motivation is blunted from moving to avoid exposing his back, so the motiveless bottom wrestler stays as motionless as possible: in wrestling lingo, *stalling* (one of my best moves). The guy on top has no vulnerabilities. So the par terre position involves one person trying to turn the dead weight of the other. That's an incontrovertible display of limited motion. The greatest United States freestyle wrestler was John Smith, who had the most graceful low single-leg takedown to leg lace you ever did see. Under the one dimensional freestyle rules (blunting possible forces, rewarding for exposures and not control) he excelled.

Under the full dynamic rules of folkstyle (the style of American collegiate wrestling), which reward controlling an opponent, not merely spinning them—and most importantly encouraging the scramble—Smith was just another great wrestler. He did not morph into a different wrestler but changed to a different discipline. Because folkstyle wrestling rules encourage scrambles and reward control, it crowns the wrestler who dominates. A discipline that handicaps motion can hardly say the same. Diminishing folkstyle programs among American universities is far more tragic than the mere elimination of an unpopular sport. It marks the fall of the bastion of the rawest display of motion.

Most peoples' failings toward wrestling amount to ignorance. Consider how the greatest challenges all folks face require their strongest, directed motion, either driving toward a goal or responding to a force intent on derailing them from obtaining it. There you have your own warrant! You've been wrestling forces all your weary days and only failed to properly name it.

Before more warrants, and I have an endless pocketful, you ought to know the history to which you belong. You wrestled your way to your greatest triumphs and so did some of the most celebrated people recorded in the annals of history.

The first great epic was written by scriveners in ancient Mesopotamia. It recorded the life of a mighty king struggling with growing old and dealing with the reality that he would one day die. To satiate his anxiety, he went on many adventures, and his final one took him to the end of the world to find eternal life. This cardinal story bears this king's name, *The Epic of Gilgamesh*.

Gilgamesh was a man caught up in his youth. He bombarded his people with his overflowing energy until his subjects demanded the gods create his equal to divert his energy away from oppressing them. The gods created a wild man, Enkidu, who lived and ran among the beasts. Enkidu was tricked into civilization after six days and seven nights by a harlot's charms. Then she convinced him to go with her to the palace of Gilgamesh. On their way, a stranger explained that Gilgamesh made it his practice as king to mate a lawful wife before the groom did, and this angered Enkidu. When Gilgamesh sought to enforce his kingly right, Enkidu stopped him.

> Enkidu approached him. They met in the public street. Enkidu blocked the door to the wedding with his foot, not allowing Gilgamesh to enter. They grappled each other, holding fast like wrestlers, they shattered the doorpost, the wall shook. Gilgamesh and Enkidu grappled each other, holding fast like wrestlers, they shattered the doorpost, the wall shook! They grappled each other at the door to the wedding, they fought in the street, the public square. It was Gilgamesh who knelt for the pin, his foot on the ground. His fury abated, he turned away.

Gilgamesh lost, but as he turned away Enkidu praised him for his valor. They became fast friends, and Enkidu accompanied Gilgamesh on many of his adventures. One of the primary lessons from the oldest wrestling match ever recorded in literature is that one's effort matters a great deal, more than the outcome (which lacks for clarity in the great epic about who really did win). Since the time Enkidu and Gilgamesh grappled in the public square, wrestling has been about exerting and responding to force to gain advantage at the risk of shattering and shaking surrounding restraints.

Our earliest great heroic tale in the English language recounts the mighty feats of a royal member of the Geats, a tribe living in Sweden. This man heard that the Danes across the sea suffered under the terrors of a monster. No one had been able to stop it for a bloodstained decade. It visited the great hall Heorot after every celebration, massacring anyone within. With a small group, the royal Geat sailed to Denmark. The ferocious monster was named Grendel, and this immortal English tale bore the name of its hero, *Beowulf*.

The king of the Danes, Hrothgar, learned that Beowulf had arrived on his shore and remarked that Beowulf was known to have *the strength of thirty men in the grip of his hand*. After his reception, Beowulf explained to Hrothgar his design. *They tell me in his vainglory the monster is contemptuous of weapons. Therefore, as I wish to keep the good opinion of my lord Hygelac, I propose to dispense with any kind of sword or shield during the combat. Foe against foe, I shall fight the fiend to the death with my bare hands.* The company of Geats entered the great hall and filled it with their confidence and merrymaking. When the sun went down, they lay down to rest as Grendel emerged from the heath. As the Geats slept, Grendel entered the hall and snatched the closest man, tearing him apart.

> Then he advanced nearer. Reaching out with his open hand, the fiend was about to take hold of the hero on his bed. But Beowulf at once saw the hostile move and propped himself up on his elbow. The archbeast soon realized that nowhere in the world had he ever met a man with such might in the grip of his hand. Grendel met his match. The monster fought to escape, but Beowulf closed with him.

Despite its efforts, Grendel could not break lose. *The furious contestants for the mastery of the hall raged till the building rang. It was a miracle that the beautiful banqueting hall withstood such combatants without falling flat to the ground.* Grendel eventually broke free and fled, mortally wounded. Beowulf recounted it all to the king, including his intention *to pin him quickly to his deathbed in so close a grapple that unless he wriggled his body loose he must fight for life in the grip of my hand.* Upon examining the destruction to the renowned hall, it was seen that only the roof remained untouched by the monumental struggle.

Their match showed at least two more truths about wrestling. There is not a more honorable contest than unaided force against force; and there might be more important assets for a successful wrestler but nothing is quite like a strong grip.

No book has had quite the effect the Bible has had. After the creation, Adam and Eve's banishment from the Garden of Eden, Cain killing Abel, Noah surviving the flood, and the pandemic confusion following the Tower of Babel's fall, we get to the point with the covenant between God and Abraham. God promised to make Abraham's descendants a great nation, and he promised to make Abraham's name great and to make him a blessing to all inhabitants of the earth (Abraham's name was still Abram and only after showing he'd give something up to bind his side of the covenant did his name get extended). God also promised Abraham a lot of descendants. Abraham took a circuitous route through Egypt before following God's directive, but eventually reared some children in the promised land of Canaan, raising his second son Isaac. Abraham was put to the ultimate test when the Lord commanded him to give up the promises by sacrificing Isaac. Abraham proceeded to obey but an angel intervened in the nick of time. Isaac lived into adulthood to raise his own son, Jacob.

Jacob was the younger and less admired of Isaac's twin sons who started fighting in the womb, but with the help of his mother Jacob gained the birthright by deceiving his father. Growing up, Jacob and the elder twin Esau knew nothing of each other but conflict. At his father's command, Jacob sojourned abroad to find a bride. During his travels he had a marvelous dream of a ladder that reached heaven, where God and his angels descended and ascended upon it; then the Lord appeared and reiterated the promises of Abraham, including the blessing that Jacob's *seed shall be as the dust of the earth, and thou shalt spread abroad to the west, and to the east, and to the north, and to the south: and in thee and in thy seed shall all the families of the earth be blessed.* Jacob journeyed on into Haran, where events developed into one of the great stories recorded in the Bible. He arrived at a well with sheep scattered about, and the daughter of his uncle Laban approached with more sheep. It was late in the day, and as the daughter approached the well Jacob removed the stone to water the sheep and romance was introduced into literature as *Jacob kissed Rachel, and lifted up his voice, and wept.*

Jacob went on to serve seven years for Rachel's hand in marriage, only to be tricked and have to serve an additional seven years before getting her, and to compound matters, Laban eventually become jealous of Jacob's wealth. The Lord commanded Jacob to return to Canaan, and Jacob did so, with Laban hot in pursuit. Laban eventually overtook him and instead of berating Jacob for taking all of his wealth, Laban lamented the departure of his daughters and children, proposing the two reconcile if Jacob promised not to afflict his daughters (he had married two) or take other wives. Jacob agreed, and his father-in-law departed bestowing kisses on all his descendants before turning back for home.

Jacob had to return to Canaan to fulfill the promises of the Lord. But when he got there he had to appease Esau, who had wanted to kill Jacob the last time they spoke. The Lord helped Jacob develop a plan to win over Esau by having his servants precede him to present all his flocks as a gift. Jacob stayed back with his family and moved them at night, sending them over a river. As he stood on a bank watching his family cross the river a man approached.

• • •

And he rose up that night, and took his two wives, and his two women servants, and his eleven sons, and passed over the ford Jabbok. And he took them, and sent them over the brook, and sent over that he had. And Jacob was left alone; and there wrestled a man with him until the breaking of the day. And when he saw that he prevailed not against him, he touched the hollow of his thigh; and the hollow of Jacob's thigh was out of joint, as he wrestled with him. And he said. Let me go, for the day breaketh. And he said, I will not let thee go, except thou bless me. And he said unto him, What is thy name? And he said, Jacob. And he said, Thy name shall be called no more Jacob, but Israel: for as a prince hast thou power with God and with men, and hast prevailed. And Jacob asked him, and said Tell me, I pray thee, thy name. And he said, Wherefore is it that though does ask after my name? And he blessed him there. And Jacob called the name of the place Peniel: for I have seen God face to face, and my life is preserved.

The most significant book in history includes a story that turns on a wrestling match. Has any match had more significance to the inhabitants of the people on earth with the God of Israel being the source of purpose for as many humans' lives as there are sands of the Red Sea? Even hurt, Jacob would not give up until he got his blessing and the rest, as they say, is history. Or it almost was until Rachel gave birth to his twelfth son, Benjamin (the younger brother to Joseph, the one with a coat of many colors, ability to interpret dreams, and the resolve to flee his host's amorous wife). Rachel paid the ultimate price, as she died in childbirth completing the Israelite tribes.

I cannot conclude as the whaler Ishmael did that *if I shall ever deserve any real repute in that small but high hushed world which I might not be unreasonably ambitious of; if hereafter I shall do anything that, upon the whole, a man might rather have done than to left undone; if, at my death, my executors, or more properly my creditors, find any precious MSS in my desk, then here I prospectively ascribe all the honor and glory to whaling; for a whale-ship was my Yale and my Harvard.* But I can attest that wrestling was my Pandemonium. I emerged with *deep scars of thunder* on my face more in common with the hideously marred Queequeg than fair Ishmael. Wrestling was not merely a metaphor for struggle, because it decimated me for five months every year as I grew up during junior high and high school. Losing match after match was a small part. Losing weight every day and every night to compete was the large part. Looking for Mark Schultz in the halls of the Fieldhouse where I never found him I came to learn how lucky I had been reading news of three, *three*, college wrestlers who died within a month of each other from cutting weight. Billy, Joseph, and Jeff's deaths shocked wrestlers with what we all knew was possible.

Their deaths ushered in regulations that restricted weight cutting for amateur wrestlers. How many afternoons had I spent in saunas and how many evenings sleeping in plastic gear and how many others gone to extremes pushing the limit like Billy, Joseph, and Jeff? Each saga to make weight culminated in no fewer than twenty-four hours of anticipation for a drink of water. I know the power of singular thought, iron concentration not because I've been able to do it for more than a few minutes at a time outside wrestling but during those hellish nights and mornings before weigh-ins I could see and think of only one thing, water. The line for many wrestlers was not triumph or fame. Though some wrestlers became titans of finance and leading professionals, the greatest live in relative obscurity outside the loyal enclave of wrestling fans.

Many supporters of wrestling advocate for the benefits of wrestling, arguing it produces work ethic, leadership, responsibility, etc., as if every other sport did not do the same; when we all know leadership, as other positions of power, are more a result of the privileged tit of fortune's breaks; even the more nuanced argument that wrestling makes someone more fit to seize fortune. Nonsense.

The line for wrestling's lasting and distinct value is learning to go on after failure, defeat, and self-induced decimation and shame. Struggling to get up and pressing the action only to survive one headwind after another is the superior value of wrestling. No disappointment is more all your own, and no reward greater than continually willing yourself to fight while everything continues to beat you down. Could there be a more effective refiner's fire for moving through life's many challenges? Could there be a more effective mold to pare everything away to the core of one's dignity? In triumph and in defeat you know who you are as a wrestler. Because no one can wrestle your match for you, you are your performance, minutes lasting far beyond the seconds you might have your hand raised. One of a wrestler's singular gifts to others is an earned self-realization that is not projected cheaply onto them. Maybe there could be a fitter mold, but there has not been since Gilgamesh emerged from it. No sport demands more or returns more as sure as the struggles that required your best efforts and unyielding will did not fail to return the greatest rewards in defeat, the hell of life.

I climbed the ladder to the south blast furnace to learn, upon reaching the floor, that I had been assigned to the north furnace. I walked across the floor and entered the passage connecting the furnaces, glancing into the control room that held enough gauges to make a commercial pilot salivate. I had worked the north furnace on many shifts, though far fewer than on the south furnace. I knew the crews, and headed to the iron side. The crew boss called me over and assigned me to the slag side, the position of operator two. I had been waiting to be Level Two since my first day, because he stood around and did nothing for the majority of the cast. I didn't hesitate to embrace my role, eager to take and send samples as each ladle filled. Obtaining a sample involved a little bit of finesse, placing the tip of the rod in the end of the trough. You couldn't leave it in too long and had to lightly tap off the covering after securing the sample. After the crew boss's first demonstration I handled the new position with aplomb for the first six hours of the shift over the course of as many casts. As a cast ended I approached the trough where the molten iron poured out into the runner heading down the iron side for my final sample as the last ladle filled. I extended the rod into the trough and took another step and tripped falling across the runner. I dropped the rod and braced my right hand just inside the trough wall a few inches above the flowing iron while my left hand caught my greatest moment of luck bracing against a sturdy plate extending off the back of the trough, my body straddling over the runner. I got up and my right hand was on fire but the trough had not seared through my glove, another but less monumental piece of good luck. Standing above the end of the trough I noticed a three-by-five-inch triangle plate connected to the runner, which I hadn't noticed before.

—Your brother said you're going to Harvard.

—At the end of the summer.

—What the fuck are you working here for?

—So I have enough money to get me there. I'd like to buy a laptop too.

But I found myself asking the same question my last three weeks on the floor when I added stretching my hamstrings and lower back on any ridge that could hold up my legs and lying on the picnic table in the break room, to my post-cast routine of changing shirts in front of the air conditioner. I packed my lunch with ibuprofen for four pills every four hours, consuming them faithfully at the beginning, twice during, and at the end of the shift. Shoveling correctly with your legs and a straight back is easier to do fresh at the beginning of the shift then exhausted at the end. When my form lagged I noticed my lower back over my left buttock tighten like a fist, starting to crack along my hip, persisting for my last weeks on the job. I stretched more and took more ibuprofen.

Josh continued to bunk with Jake and me and did his best to include us in non-steel-related chaos. On Saturday morning we got on the road early. Josh didn't enter the biggest rodeo in the world every year. His bull was in the first section of the matinee show at the Cheyenne Frontier Days Rodeo, and we had about seven hours to cover on Interstate 80 to get there from Provo. With no problems we'd arrive with enough time for him to conduct his necessary rituals behind the chutes before his ride. You can see a lot of Wyoming in seven hours, and we did. The road trip didn't faze me. I was used to taking day trips with Jeremy and Josh to rodeos in small towns throughout Idaho and Utah all my teenage years growing up with them. Heavens, I had spent enough time on the road I could have read every great Russian novel twice. Instead I listened to Chris LeDoux and George Strait and Alabama and whoever else's cassette tape was in the car, and I tried to snooze. Combining the time on the road with the hours at rodeos over the years, I could have read every classic novel written and still not missed a second of Jeremy and Josh's bull rides.

The drive to Cheyenne passed as expected for a long run. We rolled into the arena and parked between pickup trucks, and I stepped out and did the same thing I always did at every rodeo. I found a bathroom to relieve myself. Even though I didn't compete I was nervous the entire time I sat in the stands up until the announcer called Jeremy or Josh's name, and then through their attempt at eight seconds of glory. After a sturdy pee, right away I started asking God to bless them with safety, which intensified as I repeated the request faster and faster the closer it got to their rides.

The biggest show on earth was no different. Josh headed toward the chutes and after finding the bathroom I walked around the vendors with concentrated prayers keenly distracted by the staffs of the Jack Daniels and Copenhagen booths, manned by tightly fitted, hardly-clad young women. I did some of my greatest pondering at those moments whether at booths or walking around bleachers at what seemed like every rodeo, asking myself what a brave, tough, handsome cowboy had that I didn't.

The first section of the bulls rolled around and Josh's bull was in one of the first chutes. The grandstands were as tall and long as any rodeo's that I'd seen, and they were packed. Josh had drawn a bucker and it flung him high into the air shortly after it kicked out of the chute. He wasn't hurt as he stumbled out of the arena. I left my seat and loped around the chutes until he appeared a few minutes later.

—Had a good one, he said smiling and shaking his head.

—He bucked.

—Let's go.

I didn't say anything because you don't tell a bull rider who just bucked off a ton of twirling fury that you looked good while you were on it, but it was just that last split second before you bucked off you looked like a rag doll, or keep positive there, cowboy, you'll have better luck next time, or not even Don Gay rode 'em all. Sometimes being there was just enough, but then sometimes being there was just the bare minimum.

I entered my senior year of high school fit and hungry for my final year of wrestling. I had committed myself to compete close to my weight of 165 lbs. at the start of the season. For once, I had some muscle and aimed to make the most of it and was going to manage my weight reasonably, competing at the 152 lb. class. Josh came to the preseason practices. After passing on his rodeo scholarship in Oklahoma, he had a few free months before his Mormon mission. He wrestled growing up but had played basketball in junior high and high school. He came to practice to roll around for exercise, and he knew I had been working hard in the offseason, so he encouraged me to fight my best. The first tournament approached, and coach called for the first wrestle-offs of the season to determine the varsity team. A sophomore challenged me for the 152 lb. spot and, to my surprise, took me down early in the match and, to my frustration, prevented me from scoring the rest of it, beating me.

I was beside myself sitting in the locker room where I ignored the coach's consolation. I finished practice unresponsive to teammates. We left the gym in the pitch of darkness. Josh drove the yellow Chevette home in silence. I stepped out of the passenger side and Josh met me in front of the car and grabbed me and hugged me. I stood with my arms to my side and he squeezed me tight and didn't let me go. I had been hugged before but not by someone in my family. If someone had tried, I would have punched him. I had been hugged by a woman in the ward at my mother's interment. She grabbed me through a sea of people from where I had been standing, staring at my mother's casket and the large purple rug underneath it, unsure my duty as pallbearer had ended as people started moving around after the ceremonial dedication. I thought I would be asked to help lower her into the ground. Pulling me through large bodies she told me she loved my mother, and that my mother had been one of her very best friends. Her large bosom pressed out all my breath and pushed the pin from the boutonnière into my chest. Only Grammie had hugged me before like that.

We left Cheyenne with plenty of daylight. A couple hours down the road an eighteen-wheeler semi truck pulled over and turned on its flashers. A small man jumped out of the passenger side and an average sized man jumped out of the driver side and ran around the front of the tractor at the small man who swung wildly. The men twirled around and around until the bigger man landed on top as we passed them. A few miles farther down the road there were belongings strewn across the median and the other side of the interstate. Cars had rolled off the road and a large Suburban sat in the middle with a man still draped over the steering wheel.

CHAPTER 26
FAITH

—I don't know what to tell you, I said.

—I just don't know what to do about it, Nicholas said.

—I wish I were so lucky.

He laughed. Nicholas always laughed, a high trill reverberating through the whole chest, like life had only one mood, one worth laughing about. Even during a conversation with consequences we both perceived as significant—him far more than me—and him unsure of what he should do, he laughed.

—If you like her, then I would entertain the possibility of a relationship, I said.

—I just don't know. She is so beautiful.

—We are way out of my area of expertise, but I don't see the holdup.

—I just told you she left her husband because she loves me!

—But you also said she didn't love her husband. And you weren't having an affair before she left him. You only touched her all over and tossed her in the air.

He laughed, stretching back into his chair. We sat in a café outside Harvard Square he had picked for its vegetarian menu. I didn't recall his abstaining from meats when we roomed together in Provo, but his commitment to healthy eating did not surprise me. He moved to New England to join a ballet company about the time I moved to Cambridge for graduate school, and had recently taken the position as principal lead male dancer of a Boston ballet company after spending a year with a company farther up New England.

—You can meet her at the performance. You should bring someone, I can get another free ticket.

—One will do. How will I know which one she is?

—She is the most beautiful dancer in the company. And I'll introduce her after the show.

—All ballerinas are excruciatingly beautiful at every performance I've seen.

On Divinity Avenue, I passed the Peabody Museum on my left and Divinity Hall on my right. A path led between the science buildings to Andover Hall and a side street connected to Beacon Street, and I veered right and took a quick left onto another side street ending at Somerville Av'. Another left led me past outdoor basketball courts and, on the right, Central Street ran deep into the heart of Somerville where I lived with three other divinity students. I was happy climbing up Central Street or relieved, maybe both.

After Nicholas moved east to join the first company, I saw him perform flawlessly. Watching him move with the other dancers, in line with their steps, and in sync with their jumps, awakened me to the most resounding fact I should have never failed to appreciate but always had gazed over, that real grace comes from hours combining into years of practice. Nicholas had made that commitment and had succeeded brilliantly. He danced beautifully. I hardly could believe it, I commented to my date, a coy brunette I'd been smitten with since meeting at a Divinity School cultural event hosting an Islamic *tzadik*, a Muslim spiritual leader. I had attended a Quran reading group, led by a woman, with two other women and me. The leader of the reading group studied under the visiting tzadik from California, so I decided to attend to support her. She was tall and thin with a long pretty face. As the meeting opened I noticed the brunette, who I did not recognize from the

Divinity School. The tzadik interrupted my gaze on her and started talking to me.

—So what year are you, how do you like Divinity School, have you read the Quran?

He continued on and on and I politely answered his questions but tried to find a reason to move on to talk to the brunette.

—So tell me what do you think the purpose of life is? he asked.

—I have no idea, I said.

Beside himself, he fell back into the couch chuckling and hugging himself.

—You study at Harvard and you have no idea what the purpose of life is? Well, you are not alone, but you came to the right meeting, as I will discuss it before we chant.

And he did discuss the purpose of life, citing passages from the Quran. I kept looking at the brunette across the room and again was interrupted when the tzadik directed us all to make a circle. I had not planned to stay through the entire meeting but had to if I was going to meet her, so I joined the circle and for the next twenty minutes watched the group chant. I didn't know I was so conspicuous in my lack of participation until the tzadik rebuffed my thank you afterward and another man in attendance commented on my dumbfoundedness at a future cultural event. I told him I felt it would have been rude to fake it. I asked him if it did anything for him. He laughed and said no.

He carried on and told me he was a retired physician and fascinated with religions so he regularly attended the Divinity School's events. I volunteered I attended BYU for my undergraduate degree, and he responded that a prominent Mormon had been in his Harvard class, a shocking revelation, indeed. While at BYU I heard upon verifiable rumor after rumor that Harvard Medical School never admitted BYU students, and I knew of none in Cambridge. It was just understood no one got in, unlike the law school and business school that overflowed with Mormons. We all knew the medical school had a well known aversion to Mormons, treating anything BYU like a disease, so I didn't bother to ask if his Mormon classmate had attended BYU, as it mattered little to what I already knew about the medical school. After the chanting finally ended, I introduced myself to the girl with the shoulder-length black hair as she gathered her coat. She entertained my approach so, emboldened, I made my move.

—Could I take you out some time?

—How about coffee?

—Great, would love to.

I got her number and we arranged a time to meet for coffee. She wasn't the first to correct my invitation for a date with coffee. I soon caught on and quit asking girls out on dates altogether but invited them for coffee instead. I didn't drink coffee, but I was a hell of lot more successful, not to mention it was easier, at asking a girl to get some than for a date.

When Nicholas informed me of his move to Cambridge I immediately said he could stay with me until he found a place to live. I informed him that Cambridge's single ward, which I had attended on a couple occasions, included many local Mormons, and I was sure that, through the ward, he would find living arrangements that worked. I had not contemplated what I would need to host him. I was short an extra pillow and blanket and, to make things worse, I had to run a fan to drown out his snoring. He was as kind after my abuse as he had been graceful flying through the air, and quickly made arrangements to stay with another friend the next day. I appreciated fully what I had done some time after, reflecting on when I re-invited him to stay as he was leaving and he sighed heavily and said no thank you. I had felt bad since he departed, so I took the visit at the vegetarian restaurant as a positive sign he hadn't held my inexcusable indifference toward him against me. Walking home I reviewed my advice and realized I had probably failed him again, encouraging him to pursue a relationship he seemed so reluctant to. But I didn't beat myself up because I had one very important thing going for me, he would not follow my advice: he knew me.

I arrived in Cambridge wearing a baby blue windbreaker, complaining of a hurt back. The pain was intense in the lower ridge running over my left buttock but my back problems in whole started before my summer at the steel mill. My upper back had been bothering me for years, since high school. I knew only one relief, a solid bed. I entered my first apartment in Beckwith Circle off Beacon Street in Somerville on the Cambridge border, walking into the room straight ahead of me with an old hard bed frame inches above the floor, and I gladly accepted it, and when I moved to the house on Central Street I bought a new twin mattress, double thick and firm, within minutes lying atop it, having experienced nothing approaching its comfort in my young life, truly believing I knew heaven every second spent on it. And I spent as much time as possible on it. As soon as I got home I lay on it whether I was tired or not. It became my best place to read. I was incredulous that life could be so good, looking up from it.

Within days of arriving in Cambridge, classmates confirmed they were as smart as I expected them to be, and by semester's end I learned professors were hesitant to point out intellectual disparities I had apparently missed—though none known to me other than my own. I was happy they awarded everyone with at least a B. I got a lot of Bs. I wrote many C papers and tests, with some dipping below, so I didn't mind a lick that grade inflation was the norm. An A was tough to come by, but that was never my goal, passing my classes was. For two years I fed my endless curiosities, swimming in seas of ideas. I would have taken every class and read every book but I didn't have near the stamina and, no offense to the book-gods, there wasn't the time. I decided I would study the world's religions and stuck to my plan, resisting the recurring temptation each semester to take philosophy and theology classes. My only exception was including Christian history in my study of world religions. I knew bits and pieces of Christianity: familiar with the New Testament and the great falling away from the truth after the death of the apostles, otherwise known as the Great Apostasy, which made the restoration of the priesthood and true Church of Jesus Christ so necessary through Joseph Smith. Naturally I struggled to justify spending time and money on a familiar topic, however partially familiar it was to me. But upon some reflection, measuring past two seconds, I figured I did not know anything about it so included it in my plan.

I made a couple other exceptions, including a course on psychology and religion. I expected an overtly critical course but to my surprise the readings were mostly favorable, none more than Paul Tillich's *Dynamics of Faith*. Tillich's short classic was a thunderbolt over a hundred and some pages, best taken slowly with crumpets and tea. At BYU, Kierkegaard introduced me to a viable relation to God through his leap of faith and at Harvard Divinity, Tillich explained concretely what that faith was and what it was not. I chose his work that correctly defined faith and critiqued idolatrous faiths as the subject of my final term paper. Choosing to write about it provided me the opportunity to reread the book and to apply it to my Mormon religion.

In his little classic, Tillich proposed that faith was being in a state of ultimate concern. He suggested there were a number of things humans were ultimately concerned about, such as success and nationalism. Tillich was German; he didn't have to say much to make the point that nationalism could be an ultimate concern. He fled Germany as a young man and wrote his classic in the 1950s, not long after the horrific past of Hitler's Third Reich. All ultimate concerns were a form of faith. However, true faith was concerned with the infinite God and all other concerns were idolatrous faiths. Tillich argued nothing defined one's religious personality more than one's ultimate concern. He made a point of distinguishing belief based on some factual claim with a probability the claim was true, from faith that was not a truth-claim about a fact but was a state of being wholly focused on an object with ultimate importance. This was a critical distinction, because he claimed that when most people claimed to have faith in God they meant they had a belief in the truth of scriptures or historical events. He introduced a test for determining if one's faith was idolatrous by examining whether a finite object was considered ultimate. That is to say if one considered anything finite like church or a creed was ultimate (keeping in mind the distinction from having a belief in the probability that church and creeds were true, which was entirely acceptable), then you had yourself an idolatrous faith because only the infinite (God) could be the ultimate concern of true faith.

Like Kierkegaard, Tillich explained that the possibility of faith involved a participation of polarities, where a finite subject restrained by daily experiences encountered an unconditioned object, God and the subject/object framework was overcome by the infinite. He described this experience as the holy, pointing out the holy was a term just as abused as faith, when people mistakenly associated it with moral perfection rather than its appropriate definition of mysterious participation with the infinite (a point at odds with the apostle Paul's understanding of the holy, because Paul clearly held that sexual purity or a high morality identified one as holy in 1 Thess. 4: 3-8; or does Paul play both ways in 2 Cor. 7: 1 where the perfection of holiness comes through reverence, a heightened respect and extreme state of concern?).

Tillich's treatise addressed more fully what was not faith: the intellectual and emotional strains well imbedded in Christian history; additionally he pointed out the long-standing notion that the act of the will as an expression of faith was really an extension of the improper substitution of faith with belief because a person exercising his or her will was a commitment to a belief (again at odds with the apostle Paul who said faith expressed itself through volition, or love, in Gal. 5: 6). Tillich's treatise also addressed the significant roles that symbols and myths had in faith, how the truth of faith measured against scientific and other truths, and the necessary role of the community to a life of faith.

But before all that important stuff he made one point about a necessary component of true faith that banged the cymbal I had not heard save from

Kierkegaard himself. He claimed that doubt was necessary to true faith! He argued that faith associated a finite being turning to the infinite and within that relation, *Faith is uncertain in so far as the infinite to which it is related is received by a finite being. This element of uncertainty in faith cannot be removed, it must be accepted.* In my words, unless you are an infinite being or faking it, your faith will have doubt. K went on and on about despair being the sickness unto death only curable through a leap of faith in the infinite, a fair sampling of which you got a smidgen of, something far from eloquently explicated in the preceding pages. Tillich added that uncertainty cannot be removed because we are finite, with limitations, trying to comprehend an experience of the infinite. Page after page, Tillich's little work was a refreshing wave of true faith in God and confirmation that my faith in a God was valid by the very presence of my uncertainty. All of which led me to the meat and taters of my paper.

I latched onto this idea of necessary uncertainty as part of faith in God to critique my Mormon tradition's understanding of faith, which I conceded in my paper was often interchangeable with the understanding of belief, intellect, emotion, and will. Nevertheless I tarried not, pressing forward by highlighting comments by leaders of my Mormon religion to show doubt's second-class citizenship within it. Aside from its seminal place within the development of Mormon theology, the emergent concept of faith's incompatibility with doubt produces the hallmark of the strong, unyielding Mormon personality. More concisely: Mormons do not doubt.

In the *Journal of Discourses*, the undisputed greatest champion tome in Mormondom, the second great Mormon prophet, Brigham Young, said, *The spirit of doubt is the spirit of the evil one; it produces uneasiness and other feelings that interfere with happiness and peace.* This is not Prophet Young's definitive comment on what faith was, any more than any one of his statements could sum up everything the man ever said, as no one has said more or had more of it recorded, but noting the source of doubt—the devil—was sufficiently relevant to scare me into including it. Additionally, in *Mormon Doctrine*, Mormonism's great codifier, the apostle Bruce R. McConkie argued that doubt—like its sister, skepticism—came from the devil. The devil has not been busier than among the hearts and minds of righteous Mormons. These sensational examples aside, the final example provided the turn-key into the Mormon concept of faith and their religious personality, with the aforementioned nary a touch of doubt.

The definitive statement on the Mormon concept of faith is found in the *Lectures on Faith*. The *Lectures on Faith* are a compilation of seven lectures developed at the School of the Prophets in Kirtland, Ohio, in 1834 and 1835. It is possibly the first document of a systematic attempt at a Mormon theology. If it is not the first, then it clearly is the most rigorous and ambitious. The prophet Joseph Smith led the school, so I naturally give him the lectures' credit as not only its likely principal but its surely presiding prophet, although Mormonism's first intellectual, Sidney Rigdon, likely authored them. For almost a century the Church included the *Lectures* with the Doctrine and Covenants as official scripture accepted by the body of the Church in 1835, until Mormonism's intellectual paragon James E. Talmage headed the decision to remove them early in the twentieth century. This may have been a delayed response to the leadership's direction to B.H. Roberts not to include the King Follett sermon in his multiple-volume official *History of the Church*. The *Lectures'* significance can only be understated, so in lieu of that attempt I provide a brief summary here.

The *Lectures* outlined a roadmap by charting what faith is, the object of faith, and its effects. Lecture First cited the author of the Book of Hebrews to define faith as "the assurance of things hoped for, the evidence of things not seen (11: 1)" and proceeded to explain that faith caused all action in temporal and spiritual matters, showing from scripture that all great things were done by faith. Lecture Second explained God was the object of faith, that Adam conversed with God in the Garden of Eden and maintained knowledge of God after his fall from Eden. The knowledge of God's existence passed from righteous men to their posterity, traceable from Adam to Noah and from Noah to Abraham. Lecture Third explained that the foundation of faith was the idea that God existed, a correct understanding of God's character, and the proper life consistent with God's will, maintaining that a correct understanding of God was necessary to exercise faith commensurate with salvation and eternal life. Lecture Fourth expanded on this necessary connection between a correct understanding of God and the exercise of faith in God, explaining six of God's attributes: knowledge; faith or power; justice; judgment; mercy; and truth. Lecture Fifth explained the Godhead, the Father, Son, and Holy Spirit, stating the Father and Son were separate personages and they possessed the same mind, which was the Holy Spirit. Lecture Sixth addressed having an assurance that one's life was in accordance with God's will, and shared the truest tenet of the Mormon religion. If one phrase accurately summarizes Mormonism, it comes from Lecture Sixth, section seven: "a religion that does not require the sacrifice of all things never has power sufficient to produce the faith necessary unto life and salvation" (6: 7). Finally, Lecture Seventh expounded upon the effects of true faith, from moving mountains and pleasing God to becoming more like God and gaining salvation.

For the purpose of my paper, the *Lectures* also demonstrated doubt's incompatibility with faith. In Lecture Third, doubt was the result of an improper understanding of God's character (3: 20); Lecture Fourth noted there was no room for doubt when justice was properly associated with God (4: 13); Lecture Sixth shared the ringer that those who fail to sacrifice were not on the proper course of exercising faith and subsequently would have doubt, concluding that doubt and faith could not exist in the same person (6: 12). But doubt had existed in me at my most active and faithful when I considered God and salvation. My precarious place welcomed Tillich with open arms.

But highlighting doubt's dirty place within Mormonism did not reach the top ten list of significant threads in the seven lectures. While some Mormon authorities maintained the *Lectures*' official place as scripture, such as apostle McConkie, most Mormons, including Mormon authorities, could not tell you a snippet from them save the line from the sixth lecture quoted above. The reason is the *Lectures* show the evolution of Mormon theology and Mormons focus on the latest and the greatest—the direct result of their belief in modern and continual revelation—which the *Lectures* are not. They mark a mid-point in Mormonism's early history, sitting a decade and half after Joseph Smith had his First Vision of God the Father and Jesus Christ the Son, and a little less than a decade before Joseph Smith declared God's finite character and humans' potential to be Gods in the King Follett sermon.

Some noteworthy markers include Lecture Second's explanation of God's omnipotence, omnipresence and omniscience and being without beginning or end (2: 2), and Lecture Third pointing out that God does not change nor could any variance be found within him (3: 15), and if he was changeable, people would doubt him (3: 21). God was from everlasting to everlasting [or infinite] (3: 19). The Mormon theologians from B.H. Roberts to Sterling McMurrin had no choice but to ignore the theology in the *Lectures* because they have far more in common with the Hellenistic God of traditional Christianity, as codified in their Creeds, than with the finite, embodied God that Joseph Smith settled on in the Follett sermon.

And while I'm on the topic of what Roberts and McMurrin ignored, I should mention the Book of Mormon, also ignored likely because it shared an understanding of God aligned with the *Lectures* (for example, the great King Benjamin's Omnipotent Lord who reigned from "all eternity to all eternity" in Mosiah 3: 5; and the prophet Abinadi clarifying God the Father and the Son where one God in Mosiah 15: 4; and I would be remiss if I didn't mention this Trinitarian view was consistent with Joseph Smith's translation of the Bible, where he corrected Luke 10: 22 and 1 Timothy 2: 4 by adding the Son is the Father and they are one God). But even God's Hellenistic roots were not the most candid disclosures.

Lecture Second also explained that the principle of preserving knowledge of God's existence through human testimony of righteous men ensured no need for a new revelation, to man, of the God (2: 44), and Lecture Fifth revealed the whopper that God was a personage of spirit (5: 2)—not embodied—and the third member of the Godhead was not the Holy Ghost but the Holy Spirit, which was the same minds of the Father and the Son, which same mind humans could also possess, growing "grace to grace" to become joint heirs with Christ (5: 2).

These propositions could not be at greater odds with the official Mormon understanding about revelation and God's form. Revelation is ongoing, in a very big way. For Mormons, God and Jesus and the Holy Ghost are all separate, the first two have bodies and the second is a personage of spirit. And the idea that they are the same by having the same minds smells awful close to their same wills being the basis of unifying the trinity of historical Christianity. Hence, little chance of any coincidence that Mormonism's brightest member, apostle Talmage, removed the *Lectures* from the canon of Mormon scripture.

I did not explain any of this in my paper despite its all being relevant to the correct understanding of God it purported to provide, which Joseph Smith proceeded to contradict later in life, which miraculously, aided by heaps of ignorance, informs the unbreakable, impenetrable, and unyielding Mormon personality inculcated within the Mormon Church today.

What I did was sufficiently demonstrate that Mormons endorsed a different true faith than Tillich, but I did not demonstrate theirs was idolatrous. And how could I? Explaining that Mormons were not concerned with the ultimate of ultimates was like telling a purveyor of pastries his customers would never be filled. But of course they could and they would! Mormons did not need Tillich's faith any more than they needed a calorie chart, because they had revelation. Yes, revelation tended to come in finite forms, but Tillich never said snippets of the divine were idolatrous. Joseph Smith had seen God in the spring of 1820. And he was not infinite (despite the *Lectures*). He was an embodied man (more in spite of the *Lectures*). The Mormon God was more like Professor Xavier of the X-Men to the tenth power. Xavier had incredible powers, but he was at the top because of his overwhelming knowledge of mutant powers, not because he possessed them all. Similarly, the Mormon God was not himself all power, but had knowledge of all eternal principles, and that's why Mormons would unanimously agree he was omniscient. And His Holy Spirit made his omnipresent.

In the *Lectures*, Principal Smith noted in Lecture First that *Faith was the first principle in revealed religion* and supported his proposition with seven lectures about that revelation which was God. Mormons do not have an ultimate concern about something they do not know about, or something invisible as suggested by the creeds and contradicted by Joseph Smith's First Vision (later contradicting himself by lecture 6: 2, which stated God was invisible), so their task is not to be concerned about the infinite; rather their task is to obey the divine laws from that revealed God (extraordinarily in concert with the *Lectures* and all Mormon doctrines). Mormons experience the holy in finite forms, at worship in temples to weekly family home evenings. The holy takes all forms, thus removing the wall between the supernatural and the profane. Why would someone in his right mind be concerned with something more than the slice of Godiva Double Chocolate Cheesecake in front of him? The role of obedience, not concern, underscores all Mormons' understanding and expressions of faith. In my words, for Mormons there's no faith without faithfulness, because their faith presupposes a God revealed to Joseph and the Church's prophets. Tillich's did not presuppose the same revealed God.

But Tillich's explanation of faith blew me down not because it offered an alternative to the revealed God and his subsequent revealed laws that deafened my ability to think and act, which they did, but for its enabling uncertainty. I had not only lived a life of K's doubt but whenever I contemplated the possibility of God I ended in a mixture of emotion and thought of something including it. I had chalked that element up to making me a more effective Mormon missionary, able to genuinely entertain others' views, and it had been a key to my personal development, allowing for an increase in understanding and belief in my ability to think—whether the ability was actual or not, the belief counted for something helpful. Mormons' faithfulness led them to perfection, and I would not contend their goal could be any greater without unfairly misrepresenting them. Yet mine had always been more modest, as my faith in the undefined (unrevealed) possible expanded my abilities—or my belief in my abilities—to understand and to appreciate the endless variety of information and experiences I luckily stumbled upon and learned about from others.

CHAPTER 27

THE TRUE CHURCH

Shored up in my doubt, I embarked on enjoying a smörgåsbord of knowledge at Harvard Divinity. I was not naïve enough to think my graduate studies paralleled Nicholas's dancing, but I had at least discovered my own ballet and could see the road I would have to be committed to leap about, inches here and awkwardly there. The cocktail of K and Tillich allowed me to breathe deeply on a pavement of uncertainty—somehow without any understanding how—acting as the catalyst to having genuine experiences. I didn't think for a second my Mormon counterparts were not having genuine experiences on the yellow brick road to celestial bliss, but those experiences had a solidifying effect, making more concrete and formidable their decisions and paths, which did not suit me even at my most faithful. I also recognized the benefit of their certainty in the face of life's great disappointments. But these certainties were not fuel for life, and cut me off from what was.

What was the endless variety of experiences offered me vital perspectives of life and fresh breaths of it. The tradeoff was being more vulnerable to life's disappointments, yet the very exposure provided something more authentic than the buffer of certainties allowed.

For Mormons, the glory of God is knowledge or, I've heard it said, intelligence, and for me knowledge was always something experienced, or empirical, or more accurately memorized. In other words, knowledge was something achieved through processes, experience of listening, studying, reading and memorizing, more memorizing, a lot more reading, some writing and a lot of rewriting. Not a process like an abstract algorithm triggered in my noggin. More like an algorithm with variables in motion in real time, combining to form a new plateau of information with a sore ass from so much sitting. Knowledge was something far more remembered than applied, though I tried to store up and use all kinds. If I could claim any peek at real knowledge at Harvard Divinity School, it came during my study of early Christianity.

And the seed was planted a couple years earlier over beer and pizza with my brothers in Salem, Oregon. Five brothers loaded into my Saturn to drive from Salt Lake City to the Willamette Valley to visit Jami and his wife and their newborn daughter. They lived in a two-bedroom apartment within a short drive of Willamette University's campus, where Jami attended law school. We watched *Monty Python and the Holy Grail* (1975) on many prior occasions, like many well adjusted Mormons, but during this visit we upgraded to the British troupe's more ribald *The Meaning of Life* (1983), accompanied with party favors most Mormons did not have. After ordering many large cheap pizzas, and a critical run to the local party store for whatever beer was on display, we popped in the classic and thoroughly enjoyed ourselves. The visit was conceived around this very gut-wrenching event. But Jami also wanted to introduce us to his greatest discovery during law school, the Dover Thrift Edition. At a dollar each, he bought classic after classic and insisted he read a most humorous find from one of antiquity's greats. He wielded the thin Dover over us and read:

> Prometheus, for that tongue of yours which talked so high and haughty: you are not yet humble, still you do not yield to your misfortunes, and you wish, indeed to add some more to them; now, if you follow me as a schoolmaster you will not *kick against the pricks*, seeing that he, the King, that rules alone, is harsh and sends accounts to no one's audit for the deeds he does.

In Aeschylus' *Prometheus Bound*—one of the great Greek myths about Prometheus's stealing fire from the Gods for humans and suffering the punishment of having his liver eaten anew every day—Prometheus was counseled in the excerpt above to relent, which he never did, and it contained a phrase we all knew from the account of Paul's conversion in The Acts of the Apostles. Our father had pointed out Paul's futility *to kick against the pricks* more often than we could shake a stick at. And here was Prometheus being told the same thing centuries before Paul. The phrase stuck in my craw and the final term paper in the early Christianity course provided the perfect opportunity to scratch it.

During the course I learned a bundle of history about Christianity's beginnings. That the history of Christianity during the first couple centuries after the life of Jesus consisted of many different Christianities did not surprise me one lick. Of course there were many groups, because early Christians were left to follow the remnants of the true Church that Christ set up during his life that was lost with the deaths of the apostles. The loss led to a great falling away prophesied in one of the epistles of Paul. That was a significant reason why the prophet Joseph Smith was called to restore the true Church of Christ. What I was less informed about was the idea that many of Jesus' early disciples claimed to set up true but different "churches." Of course my father's affection for Paul probably influenced my interest in Paul's efforts to found churches above the other apostles. And Paul was all the more attractive because so much of what he accomplished was recorded in his letters included in the New Testament.

I learned that the history of early Christianity was not so much about the loss or survival of the one Christianity as it was about different Christianities trying to preserve their views of Jesus, with a combination of them winning out in the early part of the fourth century under the Roman emperor Constantine. A bunch of competing Christianities was news to me, but everyone in the class probably knew this history, especially my Catholic classmates who traced their membership to the winning team in Rome. Mormons were keen to point out that only two Christian religions could really claim to be the true Church of Jesus Christ: the Catholics' because they traced their tradition to the authority of the apostle Peter, or the Mormons' because Peter appeared to Joseph Smith and restored the proper priesthood to him. And Mormons won because the truth was lost, necessitating that Peter come back. But I was keen to realize news of multiple Christianities with varying messages of the meaning of Jesus' life tipped the scale to the Protestants, and in particular the Evangelicals who truncated tradition down to deal directly with the New Testament.

While all that stuff about the truest tradition fascinated me some, it did not grab my attention nearly as much as the texts of the early Christians. Many of these texts were included in the New Testament, but none of the early Christians had the New Testament since it was put together a couple centuries after Jesus' death. Out of the many different scriptures read by the early Christians, one of my favorites ended up in the New Testament, The Acts of the Apostles. The book of Acts was, in fact, a history of early Christians. I preferred its narrative format, highlighting important events like the day of Pentecost, and dramatic meetings between the early apostles. But I most enjoyed the story of its hero, the apostle Paul. Of all the apostles to write about, Acts' author recorded the life of Paul, arguably the most important Christian.

Jesus may have been the founding figure of Christianity, but he was Jewish through and through. He taught "the way," a version of Judaism, not a new religion. He taught a biblical religion on steroids: you had to love God, your neighbor and your enemies (Matt. 5: 44)! Jesus taught you went to heaven when you treated a stranger kindly as if you were treating him, and you would be going to hell if you failed to treat a stranger kindly because that would be the same as failing to treat him with kindness (Matt. 25: 32-46). The righteous will not even know they had been treating God with kindness! There is no semblance or remnant of this unknowing salvation in what developed into Christianity. Paul was chief among those who established that you get to Heaven by actually knowing the true meaning of Jesus and by accepting Jesus' sacrifice. But I digress.

The highlight of Paul's story I had known my whole life. He persecuted Christians until one day, while he was traveling on the road to Damascus, Jesus appeared to him and asked why Paul insisted on persecuting him, proceeding to tell Paul to knock it off and to fulfill a greater mission as a witness of Jesus to bring forgiveness to others. Subsequently this vision converted Paul to Christianity, inspiring him to dedicate his life to setting up churches throughout the ancient cities of the Mediterranean, and to teaching these new converts the true gospel of Jesus.

According to the author of the book of Acts, Jesus also told Paul to quit *kicking against the pricks.* Believing I was clearly onto something from my last Monty Python marathon, I proposed a paper about the phrase to my roommate, Will, who encouraged me to propose the paper to the professor before I started. So I did. One of Will's many degrees was in early Christianity, and he assured me if my paper had merit my professor would know it.

I set up an appointment with the professor's secretary because Harvard professors saw students only by appointment. At the appointed time I knocked on his office door. He warmly received me with a strong European accent.

—Come in. Sit down. Tell me about your paper topic?

—I want to trace the literary history of a key phrase in the vision Paul had of…

—Do you read Greek?

—No.

—You must learn Greek. It's the most beautiful language in the world.

—I studied Latin…

—Latin is fine. Greek is beautiful. You must learn it.

—I could hardly read Latin after years studying it, and many people have told me Greek is harder than Latin.

—Latin is fine. Greek is so beautiful and you must learn. Tell me about this phrase.

—Well, my roommate Will told me you would know if it was a legitimate phrase.

—Yes, Will is very good student. Let me see.

He rose from his chair and pulled a book from a shelf.

—Yes, it occurs in the authoritative text. You can proceed.

Phew. Will had gone on about how my research would be meaningless if the phrase was not in the Alexandrian manuscript because it would have been a clear innovation of later scribes of the Byzantine manuscript of the New Testament. These two manuscripts, heretofore unknown to me, were the sources for all translations of the New Testament, and most scholars accepted the Alexandrian manuscript as the older of the two, and developed by scribes who were far superior and more scrupulous than the later Byzantine blokes. The distinction between authoritative manuscripts was Greek to me, but I appreciated the importance of my professor's positive response and its being in concert with Will's opinion. Because it was far from me to participate in meaningless research of empty clichés, I began to execute my plan.

I knew I needed, first, to trace the history of the Greek phrase *kicking against the pricks* in ancient Greek literature and, second, to review what scholars had said about the phrase—including whether they said anything about the phrase appearing in Acts—and what scholars said about the influence of Greek literature on Acts. The search to find the answers of a term paper was my favorite part of writing one, because it did not actually include writing the paper. It included a detective's sense of poring over text after text. I prized myself as a good reader. I had no illusions of being a good writer. But even as a good reader I faced an initial challenge beyond me. I did not read Greek.

—It's not that big a deal, although you should learn Greek. Even a lot of New Testament scholars know just enough to get by, Will said.

—How is it not a big deal?

—There are resources for you to trace words and phrases, like indexes in the backs of your modern scholarship. So what you do is go to the library and ask for a popular concordance of classic Greek literature.

—What is that exactly?

—If they don't know at the library, they shouldn't be working there. They'll find it. Tell them about your paper topic, and they'll probably get excited and go out of their way to help you.

Will's words were true to form. He was one of the minority of classmates who held firm traditional beliefs in God. And, as a Catholic, he was among the oppressed under the liberal banners of the Divinity School. But he was also among those shamed by the failures of Cardinal Bernard Francis Law over the past couple of decades, while Law served as the archbishop of the archdiocese of Boston. Law would resign by the time we graduated. Priest jokes at the div school were slightly more plentiful than lawyer jokes at the Law School, even told by a few Catholic classmates, but not when Will was around.

Priests had basically raised him during an unhappy childhood deep in the cold of Maine, and he would permit no universal branding of all priests with Law's failures. On multiple occasions, even sober, Will and I had argued about God for hours. I loved his tenacity about all things theological. However, I could recall just a few others like myself who had accepted a theological duel and still considered him a friend after being nearly slain during it. He spared no one the unveiling of the weaknesses of his or her position. As consolation for surviving our debates, one day discussing our favorite books, he encouraged me to read *A Supposedly Fun Thing I'll Never Do Again* by David Foster Wallace. You'll love him, Will said, giving an introduction like others had to their favorite authors, the best of lasting urgings.

My library investigations bore many riches. I learned that the phrase appeared throughout many important ancient Greek texts, including one by the greatest of Greek playwrights, and so would be the key to unlocking the true meaning of Paul's conversion according to the author of Acts. I also learned that no scholars—within the scope of my review—had explained the phrase within the context of Paul's Christian mission. That meant I was sitting on a scholar's golden egg. Finally, I learned that scholars had a lot to say about the author of the book of Acts, who showed a familiarity with themes and formulas from Greek literature and a convincing ability to imitate the style and patterns of classical Greek writers. I piled jewels upon jewels in a treasure trove of supporting material for my paper. But the granddaddy of all finds was a benign book about the education system of the ancient Greek and Roman world. The book provided external support of what literate people in the ancient world read, buttressing the internal support within the text that the author of the book of Acts knew the literary history of the classic phrase, the importance of which I was convinced his contemporary readers would not have missed.

Teresa Morgan's *Literate Education in the Hellenistic and Roman Worlds* turned my thesis from conjecture into as firm a proposition as I could ask for. She demonstrated that, throughout the ancient world, educational models included the works of Homer and the great Greek tragedians. Extant educational writings, many of them fragments, showed models that relied most often upon Homer and the next most popular was, drum roll please, the greatest playwright of antiquity, Euripides! That is to say, the whole slew of literate people in the ancient world learned to read and write studying Euripides (and Homer; and then from lesser greats like Sophocles and Aeschylus). You can't imagine my delight having Morgan's work remove any question whether the educated writer of the Acts and his Greek readers had read Euripides. Of course they had, because they had to read him to learn to write and to read. End of speculation. I didn't need to mention all the New Testament scholars' works, including my own instructor Francois Bovon's, that showed the author of the Acts clearly demonstrated a sophistication of Greek style far above those of any other writers included in the New Testament, but of course I did, citing many big names within New Testament studies I had never heard of save one, Professor Bovon, who not only got a book mentioned but also a comment he made in a lecture, though I expected my praise of him wouldn't get past his teaching fellow who would read and grade the paper. Of course I didn't need any of this support from Morgan to Bovon because I planned to prove not only the Acts' author's awareness of Greek literature but also his engagement of it, by examining evidence within the text.

During my research I often walked up the steps to the front door of the Widener Library, opened it and flashed my student ID card for free passage into its book stacks. Harvard had as many libraries as BYU had student chapels (I never mentioned that BYU had student chapels because it didn't as such; student wards met in large lecture halls and classrooms on campus; BYU church classrooms didn't have the zing I was looking for), maybe more libraries including all the niche ones at departments, student houses, and in professors' quarters. I found every book that came up during my online topic searches in one of Harvard's libraries. I knew I had a real find when the book had to be retrieved from storage off-site. On an expedition into Widener I headed to the special collections, having reserved one particularly important book. I had to feel the great playwright Euripides' work that shed a bright light onto Paul's conversion. I approached the student behind the desk and requested my reservation.

—There are tables to sit at to read through those doors, she said.

—Thanks.

I held a copy of *The Bacchanals*. I thumbed through its pages looking at all the Greek characters. They looked more like Chinese characters than letters of the English alphabet. I ran my fingers down pages until I arrived at the one with my phrase. It matched my notes written on the crumpled paper reaching off the table, which I mashed back into my coat pocket. I closed the covers of the ancient text and returned it.

And then I had to write the damn thing. I spent the last month of each semester gathering books and articles that would be the sources for my final term papers. I then wrote the papers during the dead week before finals. My papers suffered from having an author ill-equipped to persuasively use the English language, and also short on aptitude to construct a convincing argument, but these handicaps hardly stopped me from trying.

I allocated each day between the last day of class and my first final to writing or studying, and I generally did mighty fine sticking to the plan. I locked myself in my room with books with pages marked and notes with quotations and page citations scattered around the floor, and I began typing. I drank cola after cola as the first page turned into ten or a prolific twenty by the end of the appointed day. If I had a couple hours left over, I'd reread it and upon rereading, if I was not too demoralized by its needs, I'd rewrite parts. The next day it would be due, and I'd deliver it on time. I knew papers needed more attention, but figured my peers were up against the same constraints, not enough time to rewrite, with other pressing papers and exams to move on to, hoping some occupied the aptitude space with me at the bottom of the class. And unless the paper really stank, I'd at least get an inflated B grade.

The magnitude of my paper, titled, "The Futility of Resisting Divinity: Euripides' Contribution to Paul's Conversion Story in Acts" relied heavily on a background I did not provide in it. Two large pieces of that background were the history of the Olympian god Dionysus' religion and the influence of that religion on the Greek tragedian tradition. The Dionysian religion had been around about one thousand and five hundred years when the author of the Acts started writing his definitive work on the early Christians. Dionysus represented religious ecstasy, among other things, and the Greek theater tradition began in celebration of the great life force attributed to Dionysus in the sixth century Before Common Era (BCE). This same great tradition of Greek theatre, as erudite patrons or Britons would write it, came to an end during the sixth century Common Era (CE), when Christianity outlawed it. All of which a professor of Christianity worth her salt would know.

During the course of my research, I learned that some scholars argued the early writers of Christian texts were responding directly to the God Dionysus. They pointed out big themes and similarities, such as that Dionysus had been resurrected, his followers believed they actually ate his body in his honor, and committing oneself to his worship was the beginning of a new life. All of these themes became associated with Jesus as the Christ in the beliefs and rituals of his Christian followers. All these scholars pointed out the first miracle Jesus performed would have resonated with the followers of Dionysus, when Jesus attended a wedding and turned water into wine—because Dionysus was the god of the vineyard, effectively making the statement whatever Dionysus could do Jesus could too. None of these themes had anything to do with my paper so I didn't mention them.

During the comparison of translations of Euripides' *The Bacchanals*, I gained what I believed was incontrovertible insight into how specific ideas, often shared among various texts, took on the life of a universal theme assumed to exist outside the texts themselves.

During research of ancient texts, I searched for a translation I could easily understand. But generally a more readable translation was not a literal one. William Arrowsmith's translation of *The Bacchanals* proves this point. It clearly makes sense, allowing the reader to follow the development and tensions of the story. I recommend it above all others. But the more readable the translation, often the more significant the trade-offs. During the scene between King Pentheus and Dionysus, which I developed in my paper, Arrowsmith translated the phrase under investigation by its implied meaning and not the actual phrase, or literal words. According to Arrowsmith, Dionysus, in disguise, told Pentheus, "If I were you, I would offer him [Dionysus] a sacrifice, not rage and *kick against necessity, a man defying God.*" That translation highlighted a theme that might have very well proved useful to the scholars hell-bent on showing Christianity's reaction to the religion of Dionysus. It was clearly what the phrase meant, on the scale of a great theme fit for a great term paper title. I aimed to uncover its meaning, too, but by tracing the literal words through ancient Greek literature with attention on how the author of the Acts used it.

I began my paper pointing out that Paul shared his vision of Jesus in his epistles recorded in the New Testament. In those instances Paul stated that Jesus spoke, but in none of those instances did Paul record that Jesus instructed Paul to quit *kicking against the pricks*. That occurred only in the versions recorded by the author of the Acts. As an aside, I noted the phrase occurred in the Alexandrian manuscript so that my erudite readers knew it was legitimate, but then noted the phrase appeared multiple times in the Byzantine manuscript (the basis for the King James Version of the Bible). What New Testament scholars might have identified as a slight innovation, I proposed was the result of a well-read scribe who picked up on the author of the Acts' uses of it and decided it was worth repeating.

The phrase existed as far back as the sixth century BCE in the writings of the Greek poet Pindar. Pindar used it to show the futility of contending with God, as did those who used it after him. The first great Greek playwright, Aeschylus, used the phrase in his masterwork *Agamemnon* and his aforementioned *Prometheus Bound*. By the fourth century CE, the Emperor Julian used it, referring to it as a "common proverb," which was how modern New Testament scholars I cited in my paper had referred to it. The multiple uses of the phrase in the works of the most prolific of all Greek playwrights fired up my enthusiasm. Parts of nineteen of the ninety plays written by Euripides exist today, and the phrase appeared in four of those nineteen, which led into my paper's primary exhibit of *The Bacchanals*. (Dionysus was also known as Bacchus, the accepted term in Rome; the transliterations from the Greek being Dionysos and Bakkhos.)

The Bacchanals was not what a reader might expect. Surely it would be about the religion of Dionysus filled with cultic celebrations of ecstasy in nature inspiring people to embrace it. Indeed, it had doses of the maddening life-force with wild dancing in dense forests and was graphic enough to scare all its readers into being Goodman Browns. But it was really about revenge and the aftermath of a vengeful God's acts.

Dionysus' mother was a mortal pregnant with the son of Zeus, but her family ridiculed her, disbelieving her claim of a divine father. When she convinced Zeus to prove he was the father, his glory killed her (precedent that no mortal could see god and live), but before the baby Dionysus was destroyed, Zeus saved him. Euripides' play told the story of Dionysus' purpose to see the family of his mother pay for her death, and pay they did.

The play began with Dionysus, in disguise as a prophet of the god Dionysus, returning to his mother's homeland. Playing the prophet, he had great success among his mother's family, stirring up fervor for the Dionysian religion. All his success enraged his cousin, the King Pentheus, who openly despised Dionysus. Pentheus ordered the capture and imprisonment of this prophet responsible for religious excitement in his realm, and his attendants brought Dionysus before the King. The two beautiful cousins sparred with sharp words, with Pentheus tiring of the superior Dionysus, ordering him bound and taken to prison. In short order the palace crumbled to the ground, and Dionysus emerged before Pentheus. After another volley of words, Dionysus convinced Pentheus to disguise himself to enter the forest to witness the frenzy of Dionysus' followers, among whom was Pentheus' mother Agave. Then during the wild rituals Dionysus revealed Pentheus' presence. The women tore Pentheus apart, stringing parts of his body throughout the forest. Later Pentheus' mother Agave learned of the tragedy in which she played a central part and, overcome with grief, recognized *Now I see: Dionysus has destroyed us all* (Arrowsmith's translation). In the final scene, Dionysus justified the bloody destruction because so many had blasphemed against him. Agave responded by addressing her father with her farewell, planning to leave the country with her sisters, declaring she also would leave the religion of bacchanals to others. This was no story to drum up converts to the religion of Dionysus.

So to the point: during the scene after the palace fell, Dionysus counseled King Pentheus *to make supplication instead of being all upset, kicking against the pricks, hellbent on defying the God Dionysus* (my interpretation of various English translations, which I would not have dared render in my paper, so I do here).

In my paper I connected *The Bacchanals* to the Acts based on five indisputable proofs, go ahead and try to dispute them, within the text. First, I explained the parallels between the liberation accounts of Peter (Acts 12: 6-10) and Paul (16: 25-26) to Dionysus's liberation in *The Bacchanals*. Second, I returned to the work of Professor Bovon, who identified a Greek literary submission model in Acts 21—indirect proof that complements later proofs. Third, I compared the "murderous threats" against the Disciples of Christ by Paul in Acts 9: 1 to the threats against Dionysus.

Then I got to the heart of my paper with proof number four: when Jesus appeared to Paul, he told Paul the things I've already mentioned, including the same thing Dionysus told Pentheus, *quit kicking against the pricks*. But unlike all of Paul's literary precedents, Paul did not keep kicking against divinity. He realized its futility and submitted, which turn in Greek literature was a masterful invention by the author of the Acts. The God of Christianity got his converts and could not be a clearer contrast to the popular Greek god Dionysus, who didn't. Instead of fighting against god like Pentheus and the great characters in Greek literature before him, or turning away from religion as Agave did, Paul and other early converts turned to Christ, the new god of the Christians. I learned much later this model of submission had a precedent in flood myths in the ancient Near East where heroes resisted floods up until the Hebrew version with the hero Noah who submitted, dutifully following God's directions to build his ark. Noah's precedent was also marked by receiving credit as the father of the vineyard, a much earlier attempt to trump Dionysus, the god of wine. I'm left wondering if a phrase didn't connect them.

But I promised five proofs and you've read only four, so without fanfare, five you will have. The author of the Acts reached the climax of the record of the apostle Paul during the trip to Athens, not only the intellectual nexus, epicenter, heart, and Mecca of the ancient world, but also the heart of the religion of Dionysian religion. At Athens, the author of the Acts rested his case. During the visit Paul made two converts to Christianity, one of whom was the most prominent convert in Christian history. This convert was a member of the highest legal court in Athens, the Areopagus, where gods themselves were revered to have sat in council. No convert could have been more revered in Greek culture. And this convert's name was Dionysius (Διόνυσιος). One "i" different in Latin and only one character "ι" removed from Dionysus (Διόνυσος) in the original Greek, a subtlety that carried the weight of a hammer. The author of the Acts and its readers knew from centuries of literature it was futile to resist divinity, but after the Acts they knew the value of submitting to it, and chief among them who learned was the most well-known ancient god believing in the new one of Christianity.

I sat in a chair on the front row of the Sperry Room. I had attended many lectures in the renowned lecture room but never in a seat on the front row. It was in Andover Hall, the main building housing classes for the Divinity School. All kinds of luminaries had entered there. I walked by the Sperry Room during a lecture by Huston Smith, a pioneer scholar of a comparative study of world religions, where students lined the walls and covered the floor. When I sat in a front row I had the row almost to myself to hear a former Dean of BYU's Religious Instruction Department give a talk about why Mormons were Christians. My roommate James, who focused on American religions, also attended. I leaned across a couple seats toward him.

—Why aren't any professors here?

—I asked one if he was coming, but he said the BYU professor wasn't a professor of an academic discipline and hadn't done any scholarship. I guess he did his work in religious education.

—But he's a living Mormon.

—Hey, I made it.

My first roommates at the div school were the equivalent of the social elite at BYU. They were always going out and when they weren't, they were planning parties to stay in. For one of their first parties they invested in lots of liquor, and when one roommate approached me to pay my share, James interrupted him and said it was fine. I didn't say anything and had something to read, so I left the room. When I stepped back out of my bedroom to head out of the apartment James and my roommate were arguing about my share. James was animated, insisting they wouldn't make a Mormon pay for the party liquor, and they didn't. Not having planned for party liquor in my budget and not having consumed alcohol (never liquor but a lot of Zima) since my BYU freshman year, I marked James for one of those rare ones who actually applied the cultural sensitivity professed by the many, and by a semester later I would raise a glass in his honor.

The BYU professor proceeded to read his paper for the next fifty minutes. He based his thesis that Mormons were Christians on the premises that Jesus Christ founded his church, but the truths Jesus taught, and the divine authority, or priesthood, to act in Christ's name were all lost after the deaths of the apostles. The professor cited the letter of Paul that prophesied of a great falling away from the truth about Jesus, which loss the Mormons called the Great Apostasy. The paper read like a Sunday School lesson about Mormon beliefs. The message was not only that Mormons were Christians but they were the only true Christians because that true Church of Christ was restored through Joseph Smith in the early part of the nineteenth century.

He finished with ten minutes for questions and looked startled that any time remained, having read faster than he had planned. He defensively announced he would take questions. Out of the dozen people scattered in the crowd I noticed a couple of evangelical classmates, who were even rarer than the Catholics at the div school. They asked stock questions about the inerrancy of the Holy Bible and the prohibition in the New Testament on new books like the Book of Mormon. The BYU Professor, pugnaciously disposed, not unlike his sister fundamentalists, answered accordingly. Before time expired, a student in the middle of the room caught the BYU professor's attention, and the professor promptly acknowledged the student's raised hand.

—You talked about the true understanding of Jesus being lost but the Christology you described as being restored through Joseph Smith has existed since the early centuries of Christianity. So my question is what true understanding of Jesus was lost?

I turned my head recognizing the voice of the Ph.D. candidate Philip.

—Well, I'm not a scholar of Christian history so I can't answer that question.

My jaw dropped. I was certain I correctly heard him. He did not only punt, he took off his pads, threw them down and left the playing field. Beside myself, I thought to yell, "before you take off your jockstrap, get back on the field to go for a fricking tackle." Don't let Philip get away with that shite.

Philip was terribly likable, had a stellar reputation, everyone I knew admired him, and I was no exception. He was friendly and as articulate as anyone moving in div school circles. He completed a master's degree at the Divinity School before embarking on his doctoral program at the Graduate School of Arts and Sciences, and he still spent most of his time at the div school. He had been a teaching fellow for one of my favorite courses about theology and science. That course was taught by a tall, fully-bearded, probably Californian, professor, who unlike most of his colleagues showed up prepared to lecture. He became one of my favorite professors by the end of the course and remained one even after our incidental parley at the end of one class.

—For this writing assignment you each need to do your analysis from a specific tradition? he instructed us.

—Why? Why can't we just write sound analysis? I asked.

Taken back by my retort, he paused and collected himself and continued to defend his instructions. And I disagreed back. To this day I do not recall what the hell was at stake between the differences in our positions, but I was clear on it at the time. I do recall Philip's comment during its midst.

—Actually yesterday's heterodoxy is today's orthodoxy.

—Who's point does that prove? I asked.

At which point my roommate Gallegan, who like Philip spoke an elegant British dialect, patted my arm encouraging me to stop, and upon said patting I did. After that mash-up, I would pass Philip in the hall and we continued to exchange greetings, but thereafter in those same halls I couldn't catch my still favorite, but former, professor's gaze. What killed me was that the professor finished the lecture by making a point about studying a topic by analogy to the Jewish practice of Midrash, and as God is my witness he was not Jewish. Frick, or maybe he was.

That Philip was correct in pointing out that the Christology of Jesus that Mormons espoused was not lost after Jesus' apostles' deaths and before Joseph re-restored it was beside the point, and so was the broader and terribly superficial claim about a Great Apostasy from Jesus' true Church. The great travesty of the former BYU Dean of the Religious Instruction Department was passing on the invitation to argue about the Christology, Jesus' mixture of humanity and divinity. That had to be one of the great classic questions volleyed about the div school, albeit among a mighty small group.

Arguments about God were far from reaching the top-ten list of in-vogue issues at the div school. That list included social justice; exposing oppressive colonial views of the Others (not the Nicole Kidman film but the category for marginalized, non-western traditions); multicultural equality; the saturation of postmodern or deconstructive criticisms; hegemonic obliteration; employing anti-traditional hermeneutic (or interpretive) strategies (which is actually different from the aforementioned criticisms; but, hell, don't take my word for it); decrying capitalism; decrying old white men; encouraging a deluge of opinions, any non-euro-male-centric would do over rational based arguments; and disparaging President George W. Bush. Pertinent topics I took as seriously rhetorically as anyone.

The boat was sailing and I was completely on board with the current discourse. Nothing was more important to academic institutions than maintaining and creating academic jobs and the seas of critical theory did that. And the discourse, at least the last topic, even proved the keystone to a slew of Nobel Prizes awarded to Americans the decade overlapping my stint in Cambridge and extending beyond it. No one I knew at the div school, except for the couple evangelicals and handful of Catholics, even cared that Mormons claimed they were Christians and that explained—not any latent prejudice—why so few people showed up to hear the former dean give his Sunday School lesson. "Sure, you're Christians, good on ya, cheers to ya, here's to hoping that one works out for ya."

The former dean's surrender of there being nothing lost and nothing new about Jesus after the Prophet Joseph Smith restored the true Church of Jesus was not merely representative of Mormonism's relationship to Christianity, it was representative of how Mormons in general don't know anything about Christian history. On this point, there's not a gap from the leaders at the top to the newest converts at the bottom. For Mormons it's sufficient to believe in an essential Christianity that only they have the full story about and to live like a Christian, which living part they do as well as any group on Planet Earth. If you asked for a workable definition of a Christian, many Mormons would cite a malleable proposition supported by brilliant illustration after brilliant illustration from C.S. Lewis, who has been the motherlode for ideas supporting how Mormons are Christians, and which Mormons love to point out that they independently reached long before Lewis espoused his great Christian explication, such as ideas from all religions have bits of the truth to humans' potential being nothing short of becoming gods. Lewis's inclusive ideas not only affirmed many Mormons' belief of Christianity, but also he offered an authoritative seal because he was so damn persuasive at explaining them.

While not many Mormons know dirt about Christian history, most Mormons, if not all, have been predisposed against the Nicene Creed, and against, albeit without much press, the Athanasian Creed. Rehashing, again, the pagan, I mean platonic, fix behind these creeds' inceptions would be fun but unnecessary. Of course, they came out wrong, which we can all admit almost two thousand years later; well, with the exception of a billion believing Christians. If anything marks the falling away from the truth of Jesus or the Great Apostasy, Mormons will tell you it was the Nicene Creed. Ironically, none of them will tell you that the Nicene Council got the key inquiry about Jesus and the Father being coeternal correct, which guided the very outcome of the Nicene Creed, because if Joseph Smith held firmly one theological doctrine it was that all humans, including you and me, were all coeternal intelligences.

The mighty mistake happened, as tradition goes, in Nicaea (present-day Turkey), about three hundred years after the life of Jesus when the brightest Christians dueled over the best understanding of who God is (whether he is one or more than one), and how Jesus compared to God. Tradition has it that the church scholar, Arius, lost the argument when he said God had the most power and Jesus was subordinate to God (Arius' position about God creating Jesus became known as Arianism. Incidentally, Arianism was consistent with the Apostle Paul in 1 Cor. 8: 6; 15: 24-28, where one Lord, Christ the Lord, will hand over the Kingdom to one God, God the Father, and Christ will be subject to the Father; Paul also clearly clarified the superiority of the Father who was worthy of eternal praise in 2 Cor. 11: 31, all of which is the kind of hierarchy that would have made the apostle Bruce R. McConkie giddy).

The victor was another church scholar, Athanasius, who said God and Jesus were the same simple substance (consistent with the writings of Plato's chief disciple Plotinus, who clarified in the third century CE that the highest Good was the absolute, indivisible, formless, and infinite One; Plotinus was chiefly responsible for spiritualizing Plato and Aristotle's metaphysics, or in other words their descriptions of reality, and he rightly gets a lion's share of the credit for creating the trinity of traditional Christianity). About three centuries later, the Athanasian Creed cemented the trinity's reign in Christendom.

The adherents to Athanasius' view in the Roman Church realized the doctrine of the trinity would fare much better among the faithful if it had some foundation in the Bible. It just so happens that the Alexandrian manuscript, the one any New Testament scholar worth her spit considers authoritative, does not have a reference to the trinity. But at some point in Christian history a scrupulous scribe added one to 1 John 5: 7-8. *For there are three that bear record in heaven, the Father, the Word, and the Holy Ghost: and these three are one. And there are three that bear witness in earth, the Spirit, and the water, and the blood: and these three agree in one* (the King James Version). The brouhaha over this invention was front and center before the Christian reading world when Desiderius Erasmus took it upon himself to translate Greek New Testament manuscripts in the early sixteenth century. We consumers of sharp wit know Erasmus for his masterwork, *The Praise of Folly*, but in his own day he was a reputed scholar of the Bible. Before Erasmus, translations of the New Testament were based on the Latin version going back to Jerome, with various wild justifications for affirming a translation (say French) of a translation (the Vulgate) over a translation (say French) from translations in the original language (Greek) eventually going back to the originals. During his paradigm-shifting translation, Erasmus proposed not including 1 John 5: 7-8 because it did not exist in a single one of the Greek manuscripts (in what he had, which was a small sampling of all what had been written; and what he had were not originals but translations of translations of translations and on and on of the originals). But his contemporaries excoriated him for such a suggestion, and in the end he sided with the scribe who added the trinity doctrine to the sacred text.

Cheers to Erasmus for recognizing the value of learned scribes, say a billion Christian worshipers, including the late C.S. Lewis, who made as persuasive an argument for the trinity as he did any aspect of his come-one-come-all blend of Christianity. The Mormons correctly contend that the trinity verses are among the most blatant examples of innovation in the Bible. Dare I say, they would call them "corruptions." They're right that the verses were part of the development of the Christian scriptures (which development Joseph Smith did not correct in his translation of the Bible; rather his aforementioned corrections two-upped the scrupulous scribe for the presence of the trinity in the New Testament).

While largely blind to history, Mormons have openly faced the same challenge to develop a proper view about the hierarchy of gods from Athanasius to the innovative scribe of 1 John 5: 7-8. During the golden age of Mormon thought, spanning the years Britons walked the sandy salt flats along the Great Salt Lake, the highest leadership of the Church authorized a treatise on the doctrine of the Mormon Gods, God the Father and God Jesus: *The Father and the Son* authored by the First Presidency and the Council of the Twelve Apostles and published in 1916. It tackled how the term "Father" applied to Jesus in the Bible and in the Book of Mormon. By the last section of the treatise, who the Father was and if the Father was often the Son as it insisted, was not any clearer than what in Sam Hill Jesus meant when he clearly said he was the beginning and the end (Alpha and Omega), when the treatise insisted God and Jesus had a literal relationship as a Father and a Son. The treatise included the popular Mormon doctrine of "Divine Investiture of Authority," where Jesus acted as the Father, something Jesus did when he acted as Jehovah throughout the Old Testament, for Mormons.

The method of the treatise amounted to a hodgepodge of Biblical and Mormon passages of scripture stitched together in apparent harmony, a common approach to explicating Mormon doctrine. Where the treatise failed on substance, it succeeded brilliantly in taking responsibility for defending its assertions about Jesus' divinity, the kind of effort a former dean of BYU's Religious Instruction Department talking at Harvard should not have failed to make. Tragically, he would not have felt any more to do with it than any of his peers or the Church's leaders, this kind of responsibility as much a part of its forgotten history as the Britons who once fulfilled it.

Mormonism's own challenge to define the divinity of Jesus and God has roots in its beginning, when Joseph Smith, as a fourteen-year-old youth in 1820, saw a God. Joseph's experience is referred to as The First Vision. In the earliest account of this experience, Joseph wrote in his own hand that the Lord appeared to him. A roommate of mine at BYU pointed out for the first time to me in my double-decade-plus life that in this earliest account there was no mention of two personages later described in the official version of Joseph Smith's "History." He, a returned missionary, reported this revelation to me, another returned missionary, in a shared moment of the mother of all flabbergastedness.

—What are you talking about? I said.

—My professor gave us this packet of multiple versions of The First Vision, he said.

—What are you talking about?

—Look, Joseph Smith wrote or dictated multiple versions of The First Vision over the years before he wrote the official version in '38 or '39 before he published it in 1842 in the Wentworth letter.

I knew about the Wentworth letter, as sure as I knew any part of Mormon Church history: it was Joseph's letter to Mr. Someone Wentworth who was an editor of somepaper, somewhere in the Midwest. It was subsequently included in the back of the Book of Mormon with the Pearl of Great Price, as "Joseph Smith History."

—That was written twenty-plus years after Joseph had the vision. He wrote earlier accounts.

—Give me that packet, I demanded as I pulled it from his hands.

—I'll need it back to study for the test, he protested.

If one Mormon would have a sufficient explanation of the various accounts of The First Vision, the greatest Mormon intellectual of all time, Hugh W. Nibley, would. Although he had retired years ago, Nibley kept an office in the Harold B. Lee Library. One afternoon I dared enter his office, and at the counter an old man sat, writing in a notebook. I approached, and an old woman behind and off to the right of the old man lifted her head and smiled. She pointed at the old man.

—Hello, I'd hoped to meet Mr. Nibley.

—Pleased to meet you.

And I smiled.

—What's your major?

—Literature.

—Then you know my daughter?

—Who's she?

—She's very popular among the students. You should take her classes.

And he looked back down and continued writing in the notebook. The old woman behind him turned back around, faintly shrugging and smiling. I smiled back and left the room.

Nibley's legend at BYU was enormous. He was the great defender of Mormonism. No one compared. Anyone with a smidgen of interest in Mormon apologetics knew of him. He spoke many languages and had published many, many books. And I was not disappointed when I found he had, in fact, addressed the multiple versions of The First Vision, sort of. He actually spent an enormous amount of space addressing the detractors of The First Vision. An hour into my review I was so discouraged I couldn't finish his ramblings, still not sure he ever got around to addressing the discrepancies among the versions, sure I didn't want to find out he did only to be let down further.

When Nels L. Nelson and other titans of Mormonism wrote that the truth of Mormonism hinged upon the young boy Joseph seeing an embodied God the Father and an embodied Resurrected Son, the weight of the first account penned by Joseph about seeing the Lord had the same consequence as an anchor sunk to the bottom of the sea. Did Nelson have his man? By the time Joseph wrote his history, subsequently publishing it in the Wentworth letter, he had seen two Gods and one of them said, "Behold, my Beloved Son," and then took the time to clarify that no churches claiming to teach Christianity were true. Nibley's persnickety, sarcastic style rarely provided details relevant to the topic discussed (among the sampling I could bear); his lasting hallmark was the eternal spring from which he bloviated about endless bits of obscure information even his peers could not decipher. I was surprised such a brilliant mind could be so irresponsible and so bloody disappointing. Criticism like this owes a supporting example, but I can't conceive of a redeeming excuse for wasting more of my time, or yours, for the seconds it would take you to read one. But I will attest—with every fiber of my being—you should seek out all true and virtuous books and you will not be led to Nibley's interpretation of the ancient illustrations of the Egyptian Book of the Dead, which also accompanies the Book of Abraham. Your sixth grader could likely offer a more imaginative, and certainly a more accurate, explanation.

But even competent Mormons tackled the multiple versions of the "First Vision," none more accurately than James B. Allen in the essay "The Significance of Joseph Smith's 'First Vision' in Mormon Thought," in *Dialogue: a Journal of Mormon Thought*. None did so more ably than the historian Richard L. Bushman. Bushman explained that Joseph offered an abbreviated version in the earliest account, and provided a fuller but still correct account in the later version, explaining the versions were essentially the same. Bushman might be right that Joseph saved the important details for later. But Joseph declared that, after having the vision in 1820, he proceeded to attest to it and suffered a lot of persecution for it. Does not the integrity of his account depend upon the accuracy of its telling? Not according to Bushman and other defenders of the versions' harmony, whose defenses reveal less about any harmony than they do about a singular characteristic of Mormonism. Mormons fervently cultivate the Monday-Morning-Quarterback syndrome. And it's not by choice, but results from their commitment to Revelation, which happens to be God's most recent rendition of anything. The anything always takes priority over what came before. The most recent provides real-time guidance from God, correcting Mormons' view of the past, including terribly important facts. Revelation offers the proper goggles to view true Christian religion.

Consider only one example. It's not a universally confusing example like the divinity of God(s). It's the Mormon capstone, the family. Mormon revelation established that the purpose of the Christian gospel was to fulfill the eternal design of God through the family. This Revelation taught that we knew our families in the pre-mortal life and we'll know them after this life. However, to be with them in the next life, everyone must accept the teachings of Mormon prophets and fulfill the rituals of the Mormon Church, from baptism to making sacred promises in the holy temple, so families can be sealed together forever. In 1995 The First Presidency and Council of the Twelve Apostles of The Church of Jesus Christ of Latter-Day Saints issued a Proclamation to the World titled, "The Family." These modern-day prophets proclaimed *that marriage between a man and a woman is ordained of God and that the family is central to the Creator's plan for the eternal destiny of His Children.* The proclamation espoused some Mormon beliefs and a lot of common-sense commitment to rearing children.

This Mormon Revelation on the central role of the family in the Creator's plan creates a pickle for Mormonism, which also claims to be the repository of the true teachings of Jesus Christ. There is no ambiguity in the teachings of Jesus that the family was not central to a life committed to God. One could conjecture the emphasis on the family was part of the true Christianity lost and then restored through the Prophet Joseph Smith. But Jesus did not only fail to teach that the family was central to the Creator's plan (The Creator as God the Father or Jesus as Jehovah? It's one thing for Jesus to contradict the Father and it's another to contradict himself.), he also taught that his message was designed to divide the family. When Jesus empowered his twelve apostles to carry out their mission, part of his instruction included *Think not that I am come to send peace on earth: I came not to send peace, but a sword. For I am come to set a man at variance against his father, and the daughter against her mother, and the daughter in law against her mother in law. And a man's foes shall be they of his own household. He that loveth father or mother more than me is not worthy of me: and he that loveth son or daughter more than me is not worthy of me* (Matt. 10: 34-37). There can be no misunderstanding whether Jesus sets the daughter-in-law against the mother-in-law. A table setting can do that. But does true discipleship to Jesus necessarily make him a home wrecker? Presumably, the folks Jesus' apostles came across had not heard about Jesus. So does Jesus' statement about his purpose to divide families apply to families who are unified in their belief of him? He focuses his audience on the correct answer for either scenario by weighing the love of family against the love of him. If this preeminent focus on him as a true measure of discipleship wasn't clear the day he sent his apostles out, then the next time Jesus breached the subject with a righteous young man, it was.

If Jesus of the New Testament was one thing, he was a teacher of ethics: that is he taught a correct way to live, with a focus on how one's actions influence others. In one of the best-known accounts of his life, a young man approached him to know what he had to do to gain eternal life.

And behold, one came and said unto him,
—Good Master, what good thing shall I do, that I may have eternal life?

And he said unto him,

—Why callest thou me good? There is none good but one, that is, God: but if though wilt enter into life, keep the commandments.

He saith unto him,

—Which?

Jesus said,

—Thou shalt do no murder, Thou shalt not commit adultery, Thou shalt not steal, Thou shalt not bear false witness, Honour thy father and thy mother: and, Thou shalt love they neighbor as thyself.

The young man saith unto him,

—All these things have I kept from my youth up: what lack I yet?

Jesus said unto him,

—If thou wilt be perfect, go and sell that thou hast, and give to the poor, and thou shalt have treasure in heaven: and come and follow me.

But when the young man heard that saying, he went away sorrowful: for he had great possessions.

Then said Jesus unto his disciples,

—Verily I say unto you, That a rich man shall hardly enter into the kingdom of heaven. (Matt.19: 16-23)

Which raises the question: was Jesus a pro-Plotinian, declaring that there was only one that was good, God? Or is this example of yet another innovation? At this point in Jesus' response, his disciples freaked out and asked who could then be saved, begging to know if they were worthy. After reassuring them, Jesus stated, *And every one that hath forsaken houses, or brethren, or sisters, or father, or mother, or wife, or children, or lands, for my name's sake, shall receive an hundredfold, and shall inherit everlasting life. But many that are first shall be last; and the last shall be first.* (Matt. 19: 29-30).

In this meeting, Jesus reiterated that family was not central to true discipleship. He then went further by stating one gained eternal life by forsaking family. Most of us recall Jesus' admonition to the young rich man to give up all of his possessions, the youth's dejected response, and his unlikely reward of heaven based on Jesus' comparison of his entrance into the Kingdom of God to a camel passing through the eye of a needle. But the eternal challenge to the rich set up the more significant point, that Jesus' disciples, those who forsake wealth and family, shall *inherit* eternal life. For many of those who have wealth, they were lucky enough to inherit it from family, as much in Jesus' day as our own. Jesus' poignant condemnation of wealth is a double-whammy for Mormons because it's a condemnation of family. There's no equivocation for Jesus that preferring riches and family, often one in the same, over him prohibits entry into the Kingdom and shorts the rich on the reward of eternal life. Parents who take Jesus seriously should consider whether bestowing possessions on their children is worth the bar to their eternal blessings in the next life.

The Revelation of the Mormon family is so central to God's plan that those individuals who are not married but live faithfully to the Mormon prophets' teachings are repeatedly reassured by the same prophets that righteous individuals will not be denied the opportunity to enter into celestial marriages in the next life (the one after the one we're all familiar with). It comes as no surprise that this modern Mormon promise contradicts Jesus' teachings on marriage after death, as sure as the Revelation of the central role of the family in God's plan is irreconcilable with Jesus' teachings on true discipleship. Jesus not only stated there will be no marriage in heaven in response to some wily Sadducees' attempt to trip him on the correct explanation of the union of a woman who passed through seven husbands, all of whom were brothers (Matt. 22: 28-32), but in another account of the same event Jesus stated those *worthy to obtain that world* [not this world] *and the resurrection from the dead, neither marry, nor are given in marriage* (KJV Luke 20: 34-36). No other idea is as threatening to Mormonism's framework as Jesus' straightforward denial of marriage in the eternities.

But could not all this be better understood in context? Go for it, read the passages and try as you might to temper Jesus' view of the family, but I promise you they resist being twisted. But then couldn't all these anti-family pronouncements also be corruptions of the pure Christianity that Jesus really, really, really taught? At some point, Mormons have to concede that, for the category of Christianity to have meaning, Christianity has to mean some things and not mean other things? Because Mormons won't, Christians correctly consider Mormon's view of Christianity as impossible. It is not really like getting a child to fess to eating all the cookies in the cookie jar, but getting the admission is. But didn't Jesus praise the virtues of children somewhere in the New Testament?

In all soberness, advances in early Christian scholarship have demonstrated that the most faithful early Christians often identified themselves with the commitment of discipleship espoused by Jesus—that is, a commitment to following him that included giving up wealth and family. If Jesus started a church, it was populated by ascetics. And on this point, his strongest advocate, Paul, was in complete agreement. Paul was as innovative as the author of the book of Acts when he advocated that in Christ there was no male or female (Gal. 3: 8), a radical form of equality with no Biblical precedent and no real prospect of catching on (though it did for a time before it was stamped out during the critical formative centuries of Christianity from the fourth century CE and on). Some of the most obvious innovations in the New Testament involve passages ascribing authorship to Paul that counter his landmark declaration of gender equality in Christ. The most debated was the likely insertion in one of Paul's actual letters, a supposed directive for women to remain silent (1 Cor. 14: 34-35). Again, no New Testament scholar worth his spit considers that bit about shutting up was Paul's words, nor does any scholar consider that the rubbish about restraining women's participation in church were Paul's words in First Timothy. Nothing can be more disappointing to a fan of Mormonism's bold declaration of the living God and living Prophets who restored lost truths, when the very same routinely turn off the spout of reason (e.g. failing to denounce from the Mormon view all the "corruption" passages as they do the infamous trinity passage), when it conspicuously contradicts their insistence of more-of-the-same (i.e., God's true order as the husband at the head of the household and the wife beneath him, glorifying him by bearing his children, which Paul himself, and his followers were guilty of perpetuating on occasion). These passages attributed to Paul maintain this more-of-the-same, and no Mormon leader has had the courage to denounce them. Instead Mormons embrace the reality that among all of what Joseph Smith re-restored were many of the old views, including innovations, never lost in the first instance as sure as he restored anything.

But I should ask the pertinent question: Is Mormon Revelation better than Jesus' admonition? We know that families who inherit wealth have immense advantages of success and quality of life over families who do not. Take another step and substitute wealth with the value of education or value of commitment, and what we have is convincing proof that the family provides a structure for inheriting values that is superior to its alternatives (single parents, cults, nationalism, aristocracy, etc.). So Mormons are right on that point. And is not that point more important than the nonsensical proposition that the family has always been central to the plan of God? Of course it is, especially since the incongruity between Mormons' claim about the family, and Jesus' teachings to forsake the family, is another good thing, which may just demonstrate Jesus was wrong about at least two things. God is good and so are families. But that is a discretionary conclusion, and I for one am not ultimately convinced that families are a good thing, let alone among the highest of good things.

What is not left to one's discretion is that Jesus and his chief proponent Paul were dead wrong on their apocalyptic visions. Both unequivocally believed the end was near, and God was soon going to bring justice and salvation to those who deserved both. But the end was not near; in fact, Jesus and Paul were at least two thousand years wrong, and counting. They taught a gospel of expediency, including leaving the family (Jesus) and not bothering to marry unless you were sexually weak (Paul), in large part, because the end could be tomorrow. Mormons would do well to own up to its privileging modern revelation and drop the comical (offensive to believing Christians) assertions about having the true Christianity. Mormons claim Joseph Smith ushered in the final great dispensation (or penultimate one if Jesus' millennial reign is included), where Mormonism emerged as the summation of all previous dispensations. This summit does not comport with the pinnacle of Christianity, when God became incarnate and condescended for the purpose of sacrificing for all of humanity. Two of the highest heights do not equal one paradox; the two are a mixture of pure incorrigibility. Mormons need to be happy they have their cake (all the truth through modern revelation) and stop eating it too (digesting Christianity into something unrecognizable to Christians, and to the records of Jesus too).

Maintaining the timeless role of the family may have no scriptural support, and all fallacious readings to suggest it does hardly renders Mormons' position futile. In real time, the value of family is demonstrable. And Mormons would be better served to temper their need for revelation when they have ample evidence available to justify their view of the family. The Proclamation on "the Family" could never achieve what N. L. Nelson's essay, "The Mormon Family" in October 1, 1904, issue of the quarterly magazine, *The Mormon Point of View*, does. Consider that "the family" may provide one of the best pieces of evidence to explain altruism, supporting William Hamilton's simple, and widely accepted equation justifying kinship selection, that is individuals may sacrifice themselves for the continuation of their gene pool. Or does family support altruism? Is Hamilton's formula—the relationship between one's relatives to the benefits being greater than the costs—the absolute explanation of altruism? Anyone who has read Shakespeare's history plays hardly needs to turn to hard data to see the family breaks against altruism as often as it does for it.

But what about for the other animals that can't read? Believe me, when they begin to read, tests of altruism will break just as consistently in the same way as it does for us animals who do. Kinship selection doesn't have an absolute ring about it even with evidence in support of it. So what does the family prove? The "Mormon" family proves that group selection, the far less accepted position among evolutionary biology of today, explains altruism. Acting against one's self-interest, a contradiction in the process of evolution, often occurs under the behest of a group when it benefits the group. And in Nelson's essay, his argument on behalf of the Bible family ideal proves a value of the Mormon group beyond the family unit he intends to justify. In this single essay, he removes polygamous shame and offers fair warnings for what the Mormon group must to do to evolve after the practice of polygamy's official end in 1890, nearly a couple decades before he composed his essay. Many of his points are right on and a couple others are irreparably less so. He's right that the begetting of small ones is a chief value of the group, but he is less right condemning the role of wealth that makes so much fecunding and cultural flourishing possible. Along with Nelson's other classic pieces, Mormons are not only ignorant of "The Mormon Family," but also are unable to appreciate it betrothed to authority's voice of revelation and its myriad mind-numbing consequences. What they do not miss is their place within Mormonism.

But what if Jesus was not wrong on either score? What if God is the only good? Mormons have arguably made family a matter of eternal or ultimate concern, but Jesus did not and even Nelson didn't suggest he did. Jesus made God his ultimate concern (he may have arguably made a concern of caring for the poor and sick but there is no argument that he made families one). And why would God be the only true good? Honestly I do not know or believe that God is, but Jesus' direction after proposing God was the only true good does make sense. And that direction was? Answer: complete devotion to God. Whatever is your ultimate good—if it really is an ultimate good—will require your corresponding ultimate devotion. It is simply not ultimate if it does not. Then, to come full circle, the measure of one's ultimate concern, however weakly manifested, is one's demonstrable actions, the direction of life. So if God is the ultimate good (a particularly high-value concern) then anything else is defined by an adjective other than the good. Jesus understood that the integrity of a thing required meaning a certain thing, and not meaning something else. Then Jesus was not wrong, eh. And while his failed apocalyptic vision of a messiah able to liberate the Jews has plenty

426 MY BEST MORMON LIFE

of textual support, there is another view that his apocalyptic vision found its certain end, indeed, in his crucifixion and death. His end culminated in a sacrifice that satisfied justice and provided eternal life (according to Paul and others). So Jesus may not have been wrong on either score (but we all know the apocalyptic vision of Paul was).

Mormonism promises everything and offends Christianity in its claim. Is a cost of having everything the loss of having one substantial thing? If you enjoy the whole, can you distinguish and enjoy the parts? Or in another wholly unrelated conceit, if your position can justify every conceivable thing, then can your position simultaneously mean one thing? If you look to the Mormons, the answer appears to be a resounding yes. Honestly, I do not have the slightest idea, but I suspect not. It's more likely the alternative that the claim of everything is smoke and mirrors and Mormons enjoy many substantial things, all parts of a much bigger whole neither they nor you have. Having everything would be akin to seeing God, and few have done it and lived (including Joseph Smith, who saw the Lord, who presumably was God the son, Jesus, Lord of this world, Father only as divinely invested). Whatever the explanation, it cannot be easy to live with everything; heavens, it might even be harder to believe you are living with everything but are not; for heaven's sake, a lot of us struggle in making sense of some aspects of human life eons shy of everything. What I wouldn't give for just one thing.

CHAPTER 28
CRUMBS

I stood before a granite church on Harvard Street. If I turned right I could walk into Massachusetts Avenue running into the heart of Harvard Square. On my way I could get a burger at Mr. Bartley's and then get a Sam Adams at John Harvard's Brew House. Heavens, I could get a Sam Adams at any restaurant within one hundred miles. Maybe I would do both, but not before I was certain I had tried my best to find what I was looking for, the Jose Mateo Ballet Theatre. I looked up and down the street, but sure I had the right building I just stood there. The sign out front clearly said Cambridge Baptist Church. I walked up to the door and took another glance about. A woman stepped out.

—Here for the ballet? she said.

—I am, I said.

—Inside.

I entered a sanctuary with lean pillars running along the sides. The space was a captivating white. Seats, like broken bleachers, set up against the north wall where the pulpit must have once stood. I took one and looked for Nicholas. He eventually entered with the rest of the company. They danced so close I could have reached out and pushed one of them. Nicholas was a solid force of strength, gliding at one moment and holding his position at another, leaping amidst the beautiful ballerinas, lifting one and then another. I had never seen so many beautiful women flying across space, and there was Nicholas at the center enabling them to spin faster and jump higher. He did it without a hitch. Throughout the different numbers, I fantasized being the principal lead dancer as concertedly as I ever did about being John McClane of the Die Hard films. Then, reflecting on the strength it would require, brought me back to my seat as surely as my aversion to daring stunts did. After the performance I milled about, and met Nicholas's re-entrance with a hearty pat on the shoulder.

—Incredible, just incredible, I said.

—Thank you for coming, he said, giddy with an ineffaceable smile.

—No, thank you. Where's the after party with all the angels you were throwing around the room?

Nicholas could not be embarrassed. He was too guileless, unshakeable, unwavering. He rolled back on his heels, shaking his head.

—I want you to meet one of them. She'll be out in a minute.

One of the striking ballerinas reentered the sanctuary walking directly toward Nicholas. He introduced her and I complimented her great performance, sure my favorable impression of all the dancers included her, and even more sure I had given Nicholas the best advice I had given anyone weeks before in the vegetarian café. One of the company patrons praised Nicholas to me as she exited, stating loud enough for him to hear how happy the company was to have him for the season and how they hoped he would be around for many more.

Ballet stilled time for me. Everything was a revelation. A dancer's body told a different story than words in a play or song. It was closer to music, another mystery to me. I could hardly make any sense of ballet, but its balance and grace moved me, and I knew only that to produce a flawless piece, the performers needed more than talent. The performance in this church reminded again that they needed hours upon hours, combining into years, of dedicated practice. And here Nicholas stood at the pinnacle of just such an accomplishment. I hugged him around his shoulders and thanked him again.

I saw Nicholas rarely, as I did not make it to church services and was caught up in my own studies trying to iron out what kind of Mormon I would be, aspiring to an obscure mutt of something far from the science fiction writer Orson Scott Card and the twentieth-century literary critic Wayne C. Booth. I confess this question of identity has about as much attraction for me as it has presence in this record. Yet its late arrival is a breath of "it's about time" for many faithful Mormon readers. It might be the only question they care about. And why? Because, the meaning of a religion and the members of it are inseparably bundled together—I suspect the true meaning of any religion involves its relationship to those who belong to it.

When someone who has previously belonged, no longer belongs—in accordance with the official criteria for belonging (i.e., not sharing common beliefs, participating in rituals, etc.)—that person has not only chosen an impossible alternative to the conception of all-the-truth contained within Mormonism, but has also become a direct judgment on those who remain practicing it. Because of the impossibility of other or more truths, the Mormon mind does not permit a non-threatening departure from its fold. It's possible to leave for a lot of bad reasons, such as adultery, drug use, unbelief, but not a single good one. Honestly, I cannot raise enough interest to care a lick about a question that elicits such sorry stock responses. However, the responses revolving around the nucleus of someone, in some fashion, falling from the truth serve as brilliant defense mechanisms that guard the faithful Mormon from any glimpse of another horizon. There's no alternative truth after imbibing Mormon truth, which is an all-encompassing promise that is the measure of Mormon judgment. Identifying that impenetrable Mormon pathology, I have come to believe that repeatedly focusing on the merit component of truth, and not its acceptance, is the only way to address this unfortunate Mormon condition; hence, my analytical approach and the continued lacuna of a psychological or sociological one in said record. Identifying with others has all the benefits you could possibly list, but the sacrifice of truth should not be one of them.

But despite what I didn't know—being undecided on how to devote myself to my religious tradition during this life—I was not confused with where I knew I would end up after it. Years before I had made the decision it would not be with kagillions of people I didn't like in the celestial kingdom when the one person I did like would not be there. At my home ward of Riverton, Bishop Smith had replaced Bishop Eddleston, who had replaced Bishop Patrick, the bishop during my mother's death. During Smith's tenure my brother had a daughter out of wedlock, and Smith took it upon himself to summarily disfellowship my brother from the membership of The Church of Jesus Christ of Latter-day Saints, suspending by the proper priesthood authority all his ordinances necessary for Mormon salvation and celestial exaltation. The decision was consistent with Mormon official views of morality that my father had espoused all his life, and he was beside himself to condemn my brother a couple of years earlier when he had chosen to live with his girl-friend. My father offered the kind of moral platitudes that even a halfwit like myself would know are of any worth only when measured against the whole quality of the person they supposedly describe, a conception of value that zealous believers in Abraham's deity have perennially ignored.

Moral declarations are always a projection of one's expectations, and are without exception a reflection of the declarer, as surely as they fail to classify their intended objects. No more accurate condemnation did the Jesus of the New Testament make than the clear scribal innovation in the Gospel of St. John, *He that is without sin among you, let him first cast a stone at her* (John 8: 7). I got it. Smith and the Mormons did not have something superior if they didn't have the power to say who could and could not belong, and I wasn't about to encourage them to change their rules. But the power to exclude is a measuring stick for those they apply it to, and also works backward to those who apply it. A group excluding the best among us suffers the tradeoff of a premium on quality, a trade, I reckoned, not worth the eternities.

—You should come hear the Mormon historian speak. He spent his career at Columbia, and what I hear he's pretty legitimate, I said.

—I plan to, my old roommate James said.

—He is supposedly going to talk about Joseph Smith. I guess he's got a book coming out about him.

Mormon students at the Divinity School did not fail to sponsor Mormon speakers utilizing the Office of Student Life, the nonacademic advocate of *all* student interests, using a loophole they were keen to exploit to get Mormon academics on campus. Unlike that of the former Dean of BYU's Religious Instruction Department, the talk by Richard Bushman, the Columbia professor of history, was well attended. The Sperry Room filled with Mormon students, many of whom I recognized from the handful of times I had attended the Mormon Church on Brattle Street directly across from the Longfellow House and a short walk from Harvard Square. I recognized one whose effect on me still had not worn off.

Somehow, through the Mormon grapevine, a request went out for someone studying world religions to make a presentation to Cambridge high school students and one of my Mormon div school classmates approached me. Of course I was happy to help, and when I entered the teacher's high school class to present my thirty-minute history of Hinduism, I froze. She was gorgeous. As requested I showed up early and she took me into the hall to visit for a few minutes, and despite my confused state I agreed to leave plenty of time for questions but made no promises for answers, learned she grew up in Salt Lake City, recently had her degree at Wellesley College, the all-girl liberal arts school, and had been teaching since.

I had not seen her again after that presentation, but there she sat in the midst of the sea of Mormons before Richard Bushman was to speak. While I had not seen her, I had thought about her and mentioned her in one of a few meetings I had with the local Mormon bishop, who kindly reached out to me for personal interviews, encouraging me to participate in church services and local ward activities. We spent most of our visits talking about our shared interest in Buddhism. During one interview I mentioned the great honor of speaking to the high school class of one of the members. He knew immediately of whom I spoke, mentioning she was engaged to be married but not before a light went off in his head, for shortly thereafter I received an unexpected invitation to join her and friends for some function, which I declined. Oh, but for the blighted prohibitions on polyandry!

During the question-and-answer portion of Bushman's presentation, he ably responded to many questions. None of them were contentious like those hurled at the former Dean of BYU's Religious Instruction Department.

—Brother Bushman, I've always wanted to know why Fawn Brodie's book about Joseph Smith, *No Man Knows My History*, is still in print. I mean I see it in every national chain bookstore despite its being proved wrong multiple times, a conspicuous Mormon member of the audience asked.

—It's in bookstores because it's the most academic work on the life of Joseph Smith. I don't agree with the psychological approach. My own book is more of a cultural approach.

Holy lily liver, did I sit up in my seat as a sheet of silence covered the mostly Mormon audience. I had just heard the most revered living Mormon intellectual give credit to the most reviled book in Mormon history. Every Mormon thinker before him had decried Ms. Brodie's book as the remaining trappings of Satanic excrement. Supposedly the aforementioned Mormon scholar, Nibley, had devoted an entire book to rebutting it and every Mormon apologist after him shit on it as a rite of passage. Then, in the Sperry Room, Bushman audaciously passed fresh air over us. I didn't recognize in him the Mormon scholars I knew. He moved with no apparent restraints and spoke as freely. I hadn't seen a Mormon thinker like him, nor had I believed that one existed.

I had had a lot of favorite Mormon intellectuals at BYU and none moved or spoke freely. At the top of my list were Eugene England and Duane Jeffery. England started teaching at BYU in the 1970s after the McConkie and Smith duo began tamping down intellectual value in the 1960s. In response to the new McConkie and Smith anti-intellectual landscape, England cofounded what would become the most longstanding and long-suffering journal of Mormon thinking, *Dialogue: A Journal of Mormon Thought*, its history of thoughtful and sincere contributors deserving volumes of accolades. It provided a venue for critical inquiry unavailable and unacceptable within the official publications of the Mormon Church, resulting in an overflow of benefits to every Mormon for generations to come. Both its contributors and its readers were largely faithful, practicing Mormons. Article after article evidenced a smart enclave of Mormons, and consistently marked them as an oppressed one working under the ever-looming eye of Big Brother, on North Temple, who accompanied and influenced each piece.

That contributors to *Dialogue* examined controversial aspects of Mormonism from positions of faith in Mormonism showed a persistence, yet there was a contradicting strain of homogeneity among their offerings of heterodoxies, as paradoxical as opaque is my proposition. While England was not representative of each contributor, his writings displayed the tension between being critical of Mormonism and maintaining faith in it. His work at times reads like the rambling confession of a tortured mind. Among his saddest examples is the essay, "Obedience, Integrity and the Paradox of Selfhood," in his collection of essays, *Dialogues with Myself*. The reasoning and sentences at times are as uncomfortable to read as England's attempt to make compatible being a critical but faithful Mormon must have been. In other essays, like "The Mormon Cross," also from *Dialogues*, and "Shakespeare and the At Onement of Jesus Christ," in the collection of essays, *Why the Church is as True as the Gospel*, results matched the heights of England's empathetic and intellectual prowess. Once, in the large conference hall of the humanities building, I heard him read a fictional story about a doctor accompanying his Jewish patients to a concentration camp, holding the rapt attention of his young audience, spreading over us his pulsating desire for his fellow Mormons to do good continually in the face of oppression.

I first met England in the mid-nineties, a couple years removed from the beginning of his certain fall from the Mormon authorities' tolerance (he was never in their favor). In the early nineties, he had publicly decried the actions taken against Mormon intellectuals by the quasi-covert Strengthening Church Members Committee. He recanted when the authorities pointed out that members of the Quorum of the Twelve Apostles sat on the committee. The committee's work uprooted intellectuals on par with the Spanish Inquisition, less a readily available rack. Those attacked by the Committee were as passionate about their membership in the Mormon Church as its legions of non-intellectuals, and the most famous excommunications were known as the infamous September Six. These six, like England, and others targeted by the committee, highlighted an intellectual tradition on the margins of faithful membership dating as far back as B.H. Roberts—but more accurately marked in our modern era by the publication of Mormonism's greatest novel, *The Giant Joshua*, by Maurine Whipple, in 1941. Following Whipple's classic came the publication of the most significant books on Mormonism up through the present day: Fawn Brodie's aforementioned biography on Joseph Smith, *No Man Knows My History*, in 1945, and Juanita Brooks' *Mountain Meadows Massacre* in 1950 and *John Doyle Lee* in 1961. The nonfiction works caused tectonic shifts in the study of Mormonism still being felt today.

Whipple's novel is far less known, and certainly one of England's greatest failures was not to explain (based on his own noted formalist Stanford training) *The Giant Joshua*'s rightful place among the great literature of the world. Heavens, its effective uses of free indirect discourse were a few rewrites shy of causing Harvard's professor of the practice of literary criticism James Wood to squeal with delight like a child for his pony on Christmas morning. England incorrectly concluded the artistry of *The Giant Joshua* waned as the novel closed, his error recorded in a forgettable attempt to define a Mormon aesthetic based on how much a work stoked the culture's own beliefs, regardless of form and correspondence to truth. England's ill-begotten treatise was as silly as the good Harvard Professor's title was an illusion. Maybe that's the joke. Maybe England knew his conception of Mormon art was shite as much as Wood doesn't torture his readers with literary criticism.

Joshing aside, saying something alone, never makes it so. And that even goes for what I say. Something is so when the saying corresponds to a reality separate from the saying, a possibility demonstrated throughout our days cumulating in what we refer to as our lives. *The Giant Joshua* is a masterpiece separate from my declaration that it is. It achieves the right measure of both form and content, telling of the Mormon settlements of southern Utah and the challenges faced by those people living the divine law of plural marriage. As with all great novels, the characters in *The Giant Joshua* practically sing with agency restrained by life's compounding realities, but its unique triumph is presenting a panoramic perspective of polygamy through the eyes of the protagonist, Clory, the third wife of fictional apostle Abijah.

Whipple populated her novel with actual events and Mormon leaders, including the apostle Erastus Snow, who voiced the hope of all thinking Mormons at a disciplinary proceeding for a soon-to-be-excommunicated brother in the faith. The man had openly professed his lack of belief in the prophet Joseph Smith and simultaneously justified his disbelief by citing the Mormon truth that *every man shall worship God according to the dictates of his own conscience*, pleading the court would continue to view him as one of their brethren. They did not. However, Erastus, to himself, pondered the man's situation, thinking "Some day they [the Church] would be strong enough to afford dissenters." Whipple, Brodie, and Brooks and those in their critical tradition have been testing the Mormon Church's strength since, and the answer is still "not yet." But what has proven its strength after repeated inquiries is that no Mormon names carry the value of Whipple, Brodie, and Brooks.

Shortly after England's death, I sat with my brothers eating fish and chips and drinking beers with Leslie Norris at a restaurant just off Interstate 15, a few hundred yards from the Utah Valley State College in Orem, where England had finished his career. BYU administrators forced England into early retirement, and the fledgling college soon to be a university had wisely picked him up. Leslie told us a story about England he had shared with me many years before as his student. Within days of arriving in Provo to join the English Department at BYU, Leslie and his wife Kitty received a knock on their front door. It was Eugene England and his wife. Over the course of Leslie's career, BYU heaped praise after praise upon him, adopting the great Welsh poet as one of its own, but during our many visits he did not speak more appreciatively of all he had received from BYU than of England's kind acts. He brightened in his characteristic way that denoted something of great importance whenever he mentioned them. The Mormon community took every step to save Leslie and Kitty except for binding their hands to be baptized and to enter the holy temple, consistent and sincere attempts that were truly admirable but undone by us Elison brothers over Guinness and chips during numerous lunches and deliveries of red wine to their beautiful home in the river bottoms on the Provo/Orem border. And as sign of our triumph, and like a fine British subject, he insisted on getting the tab or reimbursing us for the *vinum*.

Jacob returned to BYU after my strong urgings to study under Leslie, becoming one of his chosen pupils, writing poetry under his tutelage. Their bond so strong that after Jacob graduated Leslie sponsored him on a trip to Spain, ostensibly to reward him for graduating but more to inspire him to live within all the beautiful possibilities of the world and to celebrate writing about them.

But Jacob had almost left BYU a second time. He complained to me he had made another good effort but once again had had enough of BYU and planned to leave. I had one more card to play, so I laid it down and encouraged him to talk with Ken, my Nordic classmate who was entrenched among the finest thinking-Mormons, convinced Ken could recommend professors worth sticking around for. Jacob peppered Ken with requests for help, and sought out Ken's recommendations. One of them was Duane Jeffrey. It is challenging to set apart a humble and extraordinarily decent human being among so many of the same, but Jeffrey stood out to his students. Many, like Jacob, sought him out for his insatiable honesty and brilliantly warm personality. I mean that his honesty did not come with disclaimers or limits forced upon his other genuine peers. And he truly was known as a gentle man.

Duane Jeffrey was a professor of biology. When Jacob approached him after the first lecture in a course on evolutionary history, Jeffrey told him he could not admit any more students as the class was full. Jacob responded then he would be leaving BYU. Jeffrey stopped him and admitted him. Jeffrey was among those sincere, faithful Mormons who contributed critical pieces to *Dialogue*. But unlike so many contributors, he had the distinct advantage of not being defensive. He was, in fact, a scientist, and enjoyed being part of the premier Mormon intellectual tradition of Britons and Norwegians before him. Like England, he was excessively gracious. I knocked on England's door multiple times and, whatever he was doing, he stopped to listen and to visit, as I expected he did with every student. Jeffrey was of the same ilk. On one occasion he invited Jacob and us brothers to lunch at the Skyroom on one of the top floors of the Wilkinson Student Center. The Skyroom was the restaurant where BYU administrators hosted all visiting dignitaries. Jeffrey waited thirty minutes until we arrived, due to a dilatory

Josh who in a lapsed moment of indifference finished up some task before giving us a ride. Jeffrey warmly welcomed us as if he had just arrived himself. I was so sick to my stomach thinking that Jeffrey might have left that I could have hurled as easily as I could have struck Josh down as Cain had Abel. Unlike England, Jeffrey did not have the demeanor of one anticipating an oncoming orthodox condemnation. But like England, Jeffrey moved like he knew he belonged to a scrutinized sect of thinking Mormons, shoulders slightly hunched, aware of an invisible predator. Jeffrey wanted to know about us, asking questions about our interests and studies. I piped up that I had studied literature and loved to read.

—Do you have any favorite Mormon authors?

The question did not really make any sense to me. It was like asking who my favorite Amish player was in the NBA.

—What exactly do you mean? I said.

—There aren't many, but there are some. Have you heard of Brady Udall?

—What time period did he live?

—Ours. He has a great collection of short stories called *Letting Loose the Hounds*. His stories are a bit macabre at times, but I believe he's one of our most promising young writers.

—What's macabre mean?

I suspected I knew what made Bushman different from England and Jeffrey. Heavens, I had so many suspicions running wild that I wrote my most ambitious paper while at the div school on a topic that I was sure explained it.

Some papers are so damn good that having an A grade awarded is a mere formality. At least I've always believed that, in theory. My final term paper in Liberation Theology, yet another exception to my otherwise unwavering plan of an exclusive study of the world's religions (which resulted in an overflow of riches left for another day) taught by the Reverend Doctor Allan Dwight Callahan was one of those to test my theory. Professor Callahan shocked the class one day, when he answered his own compelling question.

—What religion most parallels the early Christian Church, who kept all things in common described in the book of Acts? he asked.

A class full of Harvard students went silent with a few wrong squeaky guesses.

—The Mormons and their law of consecration kept during its early history, he answered.

I about crapped my pants. I was taking liberation theology to get liberated from the Mormons, and the good reverend professor had the temerity to point out the closest parallel to the early Christians described in the book of Acts were the Mormons. Do you see now why having an understanding of just one single substantial thing would be a godsend? And the affirmation of the truthfulness of my tradition coming from, of all people, a Baptist preacher. If he didn't provide the standard yardstick to determine who had a right to call themselves a Christian, there never would be one. If you live like a Christian and feel so obliged to call yourself one, then you are one.

I introduced the humble aim of my paper in its title: "Mark 7 and the Controversy over Tradition: The Hermeneutic Mark Provides on How Tradition and Authority OUGHT To Be Engaged for a Relevant Proposal to The Latter-day Saint Tradition." I could have worn a headband with "Kick Ass" on it when I handed the paper in, but it would not have sent a stronger message. I wish I had capitalized "ought" back then, it looks so good now.

I began with an astute and slightly convoluted distinction between tradition and authority, proposing that the Markan Jesus engaged authority as a way to change tradition, as recorded in the seventh chapter of the Gospel of Mark. I then promised to prove that Jesus not only engaged authority but also invited his followers to engage his authority. Before developing my exegesis, I provided three examples of Mormonism's view on the great and unpardonable sin of questioning Mormon authority: in Mormondom, only killing Jesus could be worse. I shared a personal experience from my mission when my companion and I sat in the living room of an investigator on Easter Sunday to watch a *60 Minutes* piece about the Mormon Church. Mike Wallace asked then-President Gordon B. Hinckley about the perception that the Mormon Church did not permit freedom to disagree with its authority. President Hinckley honestly responded that members could think whatever they wanted but were not welcome to say or publish it.

Next I highlighted the teaching of a Mormon apostle who, in an address titled "Beware of Those Who Speak and Publish in Opposition to God's True Prophets," warned (as you might expect) against speaking unfavorably of Mormon prophets. He quoted Matthew, who warned *Many false prophets shall rise, and shall deceive many* (Matt. 24: 11) and cited a Mormon prophet who said that faithful Mormons could only accept as authoritative what came through the priesthood leadership of the Church, and when the faithful looked to another source they opened themselves to the influence of Satan. Holy bajesus, if there was a more glaring example of a thinking human's fallacy I haven't seen it. But, bear in mind, Mormon agency (or free will) is the uncompelled, or uncoerced, decision to make the right choice, not the freedom to make one's own choice.

While these prophets' cultic reasoning could be excused for their sheer enthusiasm about the heavens overflowing onto Mormonism, similar comments from the most competent living Mormon apostle are harder to disclaim. The Mormon apostle Dallin H. Oaks was a law professor at one of the best law schools in the United States and sat as a justice on a state supreme court before serving as president of one of the finest institutions of higher learning on Planet Earth, BYU, and I turned to him next. In his essay, "Criticism," Oaks stated that criticism about Church leaders at any level was not acceptable. He went further, stating it did not matter if the criticism were actually true. Holy mother of all mind blows! Oaks built a distinguished career upholding the truth, and by his own admission its integrity failed to underlie his higher calling as a Mormon apostle. How could that be? Well, I loved the quote so much I overstated its importance. To be fair, in the address Oaks advocated against "faultfinding" and "backbiting," and not abstaining from passing judgments, some worthwhile advice for an American culture saturated with the virtue of bitching and moaning about everything and everyone. But something more significant was in the mix. The leader of the Mormons is called the "president" of the Church, and all the other leaders are closer to V.P.s than to archbishops. Oaks and the others' views of criticism are less cultic than they are synergistic. The Mormon prophet is president, effectively the acting chief executive officer, and his job is to foster cooperation among the industrious, goal-oriented membership. Criticism of the president hampers his effectiveness and creates minor (sometimes major, if the disgruntled member is a professor at BYU) inefficiencies. Hence, the one-mindedness (pejoratively described as brain-washedness) is really a component of a well-oiled, responsive, productive group.

For a clearer picture yet, the image of a Mormon prophet must be viewed more like that of a king than a commoner with some physical failing who answers a divine call (think Isaiah 6: 1-8). Both the Mormon prophet and king were divinely appointed: one before this life in the pre-mortal realm and the other at his birth. That is why a Mormon's support of the role of a Mormon prophet is no different than a Manchester United fan's respect for the Queen. If either is insulted, he conjures enormous passion in response; Mormons will kill you with kindness and United fans will fight you until the pub closes. Neither the Mormon Mantle nor British Crown implies their words and actions will be true any more than support of them hinges on their truthfulness. While answering why Mormons venerate their prophet, and this runs into complications and stretched comparisons, but describing what Mormons' view of their prophet's vulnerability is, does not. There's no hint of controversy in the articulation of the Mormon position that an anti-criticism force field surrounds Mormon authority. It is no exaggeration to state that Mormon prophetic teachings make Mormon authority impervious to any checks or balances. If Mormon prophets do anything kindly, they regularly raise their opponents to the venerated status of prophets only to point out they are false ones. Mormon leadership would do well to advocate an objective test to determine the falsity of supposed propheting, including their own, by an examination of the consequences of their words and actions: "You will recognize them [prophets] by their fruit", Jesus said (Matt. 7: 16).

And the examination of those consequences goes both ways, "Judge not, that ye be not judged. For with what judgment ye judge, ye shall be judged: and with what measure ye mete, it shall be measured to you again." (KJV Matt. 7: 1-2). Which Jesus also said. Judgment is all about timing. First, if we don't have all the facts or applicable abstract concepts at our disposal to apply to the facts, we do well to refrain from judgment. But if we've taken affirmative steps to learn as many facts as we can and struggled to determine the relevant abstract concepts and to apply them (which is never a conscious process when we do our best and worse judging), then we ought to be judging because the direction and quality of our lives depends upon it. But judgers beware, because how we judge opens us to judgment in kind. If we render a premature and immature judgment, it invites just condemnation. Jesus identified at least one advantage to poor judgment, that it welcomes a reciprocation of poor judgment. The advantage to setting the bar low is that our opponent's likely response will be just as low (the way to keep a conversation dumb is to start with a dumb one: you look dumb but most likely so will your opponent). Responding to a low bar, opponents not only have to counter the initial mind-numbing propositions, but also have to work to raise the bar, which is a dual task most folks are not fit for. Make no mistake: those in authority appreciate the value of keeping their judgment dumb when it welcomes return judgment just as dumb. The Mormon draping at the beginning of my paper was more for dramatic effect than material backdrop. And the exegesis of Mark 7 rocked, quite independently of my highlighting the mental inflictions from my personal moorings.

The former Dean of Harvard Divinity School Krister Stendahl gave a lecture, "Why I Love the Bible" at the Harvard-Epworth United Methodist Church, and he said "To be a friend of God, you had to be one who argued with God." I know he said it because I was at the lecture, and I liked it so much I quoted him in my paper. Then I said Mark 7 provided the hermeneutic through the Markan Jesus for how to actualize this friendship process, including engaging those who held themselves out as mouthpieces of God but who shouldn't be mistaken as God, but in my humble yet correct opinion could not be separated from the words of God in my Mormon tradition, and I suspected in all others.

Hermeneutic is a fancy and legit way (it comes from Greek) to talk about interpreting a text. I wasn't really sure how to properly use it as a div student, but it was on my classmates' top ten list of erudite terms, so I regularly conscripted it into service. I still don't know what the hell it means, after checking many sources, having once upon a great time even consulted one of its modern fathers, Hans-Georg Gadamer. Which brings me to another point: no matter the argument at the div school, one way to get the upper hand was to invoke a German intellectual like Gadamer. It didn't matter if I knew his work or not, and I usually only did in a cursory fashion. But it didn't even matter if my opponent actually did know his work, and he often did, because the first use of a German authority was like a power punch. If I used him correctly, I probably knocked out my opponent, but if I didn't, it was like a missed windmill and was so exasperating that my opponent spent the better part of his time correcting my misuse and not supporting his position.

Think of a hermeneutic as a power interpretation, not some mere in-vogue applied critical theory that an astute reader could provide of any given text, which would not require an examination of the text because no critical theory depends upon what's actually in the text. You may be thinking I've missed the boat on this one, because my title implied the author of Mark 7 provided the interpretation as if providing a tool and not merely a point of view. Whether I understood hermeneutics correctly, I was pretty sure my inversion was a clever one. Humor me as I refer to the Markan tool as The Authority Engager, something I lacked the cojones to do in div school.

One could argue that Jesus himself, the highest of authorities, provided the example of engaging authority and that would be correct. But the power lies in how Jesus engaged the authority figures of his day, not that he was the authority of his day, and those details to some extent should be credited to the author of the events. It would be quite enough to have Jesus' example to feel confident to go crazy and keep authority in check. But to wield the tool of The Authority Engager, we must employ how Jesus actually did it, according to the author of Mark.

(As a rather important aside, Liberation theology is a singular pursuit to find the true meaning of Jesus through helping and aiding the poor and sick among us, everywhere. There's a hell of a lot of scriptural support for this premise, including the frame for the passages I discussed.)

At the end of Chapter 6 of Mark, we learn that wherever Jesus went people brought the sick, and Jesus healed them (Mark 6: 54-55). It was after being with the sick that Jesus came upon authority figures in Mark 7. In an earlier passage (2: 23-3:6), Jesus also healed the sick and subsequently turned to engaging authority. I somewhat naively pronounced that exegetes had failed to note the significance of the repeated coupling of Jesus' healing the sick and his engaging authority (naively because I was far from familiar with all New Testament scholarship on the subject). But I did point out that the famed New Testament scholar Raymond Brown noted the significance of Jesus' ministry on the suffering of others, something often marginalized for the more standard emphasis on his ministry's being about establishing faith (unsurprisingly in the tradition of Paul, where everything had its reference in the nucleus of faith); I extended the significance to be about liberating people from all kinds of oppression (in step with all liberation theologians). I proposed that passages about Jesus healing the sick followed by engaging authority were not disjointed, because if the authorities were not responsible for the oppression, they were in a better position to alleviate it. Unlike many of my div school peers I knew that authorities were not wholly and always to blame for poor people's circumstances. Heavens, I had many a job because someone had been audacious enough to start a company that provided it. But I was also convinced that the authorities who provided the work were responsible for distributing it fairly. So for change, one had to confront the source, the authorities, who made the decisions affecting everyone else. And on this point, Jesus and I seemed to agree.

The catalyst to engaging authority is generally some kind of controversy, and Jesus found his in whether one should eat without washing his hands (Mark 7: 3). The Pharisees, the Jewish sect with the responsibility to interpret the law, asked Jesus why his disciples did not conform to the ancient tradition but instead ate with defiled hands (7: 6). Jesus responded, *How right Isaiah was when he prophesied about you hypocrites in these words: "This*

people pays me lip-service, but their heart is far from me: they worship me in
vain, for they teach as doctrines the commandments of men." You neglect the
commandment of God, in order to maintain the tradition of men. He said to
them, How clever you are at setting aside the commandment of God in order
to maintain your tradition." (7: 6-9) Jesus' response provided two essential
components of The Authority Engager. The first one, he forcefully responded to their point. Sounds simple but it is not. By virtue of someone's being in
a position of authority, he or she enjoys power, and that power may be over
you or may extend to influencing people who do have power over you. These
people respond in kind, that is they pay more attention when they are confronted head on, by power. Jesus apparently understood this dynamic when
he employed the word hypocrite to describe his opponents. The word was a
common way to discredit authority, for ancients just as it is for us moderns,
but it appears only this once in the entire Gospel of Mark. One New Testament scholar I cited, a German, advanced the theory that the polemic was
the whole point of the passage, marked by the use of the word hypocrite.
This scholar was none other than the New Testament juggernaut Rudolf
Bultmann. None was ever greater. Bultmann also advanced the theory that
the controversy passages in the New Testament like the one in Mark 7 were
more likely the actual words of Jesus than other passages attributed to him
because they provided his view on Jewish piety, an issue akin to a first cause.

The second component of The Authority Engager is a rational argument. Something we moderns assume we recognize, and maybe we do, but
daily attempts prove that we (members of the human race) rarely accomplish. If you're like the philosopher Nietzsche, you don't think that's such a
bad thing or maybe even a wholly possible thing. For example, there's little
place for it in love and hatred and we spend a lot of effort with both. But
that's not the same thing as saying there is no such thing, or that a mostly
rational thing does not have immense value. On this occasion Jesus showed
there was such a thing by the structure of his response and the development
of his premises. The structure entailed setting the commandments of God
against the traditions of men in two verses (9 & 13). Then I moved to Jesus'
claims (or series of related premises). He focused on one's lifestyle, lest one
leave the commandments of God (7: 8) and make the word of God null
and void (7: 13). He advanced a life in line with God's commandments, not
in line with tradition. He concluded one should give up traditional dietary
laws and other traditional taboos because what went into a person did not
defile him or her, but rather what came out could (7: 14-23). His reason-

CRUMBS 443

ing led to a smart conclusion, and his approach handed us The Authority Engager.

Again and again, Jesus demonstrated that reason—not irrational action—muted power and effected real (actual) change (albeit most of it was delayed a few centuries). That's not to say irrational behavior doesn't bring about change, but that change is cyclical just like irrational arguments among talking heads, provide transient emotional responses, satisfying to those in their choir but, more often, not satisfying those of us who are left feeling as if we had watched a cat fight in the halls of our distant but not-to-be-forgotten high school lives. Maybe with a little practice Jesus would have favored the irrational arguments or entitlement speechifying so rampant in the early twenty-first century, but I have my doubts since they provide about as much stimulation as playing footsies under Nietzsche's writing table.

But what about the elephant in the proverbial room full of God's commandments? Having a God and knowing something about that God depend upon those with authority to speak on behalf of God, and they are hardly invisible. I proposed in the final pages of my paper that this connection was a tension that was not meant to be resolved, and the changing of traditions such as not washing hands did not resolve it. I supported my proposal by anticipating two objections to my thesis that authority ought to be engaged.

The first objection I anticipated was the position that Jesus was the real authority in the passage, and that the real authority is not engaged. I quote from my paper: *And his authority [Jesus'] is not ever called in question; hence a Latter-day Saint could respond that a correct conception of authority does not necessitate necessary engagement because the correct conception never lay with the Pharisees anyway.* But Jesus didn't appeal to himself as God in the text, and Jesus recognized the Pharisees' position of authority. I interjected a lengthy quotation from a scholar who explained that no scholars dispute that the Pharisees introduced their traditions to actually fulfill the commandments of God. The traditions were part of the Law of Moses. They were instituted for genuinely good purposes. Subsequently the Pharisees did not see a contradiction in their practices, which Jesus did, as surely as genuine Mormon leadership have not lost a wink of sleep over what they have added to God's commandments because all of it is meant to fulfill those commandments. The paper did not establish but assumed commandments and traditions were inseparable.

But, now, Jesus is God as understood wholly outside the New Testament so it would be a mistake to engage his authority, goes the second objection, which isn't all that different from the first. A quick rebuttal comes from how unlikely Jesus would be to support any tradition—even one named after him—that muddied God's words, given his position on God's commandments versus men's traditions. However, the definitive answer to both objections is found within the closing frame of Mark 7, where someone recognized his divinity and engaged his authority. And, again, I quote from my paper, not a holy and ungratuitous act, yet sure proof I called upon a German scholar:

> In this passage Jesus encounters a Gentile woman (v.25), who asks him to heal her daughter. In no other passage in the New Testament is Jesus swayed in his position. In this one he is. Bultmann says, "The main point is the change in Jesus' behaviour [sic]." I believe Bultmann is right because the change in Jesus' behavior completes the frame of the relationship between the engagement of authority and liberating the oppressed. Many reasons are given for the woman's success with Jesus, and regardless of the reason her daughter is freed from a demon (v.30). Her approach at engaging Jesus as the authority (v.25, 28) mirrors his own: she is rational, by evidence of her rhetorical skills and she is forceful, not in the overt way Jesus is with the Pharisees but in her persistence: after Jesus answers her initial plea with the brash response, "Let the children be satisfied first; it is not right to take the children's bread and throw it to the dogs," (v. 27) she does not give up and displaying her wit responds, "Even the dogs under the table eat the children's scraps" (v.28). Her engagement of authority results in the liberation of an oppressed person, her daughter, just as Jesus' engagement was meant to liberate his followers from a tradition to following the commandments of God.

I concluded by proposing my own Latter-day Saints tradition needed to discard its anti-criticism force field on engaging authority (not so people unwilling to accept such a low bar would take them seriously, but...) so the necessary tension between God and his authorities could exist. Without allowing for the tension, there can be no engagement of traditions of men that deter believers from fulfilling the commandments of God, which risk is much greater than supposed gains, by ensuring maintenance of those traditions to fulfill the commandments. If Jesus engaged authority and would be engaged, how then could anyone who claimed to be his follower not do likewise?

The Mormon scholar Bushman was a long way from the force-field surrounding Mormon authorities. He had the distinct advantage over England and Jeffrey of not being a professor at BYU. But that was not Bushman's main advantage. That could be found in his answer. He took a cultural approach.

If your son or daughter took a degree in the humanities in the past fifty or so years, then he or she was schooled in the cultural approach, otherwise known as critical theory. The history of critical theory is a quite manageable one and, as you would expect because of its rigor and success, quite German. It began with Karl Marx, was expanded by Friedrich Nietzsche and Sigmund Freud, refined by other brilliant Germans and championed by a bunch of other folks in the mid-twentieth century (including the French and other continentalists beside themselves to jump in), all of whom overlapped from one syllabus to another for courses at the div school. As a result of the cultural education, your son or daughter became smart as a whip. The trade-off was that he or she took a degree without knowing much, or anything at all, about the object of the criticism. It's a safe bet he or she probably hasn't read much of what makes up the vilified Western Canon routinely denounced by critical theorists. But this lack of knowledge is not a negative consequence of your child's critical theory education (written in large print on the academia banner as "Postmodern") because that education is about the approach to and not knowledge of a work. Your child is sharp on method and slender on substance and is damn attractive when he or she thinks aloud.

Consistent with valuing approach over substance, critical theorists do not produce value judgments. Judgment depends upon the interpretation of the substance of a work, and a critical approach does not (this claim didn't become less absurd as I wrote it, but it is not any less accurate than the artificial distinction I'm making between critical theory and interpretation, which provides a useful spotlight on critical theory as a cause célèbre, distinguishing it from the banal method of reading closely). A critical approach is an application of a theory with little, often no, demonstrable fidelity to the work. You might intuit for the application of theory to function it must have an awareness of some details, and you would not be mistaken. Details like plot and character are the pretext to the true meaning of a work derived from their association and breaks (enter Freud from stage left), not from their sentences and supporting propositions. It would be a stretch, but not an entirely misleading one, to suggest the meaning is a revelation of what is missing from the text—the latent and repressed—hiding behind the words, deep in the unconscious of the writer and the culture of her times until the critical theorist brings it to light. Postmodern meanings behind the text are more plausible the less traceable their causal connection. And a critical theorist rightly cares as much about a writer's intent as a doctor does the reason a patient ended on her operating table ready for surgery. However they got in front of them is a wasted inquiry because there they are in front of them. God hope she needs the incision because it's a-coming.

In the second half of the twentieth century critical theorists took over humanity departments in the United States like Japanese kudzu vines took over trees in the southern states. One of the most brilliant stars was a Christian Palestinian teaching literature at Columbia University, Edward Said. He is chiefly known for his seminal work, *Orientalism*, but should be known as much for being a close reader—and he was among the very best—as for his expansive intellect. Among Professor Said's many popular theories was that the Western or imperialist or colonialist (all one in the same like the trinity) category of "the other": that is, something different. The other described an object of western conquest and oppression. It could be a people, a culture, or a native tradition. Whatever the category of the other was supposed to cover, it was not merely a category, in the hands of the West it was also representative of abuse.

A discussion of the other has roots spreading from Hegel to Emmanuel Levinas long before the professionalization of critical studies. It took center stage in the reunion of Count Pierre Bezukhov and Prince Andrei Bolkonsky in Leo Tolstoy's *War and Peace*. After joining the Masons, Pierre tried to enact changes to benefit his serfs and visited Andrei to share his ambitions. The two royals, in agreement on progressive views, argued over one's obligations to act for the other, the very nexus of a human being's purpose in life. For anyone engaged in increasing humanity, the slightest reflection on one's action or inaction toward another human being is of the highest import because, aware or not, the level of engagement has consequences, both intended and most assuredly unintended.

Postmodernists or critical theorists don't lend themselves to a unified definition, but they do share many characteristics. Chief among them is the reification of their theories into truth. Their theories have *reproducible* application across contexts. The consequence of this characteristic is no small irony because, for critical theorists, there is no such thing as absolute truth.

There is only convention, or social constructs like artificial categories of truth and honesty and integrity, that can be reduced to the interests of those advocating for them, everything being reducible to its constituent parts of power.

An example of the post-modern fix is a sentence or three on the defense of natural rights of the individual (which are presumably universal if they are natural). Beginning with the proposition there is no such defense. Purist postmodernists assert there is no such thing as a natural right, because all rights are a product of the conditions and context of the community one belongs to. For them there is only context. The appeal to an absence of any universal right depends upon a universal claim that none exists across all contexts, a contradiction not as unrescueable as it appears on first blush, because a purist would presume the exhausting work of analyzing all possible contexts to reach its conclusions, which would inevitably lead to culturally-shaped values. While there is no inherent individual right of liberty (a demonstrable point in critical theorists' quiver as sure as your being born doesn't entitle you to anything, including your continued existence), that absence is not only not a stumbling block but it is a reality necessary for establishing human rights for all.

Human rights are bestowed by families, societies, and progressive bodies, mostly governments. Human rights are defined by group obligation to distribute rights, often understood as entitlements, such as education, health care, shelter, and protection. Human rights not only trump the fictional individual rights, but work against their flourishing in exchange for promoting the ever-growing matrix of fairness. I could have substituted "enlightened" for "progressive" above but nothing insults a postmodernist more than being identified with the secular movement spanning Europe in the 17th to 19th centuries from Spinoza to Kant that gave rise to individual rights, the value placed of autonomy, the irreplaceable value on dignity, all leading to expression and innovation, clustering in collaboration to advances matching the imagination. The group you fell into required your trust and loyalty above all else as surely as any king demanded the same from his subjects. Make no mistake, the difference between the bodies bestowing rights in your neighborhood and the divine aristocracies of yore, both potentially beneficent in large part by virtue of being in power, is enlightenment, albeit postmodernists are in possession of a more colloquial type.

Noteworthy: as one theory is reified into truth status (repeated application across contexts) there is often a simultaneous deconstruction of accepted convention, another colorful scale on the bellies of these modern ball-breakers.

The golden mean of postmodernism or critical theory is Nietzsche's perspectivism. All critical theories depend upon perspectivism's existence like moral law depends upon God's (that is according to critical theorists and theists). According to N's view, all we have are perspectives, none of which provides a vantage point superior to any other (but this reading of N is disputed by those who favor N's philosophy over others'). This is awful close to the quip everything is relative (to your point of view). And it's bolstered by no one point of view telling the whole truth and nothing but the truth. If anyone dares to advocate his vantage was superior, then he invites a high dose of skepticism—the air postmodernists breathe—from his progressive, critically thinking peers.

And if perspective is the mean, then difference is the holy chalice of postmodernism. Properly shouted, "la différance!" The key to understanding difference is not the quality of things but the relations of things. The irreducibility of things relating—by which they have their differences—is not only postmodernists' nectar but also their focal point, first principle, bedrock foundational underbelly of their whole project. This me-centric nexus, as referent and connector for the web of relating (steeped in irony beholden to Kant's revolution of knowledge through individual perception), is then extrapolated to champion all allies and blunt all foes of difference: difference never as category of all possible differences, but rather always meaning favored differences of the day distinguished from the hegemonic or dominant, which once so designated, are exiled from the controlling discourse. Supporters of fashionable differences marshal their strongest proofs by analogies as minute as the indeterminacy of quantum subatomic particles and as timeless as intergalactic space, far too much emphasis on the former and not nearly enough on the latter.

Absent from their proofs are the objective physical laws acting on all of us. In part, the absence results from postmodernists' understanding of "relativity" being akin to runway models' grasp of nutrition—that is things appear different according to one's point of view as sure as bony butts are attractive. Galilean relativity, of the type Einstein's Special Relativity confirmed, established that all humans are equal, not uniquely different. The upshot being that regardless of one's frame of reference, all physical laws apply to all humans the same, all of us being in uniform motion, that is, here on Planet Earth (the category of "uniform" is pliable but precise enough to land people on the moon, create complex global networks, eradicate diseases, and build the iPod). So what's relative about relativity? Time and space are not absolutes and are not even separate categories. The dilution of time and contraction of space appear different in non-uniform motion at sub-atomic levels and on galactic scales. But even for non-uniform motion, the physical laws still *generally* apply to all frames of reference, as demonstrated by Einstein's General Theory. The take-away, postmodernists like me or non-postmodernists like the most reasonable and dependable associate at your work, all interact with the same objective physical laws on Planet Earth. I repeat: relativity is the great equalizer, not divider. Relativity, correctly understood, is disharmonious with postmodernists' belief in fragmentation. An alienation best understood as an insistence to continue playing in the sand box, ever developing more elaborate explanations for old and new games by drawing on wellsprings of imagination to capture every layer, with attention to the layers of layers (the secularized "meta" layer), resisting all entreaties to step outside and address the natural world (everything *and* the kitchen sink), which are perceived as unfair attempts of inexcusable violence on difference.

All of this abstract thought has reached its limit (mine, not necessarily yours) and begs for examples, so just on-time, a cadre of Mormon scholars led by Professor Bushman has made fair use of critical theories to provide cogent explanations (and defenses) of Mormonism over the past couple of decades. But even more significantly it has allowed them to carve out legitimate space within academia for Mormon scholarship heretofore prohibited. While Bushman has served as the group's gentleman in chief, its most prolific and loyal general has been Terryl L. Givens.

Givens is wicked smart with a lion's capacity to maintain and weave complex concepts to explain the legitimacy of Mormonism. He moves effectively from one discipline to another through their shared repository of critical theories and employs them as persuasively as any peer, on any campus, anywhere. He broke in with his first book, *The Viper on the Hearth*, and proceeded to publish book after book with, and all the while introducing his Mormon associates to Oxford University Press, resulting in Oxford Press's being the undisputed platform for the turn-of-the-twenty-first-century Mormon scholarship (supplanting the longstanding role of the University of Illinois Press, which for decades served as the solitary medium of Mormon scholarship with its accompanying scarlet non-academic stain). *The Viper* included a hell of a lot of background information before getting around to

450 MY BEST MORMON LIFE

explaining early Americans' voracious appetite for books, focusing on fiction that treated Mormons as "the other." Givens relied upon Edward Said, applying his refined critical theory of imperialistic abuse of the other to explain the writings of the opponents of Mormonism. He showed how the fiction writers objectified and demonized Mormons and simplified them to remove any recognition of their humanity. He even did it with attention to the details of fictional works, an engagement the best critical theorists have yet to completely avoid. He cited Mary Wollstonecraft for the proposition that objectification was tantamount to erasing an individual's soul and Said's explanation of Western use of "the Orient" to segue to the domestication and exploitation of Mormons. As you might have anticipated, Givens largely focused on the Mormon opponents' spotlight on polygamy in their facile comparison to the Orient. In all, Givens brilliantly showed how fiction abused Mormons, and he did it unabashedly by throwing lightning bolts of critical theory.

Givens did not argue for or propound an original critical theory; instead he accepted its presumed reification into truth (which is the standard pattern of critical theorists). Said's critique of the western process to define the Orient was employed by Givens as a demonstrable truth. Givens did not have to provide an argument in support of it; he only had to assert it as unopposed as "of course it is" truth in concert with academic trends. And Said's theory may just be demonstrable.

Consider a thought experiment. Seriously, don't apply it to yourself. Keep it abstract. Take person A who desires person B. List ten actions taken by person A to win over person B. And how many of those actions objectify person B? How many aim to control person B? Now for the real abstract test, assume person A and person B take romantically. Now list ten actions taken by person A toward person B for any reason under the sun from daily cohabitation to long-term finagling (I'm intentionally picking the most neutral term available to describe what effects lasting compromise through what long sufferers call "sacrifice."). Again, how many of those actions flatten the identity of person B? How many bind person B? How many abuse person B?

We might just have agreed that Said extrapolated features of every personal relationship he ever had or witnessed and then projected them on one culture's overtures to another. But that would be awfully cynical. And there we have another postmodern characteristic, cynicism writ large. Givens showed that the reified concept of the other could be applied to a new context: fictional works abusing Mormonism. By its application, Givens reaffirmed its reification as truth and dismantled (or deconstructed) the corrosive methods used by fiction writers to abuse Mormons as the other. In a nutshell, Givens championed postmodernism, a finely sharpened tool of simultaneous destruction and defense.

Givens was just getting started. He went on to write nearly a half dozen postmodern works published by Oxford. His magnum opus, *By the Hand of Mormon*, successfully cleared space for academic work about the Mormon's sacred scripture, the Book of Mormon. His work was a specific, acceptable type: a sympathetic narrative examining how Mormons and their detractors used the Book of Mormon. What it did not do was support the book's truth claims. In fact (one of the few facts that postmodernists universally accept), establishing truth claims is antithetical to postmodernism because knowledge is an onion with layers of uncertainty, and postmodernists spend hardly any effort making truth out of an onion; what they do is peel away layers of knowledge to enlighten their readers at an uncertain and nonexistent core; that's actually their main project when they seek to destroy traditional truth claims. Few, if ever one, brave postmodern soul attempts to construct their own nourishing onions (not, nor should ever to be confused with the fountain of slick new critical theories constructing new indictments, endless weapons to slice up old conventional claims).

But I protest too much. Postmodern writers at their best create treatises of intellectual prowess. Their works have nary a hint of the descriptions I've provided above. If they have a defining characteristic, it is delineating dynamic boundaries. They explain motion, tracing causes and effects of contingencies, marking interconnections, providing snapshots of pulsating influences. The best postmodernism is a work of humility, the kind that opens a new window to the world. Givens' *By the Hand of Mormon* achieves this higher state if only because his tone and evenhandedness demonstrate responsibility for topics with multiple sides and show awareness of limits, but he also unabashedly and accurately describes the believing Mormon's history and claims.

Critical theories are wildfire running over traditional landscape. One critical theory cannot put out any other theory any more than gasoline can retard a wild blaze. All critical theories end only one way: a slow death after enveloping all the old brush in their path. And, in all their success, critical theories lack one important feature. They are entirely devoid of any reflective alloy.

(I'd have asserted reflective "quality" but anticipated "duh, like there is no such thing as quality": it's a mere conventional category, arbitrarily setting one thing above another thing. In which you have the proof of the very assertion because, if there is no possible comparison—no stratification of quality—then there is not anything objective to measure the comparison. These are interchangeable premises as one follows the other as easily as one leads to the other, like the chicken and egg—for real, just think upon it a few minutes. Thus the critical judgment is not reflexive, which is not the same thing as saying there's nothing to reexamine. The lack of an objective standard is another postmodern hallmark, and so is obscure analysis, so I'm in a pickle whether to rewrite the above obfuscating logical whatever or leave you a taste of postmodernists' flavor).

The consequence is that postmodernism is impotent in any attempt to reflect back on itself; or in other words it's not suited, able, or used to examine or to check itself or other critical theories, and lingual reflection should be a process we all value for the very fact that it separates us humans from other mammals. (This lack of self-reflection is not to be confused with post-structuralism's critique of structuralism, which ignited postmodernism's fire in intellectual corners during the mid-twentieth and early twenty-first centuries). All postmodernists are going one way. One relevant, but less than direct, proof: academic departments move on one-way streets, so a faculty member gets in line or gets left behind or, worse, run over. In a spot-on comparison, academic freedom and its popular counterpart progressive liberalism are like Mormon agency—the subject is free to choose the correct way.

The least of postmodernism's offenses is aiding and abetting Mormon scholarship. Its worse offense should be its inability to critique all cultures, primitive and industrial. Take one case study, *Mountain of the Cannibal God* (1978), a classic B movie starring the diva Ursula Andress, who oozed sexuality beginning with her breakthrough performance as Honey Ryder in *Dr. No* (1962). There is no possible postmodern critique of the natives who almost converted the captured Ms. Stevenson (Andress) to cannibalism because no one perspective is more superior than any other. I am not setting up a straw-woman. The heavens know I wish I were. The critical theorist's mental block about critiquing their favored cultures, some nonwestern and some not, is as certain as your snake handler's against the next bite (this mental instability should not to be confused with the ineptitude in criticizing dominant western cultures, the lapdog of critical theorists' work). But if its failure were the worst offense, we could probably still occasionally breathe knowing we are at least being presented with a credible alternative to accepted norms. But that is not all that is happening as we are expected to accept the natives of *Cannibal God.*

Postmodernism exposes traditional shortcomings and champions its own. Its purpose is not the destruction of traditional truths as much as it is their replacement. Permitting myself one more swing, postmodernism does not only create a void, it then fills it, intentionally to exchange power, not to replace exposed old with new or better truth but with their favored position; although the two—truth and in-vogue campaigns—thank god are not exclusive. And the most persuasive means to fill the newly voided space is with a compelling narrative, a narrative not based on facts, because no postmodern would be caught with his pants down privileging facts, but based on composites of the non-western life that advances and insulates the position of the other.

Which gets us to the most pernicious consequence of our current western cultures' saturation of postmodernism represented by the fallout of the notorious coverage of the death of Mohammed al-Durrah, who was caught in the crossfire of Israeli forces and Palestinian resistors in the Gaza Strip on September 30, 2000. This single event united the world against Israel and all western civilization, and served as the calling card for critics' righteous indignation against Israel, continually re-invoked to justify atrocity after atrocity for the decade that followed. The "facts" of the French public channel that produced the event were called into question. True to form, a postmodern narrative is not open to criticism, so the French "public" station sued for libel and defamation. And in even truer postmodern form, their position was to shift the burden of proof to the accuser, who claimed that the station staged the shooting, instead of carrying the burden to show the actual event. If the facts mattered, that is if the channel held in trust the public's faith and assumed a reciprocating duty to the public, the French public channel would insist on a neutral commission to review and to vindicate the facts. But the focus is not on the facts, as surely as it never was. The French channel upheld the integrity of its narrative, not facts, for which they are complicit. The young Mohammed may have actually been killed, but for postmodernists that becomes a tidbit in the shadow of the narrative that told the world he did. A postmodernist may offer, in the French public channel's defense, that the death of twelve-year-old Mohammed symbolized the deaths of many Palestinians, so even if it was staged—as the full footage of the event may indicate—the symbol of brutality was no less true. That has more to say about the hollow symbol based on nothing than it does the fatal engagements of the parties, as surely as other similar justifications abuse the "actual" events in life to reduce them to further a story that shifts power. If one life matters—and for many of us, one life does—then proof of the facts is not collateral to those who provide the story. It is central, which we must hold in trust if anyone is to be responsible. That progressive righteous indignation spread across all Europe and America against Israel and western values measures the danger of postmodernism's license to create a narrative for power.

Maybe aiding and abetting Mormon scholarship and other "others" might not be so excusable either. Take one foundational example, the founding prophet Joseph Smith's "First Vision." Postmodernists do not opine on whether the event of the "First Vision" has significance because the fact that it has come to have significance does. The move from inquiring into the authenticity of a thing is far less important than how people talk about the thing. The narrative or re-telling of the thing is a fact—the others' triumph. And why not the displacement of the actual event to its retelling, since determining the authenticity, that is whether something really happened, is impossible to unearth? This move could not be a more blatant excuse because at the very least the probability of the thing is still something. And getting close to the actual thing not only drives academic departments from over-populated New Testament studies to under-populated genome projects but it moves within our being to know and to feel it. Experiencing, or closely connecting to, things in the past has authenticity as surely as they influence things in our present. Postmodernism's paucity of truth is the others' ultimate gain. But another move pronounces Postmodernism's ultimate worth. The actuality of the thing in the present still depends on its purported actuality in the past—the surest sign of Postmodernism's lie. Mormons, like other "others," not only hold firmly to the narrative that emerges, but also literalize its latest version as a timeless one. Then the narrative as fact is hardly its final state, nor its final conclusion.

Nothing is more important than the role of narrative in our postmodern age. There ain't a drip of false faith in its power. Narrative is the medium by which we understand our past, communicate our fleeting present, and project our future. It is how we describe our experiences in the world. It creates and provides the backdrop for the images that startle, hold, and calm us. It connects us to events and directs us to what is possible by engaging our thoughts and emotions. It produces new ideas, warms us, challenges us, and reminds us what and who we love. It sets the criteria by which we comprehend and judge events and people. It includes the stories we share, sound bites we hear, and headlines we follow. Postmodernists know that quantity of information far outweighs the quality, not because they fail to advance a quality but because for the believing majority sheer mass of what is told kills in comparison to how and what is, given the lack of time to discriminate either. No group appreciates the information load and quality gap more than Mormons. They dump torrential rains of narrative twice a year at bi-annual worldwide conferences, and at weekly services throughout the year. It is impossible to dry off while spending all the other time serving in lay church capacities and raising an eternal unit of family. If one did have time to find truth, it requires mining tomes of narrative to reach it. Parties who get our postmodern fix, open floodgates of stories they want told and dam ones they don't. Bushman and his heralded contemporary Mormons scholars get it, flawlessly reaching into the multicultural toolbox and wielding its tools to ensure the telling of theirs.

Thank almighty God there is no hint of the application of "critical theories" in the writings of Mormonism's finest thinker, B.H. Roberts. Roberts' work bleeds a commitment to old-fashioned inquiry for truth. Truth is, or equals, a claim that corresponds to reality. For example, when Einstein asserted the curvature of outer space and later experiments proved the curvature: well, the two parts equaled a truth; all parts were true before Einstein asserted one and cohorts proved the other. That leads us to conclude there are many undiscovered truths, so get busy and discover a few.

Roberts enjoyed a distinct advantage: his approach tapped into his gigantic appetite for knowledge. During the course of his life, he ably explicated and defended Mormon beliefs, practices and traditions, including its keystone scripture, the Book of Mormon. In the early 1900s, he completed a series of works, *New Witnesses for God*, for the explicit purpose of proving the authenticity of the Book of Mormon. Twenty years later, over the last years of his life, his appetite did not wane when he became the Book of Mormon's greatest but unknown critic in a series of unpublished papers, "Book of Mormon Difficulties," "A Book of Mormon Study," and "A Parallel." In them he provided exhaustive analysis of specific threats to the book's claims to authenticity.

Copies of these later papers existed in Church archives, cited at times by prominent Mormon apologists, but they did not reach the public until half a century after they were written, when Roberts' heirs gave copies to the University of Utah, the bastion to many Mormon critical thinkers (not critical theorists). Two of the most famous Mormon Running Utes were the aforementioned Sterling M. McMurrin and Brigham D. Madsen. Both were generous, brilliant scholars, but both bore the sure sign of a Mormon critic of Mormonism, artificial condescension, revealing it in their short introductions to the compilation of Roberts' works, *Studies of the Book of Mormon*, which was published shortly after Roberts' heirs delivered the manuscripts to the university. As in his introduction to Roberts' magnum opus, *The Truth, The Way, The Life*, McMurrin complimented Roberts but was beside himself to point out Roberts' scholastic amateurism, and Madsen did the same, bemoaning Roberts' dependence upon secondary sources and lengthy quotations.

A close reading of Roberts' late *Studies of the Book of Mormon* shows not only an enthusiastic and expansive mind but also one capable of holding and explaining clearly complex subjects. His use of secondary sources reflected the lack of access to primary sources, and his commitment to readers who no doubt relied upon his excerpts for a fair context. More importantly, it showed the key to a successful interpretation depends upon accurate reproduction of the text(s) that one's interpreting. On strength of argument alone, Roberts qualified himself among the best of Mormon minds, McMurrin's included. His supreme intellect shined through but, more importantly, his final arguments demonstrated one bent on getting at the truth. And what could be a better testament to an intellectual life than having an undying will to find truth to the very end? Roberts achieved more than was possible for those behind the certainty of a prophet's collar and complacency of the scholar's armchair.

His explicit purpose for writing the later papers was not, as before, to support, nor had it changed to discredit, the authenticity of the book. He wrote the later papers for the benefit of the youth of the Church, whom he expected would inquire into the validity of the challenges to the book's authenticity, and he saw answering the challenges as his and other Church leaders' responsibility. He presented his first paper, "Book of Mormon Difficulties" to the leadership of the Church to garner their help in fulfilling his purpose. Not worried about their generation but worrying about the perennially inquisitive youth of the Church for generations to come, he noted his disappointment in the leadership's responses, some relying upon his own earlier work to refute him, in a sincere letter of concern to then-president of the Church, Heber J. Grant. But his disappointment prompted the additional and more complete "Book of Mormon Study," and the compendium "A Parallel." Mormon scholars dispute whether Roberts' belief in the authenticity of the Book of Mormon failed in his last years. What no one disputes was his standard for truth did not.

In order for the Book of Mormon to be what it claimed to be, a historic record of people who migrated from the Middle East to America and taught the mission of Jesus Christ six hundred years before the birth and death of Jesus of Nazareth in Palestine, then the information within the book had to correspond to reality—external to the book, but also within it. For example, the historical facts within in it, and its composition by ancient authors, had to pass objective standards. The seismic power of the Book of Mormon was its very claims to authentic history with a very strong emphasis on God's acting in history through his prophets, so any appeal to subjective proof such as a really, really, really strong personal divine confirmation was inadequate to carry the burden it was true. Roberts understood this better than any of his peers.

One of the many issues Roberts addressed in his later studies draws as stark a line as any on the claim of the book's authenticity. In item twelve of "A Parallel," he stated that

> Lehi's Colony brought with them from Jerusalem the Old Testament (the whole Bible) down to the days of Jeremiah—about 600 BC; yet about the only books extensively quoted before the coming of Christ to America is Isaiah! Jacob, the brother of First Nephi, quotes nearly all of 49, 50, and 51st chapters; and Nephi quotes about thirteen full chapters from Isaiah (see "Synopsis of chapters" in current editions of B. of M. p. 524). The Hebrew records possessed by the Nephites on brass plates are spoken of as containing more matter more than the Old Testament had among the Gentiles (I Nephi 13: 20-23). Then why are quotations and references to this great and rich Hebrew literature confined practically to Isaiah alone?....

The answer in the opposite column is that one of the possible sources for the book (Ethan Smith's *View of the Hebrews*) also quoted extensively from Isaiah. Most of the Isaiah chapters in the Book of Mormon are direct quotations from the Kings James Version of the Bible, another possible source. But Mormon apologists point out that many of the Isaiah passages include more detail than the Isaiah passages in the King James Version. They assert the more extensive passages of Isaiah in the brass plates brought by Lehi's Colony from the Holy Land to America and quoted by ancient Book of Mormon prophets evidence a more complete and original Isaiah. This is an extraordinary claim. If it is true, then those chapters alone provide sweeping justification for its value to all those with an interest in the Holy Bible.

For thousands of years the Old Testament part of the Holy Bible (the Jewish Bible, or Tanakh) was based on one of a couple of versions, and I don't mean the various revised this and standard that in your local bookstore or studied at the seminary around the corner from your favorite pub. All of those versions, including the King James Version, and the Tanakh, stem from the Masoretic Text, Hebrew manuscripts written down in the tenth century Common Era (CE). The other version, which is not widely circulated, is the Septuagint, the ancient Greek version translated from the Hebrew Scriptures over the last few centuries Before Common Era (BCE). While based on even more ancient Hebrew manuscripts than the Masoretic Text, the Greek Septuagint shares a striking overall fidelity despite many variations. The necessity of a definitive Greek version ought to come as no surprise, since Greek culture was valued above all others from the expansion of Alexander the Great's empire well into the highs and lows of the Roman Empire, including when Christianity blossomed in the fourth century CE. Then a new Bible was discovered in the late 1940s and early 1950s in caves near the Dead Sea, southeast of Jerusalem. It's taken the name, The Dead Sea Scrolls Bible. Its manuscripts date from the third century BCE to the first half of the first century CE. Its discovery was important for many reasons, including one pertinent to the matter of the Book of Mormon's authenticity. The entire Isaiah book of sixty-sixty chapters was discovered in a full manuscript and among numerous fragments near the Dead Sea. The Dead Sea Scrolls Bible largely mirrored the Masoretic text written down some ten centuries later. It had more differences with the Septuagint, but also shared an overwhelming fidelity to it. There were many variations between the three, most of which involved the Dead Sea scrolls' not including additions found in the later-in-time Masoretic text. That is to say, the Dead Sea version of Isaiah presented an earlier version without many scribal additions, consistent with the evolution of scripture.

The Book of Mormon's version of Isaiah is the opposite. While Isaiah was contained in the brass plates carried in the exodus of Lehi's Colony to the New World in the early sixth century BCE, far earlier in time than the construction of any of the other three versions, it included not fewer writings but rather more, much more than the other versions. The other three extant versions, Masoretic, Septuagint, and Dead Sea Scrolls represent a devolution from the older Isaiah in the brass plates. The contrast suggests these three were largely not projects of fidelity to older manuscripts as widely believed—and proved by the discovery of the Dead Sea Scroll Bible—but instead were heavily corrupted by scribes who made significant deletions from the originals they copied, in addition to the many more, minor additions. The recent discovery of the Dead Sea Scrolls and its fidelity to the other Bible versions may be the biggest challenge to the authenticity of the Book of Mormon that Roberts' never knew about.

The brass plates quoted in the Book of Mormon included twenty-one of the sixty-six chapters from Isaiah (chapters 2-14, 29, 48-54), and none was more significant than Isaiah 29, quoted in 2 Nephi 27. The brass plates version of Isaiah 29 differed from the other three versions from the beginning. Unlike the other three versions, in the earliest verses of the brass plates, there was no emphasis on God's laying siege to Jerusalem and forcing its inhabitants to speak as from the dust, but rather the brass plates emphasized the wickedness of gentiles and Jews in the last days, picking up on the shared theme between all the versions of nations fighting against Jerusalem. While the first passages were not insignificant variations, the major difference in the brass plates was the addition of nineteen verses to cover material in two verses in the other three versions.

Leading up to the two verses in question, God stated that people were blind to the truth *for the Lord has spread over you a spirit of deep sleep, and has shut your eyes, the prophets, and covered your heads, the seers* (Isaiah 29: 10 from the Tanakh; because the themes are less cryptic in its translation I use it here). The two verses in question follow: *So that all prophecy has been to you like the words of a sealed document. If it is handed to one who can read and he is asked to read it, he will say, "I can't, because it is sealed"; and if the document is handed to one who cannot read and he is asked to read it, he will say, "I can't read"* (29: 11-12). The next verse is often quoted, as you'll recall even by Jesus in the New Testament, *My Lord said: Because that people has approached me with its mouth and honored me with its lips, but has kept its heart far from me, and its worship of me has been a commandment of men, learned by rote* (29: 13). Prophecy was right before God's chosen people, but they were blind to it. (God had Isaiah previously seal his testimony in Chapter 8: 16 after describing the stumbling masses.)

The brass plates' much earlier version of Isaiah 29, recorded in the Book of Mormon, expands the literal meaning of the sealed book, so please bear with me to appreciate it:

6 And it shall come to pass that the Lord God shall bring forth unto you the words of a book, and they shall be the words of them which have slumbered. 7 And behold the book shall be sealed; and the book shall be a revelation from God, from the beginning of the world to the ending thereof. 8 Wherefore, because of the things which are sealed up, the things which are sealed shall not be delivered in the day of the wickedness and abominations of the people. Wherefore the book shall be kept from them. 9 But the book shall be delivered unto a man, and he shall deliver the words of the book, which are the words of those who have slumbered in the dust, and he shall deliver these words unto another; 10 But the words which are sealed he shall not deliver, neither shall he deliver the book. For the book shall be sealed by the power of God, and the revelation which was sealed shall be kept in the book until the own due time of the Lord, that they may come forth; for behold, they reveal all things from the foundation of the world unto the end thereof. 11 And the day cometh that the words of the book which were sealed shall be read upon the house tops; and they shall be read by the power of Christ; and all things shall be revealed unto the children of men which ever have been among the children of men, and which ever will be even unto the end of the earth. 12 Wherefore, at that day when the book shall be delivered unto the man of whom I have spoken, the book shall be hid from the eyes of the world, that the eyes of none shall behold it save it be that three witnesses shall behold it, by the power of God, besides him to whom the book shall be delivered; and they shall testify to the truth of the book and the things therein. 13 And there is none other which shall view it, save it be a few according to the will of God, to bear testimony of his word unto the children of men; for the Lord God hath said that the words of the faithful should speak as if it were from the dead. 14 Wherefore, the Lord God will proceed to bring forth the words of the book; and in the mouth of as many witnesses as seemeth him good will he establish his word; and wo be unto him that rejecteth the word of God! 15 But behold, it shall come to pass that the Lord God shall say unto him to whom he shall deliver the book: Take these words which are not sealed and deliver them to another, that he may show them unto the learned, saying: Read this,

I pray thee. And the learned shall say: Bring hither the book, and I will read them. 16 And now, because of the glory of the world and to get gain will they say this, and not for the glory of God. 17 And the man shall say: I cannot bring the book, for it is sealed. 18 Then shall the learned say: I cannot read it. 19 Wherefore it shall come to pass, that the Lord God will deliver again the book and the words thereof to him that is not learned; and the man that is not learned shall say: I am not learned. 20 Then shall the Lord God say unto him: The learned shall not read them, for they have rejected them, and I am able to do mine own work; wherefore thou shalt read the words which I shall give unto thee. 21 Touch not the things which are sealed, for I will bring them forth in mine own due time; for I will show unto the children of men that I am able to do mine own work. 22 Wherefore, when thou has read the words which I have commanded thee, and obtained the witnesses which I have promised unto thee, then shalt thou seal up the book again, and hide it up unto me, that I may preserve the words which thou has not read, until I shall see fit in mine own wisdom to reveal all things unto the children of men. 23 For behold, I am God; and I am a God of miracles; and I will show unto the world that I am the same yesterday, today, and forever; and I work not among the children of men save it be according to their faith. 24 And again is shall come to pass that the Lord shall say unto him that shall read the words that shall be delivered him. (2 Nephi 27)

Which brings us back to the verse in all the versions, marked as thirteen in the other three versions, *Forasmuch as this people draw near unto me with their mouth, and with their lips do honor me, but have removed their hearts far from me, and their fear towards me is taught by the precepts of men* (2 Nephi 27: 25; almost exactly as included in the King James Version).

This elaboration of the metaphor of prophecy as a book to a literal book brought forth to "the man of whom I have spoken" (2 Nephi 27: 12) has to be considered one of the most significant variations between versions of the Holy Bible. I dare you, find a bigger one. Aside from the conspicuous change in style, most obvious in the differences of vocabulary, meter, and syntax, in the nineteen verses from the three other versions of Isaiah (which differences are consistent for all the elaborated passages in the brass plates), Isaiah of the brass plates framed these verses—deleted by scribes from the other three versions—with the standard Book of Mormon phrase, "shall come to pass"

(27: 6, 24), but more importantly with revelation "from the beginning of the world to the ending thereof" (27: 7) and the "God of miracles...[who is] the same yesterday, today, and forever..." (27: 23). This passage is truly a revelation. Within the text the revelation is clearly the sealed book that will be brought forth by the man it "shall be delivered unto" (27: 9). No revelation could be more significant to the last days than one that *reveals all things from the foundation of the world unto the end thereof* (27: 10; the last days also noted in the opening verse, which is a variation unique to the brass plates) when the Book of Mormon came forth.

The passages go beyond showing Isaiah's unparalleled prophetic ability. They foretell the sequence of events highlighting a specific period in the early history of the Mormon Church—the translation of the gold plates into what is now the Book of Mormon. Joseph Smith first saw the gold plates on September 22, 1823, after four consecutive visits from the angel Moroni. He finally took possession of the plates four years later in September of 1827. From December of 1827 to June of 1829, he translated the Book of Mormon, completing the majority of the translation within three months when the third of three scribes, Oliver Cowdery, arrived on April 5, 1829. Joseph Smith described this period of translation in his own words, recorded in the "Joseph Smith History" (JSH) in the "Pearl of Great Price," appended to many editions of the Book of Mormon. Verses 27-54 of the JSH relay the visits and instructions from the angel Moroni. Verses 55-75 of the JSH relay the period of translation. In the latter set of verses, Joseph described an event involving his second scribe, Martin Harris (his first scribe was his wife Emma), who presented a copy of characters from the gold plates and a translation of them to a professor of ancient languages at Columbia University, Charles Anthon. Professor Anthon attested the characters were authentic and the translation correct, but recanted when Harris informed him an angel of God made the translation possible. Professor Anthon requested to have the book brought to him so he could translate it. Upon which Harris replied the book was sealed. To which Professor Anthon said, "I cannot read a sealed book" (verse 65).

Isaiah of the brass plates saw the men's actual verbal exchange (2 Nephi 27: 17-18). Isaiah also identified the three witnesses who saw the gold plates by the power of God (27: 12) during a visit from an angel, as recorded in "The Testimony of Three Witnesses" in the preface to the Book of Mormon. But God rightly told Isaiah he would retain discretion over who would see the gold plates "in the mouth of as many witnesses as seemeth him good"

(27: 14) as others did, including "The Testimony of Eight Witnesses" also in the preface.

If the point-on prophetic voice of Isaiah in the brass plates has failed to move you, then consider just how it must have affected Joseph and his scribes. Harris took the copy of characters and the translation to Professor Anthon in February 1828. After receiving Professor Anthon's confirmation (contradicted later by Anthon's own accounts), Harris was so inspired he went home and sold his farm to support Joseph, and he helped Joseph pick up the work of translating the gold plates. They completed a significant portion of 116 pages, the Book of Lehi. Then what followed was the darkest period of the translation, when Harris convinced Joseph to allow Harris to take the 116-page manuscript to show his wife (who had not been as supportive of the farm's sale) to justify the dramatic change in their lives. Subsequently the 116-page manuscript was lost, and the Lord commanded Joseph not to re-translate it. Then in March of 1829, Oliver Cowdery became the scribe, and the two finished the translation by June. God had anticipated the lost 116-page manuscript, because Nephi, the author of the first prophetic writings in the Book of Mormon, was commanded to keep a record "of many things upon them which are good" in addition to a record of the genealogy of his people he was already keeping (2 Nephi 5: 28-33) that covered the same time period as the Book of Lehi. Imagine how relieved Joseph must have been to see that God had anticipated a replacement to the lost manuscript. By the time Joseph translated Isaiah 29 (2 Nephi 27), Harris was no longer the scribe. But Joseph's own relief could hardly have compared to Harris's upon learning that the Isaiah of the brass plates foretold of his encounter with Professor Anthon.

What compounds the problem of Isaiah in the Book of Mormon is that a large portion, if not all, was composed *after* Lehi's Colony took the brass plates with them to America (about 600 BCE). Various interpretations of Isaiah explain the overall composition of the book, but no scholars worth their socks deny the book is separated into at least two distinct parts with multiple authors. But first, a little background about the book: Recall that Israel's monarchy split after most of the tribes of Israel refused to accept David's grandson Rehoboam as King (about 930 BCE). Subsequently Rehoboam set up shop in Jerusalem, with only the tribes of Judah and Benjamin still loyal to the Davidic Reign. This area became known as Judah, or the Southern Kingdom, while the other ten tribes remained in Israel, or the Northern

Kingdom. Enter the historical Isaiah, who prophesied in the Southern King-dom of Judah during the second half of the eighth century BCE (between 740 and 700 BCE), most notably during the reign of Hezekiah, King of Ju-dah (about 715 to 700 BCE). During this time, the Assyrians conquered the ten tribes of the Northern Kingdom of Israel (about 720 BCE), who were deported, and forever-after known as the "Lost Tribes." Condemnations of Judah and Israel, interspersed with promises, and attention to the Assyrian conquest of the Northern Kingdom and Assyria's eventual defeat make up the first part, Chapters 1-39. Chapters 40-66, the second part, cover the res-toration of Judah with attention to the Babylonian exile (as a result of the Babylonian King Nebuchadnezzer's sacking of Judah about 586 BCE), and the promise of liberation by the great Persian King (about 539 BCE).

Aside from historical markers like the destruction of Judah, its exile, and restoration, scholars have explored numerous explanations about the coherence of the book. The explorations go beyond historical analysis to in-depth comparisons of structure, themes, and language. I commend them all. Suffice it to say the differences between first Isaiah (Chapters 1-39) and sec-ond Isaiah (Chapters 40-66) are as diverse as the additional nineteen verses in Isaiah 29 in the brass plates from the other three Bible versions (but I exaggerate, as the differences within Isaiah aren't nearly that big; scholars have proposed less traditional divisions, suggesting that the chapters in the 30s act as a prologue to the second part; others have proposed a third author for Chapters 56-66; some have pointed out the Babylonian exile was pre-supposed in the first as well as the second part, reasonably concluding that the composition began in exile and concluded sometime after the liberation from Babylon and return to Judah). Some scholars propose a unified book while still acknowledging the various parts and authors. For a thorough re-view of all the points of view, I commend Brevard S. Child's *Isaiah: A Com-mentary*.

Whatever scholars have proposed, there's no dispute that the use of Isa-iah is highly favored among religious believers. Jews understand Isaiah to be about the fall and restoration of Judah (based on a close reading of the text), and Christians understand Isaiah to foretell the coming of Jesus Christ (a symbolic reading of the text). Could it be both? To answer, you must read it. Have a commentary near when you do. If you take seriously anything I say, then this advice should be it.

Mormon apologists side with the ultra-traditional claim the Book of Isaiah has one author, who was understood to have unparalleled prophetic power. Sidney B. Sperry makes this argument in his essay, "The 'Isaiah Problem' in the Book of Mormon." This traditional claim goes that Isaiah lived during the Assyrian destruction of the Northern Kingdom and looming threats to the Southern Kingdom, and God gave him the power to see the destruction of the temple and exile in Babylon a century and some later, and its restoration a half of a century after that. Isaiah's prophetic power was so great that he knew the very name of the Persian King who would liberate Judah from Babylon (referencing Cyrus in 44: 28 and 45: 1). The existence of both parts of Isaiah in the brass plates have given some of the more rigorous Mormon thinkers like Givens pause enough to propose the Isaiah passages from the brass plates must be understood by a Midrashic reading. But none of them, including Givens, explain what that entails, and for good reason. Midrashic interpretation examines a text, or seeks, for its hidden, deeper meaning. Midrash explains obscurities and incongruities. To propose that the Isaiah passages from the brass plates illuminate hidden meaning amounts to ignoring them, which the best Mormon thinkers universally do. That's because the additions in the Isaiah brass plates offer expansive elaborations. They are brazen revelations like the existence of the ordinance of baptism in Isaiah 48: 1, *Hearken and hear this, O house of Jacob, who are called by the name of Israel, and are come forth out of the waters of Judah, or out of the waters of baptism, who swear by the name of the Lord, and make mention of the God of Israel, yet they swear not in truth nor in righteousness* (1 Nephi 20: 1). This passage proves a central doctrine in Mormon theology: the principles and ordinances (such as baptism) of the gospel were necessary for everyone and were fulfilled in old Biblical, pre-Jesus Christ times.

For many Mormons there is no reason to pause, because seeing the pending exile and liberation of Judah was only the beginning of Isaiah's prophetic powers. His real power came from foretelling the coming of Christ and the restoration of the gospel of Christ (in the cited passage from the brass plates as recorded in the Book of Mormon above). For Mormons—and most Christians—Isaiah foretold of Christ throughout his book in all extant Bible versions, naming just a few: born of virgin with the name Immanuel (7: 14), the great Messiah passages immortalized by Handel such as Chapter 9: 6, and the suffering servant as in Chapter 53: 2-12 (7: "he is brought as a lamb to the slaughter"). For Mormons, Isaiah's foretelling was much more. His testimony of Christ is why the Book of Mormon prophets quoted him. The reference to "the power of Christ" in verse fourteen of Isaiah 29 in the brass plates (recorded in 2 Nephi 27: 11) shows the real power of Isaiah (and goes without saying is another slight variation from the other three Bible versions). Permit me to repeat myself. Believing a single author received the prophecies recorded in Isaiah part one and part two is hardly a challenge to its authentic existence as recorded in the brass plates brought by Lehi's Colony to the New World, in light of Isaiah's much larger purpose in concert with the Book of Mormon prophets to foretell of Christ.

Which brings us to the single greatest challenge to the authenticity of the Book of Mormon: the foretelling of Christ. The Book's Christology of Jesus Christ exceeds the horizon of prophetic possibility; that it is to say a rendition of a Christology is explication of doctrine, not prophesy. If I may repeat myself, the view of Jesus Christ shared in the Book of Mormon is not a prophetic one. It is a description of events and beliefs developed by his followers in ancient Palestine and later by Church fathers. One thirty-verse excerpt from some five hundred plus years before the birth of Christ will suffice:

1 Now I, Nephi, do speak somewhat concerning the words which I have written, which have been spoken by the mouth of Isaiah. For behold, Isaiah spake many things which were hard for many of my people to understand; for they know not concerning the manner of prophesying among the Jews. 2 For I, Nephi, have not taught them many things concerning the manner of the Jews; for their works were works of darkness, and their doings of abominations. 3 Wherefore, I write unto my people, unto all those that shall receive hereafter these things which I write, that they may know the judgments of God, that they come upon all nations, according to the word which he hath spoken. 4 Wherefore, hearken, O my people, which are the house of Israel, and give ear unto my words; for because the words of Isaiah are not plain unto you, nevertheless they are plain unto all those that are filled with the spirit of prophecy. But I give unto you a prophecy, according to the spirit which is in me; wherefore I shall prophesy according to the plainness which hath been with me from the time that I came out from Jerusalem with my father; for behold, my soul delighteth in plainness unto my people, that they may learn. 5 Yea, and my soul delighteth in the words of Isaiah, for I came out from Jerusalem, and mine eyes hath beheld the things of the Jews, and I know that the Jews do understand the things of the prophets, and there is none other people that understand the things which were spoken unto the Jews like unto them, save it be that they are taught after the manner of

the things of the Jews. 6 But behold, I, Nephi, have not taught my children after the manner of the Jews; but behold, I, of myself, have dwelt at Jerusalem, wherefore I know concerning the regions round about; and I have made mention unto my children concerning the judgments of God, which hath come to pass among the Jews, unto my children, according to all that which Isaiah hath spoken, and I do not write them. 7 But behold, I proceed with mine own prophecy, according to my plainness; in the which I know that no man can err; nevertheless, in the days that the prophecies of Isaiah shall be fulfilled men shall know of a surety, at the times when they shall come to pass. 8 Wherefore, they are of worth unto the children of men, and he that supposeth that they are not, unto them will I speak particularly, and confine the words unto mine own people; for I know that they shall be of great worth unto them in the last days; for in that day shall they understand them; wherefore, for their good have I written them. 9 And as one generation hath been destroyed among the Jews because of iniquity, even so have they been destroyed from generation to generation according to their iniquities; and never hath any of them been destroyed save it were foretold them by the prophets of the Lord. 10 Wherefore, it hath been told them concerning the destruction which should come unto them, immediately after my father left Jerusalem; nevertheless, they hardened their hearts; and according to my prophecy they have been destroyed, save it be those which are carried away captive into Babylon. 11 And now this I speak because of the spirit which is in me. And notwithstanding they have been carried away they shall return again, and possess the land of Jerusalem; wherefore, they shall be restored again to the land of their inheritance. 12 But, behold, they shall have wars, and rumors of wars; and when the day cometh that the Only Begotten of the Father, yea, even the Father of heaven and of earth, shall manifest himself unto them in the flesh, behold, they will reject him, because of their iniquities, and the hardness of their hearts, and the stiffness of their necks. 13 Behold, they will crucify him; and after he is laid in a sepulcher for the space of three days he shall rise from the dead, with healing in his wings; and all those who shall believe on his name shall be saved in the kingdom of God. Wherefore, my soul delighteth to prophesy concerning him, for I have seen his day, and my heart doth magnify his holy name. 14 And behold it shall come to pass that after the Messiah hath risen from the dead, and hath manifested himself unto his people, unto as many as will believe on his name, behold, Jerusalem shall be destroyed again; for wo unto them that fight against God and the people of his church. 15 Wherefore, the Jews shall be scattered among all nations; yea, and also Babylon shall be destroyed; wherefore, the Jews shall be scattered by other nations. 16 And after they have been scattered, and the Lord God hath scourged them by other nations for the space of many generations, yea, even down from generation to generation until they shall be persuaded to believe in Christ, the Son of God, and the atonement, which is infinite for all mankind—and when that day shall come that they shall believe in Christ, and worship the Father in his name, with pure hearts and clean hands, and look not forward any more for another Messiah, then, at that time, the day will come that it must needs be expedient that they should believe these things. 17 And the Lord will set his hand again the second time to restore his people from their lost and fallen state. Wherefore, he will proceed to do a marvelous work and a wonder among the children of men. 18 Wherefore, he shall bring forth his words unto them, which words shall judge them at the last day, for they shall be given them for the purpose of convincing them of the true Messiah, who was rejected by them; and unto the convincing of them that they need not look forward any more for a Messiah to come, for there should not any come, save it should be a false Messiah which should deceive the people; for there is save one Messiah spoken of by the prophets, and that Messiah is he who should be rejected of the Jews. 19 For according to the words of the prophets, the Messiah cometh in six hundred years from the time that my father left Jerusalem; and according to the words of the prophets, and also the word of the angel of God, his name shall be Jesus Christ, the Son of God. 20 And now, my brethren, I have spoken plainly that ye cannot err. And as the Lord God liveth that brought Israel up out of the land of Egypt, and gave unto Moses power that he should heal the nations after they had been bitten by the poisonous serpents, if they would cast their eyes unto the serpent which he did raise up before them, and also gave him power that he should smite the rock and the water should come forth; yea, behold I say unto you, that as these things are true, and as the Lord God liveth, there is none other name given under heaven save it be this Jesus Christ, of which I have spoken, whereby man can be saved. 21 Wherefore, for this cause hath the Lord God promised unto me that these things which I write shall be kept and preserved, and handed down unto my seed, from generation to generation, that the promise may be fulfilled unto Joseph, that his seed should never perish as long as the earth should stand. 22 Wherefore, these things shall go from generation to generation as long as the earth shall stand; and they shall go according to the will and pleasure of God; and the nations who shall possess them shall be judged of them according to the words which are written. 23 For we labor diligently to write, to persuade our children, and also our brethren, to believe in Christ, and to be reconciled to God; for we know that it is by grace that we are saved, after all we can do. 24 And, notwithstanding we believe in Christ, we keep the law of Moses, and look forward with steadfastness unto Christ, until the law shall be fulfilled. 25 For, for this end was the law given; wherefore the law hath become dead unto us, and we are made alive in Christ because of our faith; yet we keep the law because of the commandments. 26 And we talk of Christ, we rejoice in Christ, we preach of Christ, we prophesy of Christ, and we write according to our prophecies, that our children may know to what source they may look for a remission of sins. 27 Wherefore, we speak concerning the law that our children may know the deadness of the law; and they by knowing the deadness of the law, may look forward unto that life which is in Christ, and know for what end that law was given. And after the law is fulfilled in Christ, that they need not harden their hearts against him when the law ought to be done away. 28 And now behold, my people, ye are a stiffnecked people; wherefore, I have spoken plainly unto you, that ye cannot misunderstand. And the words which I have spoken shall stand as a testimony against you; for they are sufficient to teach any man the right way; for the right way is to believe in Christ and deny him not; for by denying him ye also deny the prophets and the law. 29 And now behold, I say unto you that the right way is to believe in Christ, and deny him not; and Christ is the Holy One of Israel; wherefore ye must bow down before him, and worship him with all your might, mind, and strength, and your whole soul; and if you do this ye shall in nowise be cast out. 30 And, inasmuch as it shall be expedient, ye must keep the performances and ordinances of God until the law shall be fulfilled which was given unto Moses. (2 Nephi 25)

• • •

The tradeoff for too plain a speech is not having any opportunity for a reasonable alternative explanation or any incongruence inviting a Midrashic reading or hope of resurrecting. 2 Nephi 25 is the banner chapter for the Christology of Christ in the Book of Mormon. Jesus Christ saves Mormons after all they can do (25: 23). The chapter also epitomizes the style of the Book of Mormon prophets: not always coherent, with thoughts leading into unrelated thoughts, or leaving thoughts unfinished, a shortcoming that perhaps I inherited through osmosis, during the many readings of the Book of Mormon in my youth and young adulthood. Despite a rough beginning establishing his credibility as one knowledgeable about the Jews, while simultaneously distancing himself from their iniquities (chief among them killing Jesus some hundreds of years hence), Nephi gets on a roll the second half, explaining his Christology of Jesus. He corrects a partial mistake that he is about to introduce his own prophecy (25: 7; when in fact he had multiple prophecies: among them exile in Babylon, 25: 11, and resurrection of Christ, 25: 13 and Israel's restorations) by pointing out an angel of God revealed to him the name of Jesus Christ (25: 19). That was no prophecy. It was nothing short of a miracle, on par with a Book of Mormon king identifying Jesus' mother, Mary, by name (Mosiah 3: 8, noting too she was a virgin, his comment about a century and some before Jesus' birth in ancient Palestine). Only Isaiah in the brass plates, outside of multiple Book of Mormon prophets, knew about Jesus, including his actual name, before he lived and died in ancient Palestine. Nephi's doctrine of Jesus includes his admirable attempt to account for the Law of Moses' being fulfilled by Jesus before prematurely announcing its death by hundreds of years. The striking Christology of Jesus in 2 Nephi 25 and throughout the Book of Mormon culminates in his status as God, the one deserving of our worship (as the Son of God, the Messiah, the Father of Heaven, the name by which to worship God and be reconciled to God) in concert with Christendom. References to Jesus Christ throughout the book emphasize his role as savior and as the Father with the proscription of the audiences' (ancient and prospective modern readers) need to come to him. This redemptive role is (so) striking because of its similarity to Pauline Christianity—where salvation comes through the death and resurrection of Jesus, inviting our fullest commitment to accept him—something Paul worked out over the course of many years, and through endless letters to religious communities he had established and a few he did not (see Romans). It's been said that all Christian sects are Pauline, and should be said with the understanding to include those before him. But Book of Mormon prophets understand Christ more than New Testament writers. For example, they understand the lion's share of Christ's atonement for the sins of the world happened before the cross, in the garden of Gethsemane where Christ bled from every pore (explained in one of the great sermons on Jesus' sacrifice for humanity by the same aforementioned king in Mosiah 3: 7), observed in a single verse in one New Testament gospel (Luke 22: 44). Book of Mormon prophets' understanding extended beyond the New Testament into the theology developed during The Middle Ages by understanding the grace of God before Augustine of Hippo (Moroni 10: 33) and Jesus' voluntary sacrifice to satisfy justice before Anselm of Canterbury (2 Nephi 2: 7). Book of Mormon prophets' understandings were generalizations akin to and innovations on controversies within the Protestantism of their translator's day. To be fair, all of whom, from Paul to Luther, understood Jesus' Christology better than Jesus did. But a heightened prescient clarity sets the Book of Mormon apart from the Old and New Testaments of the Bible. The book's prophets set a new standard for prophecy based on the miracles within the book: aptly called miracle prophecies. If God is one thing for Mormons, he is a God of an abundance of miracles, acting in history, including histories still being written.

CHAPTER 29
MARVELOUS WORKS AND WONDERS

Zach sat at the bar of O'Sullivan & Son. The pub was half a block from Beckwith Circle on Beacon Street, where I lived my first year of div school. I got to know Zach, like many of my classmates, over lagers and pale ales at O'Sullivan's. Today, in the final throes of our tenures at div school, he told me to meet him for lunch, and I happily accepted. If there was a better burger than Mr. Bartley's in greater Boston, it was at O'Sullivan's.

—Been here long? I asked.

—I worked my way over about an hour ago, he shook his head.

—How did your final exam go?

He reached into his pocket and pulled out a flask, tipping it back and forth to show nothing was left.

—Most humiliating experience of my life.

Zach and I had taken the same Introduction to New Testament course.

The grade was based on a paper (as you may recall, mine was about Euripides) and an oral exam. Toward the end of the course, the professor had provided a list of two or so dozen topics he could draw from a hat for a thirty-minute discussion.

—Which issue did you get?

—First Corinthians. Not miracles, not the Q source, not the resurrection, but a damn book I've never read!

—What'd you say?

—I started talking about Galatians and Jesus' death being the fulfillment of The Law of Moses and he stopped me and said my topic was Corinthians but I ignored him and kept talking about Galatians, quoting, of course from memory, that "circumcision availeth us nothing," and that's why the law was dead and moved on to what I knew about the development of the canon.

—Sounds like it went pretty well.

—I thought so until I noticed the teaching fellow with her arms around her head on the table. He interrupted me again to ask if I knew anything about First Corinthians and I just kept talking about the various ancient manuscripts and finished about the anti-Semitism in the Gospel of John. I said thank you, stood up and left.

—I'm sure you didn't fail.

—I'm sure I came close if I didn't.

—Well how did your paper end up?

—I got an extension.

Final papers were due a few weeks before the end of class and returned over the final class periods. I had earned one of my only A grades (actually an A- but what a petty difference now with so much time passed).

—Until when?

—Initially until the end of class but most recently until before we leave campus for the summer.

Unlike our other classmates, Zach was not graduating, not because of failing to have the required credits but because he got it in his head to study Russian our last year, committing to go beyond the surface of an introduction course at the college by enrolling in a summer course at the prestigious language program at Middlebury College, in Middlebury, Vermont. He planned to finish his degree and graduate in the fall.

—The fellow is going to take your paper home with her?

—She said she'd enter an incomplete for now and change it when she got my paper.

—Did you sleep with her?

—I think she likes me but I don't sleep with nice girls.

People knew Zach at the div school because he was one of the few open Republicans. I did not know what I was. I had been a Democrat growing up in Idaho, which decision was solidified later by living in Provo, Utah. But shortly into my graduate stint in Cambridge I learned I was not considered a real Democrat among the local ranks. I was and mostly continue to be, in a state of political limbo. While Zach would later confess he was no purified Republican, he didn't seem to have a sane choice of being otherwise living in Cambridge. When div students started a show on the local public access channel, they invited Zach to represent the conservative, white opinion. They liked him enough they invited him back. Within days of al-Qaeda's attacks on New York and Washington on September 11, 2001, Zach purchased a brand-new United States flag and hung it from his room at the dormitories next to Andover Hall. I knew the act of purchasing the flag was as big a deal as hanging it for all the div school to see. Neither Zach nor I had any money, regularly buying each other rounds of drinks on our credit cards we planned to pay off sometime after getting our first jobs. The flag cost one hundred dollars, about twenty-five pints! Shocked and convinced it had been marked up to capitalize on patriotic sentiments, I encouraged him to return it and shop around. Zach was the only one I remember who, one moment, choked up talking about the dead, and the next moment spoke angrily about those who attacked us. Other people were noticeably moved by the dead, too, but soon turned to the reasons why someone would want to attack us, stating that American foreign policies were unfair and oppressed billions.

After a few days of the Red, White and Blue hanging from Zach's window welcoming divinity faculty, students and guests, the dean asked Zach to remove it after complaints that it made people uncomfortable. One Friday afternoon on my way to the Emerson Club, a drinking club whose members met in the common space on the ground level of the dormitories, I watched Zach arguing with a classmate from Pakistan, Bahaar, about the September attacks. Bahaar justified actions against American imperialism, but deftly avoided explicitly condoning the attacks on New York and Washington. Zach responded that the attack on innocent civilians was nothing short of an act of war. We had been standing there for about an hour and both voices carried in every direction. Eventually students passing by complained about the noise, and Zach and Bahaar shook hands and parted. Bahaar later left the div school, unexpectedly. The reason given by the teaching fellow of the class in question, which I was also taking, was the need to return to care for a sick family member back home, but he had directly told Zach, who wasn't in the class, that he was caught plagiarizing a paper. He had not thought it was a big deal and did not have the time to write one. I had not heard a more reasonable justification for those of us who were incurring thousands of dollars of debt with no foreseeable promise of return on the investment, let alone loving to have free time to occasionally do other things like swim in Walden Pond.

I had an emotional connection to the claims about the divinity of Jesus going back to the fervent beliefs of my father, but I never had my own beliefs about his divinity, except one. The passage of scripture that resonated with my belief about God directed God's followers to treat others as if they were gods in Jesus' directive, *Inasmuch as ye have done it unto one of the least of these my brethren ye have done it unto me* (Matt 25: 40). I understand Jesus was saying how we treat others is *as if* we were treating him and not that everyone was a god, but by association everyone comes pretty damn close.

The existence of God always drew an enormous blank for me, but I loved the passionate arguments about God's existence and all the endless corollaries. Blanks were not uncommon for me, a belief in God exposing just one of them. I regularly drew blanks in theoretical and practical discussions, and drew even more blanks on how to act when interacting with other human beings. Most of the conceptual framework and experiences my brain, emotions, and judgment drew upon were riddled with blanks. In fact, they were mostly blanks. Nothing was there. Once in a while someone came along who seemed to function with no blanks, or ones so small they went unnoticed, including some of the most impressive human beings I've known. For a lot of folks, including me, the blanks between thoughts and experiences reveal themselves in pretty short order.

I like to think that those aware of their blanks might just be a more pure compound of their elements. For one, by their very acknowledgment (through reservation not conspicuous declaration) of what they do not know or have not experienced they provide a clearer contrast to what they do or have. For two, sometimes they are far less willing to fill the blanks with hollow supporting knowledge or fictitious experience, the surest way to eventual downfall for lack of credibility (but the fall can be a hell of a process measured in years not minutes, parsing fact from fiction). For three, and probably most importantly, they do not minimize, evade or dismiss what they do not have, a disposition allowing for unexpected development, which maintains the *sine qua non* of a meaningful life: authenticity, which is a challenge to hold, but easily forfeited.

As a non-believer about supernatural beings, I appreciated a believer's fortitude to demonstrate the contrary of such beings' absences (given the premise there was no verifiable knowledge or experience of God[s], which is no death knell to the subjective realm of one's own mind and heart, a realm with the very same parameters). I appreciated the act not because they asserted the existence of an all-mighty and all-powerful being to fill any empty blank, but because their act of asserting to fill the blank was one of creation. I longed to be with people who sought to fill the many blanks in, between, and around them to empower and to enlighten their own and others' lives with something superior, even be it supernatural. I longed for such people, because I always understood filling blanks with expansive ideas and experiences was incompatible with readily applying classification schemes to explain blanks, a control-oriented approach to life (applied by believers too), ignorance I could never stomach. The immeasurable gain to all folks shunning ready applications was the promise, and sometimes the grant, of an imaginative life.

Why I did not prefer fellow non-believers, generally, is attributable to various reasons. For one, they protested too much that all blanks amounted to markers of hidden or even more absurd latent knowledge or experience. In fact, all knowledge (such as abstract stuff and experience), all twisted and interconnected, provided the grounds to be unearthed for deeper meaning. And the all-craze, cause célèbre of the unconscious as the key to the repressed core identities was a substrate of other stuff, not of nothing. That is not to say people cannot forget most of what they know and experience as many of us do, or that ideas and experiences cannot be erased by trauma as many are. Remembering in those instances can be as fulfilling and challenging and rewarding and damning as dealing with blanks (but properly arranging forgotten and then recollected ideas and experience is as different a project from filling blanks as is classifying dark matter is from dark energy, or not when they encounter each other). And for another, my problem with fellow non-believers was the oft and cavalier self-appointed calling to eradicate the blanks, all the while failing to appreciate the simultaneous obliteration of imagination's possibilities.

I know (from experience) that they (the other: my fellow non-believers) would counter that the eradication of blanks (filled by the superstitious and fanciful) was collateral damage to the larger purpose of eradicating false knowledge that causes great harms; and, more importantly, working with the knowledge we have was the preferred practice to extend knowledge and possibilities; and, finally, they embraced blanks, too, positioning themselves for an imaginative life, a responsible relationship to ideas and to other human beings, that ultimately offered a better platform for authenticity. On those planes I agree. Progress comes from knowledge with a sustainable history, and I favor feeling and experiencing the conditions of this life with an awareness of consequences on conditions and other humans in this life to displacing consequences into a supernatural sphere in an unlikely heavenly one. However, my preference is also self-affirming because of my disposition to idleness (and lack of belief).

Believers' creations provide power for overcoming the reality they face, and the tradeoff of losing authenticity is a minor consequence when the outcome is commensurate to Olympic gold. Every Olympian takes steps to fulfill their one aim at the enormous costs of ignoring realities the rest of us cannot. Nothing short of such concerted effort could get them to the Olympics. Believers similarly sacrifice authentic experiences for their excellent end.

But believer and non-believer camps tire me when they constantly propose a false choice, their way or the highway (despite their being correct that you cannot arrive at their respective destinations without traveling their designated routes), because the choice likely abuses the role of blanks. The history of knowledge not only has blanks and always will have blanks, but layers of history benefit from those blanks. Those historical blanks, along with the current blanks in and around us, enhance possibilities (so I am suggesting there are spatial, or actual, sweet nothings based on our blanks). We need to be wary that all-consuming blanks can blunt potential (like believing in pink elephants and our modern entitlement to ride them). We also risk the stunting force of sustainable knowledge (like communism: a cherry pick of an example but a pretty damn good godless one). Blanks are the interstitial fabric of our lives; learning that they are opportunities and putting forth the effort to occupy them leads to a fulfilled life. In all that I have not said or not done, including the mere blanks I have consistently drawn for my feelings and thoughts on God, you have an accurate accounting of my many, many nothings. What I can say is that I overflow with an abundance of the stuff.

• • •

In addition to "Introduction to the New Testament," I finished Divinity School taking "Midrash: Jewish Interpretation in the Rabbinic Period." During one class the professor opened the door and yelled "That's right, we're talking about God in here." We all laughed, and he reopened the door, "Some of us still take God seriously." And if he did not say those exact words opening and closing and reopening the door, he said something a lot funnier. We cracked up because privileging a traditional view of God was tantamount to identifying yourself as a barren, surrogate wife of the reigning div school views.

I had previously taken a course on the Jewish Liturgical Year (broken into halves, and I took the first half) from the same professor. On the first day he said, "after sitting through this class you'll know more about Judaism than ninety-five percent of the Jews in America; imagine how much more you'll know by the end of the semester." He failed to forewarn that gaining the superior knowledge would require more than getting one's fanny to class. I struggled with the mid-term, barely earning a B. The class was held in the largest lecture room in Andover Hall, the Sperry Room, and that's where we wrote our exams. The final exam was scheduled for three hours, and I handed mine in under an hour, laying my blue book on a clear table in front of the teaching fellow. I had never finished first at something in my adult life; sure, I'd won cipher-downs in elementary school, freestyle wrestling tournaments, and the Elk's hoop-shoot contests but those glories of my youth had been a decade ago. And I aced the final.

On the first day of the Jewish Liturgical Year, the professor also said,

—You can call me Professor, Mr., Your Highness, anything but Jon. We're not at Swarthmore.

For many of my classmates that day, they were receiving their introduction to Professor Jon D. Levenson. All the Mormons were assigned to the Good Professor, because other professors passed on Mormons from years of frustration in trying to advise them, so my good fortune was meeting with His Highness at the beginning of each semester to discuss my course choices. "You're a serious student, Mr. Elison," he would say, having concurred with my course list (classes about Islam and about Buddhist and Hindu traditions). When our final meeting came up, I could not pass on another opportunity to take another class from His Eminence, and he was teaching "Jewish Interpretation."

Professor Levenson included, in the course materials, several essays that discussed the meaning of Midrash. They included insightful pieces that progressed in analytical difficulty from Barry W. Holtz's chapter "Midrash" from *Back to the Sources* and James L. Kugel's essay "Two Introductions to Midrash" to Gerald L. Bruns' essay "Midrash and Allegory" and Daniel Boyarin's first chapter of his book *Intertextuality and the Reading of Midrash*. The explanations had a great deal in common, but they had enough variations that Mormons scholars could find protection in the elasticity of defining Midrash, rather than accurately applying the process to their sacred scriptures. And I knew, from my postmodern literary studies, Midrash could be used in any context to justify expanding a passage's meaning.

But in short, Midrash both refers to a body of rabbinic literature and describes a way to read Biblical text; it derives from "darash" meaning "to study;" most scholars translated Midrash to mean "to search out" or "to research;" Kugel contrasted a Midrashic reading to allegorical and apocalyptic readings: an allegorical reading suggests scripture has a continuous spiritual presence; an apocalyptic reading suggests God acts in the present; and a Midrashic reading views scripture as a world of its own with Midrash as a way to access that world; it is not an interpretive strategy but it is a practice of reading, focusing on problems or irregularities in verses for the purpose of solving the problems, possibly with contradicting answers; the rabbis believed they were uncovering truth that existed in the sacred text, exercising a means of applying a biblical meaning of the past to the current situation of the rabbis.

I give you two examples: one an exercise and the other a smashing success. I will not prejudice you one way or the other about which is which.

Naturally, the final term paper had to employ characteristics of Midrash. I choose the topic of the "unidentified tree" in the Garden of Eden. If you haven't recently read the story of Adam and Eve in the Garden of Eden, do yourself a favor and pick up a Bible (Genesis 2: 15–3: 24). It's rich, and any translation will do. A critical part of the story involved one tree. *And the Lord God commanded the man, saying, Of every tree of the garden thou mayest freely eat: But of the tree of the knowledge of good and evil, thou shalt not eat of it: for in the day that thou eatest thereof thou shalt surely die* (KJV Gen 2: 16-17). Even if you've never read it, you know the rest: Adam and Eve eat from the tree. But the text does not reveal what kind of tree it is. In popular imagination, Eve and Adam eat an apple. Not likely. I drew upon the rabbinic literature to propose three possibilities: first, not a tree, but rather wheat, because people associated knowledge with eating bread; second, grapes of the vine because the taste of bitterness and its association to sorrow, the result of expulsion from Eden; and third, figs because their fruit could be eaten and their leaves were the only thing left for Adam and Eve to cover themselves with and also represented lamentation for their new mortality. In sum, I favored the figs based on the most astute analysis—all of it rabbinic commentary, none of it my own—but concluded that God left the tree unidentified for his own honor (also a rabbinic view). The Midrash wrote that God's honor was at stake because God "caused to grow every tree" (verse 9), so to safeguard from the blame of bringing death into the world on a tree of his creation, God withheld its identity. To appreciate the rabbis' point, consider only the poor rap given to—up to this very day—the revealed identity of the creature who tempted Eve.

Each of Levenson's books effected a paradigm shift, which is not saying much. There is a latent irony for an ambitious postmodernist like myself to mine, on why attributing to a book paradigm-shifting status is the highest compliment for a book in the earliest hours of the twenty-first century. If as many books as claimed brought about their alleged paradigm shifts, the earth would not still be rotating on its axis. In fact, the compliment is far more modest, meaning opening a new window on a subject (for the fresh air as much as for the new view). Levenson did not achieve multiple shifts by an enlarged intellect alone, which most of his peers also enjoyed, but by his superior ability to read closely (which means getting details straight and, more challenging, their connections). His approach was antithetical to the postmodern approach. He made coherent arguments based on elements, often disparate, of a text by excruciating fidelity to it.

A primarily sympathetic reading takes more skills than a critical reading because acknowledgment of the obligation of the first instance (the fact that a text with an objective arrangement, like the pieces of a puzzle, exists) requires one to reproduce accurately what is being examined, regardless of how well it's currently put together. The reproduction depends, in addition to its arrangement of internal form and words and influences and events in culture, on *distance*—in feet and time—from its creation more than the sober state of its new reader's preconceptions. Tabling biases is the scholar's minimum expectation, covering the distance is the scholar's Herculean task, and fashioning a new projection to move a discipline forward is the scholar's distinguishing cherry on top. The scholar's crucible is effort: more effort (e.g., learning languages, local and foreign; developing knowledge of the field during interminable periods of inquiry and observation and reading and rereading scholarship within, and relevant to, their field to catch the depth and breadth and interconnections of conversations, old and current, all before developing a largeness of knowledge—expertise—on the primary texts whether written or cultural) to understand texts corresponds to more responsible (serious) scholarship (but, God almighty, that doesn't make it more persuasive: that rarity of a thing depends upon timing, skills and a hell of a lot of practice, an unmistakable joy to discover). And the chief effort is to trace the internal development of the text, to get what rolls out in words and sentences into ideas and plot before getting to talk about it.

I read many of Levenson's books. Like all professors, he listed them as recommended reading on his syllabus, and there they were on the shelves at the Divinity School Bookstore on the ground level of Divinity Hall. I bought most of the required readings at the beginning of the semester at full price and routinely bought others that had caught my attention for marked-down prices at the end of each semester, rationalizing that, by the time I paid off my credit card, I would still have captured some savings (but never courageous enough to do the math). On one such adventure I came across a curious book, *Refuge: An Unnatural History of Family and Place* by Terry Tempest Williams. I accidently discovered the voice of moral authority from within my Mormon tradition. Williams wrote about her mother having cancer and losses to a bird refuge outside Salt Lake City. Her feeling burrowed deep, filling the void between my tradition and the natural world. Another discovery was one of Levenson's books, probably suggested reading for a course on the Jewish scriptures, *The Death and Resurrection of the Beloved Son*, which brought about a spiritual death in me, three days and counting. It relied heavily upon modern scholarship and rabbinic literature, but it was mainly a Midrashic reading of irregularities in the biblical text. It explained verses about God's command to sacrifice the first-born and beloved son, and the command's subsequent transformation into Jewish and Christian rites and stories.

The great prophets Jeremiah and Ezekiel raged against child sacrifice at the beginning of the sixth century BCE, effectively bringing about its end by the end of that century. No one disputes their success. What tends to draw some pretty strong opinions is whether their efforts included the practice of child sacrifice by Israel. One of the many controversial passages that have pained scholars is from Exodus 22: 28-29 in the Tanakh, *You shall not put off the skimming of the first yield of your vats. You shall give Me the first-born among your sons. You shall do the same with your cattle and your flocks: seven days it shall remain with its mother; on the eighth day you shall give it to Me.*

Only a detailed analysis like one provided by Levenson could do justice to this passage and many others about giving the first-born. He makes a terribly persuasive argument that Israel did. The significance of which, for his thesis, was the transformation from the practice of sacrifice to its persistence in the rites and stories of Judaism *and* Christianity.

One part of his book caught my attention because of my personal investment in it (relating to God, not sacrifice). After establishing in the first dozen or so chapters that Israel actually practiced child sacrifice until it was transformed into Jewish rites and stories, Levenson discusses the archetypical story about child sacrifice, the sacrifice of Isaac. That is how Christians the world over describe it. In Hebrew it's known as the *aqedah*, or the "binding of Isaac." While the aqedah received a surprising dearth of commentary within the Bible itself, a plethora of folks over the ages have commented upon it, including one of my favorites, Kierkegaard, who turned his attention to it into a short classic, *Fear and Trembling*. If you haven't read the aqedah, you ought to. Pick up your Bible and read Genesis 22: 1-19. Suffice it to say, God promised Abraham all kinds of blessings, including that his descendants would be a great nation, and that God's promise would be fulfilled through his beloved son, Isaac. But then God went and commanded Abraham to sacrifice Isaac, effectively wiping out his promise. The story goes that Abraham hauled Isaac to a mountain, placed him on an altar and, just before he completed God's command, an angel stopped him, providing a lamb in Isaac's place. My main man K pointed out that this was the quintessential example of faith in God's promises, leaping into the absurd of God's realm and his unexplainable ways. Levenson argues that Abraham's example was better understood as acts in obedience to God's command. Given the proof of the ancient practice of child sacrifice and the many examples of its persistence in biblical rites and stories, Levenson's point was awfully well taken. And his interpretation of the aqedah in light of that background explained what would have otherwise been a story with numerous inconsistencies (dare I say, absurdities). For example, thrice within the story Abraham uses the same Hebrew word that he is *ready*. Abraham's readiness is consistent with obeying, not with fear and trembling.

Levenson concludes his book by pointing out that the Apostle Paul did his own Midrash in his New Testament writings, to substitute one beloved son for another, Jesus for Isaac, in order to inherit the promises made to Abraham. Among the examples of Paul's Midrash, Levenson cited: *Christ ransomed us from the curse of the law by becoming a curse for us, for it is* written, "Cursed be everyone who hangs on a tree," that the blessing of Abra-ham might be extended to the Gentiles through Christ Jesus, so that we might receive the promise of the Spirit through faith. Brothers, in human terms I say that no one can annul or amend even a human will once ratified. Now the promises were made to Abraham and to his descendant. It does not say, "And to descendants," as referring to many, but as referring to one, who is Christ (Gal 3: 13-16). Levenson explained Paul based his Midrashic interpretation on a singular collective noun in Genesis 13: 15 and 17: 8, which collective noun was, in fact, associated with the individual Isaac in Genesis 21: 12. That Jesus' death had significance, beyond expiating the sins of the world, to that of inheriting Abraham's blessings, may have been obvious, but it floored me.

Paul, a trained Jewish intellectual, was not so much establishing a reli-gion that superseded the one he had belonged to, as he was arguing the new religion's entitlement to the old one's great promises. Having that connection demonstrated by Paul, after Levenson's tireless explication of the history of the rites and stories about the sacrifice of first-born and beloved son, was the moment I recognized my head back on the floor. The many great stories of brothers fighting for their inheritance, from Cain and Abel to Ishmael and Isaac (or their mothers), to Esau and Jacob, to Judah (and all the older brothers) and Joseph, provided the most accurate model to understand Ju-daism and Christianity, siblings fighting for the same thing—God's promis-es. But none of Jesus' predecessors of sacrificed beloved-sons had a physical resurrection. Yet that distinction was hardly as significant outside the Bible stories, given what I knew about the reigning Greek gods of Jesus' day. Paul's project to ensure that his gentile converts were recipients of Jesus' sacrifice and Abraham's blessings was the most significant foundation of Christianity. But I knew, as did the author of Luke and the book of Acts, it was hardly the only one.

Levenson was the Jewish Bible's interpretive reigning champion. During the fall before the class on Midrashic interpretation, he confirmed his un-disputed crown in a heated debate with other Jewish scholars about Jew-ish and Christian interfaith dialogues. In an essay "How Not To Conduct Jewish-Christian Dialogue" published in the conservative Jewish periodical *Commentary*, Levenson skewered a group of Jewish scholars over the hot coals of their ineptitude. He decried their treatise *Dabru Emet*, which was intended to profess Jewish beliefs having common ground with Christians' beliefs. He handily pointed out its weaknesses, and pounded the subsequent critiques to his essay point by point in a following issue. His sure victory was not surprising and neither were the impotent rebuttals. Suffice it to say, Levenson repeatedly relied upon the writings of the apostle Paul to point out irreconcilable differences between Jews and Christians, and not one rebuttal held him to it. Levenson outdueled his opponents for many reasons, only one being they did not use Paul too.

While Levenson used Paul's writing effectively to criticize flaccid tenets of commonality purported by *Dabru Emet*, he inexplicably dropped Paul like a spent harlot when it suited him, noticeably during his final critique of *Dabru Emet*'s claim that "Jews and Christians worship the same God." Levenson rightly pointed out Christians believe Jesus is God and Jews do not, creating a bit of a quandary for the authors of *Dabru Emet* who suggested both religions shared the same God. Yet Levenson ignored his chief proponent of the Christian position to do so, because Paul undisputedly believed that Christians, Jews, and gentiles of his day believed in the same God: there being nary a hint of the divinity of Jesus or a "trinity" in Paul's writings, and neither could it be inferred by any rational mind from the writings of his followers.

Levenson had his cake and ate it too, not because he was correct in his conclusions but because his opponents valued reading closely far less than he did. He cherry-picked Paul and got away with it. The real dispute, or risk to all Jewish parties, of the sensational debate was in the authors' bent to create a new narrative to appease the changing landscape of Jews' encounter with society in general, namely interfaith marriage. Any single one of them could have attacked Levenson, on the merits of Paul's writings, to confirm that nothing could justify interfaith dialogue with Christians more than helping Christians get back to a correct understanding of God as it existed in Paul's writings, the very same God of the Jews.

And what a gift that would have been to the confused billion or so Christians committed to the sexy superior Greek notions of Plato and his finest proponent Plotinus rather than to those of the Jew Paul. This great re-reawakening was not to have been, because the entire debate was only secondarily about the merits. It was primarily about controlling the current narrative to make interfaith congress more acceptable. And the battle of narrative was nothing new, since the narrative of God's covenant people was the very thing Paul had raged about in discussing the most blatantly conspicuously and obvious issue: for men to stop chopping off the tips of their penises to be accepted by the true God.

One can wonder if a greater issue delights the absurdities in the sky than the outpouring of consternations resulting from one single directive to shear manhood. Could there have been a more confounding image of life's purpose for Samuel Beckett's Murphy as he lay on his soon-to-be death bed than *the clenched fists and rigid upturned face of the Child in a Giovanni Bellini Circumcision, waiting to feel the knife?* Holy Mother of all fountains. Oh, biggest of all philosophers and religions' God, let our incontinent shortcomings to exist among each other account for something more.

Is Midrash the panacea for explaining the Isaiah chapters in the Book of Mormon? No. It was not a rhetorical question. The metaphor of a "sealed book" of prophecy conceivably could pose some confusion but, to fecundate the metaphor with the situation in Joseph's day—the translation process of the Book of Mormon—is not reading to connect the biblical world to one's current situation; rather it is another practice entirely, an über eisegesis of inserting one's current situation into that past world, but endowed with prophetic power.

But the Book of Mormon wants for less than strikes the eyes of many of its critics. Take only a few passages from the chapters I have shared. When the prophet Nephi explains he has not taught the ways of the Jews to his descendants because of their works of darkness (2 Nephi 25: 2), too facilely construed as hints of New Testament anti-Semitism, the unnamable abominations could well have been the practice of sacrificing the first-born and beloved son that the legacies of the prophets Jeremiah and Ezekiel routed out of God's chosen people around the time Nephi's father Lehi took his colony to the new world (consider his elision of Chapter 30 of Isaiah in his transcription of Isaiah chapters, possibly for its reference to child sacrifice?). And when Nephi explained that God directed him to make a record of his life in addition to the history he had been keeping (2 Nephi 5: 28-33), the new volume may have provided the substitute Joseph needed for the lost 116-page manuscript, but it also represented the alternative to a historical record in the ancient world. It resembled the Jewish novel in antiquity, meant to help and educate the community (e.g. the Book of Esther; or the multi-purposed short novella of Joseph in Genesis 37-50), the very declared purpose of Nephi's new volume. And revealing the eternal ordinance of a cleansing ritual by choosing baptism in Isaiah's prophecies in the brass plates (1 Nephi 20: 1/ Isaiah 48: 1) was likely a reflection of a translator's enthusiasm more than the impossibility of ancient cleansing rituals predating Jesus' life in ancient Palestine. Writings from the Qumran communities (the writings of the Dead

Sea Scrolls, which included many other religious manuscripts in addition to books of the Bible) directed purifying washing rituals within their community. At the least, Joseph kept good company projecting the necessary ordinance of baptism on his spiritual ancestors as did the apostle Paul in 1 Cor. 10: 2. These examples lending authenticity to the Book's antiquity, along with a few dozen others—many of them more convincing of its antiquity— could be mere coincidences. But they are hardly running interpolations any more than the Book's single comment condemning the most controversial Mormon practice of polygamy (Jacob 2: 23-35; 27): *Wherefore, my brethren, hear me, and hearken to the word of the Lord: For there shall not any man among you have save it be one wife; and concubines he shall have none).*

One hundred scribes in addition to the three Joseph Smith used, with all the available source material, cannot account for the cumulative coincidences of antiquity throughout the Book. Or could they? Critics wail that all the evidence of antiquity fails to mitigate the far more copious influences from Joseph's own time and culture and obvious anachronisms within it, as if the camel Rebekah rode when she first saw her husband, the patriarch Isaac, invalidates the Abrahamic promise. Grant Palmer's *An Insider's View of Mormon Origins* compiles various sources for the Book of Mormon, chief among them the King James Version of the Bible. He attends to the challenges of translating the gold plates, mentioning the scripts of reformed Egyptian and Arabic characters. These scripts are credible in themselves for their mere exoticism, as the author and narrator Cervantes himself recognized. Cervantes faced the challenge to continue the tale of the knight-errant Don Quixote when he ran out of source material. His first source ended during the fight between Don Quixote and the Basque (following the battle with the giant, or windmill). In hope of continuing the tale of this famous knight, Cervantes went shopping to find more complete records of Don Quixote's adventures. With luck he came across notebooks in Arabic, and immediately sought out a Spanish-speaking Moor to translate them. He found one, and the Moor did. The translator no sooner began then he started to laugh, and Cervantes had found the records (written by the less adorning Cide Hamete Benegeli) to continue his tale. But before continuing, Cervantes clarified that, *in this history I know that everything anyone could want to find in the most delectable history is to be found; and if anything worthwhile is missing from it, it's my belief that it's the dog of an author who wrote it that's to blame, rather than any defect in the subject.* Cervantes' conceit of exoticism, similar to the Book of Mormon, apparently had dual purposes.

The gem in Palmer's book is not the identification of any one influence on the Book of Mormon, but an irresistible influence on the life of Joseph Smith. Palmer shares some dozen-plus comparisons between E.T.A. Hoffmann's tale "The Golden Pot" to events in Joseph's life. That Joseph saw himself in that magical tale is as fantastic a revelation as the Archers' film production of Jacques Offenbach's opera *The Tales of Hoffmann* (1951).

Criticism of the Book of Mormon is on a par with its most ardent defenses. Mormons attest the Book is an authentic historical record. Critics of the Book cry bollocks. The bar is set at the whole thing's being a scam or its being all true. But what sacred text (or religion) fits into those options? Mormons are responsible for setting the bar, and benefit from it for many reasons—from the myth of the religion's completeness and authenticity to the practical synergy uniting its adherents. But the bar is fixed by two fallacies. First, Mormons subscribe to the rule that those who talk about the truthfulness of the Book of Mormon (or Joseph Smith, or the Church) are either confessing their beliefs (apologetics) or justifying their actions, such as leaving the Church (apostates). It would be an obvious false choice if anyone other than Mormons or "former" Mormons were writing about the question of the Book's authenticity (or Joseph's or the Church's; historically many non-Mormon writers decried the Church's claims; contemporary non-Mormons generally do not address questions of authenticity, but rather they focus on the culture and its relationship to non-Mormon forms of modernity). Mormons or former Mormons can, and do, comment on the Book of Mormon and their lives as Mormons for many reasons, none more important than to search out and possibly confirm the truth-claims the Book and its religion propose.

Second, no single, solitary thing within Mormonism supports the either/or choice that Mormonism is true or it is false more than Mormonism's fledgling theology based on a concatenation of proof. If I could identify who is to blame for introducing this catchy logic, I would. I have found its slithering appeal as far back as the turn of the twentieth century in the writings of Nels L. Nelson, a reminder that even the brightest among us have chinks in their mithril armor. Nothing is quite as imbedded into the Mormon personality as the logical chain that, if one knows the Book of Mormon is true, this proves that Joseph Smith was a true prophet for translating it; and if Joseph was a true prophet, the Church he set up was the true Church of Jesus Christ; and, if it's the true Church, the rites and ordinances necessary for salvation and exaltation taught within it are also true. The tradeoff for believing all things stands upon one thing, which is Mormonism's Achilles heel, not to mention that it fosters an illusionary causal relationship based on logic. Mormons often offer a "proof" that is an abstract one, which isn't a proof, because we and the chimpanzees at your local zoo can conceive of any part's not being supportable. Joseph Smith may have still been a prophet even if the Book of Mormon is not what it claims to be. And the Church may be true all on its own merits, despite its beginnings.

And the logical chain is utter nonsense. The question whether a religion is true is a fair measure of the logic's inapplicability, because that question asks whether a religion corresponds to reality, or in other words itself, and only misleadingly whether it is a sign for something else's truthfulness. Religions provide stories and sets of beliefs and practices to enhance adherents' relationships to the supernatural in order to provide guidance to their lives and ultimate status in the next. The words and actions correspond to a divine realm. It mostly goes without saying, but I will say it, that the supernatural realities are beyond or separate from the physical, mortal experience we call life, which distinction includes the Mormon religion despite their tireless insistence on a much thinner line between the sacred and the profane, if we take seriously their baseline that their God(s) are exalted beings who make their presence(s) felt through a holy spirit, and their most sacred rituals occur in holy temples that act as conduits to an eternal realm. The inapposite question of whether a religion is true more accurately asks: What religions are not true?

The question almost always festers around historical claims. But how does a religion's purpose *depend* upon the authenticity of its original claims? Its internal coherence and external persuasion might. Its truth value does not. For one, not a single religion's does; look around you. For another, a religion's genealogy of ideas and practices attests to its value, and we should measure the religion by those ideas. Genealogy, and not origin, is the basis for its truthfulness. Questions of origin are best cast in light of religions' persistence and not recreations of their first instances. That is not a shield to historical inquiry, especially when a religion like Mormonism celebrates historical incidents to shore up its foundations. Historians, have at it. But undercutting origins requires a lot of information, often more than is ever available, as sure a sinkhole for the critic as it is a hollow foundation for the adherent. Mormonism's vulnerable origins make it more like all other religions, not less. The questions about Mormonism's origins are magnified by its youth and the illusion that there is less we do not know, compared to other religions. Many religions have been around for thousands of years, while Mormonism has been around two hundred (all of it during an intense print-culture from dime novels to the blogosphere). That is hardly enough time to distance itself from the maturation process every religion undergoes and every inquiry that a religion's origins must account for.

The maturation process is not clean, pure, or without blemishes. It's full of bruises, scars, and rashes. Any transmittal from the divine to the human involves the components of life, from the fleshly to the inconsistent. God depends upon a mess to get his points across, always has and always will, which is true whether you believe in him or want to understand those who do. Which brings me back to Mormon theology's whole-cloth that claim its religion is based on the Book of Mormon, an authentic historical record (again, my contention is the logical chain is ludicrous; which is different from wrongly, if cheaply, being impugned to its parts like the authenticity of the Book, which invites analysis on its own merits). But most scholars like Givens shirk the real issue of authenticity for perpetuating silly causes of truths by focusing on how the Book is used in Mormonism consistent with the fashionable and acceptable inquiries in academia, for whom the fact it is used is reason enough to laud its significance for those who use it.

Others, like Grant Hardy in his *Understanding the Book of Mormon*, provide a more concerted effort on the internal elements of the text to argue for its authenticity. Hardy focuses on the Book's three editors, the prophets Nephi, Mormon and Moroni. Among his many fine close-readings, take one where Hardy's analysis breaks from the uncritical view about the most famous killing in the Book, the death of Laban, custodian of the brass plates, the important records that Lehi's family needs to keep the commandments of God in the New World. Nephi comes upon Laban who was *drunken with wine* (1 Nephi 4: 7); the Spirit of the Lord directed Nephi to kill Laban (4: 10-11) based on four reasons: *Behold the Lord hath delivered him into thy hands. Yea, and I also knew that he had sought to take away mine own life; yea, and he would not hearken unto the commandments of the Lord; and he also had taken away our property* (4: 11). The main reason was really the first when the Spirit repeated, *Slay him, for the Lord hath delivered him into thy hands; Behold the Lord slayeth the wicked to bring forth his righteous purposes. It is better that one man should perish than that a nation should dwindle and perish in unbelief* (4: 12-13).

The Mormon doctrinal exposition of the passage follows that Nephi did not commit murder because he carried out a commandment of God. Hardy does not stray from this position. However, he dissects Nephi's later rendition of the killing by noting his curious editorial choices, pointing out there is no reaction from his father Lehi (which likely would have been negative), but there is the interjection of a different topic by his mother, diverting judgment entirely. Hardy's analysis reveals the human crevices that make a story believable, but the crevices also make the story more complex and not as easily extrapolated as doctrine. That Laban's death was necessary to preserve God's commands is one of the major ironies within the Book, because Nephi's decedents are wiped from the earth by the Book's end.

If Mormons insist on the Book's value, then they must become better readers. As a consequence of becoming better readers, the book will be less about profession of their faith and being an inane basis for everything else's being true, but the return will be an enriched view of and credible belief in their sacred Book. They might not reap the benefits, but I promise their children will. The Bible has meaning for so many people because of its intricacies and layered conversations, not despite them. Rigorous analysis and responsible readings tend to demystify but do not necessarily destroy belief. That so many Mormons' belief in the truthfulness of their religion depends upon that religion's being free of faults is immature at best, and terribly and poorly thought through at worst. The Book of Mormon is full of its own faults; none of them, separately or together, upends its value or initiates the fall of the Mormon religion. Its faults enhance an authentic experience, which depends upon struggle for truth. Its faults don't beg for the academic shield to excuse those necessary struggles. But just what can one say about the Book's prescient Christology? Well for one, if Jesus's sacrifice for humanity applies to all humankind, including the humans who lived before him, then is there any greater testament than the Book of Mormon?

What Levenson's *The Death and Resurrection of the Beloved Son* traces is the power of promise, not its fulfillment but its guiding light that Jews and Christians separately seek. Abraham's blessings were resurrected again and again throughout the Jewish scriptures and New Testament. Could those promises be worth all the actions spent on claiming them? Volumes of the fairest thinking have attempted to answer, and even more lives have been spent fulfilling them.

Mormons have thrown their hat into the mix for God's blessings no less forcefully than Paul did. Mormons claim for themselves Abraham's promises, and they make their claim as adopted heirs of Ephraim, the son of Joseph (the son of Jacob/Israel, the wrestler, you might recall). The first prophet of the Book of Mormon Lehi was a descendent of Joseph (1 Nephi 5: 14). God made covenants with Joseph (2 Nephi 3: 4). In fact, the visionary Joseph while in Egypt saw Lehi's day (2 Nephi 3: 5) and the seer who would bring forth God's word in the last days (2 Nephi 3: 7). Like Paul, Lehi did his own Midrash, identifying the sticks discussed in Ezekiel 37: 15-19 in the Bible, as the stick of Judah, and the Book of Mormon, as the stick of Ephraim, the son of Joseph (2 Nephi 3: 12), closing by identifying Joseph of Egypt's vision (obviously in addition to the two noted in the Biblical account) the very name of that seer who would bring forth the stick of Ephraim, *And his name shall be called after me; and it shall be after the name of his father* (2 Nephi 3: 15), Joseph (Smith, Jr.). If any heir has made a case for claiming God's covenant and honoring it (Genesis 9: 1) by being fruitful, multiplying, and replenishing the earth, then the adopted heirs of Ephraim, the Mormons have.

The last time I saw my mother was in Pocatello, Idaho. Bishop Patrick drove the five youngest brothers to join our father and Jami, who had been staying at the hospital with her. Bishop Patrick explained that he and our father had decided we should see her because she was being moved to a hospital in Salt Lake City the next day.

We rode in silence, and I stared out the window of the car into the night as we traveled south past open fields along the side of the freeway. Then darkness turned bright under the lights of the hospital. We walked through the sea of encouraging smiles and pressing hands, members of Riverton Ward filling the lounge, to a door and peered through its small window. We had all gathered together in great ceremony once before to see my mother: the morning she gave birth to Jed in Old Red. She lay on the bed facing all her boys lined up against the west wall. She squeezed plastic combs in her hands as the midwife encouraged her to breathe and to push, and she responded by breathing and pushing and screaming until Jed's head popped out into his new world with us. I had seen my mother animated before, hollering for us to do this or that, but not as concertedly as over those minutes having Jed. We all moved closer to the bed and welcomed our new brother. I asked her if I could have the yellow comb she had been using, and she said yes.

The doctor pushed the door open and led us in. He directed us to move along the foot of the bed where our mother lay with eyes closed in a white gown under white sheets with her hands placed on top. The doctor and our father spoke to her.

—Chris, your boys are here to see you.

She opened her eyes, and she smiled.

"Jesse."

I stood at the foot of her bed and moved around to her, and she closed her eyes. We stood looking on her for a couple of minutes as the doctor and our father made more comments, but she did not hear or failed to respond. She struggled to see behind an invisible wall. She was there but not, wanting to be and was. We walked back into the lounge. The members assured us she was improving and the doctors in Utah would give her the help she needed. The warmth showered upon us after the shock of seeing her unable to communicate caused a knot of guilt in us. Someone offered to buy us soda pops from the machines in the lounge, and we shook them off. I had never passed on a soda pop, one of life's great luxuries, but I did not open my mouth fearing I would cry out loud. Years after that night our father recalled our visit as the night of promise. Our mother's unexpected responsiveness buoyed everyone's expectation for the coming two-week saga to save her life in Salt Lake City.

The death of our beloved mother was an event as old as time, no greater or less than any other. Yet her death continues to have an unparalleled effect on the lives of those who knew her. Her boys still sing, with Oliver, each dawn, "Where Is Love?" never under the illusion that love is anything but her. She rises in our memories, an unheralded resurrection, not miraculous but there, witnessed individually, by us few. Her common, most unoriginal death tilts the scale of meaning by her temporary life. A cosmic backdrop may extend the common and unoriginal, but it is the words, gestures, and actions, all composite parts of her life that weigh so heavily, leaving its imprint. My mother fulfilled her role in honoring God's cyclical covenant, but her blessing to us was all her own, extending her life to ours. Trying to justify her gift would end impossibly, but failing to honor it would be unpardonable, and getting regularly mired in both as expected as they are also unoriginal. If life's end is as unoriginal as its beginning, then the life they frame could be, too, save that a life distinguishes itself by what one does with it, as surely as anything is.

I sat with Zach one last time before I left Boston.

—I enjoyed your paper, I said.

—Really? I wasn't so sure how it would be received.

—You made a persuasive argument that Luke's account of Jesus showed him concerned with economic reform. I mean all that stuff you quoted in Luke about changing the economic system.

—Exactly. Jesus focused on the poor, not the poor in spirit, and tried to overturn the economic evils they faced. The big things were it would have been impossible to build capital in first century Palestine after all the officials' shares. And the idea of getting out of debt was just as impossible. I truly believe Jesus' main goal was to reestablish the Jubilee year for the forgiveness of debt, but like I said in my paper that wouldn't have changed anything long-term because there will always be poor people since erasing problems is only temporary. Which Jesus may have said somewhere.

—Your comment about Jesus being lazy wasn't so well supported.

—Well there's no evidence he worked.

—He walked around a lot.

—Won't argue with that but that is hardly the equivalent of working.

—You know I always thought the early Christian community demanded a full devotion of faith but you pointed out their complete devotion of material possessions to the community. Like that unlucky married couple who failed to give up all their possessions to Peter in the books of Acts. That was a strong connection to the economic focus throughout Luke. And, I might add, another proof the same guy probably wrote both books.

—Communism was the ideal of Peter's earliest community. The early community in Acts based their understanding on Jesus' main goal of economic reform. But that failed. Instead, Jesus' teachings evolved into a religion a few centuries later. Let that be a lesson before you spend a lot of time trying to carry out your ambitions. You might mean well but people will make something else of it.

—How did the party go at your Russian teacher's house?

—They were surprised to see me. Only one of my classmates knew I was coming, the girl who gave me the address. None of them liked me much. It got so ridiculous during class I'd go out of my way to harass them. Someone would say something smart and I'd agree, saying, "I was just telling my friend that earlier today." Or after they'd say something, I'd say, "That's exactly what I think." All they had was expensive vodka. We started doing shots as soon as I got there.

—How long did that last?

—All night. After a few rounds I barely made it to the kitchen before I threw up.

—You didn't go to the bathroom?

—Didn't know where it was.

—What'd they do?

—They tried to get me to stand to catch a cab, but I wasn't in any shape and was happy on the floor at the time. Then they gave up and left me. I spent the night there.

—Sounds like an awful night.

—It was cold but not so bad. I had to get up a couple times to throw up some more. Fortunately I did not have to go far. But if you find yourself on the cold side of a kitchen floor, try to grab yourself a blanket on your way there.

—I will.

—Do you have time for another round?

I finished Harvard in a scandal. When classmates found out I planned not to attend Harvard Commencement on the green between Widener Library and Memorial Hall, known as Tercentenary Theater, inquiries poured in about acquiring my tickets. A graduate got only two tickets because of the limited area to cram loved ones on the theater, and for most graduates two was not enough. Of course, I overpromised because one of my roommates asked me after I had committed my tickets, and I could hardly deny him one. I partially rescinded my initial bequeathal, which ended awkwardly, so much so that I should have fully reneged. If I may impart some advice to you, be careful what you promise and to whom, but be even more forceful when you go back on it. Jeremy arrived the weekend before graduation. We loaded the car with new books and headed back west on Interstate 90.

Acknowledgments

I owe a bushel of thanks to supporters of my book. Matt Kuntz got me to Montana so I could write; then he encouraged me to write about my life and my thoughts about religion. My father offered candid and encouraging responses to multiple drafts, and all my brothers provided positive feedback. Keith Williams, Nateijie Hamilton, Kenneth West, Robert St. Hilaire, and Theresa Boyar made helpful comments and edits. Andrew Cannon read multiple drafts and helped develop parts and correct others. Barbara Fifer's superb editing improved the whole book. All were generous, and their efforts made the book much better. I can't thank them enough.

Made in the USA
Lexington, KY
30 April 2017